Dying
and
Death

DYING
AND
DEATH

A Clinical Guide
for Caregivers

Edited by
DAVID BARTON, M.D.
Associate Clinical Professor of Psychiatry
Vanderbilt University School of Medicine
Nashville, Tennessee

With 7 contributors

The Williams & Wilkins Company · Baltimore

All content except CH. 12
Copyright ©, 1977
The Williams & Wilkins Company
428 E. Preston Street
Baltimore, Md. 21202, U.S.A.

Chapter 12 ©, 1977
Robert M. Veatch

Made in the United States of America

Reprinted 1979

Library of Congress Cataloging in Publication Data
Main entry under title:

Dying and death.

Includes index.
1. Terminal care. 2. Death/Psychological aspects. I. Barton, David, 1936–
R726.8.D89   616   77-2183
ISBN 0-683-00440-9

Composed and printed at the
Waverly Press, Inc.
Mt. Royal and Guilford Aves.
Baltimore, Md. 21202, U.S.A.

This book is dedicated to those persons who are most important in my finding meaning and a sense of aliveness in my life—my wife, Lynn, and my children, Kirk, Amy, and Daniel.

Foreword

Vex not his ghost; O! let him pass; he
  hates him
That would upon the rack of this tough world
Stretch him out longer.

KENT'S PLEA before King Lear's death rings true throughout the centuries and speaks to the agony and relief of man's death. The words and the meaning behind them are in no way antiquated, and perhaps even today hold deeper wisdom when one is confronted with the dying person in our modern medical system. I suspect there is little creativity in the dying process just as there is no dignity in death — all becoming shibboleths when one is faced with one's own death, the death of loved ones, or patients whom one has cared for. This book deals with the struggles of David Barton and his attempts to come to grips clinically, existentially and humanistically with the world of the dying. He is not concerned with life after death but rather with the life of the dying patient and with a clinical framework from which those involved in his care can work.

As a close personal friend and colleague, I have watched David's development in this field and his immersion in it. The reader will find this book no armchair monologue but instead the writings of those who are at the front lines of death as it involves themselves or patients whom they actively treat. Nor will the reader find this book a how-to-die one. To the contrary it offers multifaceted and multidisciplinary information that provides the caretaker with insights into the psychology and pathos of dying, allowing him the freedom to formulate his own approach to the problem.

As is evident in this book there is now a vast, perhaps even an overwhelming, amount of literature related to death and dying. Indeed the question is being asked in one form or another, "Is there an overkill of death?." An editorial in the *Journal of the American Medical Association*,[1] for example, with the title "Dying is Worked to Death," notes that "It is much too easy to write about death . . . perhaps because it is so easy to write about dying, so much is written about it without saying anything new." Even within the field of thanatology Weisman[2] observes that "people who find death so glamorous often forget that people are very sick before they die, that people may be killed in vastly brutal ways. Death as a new chic may mask reality just as effectively as the older systematic denial we rail against." Barton, like Weisman, refutes that it is easy or simplistic to write about dying. To the contrary they demonstrate the complexity of the subject and the depths to which one must delve to understand it. One can postulate that a backlash will develop against thanatology, and that some of this reaction will result from the speculative quality and the romanticism which has developed in the field. Yet man will, as always and forever, inevitably face death and die. As our society moves toward a state in which dying becomes increasingly institutionalized and prolonged by advancing technology, we need thinkers and doers like David Barton and his contributors and are indebted to them for producing this important book.

HARRY S. ABRAM, M.D.
Professor of Psychiatry
Vanderbilt University School of Medicine
Nashville, Tennessee.

1. Editorial, *JAMA 229*:1909–1910, 1974
2. Weisman AD: *The Realization of Death: A Guide for the Psychological Autopsy.* Jason Aronson, New York, 1974

Preface

IN RECENT YEARS, there has been an increasing interest in matters related to caring for persons in the areas of dying, death, and bereavement. This book is a reflection of that increasing interest; and it is my hope that it will prove to be useful to practicing physicians, community clergymen, pastoral counselors, social workers, psychologists, nurses, mental heath counselors, students in these areas, and others working or interested in the process of caring for dying persons and their families.

This book is based on the idea that in order to develop more effective approaches to caring for dying persons, one needs to be able to discern and respond appropriately to the myriad of needs of the person and the members of his or her family, to have a working knowledge of basic theoretical concepts and basic knowledge about the areas of dying, death, and bereavement, and to develop the ability to appreciate the perspectives and abilities of a wide variety of health-care and health-care-related personnel. An approach that achieves a synthesis of these dimensions of the care process is felt to be one which will best equip caregivers to provide optimal assistance to all those involved.

The concept of caring is central to the design of the book. Here, caring refers to the ability of the caregiver, regardless of his discipline, to remain in an approximated relationship with the dying person, his family, and other caregivers in such a way as to ascertain needs over time and to utilize sets of knowledge, skills, and attitudes to facilitate a reasonable level of adaptation for all concerned. A caring approach not only requires an appreciation of the vast spectrum of needs of the dying person and his family, but also serves to help understand the needs of other caregivers and provides an atmosphere of mutual support for those working in the care situation. In the process of caring, it is also necessary that the caregiver manage those feelings within himself or herself which might result in avoidance, distancing, or any form of diminution of need-discerning presence and responsiveness.

The dying and death of a person evokes in that person, and in all of us relating with him or her, basic anxieties and fears related to our finiteness. The death-approximated individual, and those caring for him or her, manage this confrontation with increased death awareness through seeking and engaging in activities aimed at finding a continued sense of being alive — even while facing death. In order to continue to view ourselves as living individuals in the presence of our increased knowledge of death, we are dependent on caring interactions with others to affirm our sense of aliveness. Caring relationships, in which one is cared for or provides care for another human being not unlike oneself, create a life setting that provides activity which allows individuals to find meaning, hope, personal significance, and the sense of continuing to be alive. Thus the process of caring itself forms the very matrix from which we generate our meaning, our hope, our personal and professional significance, and our sense of aliveness in our confrontation with death.

Because the needs of the dying person and his family are highly individualized and cover so vast a spectrum, caring for these persons often requires the blending of care and knowledge derived from a number of health-care and health-care-related disciplines. Thus, those persons providing care need to have a knowledge of the manner in which disciplines other than their own might provide care or contribute knowledge valuable to the care process. Those issues which may disrupt a "working together" posture need to be understood and overcome. Such disruptive issues include preconceived stereotypes held by various caregiving disciplines about one another, varying sets and levels of knowledge and skills, differences in professional language, role conflict resulting from overlap in areas of care, interference from institutional hierarchy, poor communication patterns, and the lack of suitable settings for overcoming conflict and integrating differing approaches. Only when such issues are managed and overcome, and the process of care is understood in terms of the totality of needs and efforts, can a collaborative, cooperative, mutually supportive approach to the care of the dying person be achieved. This concept, that of supportive collaboration, the "working together" of caregivers from many disciplines, would provide a flexible and complementary approach to providing care for the dying person and his family which has not heretofore been used to its fullest potential. Mutual support, collaboration, and integrated approaches to care are viewed as superior to the compartmentalized care provided by a single discipline.

Part I of this book is intended to provide an overview of basic material and an approach to caring for dying persons and their families. The literature in the areas of dying, death, and bereavement has become vast; this section of the book is not intended to be an exhaustive review. I have, however, attempted to selectively gleen important concepts from the literature in order to offer the reader exposure to the underpinnings of care in the area. Woven through these chapters is an approach to the dying person and his family stated in terms of the interpersonal relationships and interactions that may foster or impede the effective care of the individuals concerned. A central theme in this portion of the book is the concept that those problems and conflicts involved in adapting to dying and death are largely related to the problems and conflicts related to living in the context of dying and the threat of death.

Part II of the book consists of a number of contributions from people representing varying caregiving disciplines, and includes the reflections and thoughts of two dying patients. Undoubtedly there are other disciplines and contributors who should be represented in this section, and determining those dimensions which were finally selected to be included was a difficult task. I think it important to mention that as the book was planned originally, a chapter written by a social worker was to be included, but circumstances arose which kept this from occurring.

I remain firmly dedicated to the concept of a multidisciplinary approach to caring and am hopeful that these perspectives from professionals representing various disciplines and views will serve to underline what I believe to be a necessity for an approach to effective therapeutic care in the area. It is hoped that the various contributions will help the reader begin to integrate the views of varying disciplines in the overall process of caring for dying persons and their families, thereby moving toward achieving the concept of supportive collaboration mentioned above.

I hold the basic belief that a book such as this one, like the process of caring itself, should as nearly as possible evolve from and reflect the total interactional process and experiences of its writers. Thus those persons who have been part of my experiences in the relationships relating to my work with patients and colleagues in the area of dying, death, and bereavement, in the meetings, classrooms, and innumerable discussions, and through scientific and other writings should all form the experience that comes together as this book. In caring for a dying person and his family, the immersion of oneself in the experience of the relationships involved in caring constitutes a vital part of care and its ultimate outcome. Similarly, the writing and editing of this book must represent the point in my own experience, and that of the contributors, which we have reached through the interactions involved in the process of working in the area, as well as reflect the influence of countless encounters with others sharing similar interests.

I could not, in any complete way, list those persons who have so helpfully participated in this process and have, over a number of years, aided me in giving some form to my ideas. Those patients who have shared with me aspects of the most precious transition in their lives—their dying or the loss of those dear to them—form the nucleus of my experience. To these persons I am most grateful. Certainly the book could not have come into being without the contributors who so willingly undertook the task of placing their feelings, ideas, and experiences into the chapters that comprise the second portion of the book. Undoubtedly, I have been strongly influenced by the group of multidisciplinary persons with whom I have worked, many of whom are not directly represented in the book. These colleagues have added new dimensions to my thoughts, feelings, ideas, and concepts of the psychology of human existence; they deserve my deep appreciation. The works of Avery D. Weisman, Robert J. Lifton, and Elisabeth Kübler-Ross have had a profound impact on my thinking and their thoughts have found their way into both many parts of this book, and my work in the area. Harry S. Abram, a friend and colleague, has strongly influenced my thoughts and work. When I have despaired about both my work and the creation of this book, his friendship and dialogue, his help in clarifying ideas, and his editorial assistance has often served to provide an impetus to continue my efforts. Unquestionably, without the support and guidance of Jim Gallagher of The Williams & Wilkins Co., this book would not have come to fruition. I am deeply thankful for his belief and faith in the project and his patience and help along the way. My family perhaps deserves the most credit for their patient tolerance of my absences during the long hours of emotional and intellectual absorption in the writing and editing of the book—time that often rightfully belonged to them. I am deeply grateful for the help, support, and encouragement of my wife Lynn. Without her support and encouragement, her assistance with the editing of the book, her aid in helping me clarify many of my ideas, and, as is true of most of what I do, her belief in me, I do not believe that the book would have been completed.

Mrs. Linda Hardy skillfully typed most of the manuscript, assisted with the editing, corresponded with the contributing authors, assisted me in library research, and made countless other contributions to the preparation of the manuscript. Her skill, interest, and untiring devotion to the preparation of the manuscript were significant contributions to the creation of this book.

I could not have known when I began the preparation of this manuscript that in the midst of my writing and editing, I, myself, would experience a great personal loss. My father died unexpectedly almost a year after I began work on the manuscript and a year before its completion. The death of a loved person is indeed a powerful and painful human experience. His dying and death and my subsequent grief provided an intense need to complete the book, yet brought death so near to me as to cause me at times to want to abandon the project. He was proud of what I was doing; he was a caring man, and I am certain that some of what I have written here bears the mark of his caring way of living, his dying, and his death. He, himself, always spoke of writing a book. He did not; and so, as his son, this book is for him.

DAVID BARTON, M.D.

Contributors

Jan van Eys, Ph.D., M.D., Professor and Head, Department of Pediatrics, M.D. Anderson Hospital and Tumor Institute, The University of Texas System Cancer Center, Houston, Texas.

John M. Flexner, M.D., Associate Professor of Medicine, Department of Medicine, Division of Hematology, Vanderbilt University School of Medicine, Nashville, Tennessee.

Ann B. Hamric, R.N., M.S., Assistant Professor of Medical-Surgical Nursing, Virginia Commonwealth University, Medical College of Virginia School of Nursing, Richmond, Virginia.

Liston O. Mills, Th.D., Oberlin Alumni Professor, Pastoral Theology and Counseling, Vanderbilt Divinity School, Vanderbilt University, Nashville, Tennessee.

Daniel T. Peak, M.D., Medical Director, Continued Treatment Unit, John Ulmstead Hospital, Butner, North Carolina.

Charles E. Scott, Ph.D., Professor of Philosophy, Department of Philosophy, Vanderbilt University, Nashville, Tennessee.

Robert M. Veatch, Ph.D., Senior Associate and Director of Research Group on Death and Dying, Institute of Society, Ethics and Life Sciences, Hastings Center, Hastings-on-Hudson, New York.

Contents

part **I**

AN APPROACH TO CARING FOR DYING PERSONS

1

DYING, DEATH, AND BEREAVEMENT AS HEALTH-CARE PROBLEMS

David Barton, M.D.

If one views the number of articles and books on a subject in the medical and nonmedical literature as an index of the current interest in an area of health care, then one must certainly conclude that dying, death, and bereavement have been identified as salient issues in current medical practice. Indeed, one bibliography containing over 1,400 references[1] and another containing over 2,600 references[2] would seem to present impressive evidence that the subject has been addressed from every quarter and is highly visible. Yet in 1963, the topic of "Death" was included in a book entitled *Taboo Topics*[3] and, in many medical care settings, the topic remains taboo or is viewed as "soft data" and of questionable relevance. Clearly, a topic may be highly visible and still be taboo. Likewise, a large body of knowledge about an area may be available and the application of that knowledge be limited. Visibility in itself does not necessarily mean that the knowledge and skills related to an area have been integrated into the care-giving process.

The practice of medicine involves the identification and delineation of problems, their clarification through clinical observation and systematic study, and the application of derived knowledge, skills, and attitudes to care situations. Commentary is no substitute for the development of actual approaches to problems in care. Thus while phrases such as "death and dying" and "death with dignity" may be echoed through the halls of the medical institutions, and in fact provide a necessary focus and emphasis, the critical issue remains one of integrating approaches to care for dying persons and their families in actual care situations. To do otherwise is to isolate the area and set it apart from the mainstream of medical practice. Without integration of the knowledge into an approach, there is the danger that the topic and its many ramifications will become like the dying person— often isolated and set apart on the periphery of care. The purpose of this chapter, then, is to describe those aspects which legitimize dying, death, and bereavement as health-care concerns as well as those aspects which create difficulties in the development of approaches to care.

ADVANCES IN MEDICINE

The current interest and emphasis on problems related to the dying person stem from a number of changes that have occurred in this century within medicine and the society it serves. Tremendous advances in medicine have been achieved in this century; the techniques of preventive medicine, the advent of the antibiotic era, and the development of medical technology have had a substantial impact on illness and medical practice. The infectious diseases such as pneumonia and tuberculosis, which were at the top of the list of causes of death in the year 1900, have been replaced there by the so-called chronic and often protracted degenerative diseases such as heart disease, cancer, and vascular diseases affecting the central nervous system.[4] Medical science has developed replacement techniques with physiologic fluids, blood, artificial heart valves, and organ transplantation of such vital organs as kidneys and hearts. Life-sustaining measures include the ability to feed an individual almost indefinitely through total parenteral alimentation, highly efficient artificial respirators capable of sustaining respiration for prolonged periods of time, renal dialysis, and cardiac pacemakers to stablize cardiac conduction patterns. Diagnostic procedures are refined, extensive, and capable of analyzing small quantities of blood for its numerous chemical constituents or pinpointing lesion within the brain with the use of radioactive materials or computer methodology. Resuscitation methods a few years ago termed "heroic" are now commonplace in the hospital setting, and are frequently used systematically to restore vital functions after their brief or sometimes prolonged cessation. Highly specialized and technically skilled special care units such as medical and surgical intensive care, cardiac care, burn, and renal dialysis units are now common settings in the general hospital.

The hospital itself has developed into a complex social institution with all of the structures inherent in such a setting. In the medical institution one can expect to encounter social hierarchies, highly specialized role designations, and complicated, sometimes burdensome, administrative protocols. The hospitalized or the ambulatory patient can expect to come into contact with a myriad of caregivers, including his* physician, specialists called in as consultants, nursing staff, administrative, diagnostic, and support personnel, and often trainees. Additionally, the patient and his family may receive or require the care and assistance of social workers, hospital chaplains, and community clergy. They also may come into contact with personnel who reflect the rapid changes in medical care, such as clinical nurse specialists, nurse practitioners, and a variety of paramedical personnel.

The results of this technology are impressive. In the United States, life expectancy increased from approximately 47 years in 1900, to over 70 years in 1967.[4] Not only

has life expectancy increased but there have been significant shifts in mortality rates in certain age groups. In 1900, over 50% of recorded deaths were children under the age of 15, while only 17% of recorded deaths occurred in the 65-and-over age group. At the end of the 1960's, 67% of deaths occurred in the 65-and-over age group and death in the younger age group had markedly decreased.[5]

Earlier diagnosis, newer treatment methods, advanced surgical techniques, potent chemotherapeutic measures, and high-voltage radiotherapy have also brought about significant changes in the duration of life after diagnosis of disease. This is apparent in the statistics related to certain types of malignant illnesses in which the percentages of individuals surviving five years after diagnosis have shown significant increases from the 1940's to the 1960's.[6] Survival rates have not decreased for any cancer site in the past 25 years; five-year survival rates for a number of cancer sites have increased steadily from the 1940's to the 1960's. Thus, people now live for longer periods of time with the knowledge of having or having had some life-threatening illnesses.

Changes derived from improved technology and organization of health-care delivery, while often life-giving and beneficial, have not been without significant economic costs and psychosocial stress. Changes in technology and advances in biological care are inseparably intertwined with psychosocial stresses and often new psychological dilemmas — stresses and dilemmas for patients and their families, and in many cases for caregivers as well.[7–11]

INCREASED INTEREST IN PSYCHOSOCIAL ISSUES

Since the early 1950's the field of psychosomatic medicine has substantially broadened. While once more limited to the study of psychogenicity in diseases (such as duodenal ulcers, ulcerative colitis, and asthma), the field now encompasses the entire area of psychosocial adaptation to illness and surgical procedures including the effects of the

---

* In Chapters 1 through 8, I have used the pronouns "he," "him," and "his" for ease of reading rather than "he or she," "him or her," and "his or hers." I ask that the reader view this as literary convention rather than as discrimination, as the latter is in no way intended.

diagnostic process, the treatment process, and the effects of the health-care system on the patient's overall psychosocial adaptation. This emphasis has given rise to a large amount of literature devoted to the study of the psychosocial aspects of health care and has served to significantly heighten awareness about psychosocial care. Psychiatrists, other physicians, nurses, social workers, psychologists, hospital chaplains, and other health-care personnel have devoted increasing energies in the direction of psychosocial medicine and their efforts have served to bring to light a variety of individual, interpersonal, and social problems involved in adaptation to illness. The numerous disciplines working in the area have provided varying viewpoints and have pointed to the need for a blend of interdisciplinary knowledge and efforts. By representing many disciplines, they have brought not only the knowledge and skills from their respective fields, but also have drawn on principles of sociology, law, anthropology, ethics, religion, and the more traditional branches of psychiatric practice.

In many teaching centers, psychiatric consultation-liaison teams involving the collaborative efforts of psychiatrists, nurses, social workers, psychologists, and chaplains assist in the psychosocial care of patients in the general hospital. Along with their interest in individual patient care, they have directed their efforts toward both preventative aspects and the facilitation of a psychologically therapeutic hospital milieu. They have concerned themselves with the interpersonal attitudes of not only the patients and their families, but also have turned their attention to the therapeutic and sometimes nontherapeutic attitudes and interactions of caregivers toward patients and their families and among themselves. These teams have also been concerned with the hospital environment—the physical plant itself, its administrative protocol, its machinery, and its spatial features, all as they affect the patient's adaptation to illness.

INCREASED INTEREST IN HUMANISTIC CARE

There has also been an increasing interest in the humanistic aspects of care. Humanis-tic medicine encompasses an appreciation of the psychosocial aspects of medical care while extending the concept to meet the needs of the individual as a unique human being with rights and with dignity. Humanistic care assumes a less reductionistic, more holistic approach and acknowledges the uniqueness of the individual patient. When receiving individualized, humanistic care, the patient assumes a more active role as a knowledgeable participant in his care, is concerned with human rights, and expects far more dialogue with those giving care. In the context of the desire for more humanistic care, medical technology is viewed ambivalently with both appreciation and as a threat. Its life-prolonging potential is, on the one hand, welcomed, while on the other, the technology involved is seen as a threat to individualized treatment. While appreciating the need for technology, the public fears being reduced to dehumanized computer numbers. In terms of the reactions to issues surrounding dying and death, this need has been expressed in the plea for "death with dignity."

Within the medical institution many have perceived the danger of a reductionistic, techical view of patients and have recognized that those who receive health care are more than vital signs, blood counts, and electrolytes. The patient with a myocardial infarction is more than a "coronary in bed four," yet this impersonal view is sometimes fostered by a technology which tends toward sameness. Life-threatening illness does not lend itself to impersonal care, for each person sees his life as his most valuable possession. He views his life as unique and is unwilling to see it reach its end in a specified, predetermined, prescribed manner which compromises uniqueness.

THE INCREASED SENSE OF FINITENESS

In the past three to four decades we have experienced the profound impact of continual wars; thus, with the development of television, capable of bringing the battlefield into the living room, we live in a world which is attuned to death. The use of nuclear weapons capable of leveling cities looms as an ever-present possibility of the next moment. What has been described as "future shock" provides a steady flow of rapidly passing sensory inputs and creates a sense of transience.[12] Both individual death and the annihilation of our entire culture is possible at an moment. Not only must we deal with our individual finitude, but we must also deal with the possibility of the extinction of the totality of human existence and live with the resultant sense of cultural finitude.[13-15]

One method of coping with constant awareness of death is to move toward the elaboration of a romanticized view of death. This view and its accompanying mood has found its way into the literature about dying and death. Being "next" to death, talking about death, talking with dying people, and being able to handle the "heavy" subject of death are abilities endowed with considerable romantic qualities. Some associate the movement toward caring for dying persons and being concerned with death with this view and see the interest as a fad or bandwagon. But the interest in this area of care extends far beyond this romanticized view and mood. Lifton has noted the importance of viewing death as a central theme related to the events of our times.[13-16] As sexuality was the "hidden" force of the 19th century, so death and finitude is the "hidden" force of the 20th century.

SOCIAL CHANGE AND INSTITUTIONALIZED DYING

Dying is rapidly becoming an institutionalized process. Changes in society and family structure, along with the hospital-based availability of modern life-saving and life-prolonging procedures, have moved the dying process toward the institutional setting. Our society has evolved into a highly mobile, industrialized social order. The extended family structure of the past, with its ability to provide support and care for the sick, has given way to the smaller isolated nuclear family. Although the nuclear family is more mobile it must rely on outside support rather than close relatives when one of the family members is ill. Necessarily, the isolated nuclear family seeks support from close friends, neighbors, and community institutions and agencies rather than abundant relatives living in close proximity as in the past. Dying at home in the company of fa-miliar faces and surroundings has given way to dying in institutions amidst a complex array of caregivers, machinery, social organization, and administrative protocol.

In 1958, over 60% of all deaths in this country occurred in institutional settings (hospitals, convalescent and nursing homes, and in the hospital units of institutions such as mental hospitals). Less than ten years earlier, this figure was slightly under 50%. The largest percentage of institutional deaths in 1958 occurred in general hospitals, the next highest in convalescent and nursing homes, and the next in hospitals for the mentally ill. Additional data available for later years indicate a trend toward even higher percentages of the population dying institutional deaths.[4] Society is increasingly delegating the responsibility for the care of the dying to the institutional setting. These findings indicate that increasing numbers of health-care professionals are placed in close approximation to dying persons and death. These caregivers must necessarily utilize available technology and, at the same time, provide humanistic care. They must also develop the knowledge and skills to enable them to care for dying persons and their families and to deal with constant exposure to reminders of their own finitude.

Those individuals providing care within the medical institution often experience intense feelings related to their interaction with patients — especially the dying and their families. When perceived and managed, these feelings may be used to enhance and facilitate therapeutic care, but in some situations the feelings may significantly interfere with the provisions of care. In caring for dying persons, health-care providers may feel helpless, drained, physically and mentally fatigued, anxious, saddened, grieved, and overwhelmed by the constant stimulus of human suffering. Physicians, nurses, clergy, social workers, and other caregivers are as human as their patients and, in spite of attempts to modulate their level of involvement, often experience the full range of human emotions and attitudes. In response to these feelings, they often use the same coping strategies and defensive maneuvers used by those who receive their care. Thus, caregivers need to develop a self-awareness which will allow them to use their feelings as an indicator of reactions to patients' behaviors and attitudes. Feelings may then be evaluated in terms of their therapeutic or nontherapeutic potential. To facilitate this, an atmosphere that allows communication about these feelings and the support and guidance of other caregivers must be developed.

Thus, advances in medical technology, an increased awareness of psychosocial issues in medical care, the humanistic emphasis in patient care, an increased awareness of finitude, changes in family structure, the institutionalization of dying, and increased proximity of health-care personnel to the death situation have all resulted in an increased identification of dying and death as health-care problems. These trends have reached a level that creates a need for the development of effective approaches to care in the area. A basic thesis of this book is that dying and death must be viewed as a part of the life cycle; dying and death are so much a part of the everyday work of the medical institution that the development of the systematic use of knowledge, skills, and attitudes is required to effectively provide care in the area. All illness and disease is perceived as a threat to one's existence. As such, illness is proof to the individual of his humanness and a reminder of personal finitude. The creation of an atmosphere that conveys the medical institution's acceptance of the responsibility of caring for the dying person is now a necessity. Dying and death are indeed health-care problems.

THE PROBLEMATIC NATURE OF PAINFUL FEELINGS EXPERIENCED IN THE CONTEXT OF DYING AND DEATH

It now becomes appropriate to explore ways in which dying and death are problematic areas in the overall scheme of health care. These problems arise from the subtle intertwinings of the biological, psychological, social, and cultural dimensions of dying and death. In the context of this discussion a "problem" refers to a medical event, a series of events, or a process of medical care which is likely to create considerable personal and interpersonal discomfort at a feeling and experiential level in the dying person, his family, or the health-care givers. The situation is not only difficult in terms of

cognitive knowledge or performance skills, but also generates a wide spectrum of painful and dysphoric feelings. These feelings may range from intense anxiety to apathy. They may take the form of paralyzing uncertainty, deep sadness, or nameless feelings experienced only as a painful, free-floating discomfort. They may cause the caregiver to question the very meaning of his profession, for, at these junctures, the usual activities which allow him a sense of aliveness and caring are compromised in his confrontation with dying and death.

Perceiving this discomfort, the caregiver tends to avoid those circumstances which produce the dysphoria. Any circumstance that has the potential to create distance between the caregiver and the patient brings a distorted, nontherapeutic quality to the relationship. The caregiver is driven from the position of being available and away from the need-discerning presence so important in the care of dying patients. The circumstances producing this withdrawal response engender a reaction similar to that of the body to a splinter. The care situation is walled off and isolated from the rest of the medical care process. However, this avoidance response continues to exert considerable influence on the milieu and retains the potential to disrupt or interfere with communication among caregivers. It is imperative then to appreciate those aspects of caring for dying persons and their families that contribute to the production of a myriad of dysphoric feelings.

THE UNIQUENESS OF THE DYING PERSON'S ADAPTATION

Dying and death involve unique adaptive processes for the patient, his family, and caregivers. Each dying person and those around him respond to the threat to life in terms of the past, current life circumstances, and aspirations for the future. These often unique responses tend to interfere with a desired sense of conformity, and the needs, feelings, and responses in one person as contrasted with another are often so dissimilar as to create a sense of disorder bordering at times on chaos. As a changing, dynamic process, the physical and emotional elements of the individual's adaptation must constantly be evaluated and re-evaluated by caregivers. Attempts to identify orderly and predictable physical or psychosocial lines of progression are often highly frustrating. The attempt to coerce specific patterns of adaptation from or superimpose conformity on any given patient may lead to a reductionistic, often mechanistic and impersonal form of care. While the caregiver and others may feel some comfort from the sense of closure derived from a specific theory or cognitive position (thereby reducing the painful intensity of their own feelings), the dying person may only suffer more by feeling that he is not fulfilling the expectations of those providing care.

THE VISIBILITY OF HUMAN SUFFERING

The dying person often presents a care situation in which human suffering becomes highly visible and not amenable to available medical intervention. The feelings of helplessness in the face of an irreversible process of suffering and progressive debilitation and loss are not limited to the dying person. They are experienced by all those caring for him. There is in medical practice the subtly perpetuated idea that death represents a failure. This posture is reasonable in a profession that has throughout its history provided services aimed at ensuring or restoring health. However, this professional expectation creates a paradox; for while a patient's death is held consciously or unconsciously as a failure on the physician's part, the physician continues to be confronted with death. The forces generated by the continual anticipation of failure and loss perhaps produce a counterforce that generates the need to ensure and restore health. It has been hypothesized that the fear of death has played an important part in some physicians' choice of their profession; i.e., that some physicians enter medicine to adapt to their own "above average" fears related to death.[17, 18] Others[19] have studied the role of death anxiety in the physician's choice of specialty and demonstrated the presence of higher levels of anxiety about death in medical students choosing internal medicine, pediatrics, and psychiatry than in students choosing surgery as a specialty.

These issues appear far broader than just the fear of death. They relate to the acceptance of dying and death as reality, as part of the life cycle, and as a legitimate end to the life process which ultimately defies control and mastery. The acceptance of dying and death as part of the life cycle and a legitimate end to the life process needs not to be equated with the acceptance of the suffering and decline brought about by a disease process, for there is much that can be done to comfort and aid the dying person and his family.

INCREASED UNCERTAINTY IN THE CONTEXT OF DYING AND DEATH

A related difficulty is that of the physical and emotional issues connected with dying and death crossing the boundaries of medical certainty and extending beyond the limits of medical knowledge. Precision and certainty are the desired ends of scientific inquiry and effort. Medical personnel from the beginning of their training are taught an ethic of performing at the highest possible level. Certainty is desired and sought. Professional excellence is encouraged and expected. But each caregiver at some point in his training may expect situations in which every resource of knowledge is exhausted. This is often a sobering and disenchanting experience for the trainee and represents a time in his professional career when he must accept his humanness and his limitations. It is a head-on confrontation with uncertainty, and one for which he is often not prepared.[20, 21] The same is true for the emotional aspects of dying as for the more purely physical aspects. No caregiver can truly appreciate with certainty the totality of the emotional responses of the dying individual for whom he is caring. But in spite of this, the caregiver can develop a process of care which will, to the best of his abilities, serve to appreciate the needs of the person, be they physical or emotional, and to meet them to the extent possible. Tolerance for uncertainty is necessarily a part of the health-care professional's armamentarium and nowhere in medicine does the issue of uncertainty became more blatant than in the room of the person close to death. Achieving a balance between the recognition of the uncertain aspects of medicine and the quest for certainty that is sought in the science of medicine represents a constant and often painful struggle in the caregiver. At each juncture in caring for the dying person there is the threat of this balance being painfully upset.

MODULATION OF INFORMATION EXCHANGE

The care area is treated as an issue to be dealt with in secret, or at least partially out of the context of full awareness, and a number of factors contribute to this aspect of the care of the dying patient. There is a tendency on the part of the patient's family and caregivers to react to the threat of death by modulating the amount of information exchanged about the issues connected with a person's dying.[22] Aside from the topic itself being painful and promoting a sense of uneasiness in all concerned, the information exchanged is shared against a background of conscious and unconscious prohibitions about communications related to death. Unconsciously, the process of denial is generally operant at some level, restricting the amount of real information available to the interacting persons. This powerful process of not acknowledging information is central to the problem in communication with the dying person and also plays an important part in the often obscure communications between the family and caregivers as well as among the caregivers themselves. The "secret," as it appears in the interactions, frequently is maintained even when some or all concerned would have it otherwise and wish that "all was in the open." In addition to unconscious processes there are various consciously conceived coping maneuvers designed to protect the dying person and those around him. Cognitively, these take the form of withholding information in its entirety or by communicating in such a way as to say very little. Emotionally, the information may be dampened through restriction of the expression of feelings. Behaviorally, the information may be changed significantly through actual physical avoidance of the person involved or by utilizing motility and modulating presence to an extent that in-depth communication is not really possible. To further complicate the communication patterns, information withheld in one mode, *e.g.*, cognitive information, may be communicated in another. In such situations, the information is communiated in a behavioral mode through nonverbal gestures and facial expressions or emotionally through anxiety and uneasiness in the presence of the person. The "secret" and its ramifications in terms of information exchange contribute an uncomfortable, fragile feeling to the sense of relatedness. It appears quite likely that some of this constriction of information serves an adaptive function by allowing certain aspects of the process of care to proceed even in the face of emotionally overwhelming data. In this, however, a paradox is evident; for the same mechanisms utilized to assist in managing the information also have the capability to disrupt or at least compromise the effectiveness of relationships.

THE USE OF CLINICAL JUDGEMENT

Caring for the dying person involves the application of considerable clinical judgement in which there is a wide range of opinion and often disagreement. In medical care there are situations where there may well be more than one option in the management process. In these situations there is often no "one best answer," and the decision rests on the judgement of the caregiver. Obviously, in these situations the stage is set for disagreement among those involved. A frequently encountered decision requiring clinical judgement is the question of whether a dying person can best be treated at home or in the hospital. Often in these decisions psychosocial data play an important role. In this case it is important to know the kinds of support systems available or not available at home, the involvement of children, and the availability of supportive friends. Unfortunately, this type of data is often either not gathered or is not integrated into the overall process of care. Psychosocial data related to the person's personality traits are also important. If, for instance, the dying person who desires a great deal of control over his life circumstances is left out of the decision-making process, this is likely to evoke considerable feeling in the person. On the other hand, if a decision is left to a person and his family who wish to view the physician as "having all the answers," one finds that the situation has again stirred feelings which may disrupt care. The technological set of medical practice creates an atmosphere in which decisions are more likely to be made on the basis of biological "hard data." There are times when physical data must be given priority and decisions made on this basis. For nonphysicians some of these decisions may, while being medically necessary, be viewed as insensitive and uncaring when in fact they reflect a necessary and even life-saving professional position.

ETHICAL DILEMMAS

Modern medical technology has created any number of significant ethical dilemmas for both medical caregivers and society, and ethical considerations are intimately involved in caring for the dying person. Many of the dilemmas appear insoluble and questions associated with them remain without definitive answers or even established procedure which might lead to answers. Issues such as the development of life-sustaining machines and the effective use of organ transplantation have created the need for establishing precise definitions of death. Traditionally death was pronounced at the time of cessation of vital cardiac and respiratory functions. With modern technology these vital functions can often be restored and maintained. This development has led to the concept of "brain death" with the focus of life shifting from the heart and lungs to the brain. The "brain wave" or electroencephalographic measurement of electrical potential on the surface of the brain has come to be utilized as a measurement of activity of brain function with the flat or "isoelectric" electroencephalographic tracing viewed as one of the important confirmatory procedures in determining the presence of irreversible coma. To avoid error, however, a broader group of criteria has been elaborated by the Ad Hoc Committee of the Harvard Medical School to Examine the Definition of Brain Death.[23] This committee has established criteria to define irreversible coma as a criterion for death. The relationship of such issues to the law is demonstrated by legislative involvement in the concept of brain death, such as that in the state of Kansas.[24] While criteria

which would provide certainty are sought, this entire area continues to be refined and appraised.[25]

To respond to the plea for "death with dignity," the health-care profession must struggle with questions related to the dilemma of the Hippocratic Oath's mandate ". . . give no deadly medicine to any one if asked, nor suggest any such counsel,"[26] while at the same time feeling the personal convictions and societal mandates toward relieving suffering. Terms such as "active" and "passive" euthanasia have come into use with discussion of the moral differences between the active use of medications or procedures to hasten death and withholding medications or procedures to allow someone to die. In 1973 the House of Delegates of the American Medical Association adopted the following statement " . . . to serve as a guideline for physicians confronted with ethical problems related to euthanasia and death with dignity."

The intentional termination of the life of one human being by another — mercy killing — is contrary to that for which the medical profession stands and is contrary to the policy of the American Medical Association.

The cessation of the employment of extraordinary means to prolong the life of the body when there is irrefutable evidence that biological death is imminent is the decision of the patient and/or his immediate family. The advice and judgment of the physician should be freely available to the patient and/or his immediate family.[27*]

Even with such guidelines, the question of " . . . when there is irrefutable evidence that biological death is imminent . . . " involves clinical judgment and may enter the realm of uncertainty. The case of Karen Ann Quinlan demonstrates the difficulties involved in the questions surrounding individual patient rights, rights of family, the positions of physicians, and the interaction of these determinants with society and the legal system.[29-36]

Absolute guidelines are absent, and the health-care profession and others continue to study, consider, and struggle with these

---

* For one author's view of the implications of this statement in terms of active and passive euthanasia, see Rachels J: Active and Passive Euthanasia. *N Engl J Med 292:* 78-80, 1975 (Ref. 28).

painful issues. These considerations, while not new in the practice of medicine, are far more visible with advancing technology. Feelings and opinions differ and a consensus is not readily obtained. When issues such as these arise in the care of the dying person, there is likely to be considerable emotion and often divergent opinion. These feelings and opinions have the ever-present potential to disrupt the relationship between caregivers, family, and patients.

PERSONAL VALUES AND BELIEF SYSTEMS

In the context of dying and death, personal value systems often become involved in care of the patient. The caregiver is likely to have any number of personal religious or philosophical views as to how the patient might best adapt and yet the patient's adaptation is highly individualized and unique. At best, the caregiver is comfortable with his own values and can allow the dying patient to use his own means of adaptation. At worst, there is intolerance which creates an atmosphere of tension and guilt. There are as many ideas as there are people regarding the best way to face death and manage the life crises involved in dying. But often a caregiver would have the person respond as he would respond and, when this attitude is communicated to the patient and his family, highly personal feelings are potentially hidden, resulting in a sense of isolation for the dying person and others.

To care for another is to place oneself in a position of possible change in oneself. In true acts of caring the caregiver changes in some respect, whether it is to increase his experience or to enable him to move closer to working with some aspect of personal concern. But if the caregiver is not prepared to act and react flexibly or is not prepared to allow some aspects of the interaction to move him toward different patterns of response, he ceases to give care. If the caregiver is so inflexible as to disallow any change in himself while participating in the care of another, he is likely to fit the persons with whom he is working into his own theoretical framework or value system and insist that the person act and react in that manner. In this case, the caregiver is likely to be caring more for himself than for another.

He is attempting to reinforce his own beliefs and approaches without allowing the other's response to be integrated into the care process. True caring can only be achieved when people can relate, when the caring is for both, when data are derived which can potentially change preconceived notions, when reactions that are therapeutic are evoked by distress, and when struggle may be stirred in such a way that a constructive set of responses is engendered by the struggle.

DEPLETION OF RESOURCES

Dying often requires the use of costly, time- and emotion-consuming, and at times extraordinary medical efforts; frequently the return in terms of restoration of health is minimal. It is not uncommon for a family's financial resources to be depleted by the care involved in a life-threatening illness. Similarly, the emotional and physical resources of the family and caregivers are often exhausted by the energies required to provide care for a dying person. Long hours of watchful waiting and emotional investment in a life crisis deplete individuals and add many additional responsibilities to their life circumstances, taking considerable toll. Support systems, which may under ordinary circumstances be adequate, are taxed beyond their capacity. Care of the dying in the hospital setting as well as the home setting may totally disrupt routine and usual functioning. In the hospital, physical resources may become depleted when intensive care units are filled to capacity and there is another person in need of the unit's services. In a home where interpersonal support is crucial, there is often simply not enough available. Helplessness, grief, depression, guilt, and anxiety serve to drain caregivers and others involved with the dying person, rendering them unable to provide care. In summary, dying can be an excessive financial, emotional, and physical burden that is capable of disrupting the function of any social unit, be it the marital unit, the home, or the hospital ward. At some point, ordinary support may not be enough and the individuals involved are often compelled to rely on others. The support required for bolstering the system may be drawn from persons more removed from the patient who have less knowledge of the individual as a total person. Again care is compromised, resulting in an impersonal approach.

DIVERSITY OF CAREGIVERS

Life-threatening illness and the process of dying and death require the services of a large number of caregivers representing diverse fields. Physicians, nurses, social workers, clergy, other hospital personnel, family members, and friends all enter into the caregiving process. Each of these persons brings to the care process a specific personal or professional identity and his or her own attitudes and feelings about dying and death. While each person involved in this process may have a specific role based on professional identity, the roles and tasks may not be clearly delineated. Long-established tradition and institutional hierarchy may designate functions of individual professionals while the dying person and his family have different expectations. There is overlap in role and functions that is not always clearly delineated. Thus patients and their families may have similar expectations of caregivers in differing disciplines. A nurse, for example, is expected to have a clear idea of the status of the patient's illness. The nurse, depending on the mode of communication in that particular setting, may or may not have this information, or because of established roles, the nurse may defer to the physician when asked questions by the family or the patient. Because these conflicts in role elicit considerable feeling, the stage is then set for a subtle disruption in the flow of communication. The same is true of other caregivers. The patient may ask medical questions of the clergyman. Family may ask theological questions of medical personnel. The possibilities for communication difficulties are unlimited.

In caring for the dying person, interaction and communication among caregivers is frequently limited. There is poor utilization of a badly needed mutual support system which might be derived from more effective interaction. Lack of access to communication with one another results in each caregiver being left to fend for himself in relating to the patient and his family. Further complicating the communication is the pretense and secrecy which tends to surround the situation. Mixed feelings and attitudes and poor communication severely compromise care.

THE TENDENCY TO STOP CARE WHEN DEATH OCCURS

All too often, formal care for the dying patient and his family ends at the time of the death of the patient. For the family, however, the work of mourning and the reorganization of life continues. During this period of time health-care needs often increase. Complicated grief reactions are not uncommon and studies[37] indicate that for many persons, the bereavement period is associated with significant emotional and physical distress. Care aimed at facilitating the effective resolution of the grief process becomes an important part of the overall care process and must be included in any approach to working in this area. The mood of the bereaved person and his immersion in loss is likely to stimulate an avoidance response, evoking in caregivers painful feelings similar to those experienced in working with the dying patient.

DEFICIENT EDUCATION IN THE AREA

Education for health-care professionals about death has been limited and poorly integrated into health-care training. Until recently, formal courses in the medical curriculum related to the problems of dying, death, and bereavement were virtually absent. Even though in close proximity to the dying, health-care professionals tend to learn about the management of these persons through informal means. Systematic instruction about the process of dying and issues related to death and bereavement have only recently become available for the persons caring for the dying.[38-48] The absence of education in this area is a powerful communication and serves to deter the development of a systematic approach. Students' perceptions about the absence of instruction serve to perpetuate the attitude that the subject is taboo. It indicates to them that there is little known about the area and therefore there is no attempt at instruction. When teaching has occurred, it has been in the form of instruction by learned panelists with little discussion by students. This form of education communicates to the student that the panelists have firm answers to the questions about dying and death. The student, then, finds himself even more uncomfortable in the presence of the dying person when he experiences uncertainty.[38] Cognitive content education alone does not adequately prepare the student to deal with the issues connected with dying and death. There is a vast experiential component of caring for the dying person and his family, and it can only be learned through the process of caring for the patient and his family. Too much dwelling in content alone allows the student to stay within the content without experiencing and becoming reasonably comfortable with his own feelings and attitudes. The student achieves closure and certainty, thereby reducing his anxiety. The experience of the student and the dying patient are compartmentalized in favor of specific, iron-clad, theoretical frameworks.

Although there are those who continue to question the directions of the movement toward caring for dying persons and their families, the area remains a legitimate one in medical care. Editorials in medical journals have noted the phenomenon of the increasing number of books and journal articles on the subject and have reflected on the phenomenon with varying feelings.[49, 50] They voice concern over the general question of the legitimacy of this field of study and raise the point that mere philosophy is no substitute for developing experience through actual patient care. To ignore it as a viable part of the health-care profession is further denial of dying and death. To involve oneself in armchair philosophy without being with the patient and his family accomplishes little. On the other hand, in any movement toward providing care, visibility is desirable and the development of a philosophy of care is a necessary beginning.

Undoubtedly the area needs well-designed and systematically applied scientific study.* But because of the nature of the feelings and the uniqueness of the individuals' responses, these studies will require time and must be done in a sensitive manner. There is no reason, however, why these studies cannot be conducted in the context of patient care, elucidating and clarifying not only the needs of the dying person, but also the most effective means of meeting those needs.

REFERENCES

1. Vernick JJ: *Selected Bibliography on Death and Dying*. The National Institutes of Health, U.S. Government Printing Office, 1970
2. Fulton R: (Comp) *Death, Grief, and Bereavement, A Bibliography 1845-1972*. Center for Death Education and Research, University of Minnesota, 3rd Ed, 1973
3. Feifel H: "Death," in *Taboo Topics*, Farberow NL (Ed) Atherton Press, New York, 1963
4. Lerner M: "When, Why and Where People Die," in *The Dying Patient*, Brim OG, Freeman HE, Levine S, Scotch NA (Eds) Russell Sage Foundation, New York, 1970
5. Krant MJ: *Dying and Dignity: The Meaning and Control of a Personal Death*. Charles C Thomas, Springfield, Illinois, 1974
6. Silverberg E, Holleb AI: Major Trends in Cancer: 25 Year Survey. *Ca—A Cancer Journal for Clinicians, 25:*2-7, Jan/Feb, 1975
7. Abram HS: Psychological Aspects of Intensive Care Units. *Med Ann DC, 43:*59-62, Feb, 1974
8. Abram HS: Psychological Dilemmas of Medical Progress. *Psych Med, 3:*51-58, 1972
9. Vreeland R, Ellis G: Stresses on the Nurse in an Intensive-Care Unit. *JAMA, 208:*332-334, 1969
10. Glaser RJ: "Innovations and Heroic Acts in Prolonging Life," in *The Dying Patient*, Brim OG, Freeman HE, Levine S, Scotch NA (Eds) Russell Sage Foundation, New York, 1970
11. Hay D, Oken D: The Psychological Stresses of Intensive Care Unit Nursing. *Psychosomatic Medicine 34:*109-118, March/April, 1972
12. Toffler A: *Future Shock*. Bantam Books, Inc, New York, 1971
13. Lifton RJ: *Death in Life: The Survivors of Hiroshima*. Random House, New York, 1968
14. Lifton RJ: *History and Human Survival*. Vintage Books Edition, New York, 1971
15. Lifton RJ, Olson E: *Living and Dying*. Praeger Publishers, New York, 1974
16. Lifton RJ: *The Life of the Self: Toward a New Psychology*. Simon and Schuster, New York, 1976
17. Feifel H: "The Function of Attitudes Toward Death," in *Death and Dying: Attitudes of Patient and Doctor*. Group for the Advancement of Psychiatry, Vol V, Symposium 11, Oct, 1965
18. Feifel H, Hanson S, Jones R, Edwards L: Physicians Consider Death. *APA Proceedings*, 75th Annual Convention, 1969
19. Livingston PB, Zimet CN: Death Anxiety, Authoritarianism and Choice of Specialty in Medical Students. *Journal of Nervous and Mental Disease, 140:*222-230, 1965

---

* The "Psychological Autopsy," a case study method in which the attempt is made to clarify and understand the psychosocial aspects of a person's dying and death from a number of perspectives, represents such an approach to the study of death (see Ref. 51).

20. Fox RC: "Training for Uncertainty," in *The Student-Physician*, Merton RK, Reader GG, Kendall PL (Eds) Harvard University Press, Cambridge, Massachusetts, 1957

21. Knight JA: *Medical Student—Doctor in the Making*. Appleton-Century-Crofts, New York, 1973

22. Glaser BG, Strauss AL: *Awareness of Dying*. Aldine Publishing Company, Chicago, 1965

23. A Definition of Irreversible Coma: Report of the Ad Hoc Committee of the Harvard Medical School to Examine the Definition of Brain Death. *JAMA*, *205:*85–88, 1968

24. Kennedy IM: The Kansas Statute on Death—An Appraisal. *N Engl J Med*, *285:*946–950, 1971

25. Refinements in Criteria for the Determination of Death: An Appraisal. *JAMA*, *221:*48–53, 1972

26. Hippocratic Oath. Blakiston's *Gould Medical Dictionary*, 3rd Ed, McGraw-Hill, New York, 1972

27. The Physician and the Dying Patient. AMA Grams, *JAMA*, *227:*728, © 1974, American Medical Association

28. Rachels J: Active and Passive Euthanasia. *N Engl J Med*, *292:*78–80, 1975

29. A Life in the Balance. *Time Magazine*, November 3, 1975

30. Sentenced to Life. *Time Magazine*, November 24, 1975

31. Kron J: The Girl in the Coma. *New York*, October 6, 1975

32. Kron J: Did the Girl in the Coma Want "Death With Dignity"? *New York*, October 27, 1975

33. McCormick RA: The Karen Ann Quinlan Case. Editorial, *JAMA*, *234:*1057, 1975

34. Connery JR: The Moral Dilemmas of the Quinlan Case. *Hosp Prog*, *56:*18–19, 1975

35. Dorf I: Quinlan Case Leaves Physicians With Life-Death Decisions. *Hospitals*, *50:*83–85, 1976

36. Kittredge FI: After Quinlan. *J Legal Med*, May 1976, pp 28–31

37. Parkes CM: *Bereavement: Studies of Grief in Adult Life*. International Universities Press, New York, 1972

38. Barton D: The Need for Including Instruction on Death and Dying in the Medical Curriculum. *J Med Ed*, *47:*169–175, 1972

39. Barton D, Flexner JM, van Eys J, Scott CE: Death and Dying: A Course for Medical Students. *J Med Ed*, *47:*945–951, 1972

40. Liston EH: Education on Death and Dying: A Survey of American Medical Schools. *J Med Ed*, *48:*577–578, 1973

41. Olin HS: A Proposed Model to Teach Medical Students the Care of the Dying Patient. *J Med Ed*, *47:*564–567, 1972

42. Barton D: Teaching Psychiatry in the Context of Dying and Death. *Amer J Psych*, *13 0:*1290–1291, 1973

43. Block J: A Clinical Course on Death and Dying for Medical Students. *J Med Ed*, *50:*630–632, 1975

44. Liston EH: Education on Death and Dying: A Neglected Area in the Medical Curriculum. *Omega*, *6:*193–198, 1975

45. Wise DJ: Learning About Dying. *Nursing Outlook*, *22:*42–44, 1974

46. Dickinson GE: Death Education in U.S. Medical Schools. *J Med Ed*, *51:*134–146, 1976

47. Kübler-Ross E: *On Death and Dying*. The Macmillan Company, London, 1969

48. Simpson MA: Teaching About Death and Dying. *Nursing Times*, *69:*442–443, 1973

49. Vaisrub S: Dying is Worked to Death. Editorial, *JAMA*, *229:*1909–1910, 1974

50. Schnaper N: Death and Dying: Has the Topic Been Beaten to Death? *Journal of Nervous and Mental Disease*, *160:*157–158, 1975

51. Weisman AD: *The Realization of Death: A Guide for the Psychological Autopsy*. Jason Aronson, Inc, New York, 1974

2

DYING AND DEATH:
Theoretical Considerations

David Barton, M.D.

The approach to caring for dying persons and their families developed in this book takes as a basic thesis the view that dying and death are integral parts of the life cycle. As in other stages of the life cycle, this stage is accompanied by many struggles and tasks. During the period of a person's life when he is dying, the primary struggle is one of an attempt to continue living while at the same time giving up life. In this struggle, the dying person thus experiences problems in living in the confrontation with death. The same is true of the family and caregiving persons, for they too must adapt to the dying and death of the patient and the reminder of their own dying and death. In so doing, they also are confronted with problems in living. The dying person, then, is "living with" his dying and the survivors, whether family or caregivers, must not only "live with" the person's dying, but also "live through" his death and their survival.[1] The focus, then, of this and the following chapters is on those aspects of living which are disrupted in the process of dying and the death of an individual.

There is a growth potential in any stage of life, but in moving past that stage the person "loses" that part of his or her life. In earlier stages of development, the achievements of adaptation to the stages are incorporated as part of the person's life experience. The paradox inherent in dying and approaching death is that whatever is achieved through growth and maturation by the dying person is simultaneously accompanied by a sense of transition and diminution. Ultimately, whatever is gained must be given up in its entirety. This paradox is responsible for the sense of loss, futility, and despair that permeates this stage of life, the feelings that provide the background against which adaptation and growth occur. It is a life stage characterized by growth through the process of letting go and adaptation to the gradual giving up of life, by learning to live with an increasing sense of loss and being directly in contact with the threat of nonexistence. In this sense, this stage of life becomes the most intense form of replication of what much of life has been up to the time of dying, for throughout the life cycle, living, growing, and adaptation entail progression through a series of transitions and losses. The growing child loses his childhood; the adolescent loses that period of his life in which he may make certain choices regarding his or her identity; the adult loses the newness of a relationship, a job, a friend, a spouse, a child, or a period of growth. Shneidman refers to endings involved in the inevitable transition of life as "partial deaths."

Death is the most final and most complete ending in life, but it is not the only one. There are many alterations in our lives that we can appropriately refer to as *endings* — conclusions of phases or aspects of our lives, the closing of episodes that irreversibly put a stop to habitually expected stimuli, psychological states, interpersonal relationships, and living patterns. Such ending short of death . . . often involve mourning and grief as intense as the mourning caused by death, and as appropriate.[2]

Such losses are but preludes to the ultimate loss in death. Loss and transition permeate life, and much of living is related to adapting to these occurrences. Each of us in becoming an adult has, for example, "lost" that part of ourselves that was our "child" — a fact which perhaps relates to the adult's intense sensitivity to the death of children. Dying and death represent the ultimate loss — the loss of the self and those with whom we relate. To those most closely related to the person, the loss is experienced as the loss of that part of the self which is most significantly intertwined and interrelated with another person.

Loss and nonexistence are inherent in life. The knowledge and representations of the threat of losses, be they partial ones as in experiencing endings throughout the life cycle or the recognized and anticipated total loss of self through death, exist at some level in everyone. Each of us goes on living with the knowledge of the possibility of death and in the face of transition and actual loss throughout our lives. No one can actually experience his own dying and death prior to the event or experience the death of another exactly as that person does. Even so, transition, loss, and the knowledge of the possibility of death is so much a shared aspect of being human that in fact, dying and death in some form are phenomena with which we have had more experience than we might like to acknowledge. The final stages of life — dying and death — are only the most extreme forms of the experience of transition and loss.

Adaptation to dying and death is an integral part of living, whether this adaptation is in response to losses and transitions or to one's own dying and anticipated death. The caregiver is concerned with the phenomena of dying and death in an individual and those issues connected with the person's attempt to *live* with the knowledge of progressively giving up life. The witnessing of this happening to another, so like oneself, is reflected in the experience of the family and caregivers as a sense of being connected with the person's living, dying, and death. This gives rise to needs, responses, concerns, and perceptions similar to those of the dying person himself. The reverberating circuitry in the relationships thus grows out of the shared sense of mortality and the adaptive maneuvers aimed at living engaged in by all concerned.

Caregivers should familiarize themselves with certain concepts and observations that have been made by others in their work with dying persons and their families. This chapter thus presents an overview of material basic to providing care in the area. The caregiver is, however, cautioned against prematurely taking refuge in a specific framework in order to provide a sense of iron-clad certainty for himself. While an individual's adaptation to dying and death has the quality of being unique, many of the concepts and observations are useful in certain clinical situations and need to be applied where appropriate. At the outset, the caregiver should recognize that adaptation to dying and death occurs as a process rather than an event. This adaptation thus has a temporal dimension, and the needs, concerns, and responses of the persons involved have a changing dynamic quality. Orderliness and highly predictable patterns of coping are the exception rather than the rule. The care of the dying person often has an unpredictable, random, almost chaotic quality which in itself is capable of stirring feelings of utter helplessness in those persons working with ·dying patients. Theoretical frameworks are useful, but should not be used to overcome the sense of helplessness and bring premature closure. To do so is to force a person into a theory rather than applying the theory to the particular situation.

THE PERCEPTION OF THE REALITY OF DEATH

In a paper entitled "Thoughts for the Times on War and Death," Freud stated:

Our own death is indeed unimaginable, and whenever we make the attempt to imagine it we can perceive that we really survive as spectators. . . . at bottom no one believes in his own death, or to put the same thing in another way, in the unconscious every one of us is convinced of his own immortality.[3]

This statement has far-reaching implications which have markedly affected the entire field of study of the psychology of death as well as the care of the dying person. At varying levels the statement has been interpreted to mean that an individual has no ability to subjectively perceive the reality of his own death. But the thoughts, feelings, and behaviors of both dying persons and those working with these patients would seem to contradict this concept. If we do not believe in the reality of our own death, and at some level of our mental apparatus we are convinced of our immortality, then we would have little investment in engaging in activities which grow in direct relationship to an awareness of death. Indeed many acts of civilization are geared to foster survival and overcome the awareness of ultimate extinction. Lifton, in questioning Freud's statement, believes " . . . it is more correct to say that our own death—or at least our own dying—is not entirely unimaginable but can be imagined only with a considerable degree of distance, blurring, and denial. . . ."[4] Freud's statement must be interpreted relatively rather than absolutely. It cannot be applied in an absolute manner to every person, although there are individuals who, when confronted with death, at times maintain this sort of disbelief. The perception of the many levels of denial operant in the death-approximated person tends to reinforce the concepts derived from the statement. Even so, to account for the intense and complex feeling states experienced by the dying person and those in his presence, a relative rather than absolute interpretation of the statement is necessary.

When we as caregivers watch or experience aspects of the deaths of others and attempt to apply the fact of this happening to ourselves, it is perhaps cognitively unimaginable. However, we experience ourselves not only in terms of our cognition but also in the experience of our feelings. At times we perceive what we feel to be as true as what we imagine or think. There are perhaps in each person parts of our physiological and mental being which represent our nonexistence as an ever-present, distinct possibility.[5-7] Thus persons confronting death respond to its nearness with varying feelings, ideas, and behaviors related to the perception of their deathliness.

The experience of surviving as a spectator is in reality no different from the experience of surviving as a potential nonsurvivor. One can know about feelings in relation to a fact that can have any number of implications in his mental functioning without actually accepting that the implications of that fact are happening to him at that moment. The difficulty in imagining the self as nothing comes about through the mental apparatus' filling in or elaborating activity when there is the threat of nothing. This activity serves to manage the perception of being nothing and ensures a sense of aliveness.

Frequently the caregiver observes the dying patient and the family moving the possibility of death to the future. The individual acknowledges that death will occur, but not yet. This projection of death into the future serves the purpose of allowing the person to perform certain anticipatory maneuvers and coping strategies and to maintain hope, while at the same time not being overwhelmed by the knowledge of his impending death. This distancing of death or projecting it into the future is a form of denial. The phenomenon varies considerably in the same patient at different times and objectively is perceived as a fluctuating sense of personal awareness of death. As one patient near death said, "I know that I am dying, and that I will die . . . it may be several months or even a year . . . I'll deal with that when the time comes . . . I'm just not ready to deal with my death now." This projection of death into the future must be clearly distinguished from the individual's viewing himself as immortal, for even though death is distanced, its reality is acknowledged. But even with this acknowledgment, there continue to be fluctuating levels at which the person accepts his impending death.

DENIAL AND THE AWARENESS OF DYING AND DEATH

Denial and the level of awareness surrounding a person's death are key aspects of the dying person's adaptation and communication with him about dying. Regardless of the directness with which information about a person's illness is communicated, there is some level of modulation of the acknowledged reality of the true state of affairs. The process by which this occurs is called denial and is viewed by many as a central phenomenon in the adaptation of the dying person.

The term "denial" has some unfortunate connotations, particularly as it is used with the dying person. Originally viewed as a term to designate an unconscious defense mechanism employed to avoid recognition of painful reality, denial is often viewed as a psychopathological mechanism that usually interferes with adaptation. This is not the case in many circumstances related to the dying person. Until recently the adaptive use of denial has received little attention. Weisman has correctly addressed the issue of denial as a central issue in the care of the dying person and has directed interest in the phenomenon away from a purely mechanistic view of the process. He distinguishes between denying as a process and denial as a fact.

We must distinguish between the *process of denying* and the *fact of denial*. Denial is a total process of responding within a specific psychosocial context. Negation is only one of the consequences of this process; denial is a final fact, not the process itself.[8]

In this view, denial cannot be separated from the interacting observers and denial is in part a process belonging to the total interpersonal field in which it occurs. This view of denial moves away from a mechanistic interpretation of its use and places it in the position of being part of the interpersonal adaptation of the person and those relating with him. Weisman states,

The mechanistic interpretation of denial is static, because it does not allow for the modulating participation of the other person to whom the denial is expressed. It assumes that denial is a constant, and that someone who denies does so out of his inner workings, not in order to redefine a relationship with another person in a specific context.[8]

In regard to the purpose of denial, he states,

Although a potential danger is apt to evoke denial . . . a common threatened danger is a *jeopardized relationship with a significant key person*. Hence, the purpose of denial is not simply to avoid a danger, but to prevent loss of a significant relationship . . . Denial helps to maintain a simplified, yet constant relationship with significant others, especially at a moment of crisis.[8]

This concept of the use of denying as a means of protecting a relationship becomes extremely important when one notes that the dying person communicates with various persons around him not only about different issues but with varying levels of intensity and acknowledgement of reality about the same issues. This phenomenon may serve to provide clues to the meaning of a particular relationship.

Denial is often viewed as an all or none phenomenon, yet there are varying levels and degrees of this process operant in the dying person. Weisman's elaboration of the degrees of denial is helpful in clarifying this point.

First-order denial is based upon how a patient perceives the primary facts of illness. *Second-order denial* refers to the inferences that a patient draws or fails to draw, about the extensions and implications of his illness. *Third-order denial* is concerned with the image of death itself: denial of extinction.[8]

Weisman also refers to a level of awareness which is known as "middle knowledge."[8] Middle knowledge is a form of "uncertain certainty" falling between the acknowledgment and nonacknowledgment of death.

The issue of denial enters significantly into the process of care, for it markedly affects the perception of individual needs. Importantly, however, many times a basic individual need may be the need to dampen, to play down, to modulate awareness about an illness or its outcome. The spectrum of acknowledgment from acceptance to denial is in many ways a shifting, adaptive, dynamic process. Both denial and acceptance may be viewed as "social strategies."[9]

Glaser and Strauss provide insights into the manner in which varying levels of awareness affect patients' care. In their discussion of awareness, "What *each* intereacting person knows of the patient's defined status, along with his recognition of the others' awarenesses of his own definition . . . " is referred to as an "awareness context." These authors define four types of awareness contexts based on the shared knowledge of the defined and actual state of the dying person by the person and those participating in his care. These are: closed awareness, suspected awareness, mutual pretense awareness, and open awareness. Each type of awareness context is important as patients and caregivers interact in terms of who has what knowledge and how much each knows for certain.[10]

In the closed awareness context, the hospital personnel are aware of the patient's nearness to death but this information is kept from the patient. The patient, in these circumstances, is unaware of his proximity to death. In the suspected awareness context, the unknowing patient can only surmise or suspect that others think he is dying. A mutual pretense awareness context exists when hospital personnel are aware of the patient's dying but feign ignorance, acting as if the patient will continue to live. In this case, the patient participates in the pretense. An open awareness context is present when there is shared knowledge of the patient's dying and affirmation of this in the behaviors of caring.[10, 11] These varying contexts of awareness have differing effects on patient care and interaction in the care setting.

DEATH AS A LIFE CRISIS

Whatever the case, the patient, family, or caregivers call forth a series of responses that contribute to the individuals' adaptation to death. The knowledge (no matter how presented, acknowledged, and managed in the interpersonal setting) becomes a profound part of the person's life and all who relate with him. At some level, be it purely intellectually or otherwise, the person becomes aware of the cessation of his existence, or someone close to him becomes aware of the possibility of the end and is moved accordingly.

Pattison describes death as a crisis event in the person's life. As a crisis, the ". . . situation awakens unresolved key problems from both the near and distant past. Problems of dependency, passivity, narcissism, inadequacy, identity, and more are all reactivated by the process of dying. Hence one is faced not only with the problem of death per se, but a host of unresolved feelings from one's own lifetime and its inevitable conflicts."[12] Dying, as a process, builds on the person's past life, his current circumstances,

and his anticipated future. The sum total of the adaptive maneuvers called into play by the person over time receives input from all of these dimensions of the person's life. A person thus dies as he has lived or wishes to live. His adaptation is also strongly influenced by the interpersonal, social, and cultural context in which his dying occurs. How complex this mass of determinants and interactions is in any one individual, and how comforting it might be to find some orderliness in the chaos of reality! But only in the most general way can a life stage be viewed as occurring in an orderly progression of discrete happenings.

ADAPTATION AS PROCESS

Adaptation to dying and the threat of death does, however, occur as a process over time. Along the way, the patient, his family, and caregivers encounter numerous psychological and social tasks which tax the individual's adaptive skills. As a process occurring over time, the adaptation has a longitudinal, temporal dimension. As a means of attempting to clarify the numerous occurrences during this period of time, sequences of emotional events occuring during the person's adaptation have been delineated.

One such move toward establishing a sequence of emotional events in the dying person's adaptation, and perhaps the best known contribution to this concept, is described by Elisabeth Kübler-Ross. Drawing on her experience of interviews with dying persons, Kübler-Ross conceptualizes the person's adaptation to dying and death as occurring in a series of five stages. In the first stage, the person's response to the knowledge of dying is one of shock and denial. An attitude of disbelief characterizes this stage. The person may appear uninvolved in the serious nature of the happenings, feeling that an error has been made in the diagnosis or acting as if it were someone else rather than he who has the illness. The second stage is one of anger. This anger may be expressed indirectly or displaced to persons around the patient. The next stage is one of bargaining. The patient acts as if he will be spared if he acts in a prescribed, pleasing manner. It is as if this good and pleasing behavior will be rewarded with cure or at least prolongation of life. Following the stage of bargaining, there is a stage of depression in which the impact of the illness is felt and the losses perceived evoke sadness and despair. Finally there is the stage of acceptance in which the person accepts his illness and its ultimate outcome.[13] In the dying person, the stages do not necessarily occur as outlined. More than one stage may be present at once, or the individual may be observed to move back and forth in the sequence. The family and caregivers may also manifest these stages in response to the person's death.

In working with the dying person, his family, and other caregivers, we must look beyond observed phenomena and attempt to appreciate the determinants and adaptive or nonadaptive effects of the phenomena. It thus becomes important to try to understand the responses of the dying person and those about them as adaptive maneuvers, and to ask the basic question, "What is the adaptive end sought in these responses or behaviors?" It would then be appropriate to ask, "What are the determinants and effects in the interpersonal environment of the denial, anger, bargaining, depression, or acceptance?" This approach addresses the processes of interactions and the person's dynamic attempt to adapt. It asks the questions, "What is the *source* of the ánger?" "What is the *effect* of the anger on the interpersonal setting?" "With *whom* is the person bargaining?" "Is the person accepting *for himself* or *to please another* person?" In the process of interpersonal adaptation, responses represent an attempt to deal with the basic underlying knowledge of the threat of nonexistence. Whether or not they are effective depends upon the environment and the maintenance of a relative sense of well-being in the individuals concerned. Thus the dying person reacts to his dying, and those who are responding to the person's dying react in turn. The outcome of this subtle equation is responsible for establishing an adaptive equilibrium or a disruptive state.

In another orientation to the process of dying, Weisman delineates psychosocial stages representing ". . . *time intervals* in which different events occur along with changes in anatomical and clinical status." There are three such stages. Stage 1 is the "prediagnostic stage and diagnostic period." This stage starts when the first symptoms or signs are noted and ends when the definitive diagnosis is made. Stage 2 is the "period of established disease." During this stage the patient is under care, observation, and treatment. Stage 3 is the stage of "decline and deterioration." During this stage the person is likely to fail to respond to treatment, and to develop new symptoms as well as the complications and side effects of treatment.[14, 15] The value of this type of staging is that it provides a framework that temporally approximates biological events which may then be correlated with the psychosocial dimensions in the person's life.

Psychosocial phenomena are observed in different degrees in these stages.[9, 14, 15] For example, the salient problems of Stage 1 relate to delay and denial. In Stage 3, the dying person is faced with less autonomy, must deal with yielding control to others, and come to terms with the cessation of his existence.

Because the psychosocial aspects of dying and death are so closely tied to medical events, any sequential approach incorporating these events might well be helpful to caregivers in assisting with the dying process. It would enable them to view psychosocial adaptation as being intertwined with the disease process and the process of medical care. An even more extensive staging which might be useful in delineating medical events and observing psychosocial needs might be outlined as follows:

1. State of health
2. Perception of symptom or sign of illness
3. Approximation with the health-care system
4. The diagnostic process
5. Reporting of the results
6. The treatment phase
   a. Treatment out of hospital
   b. Treatment in hospital or institutional setting
7. State of relative health
8. Decline
9. Loss, incapacitation, and debilitation
10. Acceleration toward death
11. Lingering
12. Death

13. Pronouncement of death
14. Immediate response of survivors
15. Prolonged response of survivors

Each of these stages, dependent on a multitude of factors, is characterized by varying psychosocial responses and concerns. Each explicit development is accompanied by a multitude of feelings, thoughts, and responses. Orderliness of progression and sameness of response are not characteristic of dying any more than one can find much semblance of definite order during the life stage which we designate as adolescence. Indeed, as in other stages of the life cycle, the individual reacts to the stresses and changes involved in terms of his own psychological makeup, his interactional field, and his aspirations for the future. The temporal dimensions (*i.e.*, the time involved in the progression through the stages) also affect adaptation and coping. The individual adapts with those skills in his coping armamentarium and with those with which interacting persons can usefully and effectively assist. While areas of coping and adaptive struggle may be delineated, the precise manner in which an individual manages his adaptive struggles is a function of so many variables that we encounter marked difficulty in establishing a definite sequential framework of adaptation to dying and death. Importantly, it should be noted that the dying person's stages of progression through an illness also call forth changing tasks of adaptation for family members and caregivers.

FURTHER TEMPORAL CONSIDERATIONS

The delineation of any sequential series of events acknowledges the concept that dying occurs over varying periods of time. The manner in which a person and those about him adapt to dying and death are markedly affected by this temporal dimension of dying. Not only does the process occur over time, but the ups and downs, progressions, and regressions obliviate a sense of order. The whole matter of caring for the dying is couched in temporal perception and is determined by a largely unpredictable time frame.

Glaser and Strauss refer to the temporal interrelationships related to the activity surrounding the dying person as the "temporal order."[16] The temporal order or the work of caring for the dying person includes the ongoing reorganization and changes of staff effort over time. The organization of the care of the person is highly influenced by the temporal aspects of the person's dying. These authors refer to the temporal course of dying as the "dying trajectory." This "trajectory" has at least two outstanding properties, duration and shape. It may plunge straight down, move slowly downward, vacillate, move up and down, or follow an infinite number of routes before reaching the point of death. Dying trajectories are based to some extent on the subjective perception of the person's status rather than the actual course of dying, and the perception of the particular trajectory by those persons taking part in the care of the patient becomes intimately involved in his care. In dying trajectories there are a number of "critical junctures" which appear in the course of dying. The point at which the person is defined as actually dying, the time at which staff, family, or the person himself make preparation for dying, the point at which there is nothing that can be done to prevent death, and the occurrence of death itself are examples of critical junctures. The occurrence or nonoccurrence of these critical junctures at a point when they are expected becomes an important part of the care organized about the patient. Unexpected occurrence (or nonoccurrence) of the juncture is likely to find the family and caregivers unprepared. Expectations around a juncture's occurring on time play an important part in the care of the person and the organization of the work of caring.

There is little certainty about the dying trajectory of an individual. The course of an illness is for the most part extremely unpredictable, and in caring for the dying person one is as often as not disoriented by the unpredictable nature of the "dying trajectory." Thus family and caregivers often have no definite temporal frame of reference in which to operate. This fact lends great difficulty to the actual planning for care and means that frequent changes in direction often become necessary. The unpredictable temporal nature of dying also means that any aspect of care must be frequently reassessed in order to keep pace with the changes which occur and those which do not occur. Such changes and the need for constant reassessment often tax the individual's coping skills and the coping skills of the caregiving milieu.

APPROPRIATE AND CONGRUENT DEATHS

Weisman and Hackett, in noting that a series of patients faced death with minimal anxiety or conflict, developed the concept of an "appropriate death." Their findings suggested " . . . that it is the sense of being appropriate that robs subjective death of its terror." They advanced the hypothesis that an appropriate death must satisfy four requirements: "(1) conflict is reduced: (2) compatibility with the ego ideal is achieved: (3) continuity of important relationships is preserved or restored: (4) consummation of a wish is brought about."[17] In *On Dying and Denying* Weisman writes, "An appropriate death, in brief, is a death that someone might choose for himself—had he a choice."[8] In *The Realization of Death* he states, "The key concepts of appropriate death are awareness, acceptability, resolution, relief and these are the concepts used to characterize successful coping."[14]

In other comments on the "appropriate death," Weisman states:

Appropriate deaths are those in which suffering is at a low ebb, conflict is minimal, and behavior has been maintained on as high a level as is compatible with physical status. Moreover, the dying patient indicates that what has already been done corresponds to what he expected of himself, of the people who matter most, of those to whom he turned for relief, and, finally, of the world in general. Literally and metaphorically, it is time to die. Relief of anguish and resolution of remaining conflicts join in a harmonious exitus. The patient both accepts and expects death, and is willing, albeit ruefully, to die. It is the ultimate of successful coping . . . "[18]

The concept of an appropriate death is of immense importance in caring for the dying person, for it conceptualizes a type of death in which the individual is maximized as a person through realization of his needs as he approaches death.

Dying may also be conceptualized as being holistically congruent or incongruent with the individual's total being dependent upon how closely the interactional process fits the biological, psychosocial, and other needs of the individual and all those relating with him. The death of a person may approach being congruent or incongruent with the person's, the family's, and caregivers' needs, responses, concerns, and perceptions. But this concept represents an idealized circumstance and problems arise because the dying and death of a person is never totally congruent in all of these dimensions. When the needs of the individual are incongruent with those of the family and caregivers, there is conflict and often disruption of care. However, congruence achieved as best as possible as the individual progresses toward death is the hallmark of effective care for the dying person. In reaching a state of congruence the needs of all concerned are perceived, understood, and met to the greatest extent possible, and interactional conflict is minimal.

The concepts of appropriate death and congruence are central to caring for the dying person. The concept of an appropriate death involves the interpersonal and social context but is more concerned with the subjective state of the individual and the manner in which he is desirous of facing death. As has been stated, it is in essence the way the person himself would choose to die were he to have a choice. The concept of congruence not only refers to individual needs but to the needs of all persons encountering the dying person and his death. Congruence is related to the overall acceptability of the process of a person's dying and death in a social context or in a specific care situation. It involves all working to achieve maximal adaptation and minimal disruption in the circuitry of the relationships. Conversely, incongruence involves the mismatching of interactions, conflict, screening out of important perceptions, inattention to the needs of the person, his family, and caregivers, and compromises adaptation. In incongruent care, support is lost, feelings misunderstood, and vital needs neither perceived nor met. Basic to the concept of congruence is the recognition that the potential for personal death and the responses to this potential are parts of all persons concerned with the dying person, for the dying and death of another is an intimation of mortality for all those in the social field of the individual. Ultimately in the care of the dying person, the point is reached when the anticipated death of the individual and the emerging absence of that person is as congruent as possible with each approximated living individual's needs and concerns. Acceptance of death as a part of living is a critical part of even approaching this point.

CONSIDERATIONS ON THE PSYCHOLOGY OF DEATH

The recognition and acceptance of dying and death as integral parts of living are of critical importance in the care of the dying person and his family. There is thus a need to look further at the effects of the awareness or nonawareness of dying and impending death on a dying patient's life and on those individuals with whom he is approximated. There is also a pressing need to integrate psychological principles based on phenomena related to individuals' adaptation to death into the mainstream of contemporary psychological thought.

Freud, in postulating the presence of a death instinct, conceptualized an internal need in the organism to return to its original inorganic form, *i.e.*, an investment of energies in an active tendency toward destruction. In so doing, he directed his attention toward movement of the organism in the direction of a state of quietude of inner forces rather than the organism's adaptation to the anticipation of inevitable death. He stated, "If we are to take it as a truth which knows no exception that everything living dies for *internal* reasons—becomes inorganic once again—then we shall be compelled to say that '*the aim of all life is death*' . . . ."[19] Psychological principles based on phenomena related to the person's adaptation to his anticipated inevitable nonexistence would require a restatement of Freud's statement to say, "the aim of much of life is to adapt to the inevitability of death."[20] These principles would by no means ignore or supplant theory based on the determinism of the past, but they would also encompass those thoughts, feelings, and actions which evolve in relation to the individual's anticipated future.

Lifton, in a number of books and essays, emphasizes the relevance of death in the study of human behavior.[4, 6, 7, 21, 22] In connection with his studies of the psychosocial phenomena observed in survivors of the Hiroshima disaster, he put forth the following propositions relevant to a "death-oriented psychology of life." First, "Death is anticipated as a *severance of the sense of connection*—or the inner sense of organic relationship to the various elements, and particularly to the people and groups of people most necessary to our feelings of continuity and relatedness." Second, "Death is a test of the meaning of life, of the symbolic integrity—the cohesion and significance—of the life one has been living." Third, "Death, in the very abruptness of its capacity to terminate life, becomes a test of life's sense of movement, of development and change—of sequence—in the continuous dialectic between fixed identity on the one hand and individuation on the other."[4] In further elaborations of these concepts, Lifton and Olson, importantly, postulate the presence of psychological representations of death from the beginning of life, these representations subsequently evolving as increasingly complex "inner imagery" and symbolism. They state: "We can understand the child's earliest images of life and death as organized around three sets of opposites: *connection–separation*, *movement–stasis* (lack of movement), [and] *integrity–disintegration*."[5] Imagery of separation, stasis, and disintegration are related to death anxiety and the threat of death of the organism, and imagery of connection, movement, and integrity are related to life and the continuity of life. As the person moves through the life cycle, there are continued elaborations of this imagery into more complex symbolic forms. At a number of "critical points" in the life cycle there are important transitional stages which give rise to increased death imagery. Adolescence, for example, in being a death and rebirth experience, represents such a critical point. In adolescence, ". . . one dies as a child and is reborn as an adult." The threats that occur in a critical point such as adolescence give rise to increasing anxiety related to death imagery and move the person toward seeking new means of finding imagery connected with life.

The ability of the organism to continuously create and recreate images and symbols is accomplished by the "psychoformative" process. A sense of aliveness and vitality can continue only when this symbolizing process gives rise to imagery which is able to guide behavior in a meaningful way. An inability to elaborate imagery which is effective in providing a sense of continuity of life is related to the phenomenon of "psychic numbing." This is associated with a disturbance of the psychoformative function of the organism and causes the individual to feel numb and distant from his life. Psychic numbing may occur in circumstances which represent or symbolize overwhelming immersion in the death experience.

These authors stress a need for a "sense of connection" extending beyond the life of the individual. The process of elaborating meaningful imagery is central to what they call " symbolic immortality." There is thus a human need to create meaningful imagery which provides a sense of continuity of life, symbolic survival, or a sense of immortality which establishes connectedness beyond the existence of the individual self. According to this framework, the sense of immortality may be expressed in a number of modes: biological, creative, theological, natural, and experiential. For example, in the biological category one may sense himself as living on through his children. In the creative mode one lives on through acts of creativity or his works. The theological mode involves the various religious images of living on after death. A sense of immortality derived from the natural mode relates to living on through images and symbolism related to the survival of nature. The experiential mode involves transcendence and depends on intense psychic states in which the perceptions and images of time and death are altered.*

These concepts are applicable to the dying patient. The threat of death from ill-ness and disease undoubtedly evokes imagery and symbolic forms related to separation, stasis, and disintegration along with increased death anxiety, and there is activity in the direction of seeking continuity with life in the imagery or symbolic derivatives of connection, movement, and integration. Continuity of life is sought after, and for many is achieved through the search for certain modes and forms of immortality. An ability to continue to elaborate meaningful images and forms related to life and the continuity of life, the preservation of the integrity of the psychoformative process, is an important aspect of the dying patient's adaptation.

Thus, in caring for the dying person, attention to the phenomena associated with these principles may be seen as an important part of the caring process. The caregiver's task is to foster a setting in which the imagery and symbolic derivatives associated with life and the continuity of life may be effectively elaborated. For example, the relatedness of caring might encourage the maintenance of the sense of connectedness. The activity of caring as a dynamic need-discerning process might provide a sense of movement, and the attempt to assist the dying individual and those approximated with him to maintain a sense of wholeness over and against the sense of fragmentation associated with dying would facilitate imagery and experience related to integrity.

The paradigms and subparadigms evolved by Lifton and Lifton and Olson present a psychohistorical perspective in that they are intimately concerned with death and life, the continuity of life, symbolic immortality, the survival of human existence in creative forms, and the persistence of a matrix for the development of these creative forms extending into the historical future. This paradigm is associated, however, with the immediate existence of the person as well as the flow of history beyond the self. Thus, Lifton writes, ". . . at every moment, the self is simultaneously involved with both proximate and 'ultimate' matters."[7] The approach that I am presenting in this book

---

* For a more detailed exploration of the concepts presented here in bare outline form, the reader is referred to the original works of the authors. They are of importance to the overall study of this area and are profoundly related to the emerging acceptance of death as a vital aspect of the psychology of living.

leans more in the direction of proximate matters related to th dying patient, his family, and caregivers, though quite likely, as I understand Lifton's formulations, the matters which he refers to as "ultimate" are intimately intertwined with proximate ones.

For the purposes of the discussions to follow, it now becomes necessary to describe the manner in which caring for dying persons and their families is conceptualized in this book. It will be assumed that in every individual there are, as Lifton and Olson have proposed, mental representations of death. These mental representations relate to that part of the human organism which always has the potential to no longer exist— to be "nothing." At some levels of mental functioning, the representations of this state (or non-state) may only be perceived in association with forms of imagery, their symbolic derivatives, and the associated feelings. However, the individual may also experience the awareness of his deathliness in a primitive, physiologically related feeling state alone, a state accompanied by exceptionally high levels of death anxiety and other feelings.* This experiential state which is associated with the potential for no longer existing may be felt and experienced as dread and anxiety. Other feelings might include feelings of terror, urgency, timeliness, transience, despair, disintegration or non-wholeness, isolation, alienation, and estrangement. The reactions to these feelings would come as bursts of activity aimed at the individual's affirming his personal significance and his sense of aliveness in the here and now—the moment of his sense of annihilation. This state of death awareness and its accompanying feelings can be viewed as being a potential response to the threat of death at any or all of the levels of human functioning—biological, psychological, social, and cultural. These feelings are experienced most intensely at times of threat of loss of the self when transition and the loss of the moment are directly in the awareness sphere of the person. The feelings are the physiological concomitants of the threatened loss of self and signal the threat

of cessation of function of all that otherwise represents the presence of life.

The intensity of the feelings associated with death awareness depends on the perceived proximity of the individual to the threat of death or the threat of the death of a significantly related individual not unlike the self. The dying person is brought increasingly closer to the reality of his death and experiences the anxiety and other feelings associated with this death awareness in an intense form. Those family members and caregivers who are significantly related to the dying person (those persons caring for the dying individual) are, in the process of care, brought closer to the recognition of a shared sense of finiteness and their awareness of death is also increased. They, too, experience a wide variety of feelings related to this increase in death awareness, loss, and intimation of their own mortality. The stronger the relationship with the person, the more intense is the experience of the loss of the significant other and the experience of the threatened loss of the self.

The expanding confrontation with death and the recognition of potential nonexistence in the person generates activity aimed toward seeking out personal significance and a sense of aliveness in the moment. The strivings of the death-approximated individual are, then, directed toward any activity (feeling, thought, or behavior) that generates a sense of personal significance or meaning and leads to a sense of aliveness. These strivings are unique for each person approximated with death and take place in all dimensions of human existence. In the framework of this discussion, meaning, or the sense of personal significance, is viewed as the structure of the sense of aliveness. Meaning, as defined here, is found in that unique activity or combination of activities which enables a unique individual, while in the moment of approximation with the threat of his own death, to experience himself as being alive. Meaning, or personal significance of this kind, may be found in biological, psychological, social, or cultural activities. I believe that this concept of

---

* Lifton and Olson, in their writings, refer to the physiological underpinnings of the more complex symbolism and imagery associated with life and death (see Ref. 5–7).

meaning is close akin to the concept of meaning as described by Frankl.[23] For each person, the path to meaning and a sense of aliveness when approximated with death is a unique combination or series of activities. In the dying person, when there is an absence of meaning, an inability to find meaning and personal significance, there is an accompanying increased sensitivity to loss and a heightening of the feelings accompanying death awareness.

In the framework of this book no means of finding meaning or personal significance is necessarily excluded, but the caring relationship which provides a discerning and meeting of needs is viewed as a primary matrix for meaningful activities and the structure for the sense of aliveness. When no other source of meaningful activities is available, the dying person may attain personal significance and affirmation of his existence and aliveness in the context of a caring relationship.[24] When caring falters, the dying person is forced to attend those painful feelings that signal his potential for nonexistence and death.

Thus for dying persons, their families, and caregivers, the needs, concerns, perceptions and responses in all dimensions of their living with and living through death have to do with the ultimate need for finding meaningful activity and a sense of aliveness. The activities of the organism toward this end are unlimited and the interpersonal transactions elaborated around these activities become increasingly complex. When confronted with one's death, the acknowledged ability to maintain this legitimate quest for meaning and personal significance in the social context is what I believe is meant by the term "death with dignity." The quest for meaning is affirmed by the individual himself, but at some point in the dying person's decline, the legitimacy of the quest can only be affirmed and granted by others. This balance between affirmation of the search by the dying person and those caring for him is, I believe, closely related to what Weisman refers to as "safe conduct" for the dying person.[9]

Summarized, the formulations of this framework would state that each human being carries within himself inherent representations of the absence of life. The state of

affairs in which a person is more in touch with that part of him which is potentially nonexistent or dead carries with it feelings of death awareness including anxiety, terror, timelessness, and urgency. The feelings are dealt with by the person and those relating with the person with a wide range of coping responses which involve activity in the form of feelings, thoughts, and behaviors designed to attain meaning and personal significance to counter this death awareness and generate a sense of aliveness in the very moment of approximation with their deathliness. For many, the activity associated with caring relatedness provides the matrix most capable of generating meaning and personal significance during the person's decline to death. In the individual relating with the dying person, be he a family member or a caregiver, there is also a gradual increase in his own perception of his potential for nonbeing that is closely related to the loss of personally significant activity which emanated from the relationship. After the death of the person, restoration of personal significance and aliveness through activities which result in meaning must be accomplished to restore the person's sense of being. The tendency in a living person is to avoid situations which lead to an enlargement of his sense of potential nonexistence.

Now the task of caring for the dying person and his family becomes clearer, for caring itself is meaningful activity and noncaring is meaningless. Caring, approximation, and determination of needs provide the activities of relating for the dying person and others from which personal significance or meaning can be derived and a sense of aliveness maintained. Caring over time and the maintenance of interpersonal interest in changing needs is a dynamic, active process affirming and creating the ability for all concerned to gain structure for the sense of aliveness when approximated with death.

REFERENCES

1. Scott CE: Reflections on Dying. *Soundings* *55:*472-479, 1972
2. Shneidman ES: *Deaths of Man.* Penguin Books, Baltimore, 1974
3. Freud S: "Thoughts for the Times on War and Death," in *Collected Papers.* Vol 4, Basic Books Inc. New York, First American Edition, 1959
4. Lifton RJ: On Death and Death Symbolism: The

Hiroshima Disaster. *Psychiatry 27:*191–210, 1964
5. Lifton RJ, Olson E: *Living and Dying*. Praeger Publishers, New York, 1974
6. Lifton RJ: On Death and the Continuity of Life: A Psychohistorical Perspective. *Omega 6:*143–159, 1975
7. Lifton RJ: *The Life of the Self: Toward a New Psychology*. Simon and Schuster, New York, 1976
8. Weisman AD: *On Dying and Denying: A Psychiatric Study of Terminality*. Behavioral Publications, New York, 1972
9. Weisman AD: "Thanatology," in *The Comprehensive Textbook of Psychiatry*. 2nd Ed, Vol. II, Freedman AM, Kaplan HI, Sadock BJ (Eds) The Williams & Wilkins Co., Baltimore, 1975
10. Glaser BG, Strauss AL: *Awareness of Dying*. Aldine Publishing Company, Chicago, 1965
11. Glaser BG, Strauss AL: "Awareness of Dying," in *Loss and Grief*, Schoenberg B, Carr A, Peretz D, Kutscher AH (Eds) Columbia University Press, New York, 1970
12. Pattison EM: The Experience of Dying. *Amer J Psychotherapy 21:*32–43, 1967
13. Kübler-Ross E: *On Death and Dying*. Macmillan, London, 1969
14. Weisman AD: *The Realization of Death: A Guide for the Psychological Autopsy*. Jason Aronson, New York, 1974
15. Weisman AD: "Psychosocial Considerations in Terminal Care," in *Psychosocial Aspects of Terminal Care*. Schoenberg B, Carr A, Peretz D, Kutscher AH (Eds) Columbia University Press, New York, 1972
16. Glaser BG, Strauss AL: *Time for Dying*. Aldine Publishing Company, Chicago, 1968
17. Weisman AD, Hackett TP: Predilection to Death: Death and Dying as a Psychiatric Problem. *Psychosomatic Medicine 23:*232–256, 1961
18. Weisman AD: Coping with Untimely Death. *Psychiatry 36:*366–378, 1973
19. Freud S: *Beyond the Pleasure Principle*, Strachey J (trans) Liveright Paperbound Ed, New York, 1970
20. Barton D: Death and Dying: A Psychiatrist's Perspective. *Soundings 55:*459–471, 1972
21. Lifton RJ: *Death in Life: Survivors of Hiroshima*. Random House, New York, 1967
22. Lifton RJ: *History and Human Survival*. Vintage Books Ed, Random House, New York, 1971
23. Frankl V: *Man's Search for Meaning: An Introduction to Logotherapy*. Beacon Press, Boston, 1959
24. Weisman AD: *The Existential Core of Psychoanalysis, Reality Sense and Responsibility*, Little, Brown and Company, Boston, 1965

3

THE DIMENSIONS
OF CARING

David Barton, M.D.

To develop an effective approach to caring for dying persons and their families, it is necessary to look more closely at conceptual issues. One cannot do so without exploring the operational definitions of the component parts of the care process. For the purposes of this book, care is defined as the ability to become and remain approximated with the dying person, his family, and other caregivers in such a way as to ascertain needs and to utilize a set of knowledge, skills, and attitudes to facilitate a reasonable level of adaptation for all concerned.

APPROXIMATION

Becoming approximated involves the development of a relationship and requires a form of need-discerning presence which is actively developed and maintained over time. Approximation and the development of need-discerning presence is a far more complex matter than simply talking with a person, being with him, or taking a history through usual interviewing methods. While these approaches are also vital to the care process, approximation involves a particular type of relationship with another human being. This relationship provides a level of relatedness that creates and fosters an atmosphere in which the awareness and communication of needs and concerns emerge and are encouraged. In caring for the dying person, approximation also refers to a special quality in the relationship. This special characteristic of approximation involves a dimension of the caring process in which the caregiver approaches, comes close to, and reaches experiential resonance with those shared aspects of the human experience that relate to being finite. At times peaceful, at other times excruciatingly painful, this aspect of approximation includes the intimations of one's personal mortality. In caring for the dying person a blatant confrontation occurs with the feeling dimensions related to death. Through this process, the caregiver goes beyond the purely cognitive appraisal of an individual's needs. He comes to appreciate not only the facts and medical events related to the happenings surrounding death, but also the range of human experience related to these events in the dying person and those around him. Approximation thus involves not only a relationship which provides an accurate technical approach and assessment of needs but also is conceptualized and entered into as an experiential process. The caregiver gains an awareness of the experience of patient, family, and other caregivers. Most importantly he approximates his own experience and derives from self-awareness an understanding of the needs, concerns, perceptions, and responses of any person as he relates to the events of dying and death.

Frequently, the caregiver concentrates only on those aspects of caring for the patient with which he is most comfortable in his own experience. For example, he may focus on some highly technical aspects of the disease process. This can serve to avoid the intense, discomforting feelings related to the shared sense of human transience and loss evoked in the context of dying and death. But in the attempt to achieve distancing from these uncomfortable feelings, there is an increase in distance between the caregiver and patient. Thus, intense feeling states related to the experiential dimensions of caring may drive caregivers out of an approximation with the shared humanness of the dying person and hence out of the insightful, need-discerning presence necessary for effective care.

There are times in the dying process when the patient needs to be alone or needs the physical presence of the caregiver, and no more. Interviewing, making conversation or anxious prattle may be undesirable or even counter to the person's wishes. The need is only that the caregiver "be-there"* as another human being relating *only* in the experience of their being human.[1] At other times, the need state of the dying person dictates the necessity to pursue active means of intervention in a variety of dimensions designed to assist the dying person or those related to him. Approximation, then, implies a flexible relationship in which the caregiver has at his disposal and choice the ability to physically be there or not, to do or not do, to react or not react, to inquire or not inquire, to inform or not inform, to talk or remain silent, to demonstrate emotion openly or to contain his feelings.

The manner in which a caregiving person is approximated with a dying person and his family is dependent on the professional identity of the caregiver and the knowledge, skills, and attitudes he possesses. Patients sometimes expect a different type or level of care than the caregiver can provide. With rapidly changing identities and overlap of skills and knowledge within the health-care profession, individuals often possess abilities which extend beyond those expected by the patient who expects only certain acts of caring from various professionals and the specific disciplines they represent. The needs of the dying person and his family are so diverse as to require the approximation of a number of people. This means that a variety of persons possessing differing professional identities, not only as perceived by themselves but also as perceived by the patient, his family, and other caregivers, will be interacting in the interpersonal field

of the dying person. However, approximation remains the same regardless of the caregiver's discipline. For all concerned, approximation is sometimes a cognitive, sometimes technical process, but the central and necessary underpinning is the experiential process. The caregiver may at times shift away from the experiential dimension to employ his discipline-related knowledge and skills in his acts of caring, but to achieve true approximation he must still be able to return to attend the experiential dimension when this is necessary.

Approximation is not easy to achieve and maintain. Regardless of the skills and knowledge of the individual caregiver, approximation is capable of evoking a vast array of disquieting and uncomfortable feelings which may lead to various forms of avoidance. As will be discussed in a later chapter, distancing based on a knowledgeable awareness of the intensity of the circumstances may at times be necessary to preserve integrity of care. As such this distancing of oneself becomes a therapeutic measure. This should not, however, be confused with the avoidance phenomenon discussed here.

THE AVOIDANCE PHENOMENON

Perhaps the greatest single deterrent to the development of a caring posture involving approximation grows out of the avoidance phenomenon. This phenomenon is not as simple as mere physical separation. In it various maneuvers may be utilized to avoid approximation and this important dimension of caring is either denied, ignored, or isolated. The painful, uncertain, and often incomprehensible feelings lead to physical avoidance and interpersonal distancing, resulting in dramatic reduction in communication with the dying person and in time spent with him. Also, because many psychosocial issues involve the experiential dimension of care, a failure to attend these issues may occur as a means of avoiding one's own painful experience related to psychological or social matters.

An equally important form of avoidance is the caregiver's viewing the care situation

---

* Weisman also refers to " . . . the capacity to be there . . . " as an important aspect of the management of dying patients. Weisman AD: "Thanatology," in *The Comprehensive Textbook of Psychiatry*. 2nd Ed, Vol. II, Freedman AM, Kaplan HI, Sadock BJ (Eds) Baltimore, The Williams & Wilkins Co, 1975

in a reductionistic manner, bound in a discipline-related set of skills, knowledge, and attitudes. In this case, the tools of caring of the discipline are applied in order to strip the care situation of the feeling dimension and its experiential component. Physicians in this mode consider the person's difficulties strictly in biological terms and view the happenings only in terms of diseased organs, pathological physical findings, or disordered laboratory values. Nurses may come to view the care situation only in terms of their own discipline-related knowledge and skills, giving attention to administrative matters related to care, routine giving of medications, and detached provision of skills designed only to provide physical comfort. Similarly, the clergyman may focus only on a constricted spiritual view of the person, or the social worker may take refuge in the myriad of matters related to administrative interactions within the social system, such as the patient's relationship with agencies or his financial straits. Still another form of avoidance is found in the rigid adherence to an iron-clad theoretical construct which disallows an appreciation of the unique individual's modes of adaptation. It should be noted that all of these activities are frequently not only important but necessary aspects of caring and approximation. But they may also be utilized as a comforting set which allows the caregiver to dwell defensively within the realm of the certainty of his discipline, thereby avoiding personal experience and that of the patient and his family. In so doing, the caregiver effectively screens out psychological pain but avoids that aspect of approximation which would allow him to relate to the dying person as another human being not unlike himself.

Another form of avoidance is found in a caregiver's focusing on or encouraging divisive interactions among various caregiving disciplines. In maintaining distance or participating in disruptive interactions, persons from one discipline may effectively avoid important data obtained by those from other disciplines, thereby considerably narrowing the focus of their activities. This form of avoidance not only results in a caregiver's failure to appreciate many of the needs, concerns, and perceptions of the patient and his family, but disallows the recognition of similar responses in other caregivers. Mutual support and gathering of data are therefore severely compromised.

Through the use of approximation, the caregiver attempts to determine the needs of all those persons in the care constellation. In the presence of shifting needs of the patient and others, the experiential dimension of care also changes. Only through the process of ongoing evaluation of the needs and experiences of the self and those cared for can approximation be maintained and the tendency toward avoidance overcome.

THE NEED BASES

When avoidance is overcome and approximation is developed and maintained, the caregiver learns that dying persons, their families, and other caregivers have numerous and varied needs, concerns, perceptions, and responses. At times, these are straightforward and easily comprehended, but at other times they are extremely subtle. Sometimes they are so blatant and intense as to be overwhelming. Any individual approximated with his dying and death is at the point of his most unique mode of being. In order to appreciate and respond to this unique state, the caregiver must be most perceptive of needs and flexible in his responses. While no classification of needs is all-encompassing and any listing has overlap, the following classification is proposed in order to focus on a number of dimensions related to the dying person.

The Biological or Physical Need Dimension

No health-care professional would deny the importance of needs related to the actual physical state of the dying person. Many in direct approximation with the dying person are educated and trained in the biomedical sciences. The needs perceived as related to this dimension are more often recognized as valid and attended to more readily. Also, biological needs possess characteristics which make them appear more amenable to management, control, and certainty. Many of the indicators can be measured or at least are readily visible. Similarly, many may be responded to with more definite forms of intervention. But while many of these indicators such as blood pressure, temperature, respiration, and fluid balance are measurable, many biological and physical needs remain in the areas of the subjective and unmeasurable.

Pain is an example of a complaint which reflects a need that is largely a subjective state. Pain thresholds vary. A person may report that he is in pain, and the caregiver has no way of measuring this complaint. Similarly, the person may state that he feels vague, often generalized physical discomfort and never really be able to communicate the precise character of his discomfort. The manner in which these less measurable and quantitative forms of physical and biological needs are discerned and the interventions employed also depend on the subjective interpretation of the complaint by the caregivers. A physician, for example, may know from his experience that a certain level of pain is to be expected with a particular diagnostic or operative procedure and have a concept of the level of pain which may be experienced by the individual. A family member, on the other hand, may be extremely alarmed by the ill person who is experiencing even minimal pain. Similarly, the nurse who must remain in contact with the patient over long periods of time may find the pain, suffering, and complaints personally upsetting or disruptive to the overall functions of the ward setting and respond in still another frame of reference. Thus, the perception of biological needs is not always as consistent as one might expect, and the perceptions and interventions employed are also strongly colored by the variability of the patient's complaint. The varying levels of complaint and the variability involved in assessment, interpretation, and response may become the basis of considerable disagreement and disruption of care. This is often the case in the latter stages of a disease process, or when the time comes that the biological state of the person becomes uncertain or beyond the limits of intervention.

It is beyond the scope of this book to explore all of the ramifications of the biological needs of the dying person. The variability associated with each disease, the manner in which the patient suffers and is affected by it, and the responses of the caregiving personnel to that suffering bear heavily on assessment and the responses related to biological needs. While some diseases may be characterized by somewhat predictable courses, most often the physical needs associated with an illness follow an unpredictable course. They may change rapidly, show minimal change, present blatant catastrophic medical events or manifest themselves in more subtle ways. Care of biological needs of the dying person is central in care, but it can never in reality be isolated from considerations of other needs as they affect the total person and those in contact with him.

The Psychosocial Need Basis

Intertwined with the wide spectrum of changing biological needs and the progression of illness are needs which are sometimes far more subtle than the purely physical needs, and these often go unappreciated in the patient's total care. This dimension encompasses the subjective or intrapersonal psychosocial needs of the person, the interpersonal psychosocial needs growing out of ever-changing relationships, and the social context need basis. The social context need basis concerns all of the interactions and responses connected with dying and death that are related to institutions, the social system, and the culture in which the person lives and ultimately dies.

Dying and death elicit any number of internal reactions and concerns related to past psychological development, current life circumstances, and aspirations for the future. These reactions and concerns relate to the person's unique feeling states and symbolic designations of dying and death, the means by which he manages and gratifies his internal impulses and strong feelings, the sense of changing self-concept both in the physical and psychological realm, and the comfort or discomfort experienced as he brings his changing physical and psychosocial being into some adaptive congruence with the interpersonal and social surroundings in which he lives. The subjective needs and responses are driven by the core difficulty of the progressive "giving up" of life and all that this means to the person — the temporal constriction, the constant sense of transience and loss, the reactions to real or fantasized losses as the disease progresses, and the projected sense of loss derived from the person's fantasized concepts of life as it will go on after his death.

The interpersonal need basis of the dying patient includes all of the subjective responses brought into relationship with those around him. These include family, friends, significant others, and a host of new persons brought into the relational field by the process of medical care. In the context of dying and death, the persons involved continue to react to all of the usual and established nuances of their interpersonal relationships, but now with the added dimension of each interaction probing at the most painful aspect of their being, that of the recognition of their own finitude. This recognition, whether it be conscious, partly out of awareness, or unconscious, is a powerful force which forces the interpersonal relationships of those involved in new directions. Because of the shared aspect of being human and finite, and the resultant feelings and experience, those in the interpersonal field of the dying patient are frequently subject to many of the same responses. While not actually "giving up" their own lives, they are forced to come to grips with the recognition that the "giving up" of life is an intimate part of relatedness and the human condition.

These forces and the threat of loss create a sense of fragility and vulnerability in which internal and interpersonal conflict is usual. Caregivers working in this area are also touched by these factors in the dying patient's adaptation, and regardless of the way in which the caregiver defines his relationship with the person and the family, he must also call into action his own intrapersonal and interpersonal skills in encountering and adapting to the most human of losses. In summary, each person confronts the loss of a significant person as well as the reality of his own ultimate obliteration.

Along with the powerful driving forces of loss and the sense of finitude, other important issues arise in one's relationship with the dying person and those around him. There are the struggles growing out of the increased dependency on others and the compromised sense of self-sufficiency. Subtle matters related to the expression of information and feelings, the renewal of old conflicts, and the emergence of new conflicts are often involved. In this time-limited setting, long established relational patterns are often changed and even reversed. The perceived pressure of a foreshortened future enforces a sense of urgency and the need for rapid resolution of conflict. An emerging sense of helplessness, uncertainty, unpredictability, chaos, and the pressures stemming from time and economic depletion may further stress interpersonal relationships. Many of these factors will also play a part in the bereavement that follows the death of the person.

In the social context, certain attitudes may further complicate issues related to the dying process and death. At any particular time, the social system, its institutions, and the culture designate life happenings with certain meanings and respond accordingly. Components of society and the culture, however, may be deficient and less than supportive in response to the point of even ignoring an event as one which has social significance. The failure of a society to accept a life happening as one which requires support means that support systems designed to facilitate adaptation of those experiencing the occurrence may be lacking, poorly coordinated, or even dislocated from the care situation. This is often the case in matters related to the care of the dying person and his family. In view of the dislocated elements of support systems, those persons capable of providing support may, because of the social system, not be allowed access to the care setting at a time when they may be helpful. If allowed access, the social system may be structured in such a way as to disallow a caregiver, be he family, clergy, or other, from effectively participating and sharing in the care of the individual. This is particularly likely to occur in a social institution or a society which does not accept dying and death as part of the life cycle and fails to delineate this area as one requiring a specialized caregiving process. It may occur in a setting where there is a rigidly established authority structure and hierarchy (often established and maintained for good reason) but is, when so established, capable of causing one caregiver to feel his domain invaded or threatened by another. Support by the social system is also likely to be compromised when there is significant overlap of effort with diverse approaches. Often the resulting conflict drains considerable constructive energy away from the process of caring and the total effort. Poor communication in a social system may also play an important part in compromising care, thereby rendering collaborative and cooperative effort nearly impossible.

The basic needs in the social context are those of accepting death as a legitimate part of the life cycle and creating a collaborative and supportive system which addresses the needs of the dying patient. Social difficulties of the dying patient and his family are likely to occur in the vocational area, and in matters related to being a survivor following the death of a family member. The dying person's needs and those of the survivor cannot be separated from the manner in which the various aspects of the social system address those needs.

The Meaning Need Basis

For the dying person and his family, caregivers must begin to deal in operational frameworks with concepts such as meaning and hope. While these are often referred to as important parts of the care process, minimal attempts have been made to define them in operational terms. In this regard, meaning needs are not only important but often central to the effective care of the dying person.

Confronted with the threat of death, the dying person needs to continue to feel some sense of aliveness and participation in the living community. This sense of aliveness is found by the person in deriving meaning from his living activities. As it has been defined for the conceptual framework of this book, meaning or personal significance is found in those activities which enable the individual, while in the moment of approximation with the threat of his death, to continue to experience himself as being alive. Meaningful activities are found by any particular person in a unique manner, and thus those activities which result in meaning for any individual will differ significantly.

Meaningful activity may be derived from the biological dimension (*i.e.*, a sense of physical aliveness), the psychosocial dimension (*i.e.,* a sense of psychological and social well-being that results in a sense of aliveness) or for many from the spiritual dimension. For an activity to be meaningful, to provide some structure for the sense of aliveness, the individual must be able to utilize biological, psychosocial, or spiritual activity in such a way that the sense of aliveness persists even when confronting dying and death. The feeling of aliveness derived from achieving meaning is capable of overcoming the overwhelming sense of despair, futility, helplessness, and hopelessness in the dying person and those around him.

If caring is now further redefined with the concept of meaning included, caregivers from any number of disciplines are capable of assisting and facilitating the dying person's finding or engaging in some activity related to his meaning needs. Through approximation and in the context of a relationship, activity aimed at discerning and meeting needs is generated. Discipline-related skills and knowledge may at various junctures in care serve to facilitate the individual's attaining meaning and a sense of aliveness. But it should be emphasized that attaining meaning involves a unique set of operations that fluctuate in various directions throughout the course of the illness. For most individuals, meaning and the sense of aliveness are found in living activities derived from a wide variety of needs. A problem arises in that the individualized manner of finding meaning may be at considerable variance with the value system and meaning pursuits of a particular caregiver. Since many persons place considerable value on one form of achieving meaning over another, they may tend to undermine an individual's meaning-directed activities and hence his sense of aliveness.

Meaning may also be viewed as having subjective, interpersonal, and sociocultural components. The first includes abilities the individual has developed in cognitive activities, personally valued solitary experiences, or creative pursuits. An individual may also find a sense of aliveness interpersonally in a relationship which affirms him as a living person regardless of what constitutes his life activities. For the dying person, the perception and knowledge that another person is caring, is affirming him as being alive, and is involved in activities to ensure his humanness, serve to validate the sense of aliveness and generate meaning. The process of caring itself, the approximation of one living person with another in a need-discerning manner and responsiveness to meeting needs to the extent possible are activities which in themselves serve to increase the sense of aliveness. A social system or a culture which validates the dying person as living and makes provisions for his and his family's unique adaptive needs also affirms the individual as a participant in the living community.

Caring in a manner that affirms another's aliveness and provides meaning may extend beyond discipline-related methods of providing care. When the health-care professional is no longer able to utilize a set of skills and knowledge, the activities connected with approximation, presence, and the maintenance of the relationship may offer meaning. In order to fulfill this need of the dying patient, the caregiver must deal with the personal experience associated with the care process, develop self-awareness, and overcome the avoidance phenomenon. In so doing, he remains approximated. To do otherwise is to distance oneself from the dying person and to fail to share reciprocally in the search for meaning. The shared sense of struggle with the recognition of finiteness affirms the caregiver, the patient, and others as alive and affirms the struggle of the dying person as a living one. When care is provided in a distant manner based more on avoidance than presence, the confrontation with death becomes a struggle without meaning, without a sense of aliveness, and one filled with a sense of isolation, futility, and ultimately despair.

Hope is closely associated with meaning and refers to an anticipated sense of continued availability, endurance, and persistence of an activity which will provide meaning over time. Operationally, hope is a form of meaningful activity which is experienced as having a sustained quality and continuity with the future life of the person. Hope is not always derived from a sense of immortality. Although the latter provides hopefulness for many, this is only one form of hope. For the dying person, hope refers to all of those meaningful activities which sustain the sense of aliveness until death. Medicine has traditionally been concerned with providing hope in the biological dimension, thereby ensuring the persistence of physical activity. In caring for the dying person one ultimately reaches a stage when this is no longer possible. Hope must then be provided through the interpersonal dimension and the commitment to approximation and presence. For many, the spiritual dimension is looked to as a source of meaning and hope. It may be a vital aspect of the caregiving process and one which should not be overlooked regardless of the caregiver's religious beliefs.

Meaning and hope should not be viewed merely as abstract conceptual issues. Living and dying persons have real and valid meaning needs. The meeting of these needs derived from this dimension of living can be practically incorporated into the overall care process. A dying person can be helped by caregivers to find meaning and hope in living, even when confronted with death. This is provided by assisting the individual in meeting his biological, psychosocial, and spiritual needs to the extent possible. It can be furthered by a culture's acceptance of dying as part of the life cycle and cultural validation of the dying person as a living individual. Importantly, caring itself represents an important way of assuring meaning, hope, and a sense of aliveness for the dying person.

ADAPTATION IN THE CONTEXT OF DEATH

Achieving a reasonable level of adaptation for the patient, family members, and caregivers constitutes another goal of caring for dying persons. Adaptation is an active process which occurs over time and involves modification and change. It involves the utilization of psychological and social processes, maneuvers and strategies designed to achieve a relatively comfortable state of well-being.

Adaptation implies that there is a level of comfort and psychosocial well-being even in the presence of a painful, often unacceptable situation. To achieve adaptation, individuals employ various psychological mechanisms and coping strategies. Psychological mechanisms are utilized to provide an increased acceptability of the unacceptable. The designation of these mechanisms as defense mechanisms has frequently led to an interpretation that they necessarily represent psychopathology. To the contrary, they are employed by all individuals. It is only when they are utilized rigidly and inflexibly that they lead to maladaptation rather than adaptation. When a circumstance is too painful to achieve total recognition, it is relegated to a nonreporting or unconscious level through the process of *denial*. This often occurs at junctures in the dying process when the threat of extinction is more apparent. When the feelings connected with a fact make it unacceptable, the process of *intellectualization* comes into play, stripping the fact of its emotional value and its assumed consequences. Thus a patient may react to the knowledge of having a particular disease through attempts to secure extensive knowledge about it, reading medical texts and literature to provide a cognitive nonemotional framework in which to submerge his feelings. When a strong feeling is experienced toward someone or thing and its expression is unacceptable, it may be *displaced* to another person or thing or expressed in a diffused manner. This accounts for the expression of anger toward persons or objects which have quite obviously done nothing to provoke the anger. The process of *reaction formation* results in the person behaving in a manner exactly opposite to the unacceptable way. Thus a dying person who feels exceptionally helpless or dependent may go out of his way to prove his independence and self-sufficiency. *Regression* is a return to utilizing earlier forms of behavior which provided adaptation under other circumstances. Thus, the patient may become childlike and demanding in response to the threats of illness. These means of achieving adaptation may operate in the dying person, the family, and caregiver. Rather than facilitating adaptation, they may serve to compromise adaptation in some situations. Interpersonal responses to

these methods of adaptation become particularly important in the process of care.

Adaptation is closely associated with the ability to cope. Coping as defined by Weisman is " . . . itself a goal-directed process related to defined problems, and is intended to bring about relief, reward, quiescence and equilibrium."[2] Based on an outline first suggested by Sidle *et al.*,[3] Weisman has developed a list of general coping strategies which provide a useful categorization of maneuvers utilized by persons achieving adaptation. Using these strategies the person may:

1. Find out more before acting [Rational investigation]
2. Talk it over with someone to relieve distress [Share concern]
3. Laugh it off, see humor in the situation [Reversal of affect]
4. Try to forget, don't worry, wait and see [Suppression/isolation/detachment]
5. Put mind on other things, do something for distraction, carry on, business as usual [Displacement/diversion]
6. Carry out positive action based on present understanding [Confrontation/negotiation]
7. Rise above it, accept the situation, find something favorable or encouraging, make virtue out of necessity [redefinition/rationalization/reinterpretation]
8. Submit to the inevitable, stoic acceptance of the worst [Passivity/fatalism]
9. Do something, anything, however ambiguous, impractical, reckless, irrelevant, or magical [Acting out/impulsive acts/compulsive rituals]
10. Consider alternatives based on past situations [Rigid or uncorrected repetition]
11. Drain off or reduce tension with eating, smoking, drinking, drugs, etc. [Tension relief by physiological means]
12. Get away from it all, fantasy or pretend for purpose of relief [Social withdrawal/stimulus reduction/avoidance]
13. Blame someone or something, disown responsibility, get angry [Projection/externalization]
14. Comply, do what I'm told, yield to authority, seek direction [Adopt a role/obedience/compliance]
15. Blame self, atone, sacrifice [Masochistic surrender][2]

These strategies may lead to successes or difficulties in coping and vulnerability. Weisman's discussion includes a rating scale aimed at deriving an index of vulnerability related to coping strategies. These strategies may operate in the family and caregivers as well as the patient. While some of the mechanisms and strategies may lead to compromised adaptation and difficulty, in many cases they represent a means of achieving adaptation, coping, and maintaining a sense of relative well-being. With adequate adaptation the person's interpersonal relationships are characterized by some degree of comforting continuity. He can withstand considerable stress and still relate positively with others. Adaptation involves a sense of personal intactness, integrity and wholeness, as well as the individual's being able to assess what is real and unreal. It also consists of the efficient use of psychological mechanisms and coping strategies in a manner which results in the management of unacceptable feelings, the maintenance of reasonable function, useful exchanging of information, the maintenance of comfortable interpersonal relationships and a relative sense of equilibrium and well being. It involves using intelligence, perception, motility, cognition, and memory as means of developing and maintaining some sense of overall comfort and well-being to the extent possible.

Attaining a reasonable level of adaptation in caring for the dying person and his family has as its goal both the facilitation of the adaptation of the dying individual and those persons approximated with him. In aiming for this, the highest level of adaptive flexibility can be achieved.

THE PROCESS OF CARE

In contrast to care directed at meeting the needs of a person occurring at one point in time, effective care for the dying person and his family is provided as a process. It not only provides continuity, but also is aimed at insightfully perceiving and responsively meeting needs. As a process rather than an event, care for the dying person may at the outset be designed to follow an orderly, specified pattern; however, it is characterized by the ability of the caregiver to alter his approach and interventions based on the shifting needs and interactions of the circumstances. While the caregiver may have

at his disposal set theories of adaptation, process care includes the recognition that one set of theoretical constructs does not necessarily apply to all situations and the persons involved. He has at his disposal a number of theoretical frameworks, approaches, and interventions which are called into action as the situations and emerging process dictate. Alteration of care by feedback from the patient is necessary in such an approach, and the maintenance of approximation and presence is essential to allow the integration of this feedback into the care process.

The levels of perception related to communicated content play an important part in both the assessment of needs and the responses engendered. In discerning and responding to the needs of a patient, a family member, or another caregiver, the caregiver takes a posture based on explicit and implicit content care orientations. In an explicit content care orientation, the caregiver's attention is focused on those communications which are perceived and reacted to as factual. Implicit content care orientation is directed toward the feelings and facts associated with or hidden in the explicit communications which may not be clearly or directly expressed or understood. The subtle aspects of communication involved in the implicit content often represent the subjective, experiential, or feeling dimension of the person. These elements of the individual's experience are often communicated by the manner in which the words and facts are presented, in nonverbal communications, or through behavior and the subtleties of interpersonal interaction. The aspect of communication which extends the literal meaning of words is often referred to as metacommunication and represents those aspects of verbal exchange such as tone of voice, gestures, and facial expression.[4] According to Satir, "Metacommunication is a message *about* a message."[5]

In an explicit content care orientation, the patient's medical complaint may evoke a response primarily designed to meet the need in a more concrete manner. The patient may state, "I have developed this lump in my breast." The statement then triggers a set of responses based on the knowledge and skills of the professional, responses that address the explicit needs as stated. In this case that might consist of activities such as history-taking, examination of the physical abnormality, further diagnostic procedures such as biopsy or tissue examination if indicated, and the implementation of appropriate treatment. Responses are made primarily on the basis of the explicitly stated and observed need basis.

A statement such as "I have a lump in my breast" is, however, generally associated with many implicit feelings and thoughts. In gathering historical data, the caregiver may learn that the lump was discovered some months previously, and its presence has been a well-guarded secret. The communication about the lump may be made in a tremulous voice, and the patient may be observed to be extremely anxious. The knowledgeable caregiver knows that the explicit statement regarding the growth may be associated with such implicit concerns as:

I am frightened.
I am terrified of having cancer.
I am ashamed of myself for having waited this long to seek attention for this problem.
I am fearful that I may lose part of me.
The part of me that is involved is important to my overall concept of myself, my bodily integrity, and my sexual identity.
If I lose this part of my body, the feelings of persons important to me may be changed drastically.
This part of me is very private.
I had a friend who had cancer of the breast and she died when she was younger than I.
If I die, who will raise my children?
I may have to have surgery and that frightens me.

The list by no means covers the wide variety of implicit feelings and concerns connected with the unique experience of the person. All too frequently, however, these implicit content issues are not discerned, discussed, or included in the process of care, yet they are significantly involved in care transactions. Because implicit feelings are seldom directly verbalized, the caregiver must often appreciate their presence from other modes of communication. Most often this type of information is obtained through the development and maintenance of an on-going relationship, and the data frequently change with the shifting needs and course of the patient's illness. The knowledge of implicit feelings and concerns is derived not only through the caregiver's relation with the patient but also through the caregiver's self-awareness as it relates to the threat of dying and death. Also, the manner in which the dialogue among the patient, his family, and the caregiver is conducted influences the data obtained. Questions designed to delineate complaints more clearly or statements phrased in such a way as to allow "yes" and "no" answers generally elicit explicit communications. Inquiries about feelings and concerns as they relate to explicit content, coupled with thoughtful observation, are likely to result in the gathering of implicit data.

A caregiver gathering implicit data may respond to the statement of the presence of the lump with the following statement and inquiry: "Well, we need to try to find out just what this is. There's a great deal of concern about these sort of things, and most people have a lot of feelings and may become rather frightened when they notice a lump like this. How did you *feel* about coming in to see me?" This opens the lines of communication and is likely to yield information vital to the patient's care. The expression of feelings and concerns is encouraged and legitimized.

Care is a transactional phenomenon involving many subtle interchanges. Not only do the communications of the patient have explicit and implicit dimensions, but the responses of the caregiver also markedly affect the dialogue and relationship. A caregiver who says to the patient, "It's good that you came in — sometimes a lump such as this can be serious," communicates a number of explicit messages. The statement also has a number of implications that may be interpreted in various ways. Implicit messages contained in this communication might be perceived to include:

You were certainly smart to come in, this may be cancer.
I am concerned enough about this disorder to let you know that you were wise to bring it to my attention.

My experience tells me that some "lumps" such as this are serious.

If this is cancer, you are likely to require extensive medical treatment to take care of this serious disorder.

You are a bad person for having waited as long as you did to bring this to my attention.

You are a good person for bringing this to my attention.

You would have been an even better person and I might have been able to do more if you had come in earlier.

As with the patient, the caregiver can explore the implicit content with a family member by reflecting on the presence of feelings and concerns. The caregiver might say, "My guess is that you have a lot of questions about what is going on. I'll do my best to help with them if you can tell me what your concerns and questions are." Again, in dealing with implicit content it is important for the caregiver to pay close attention to his subjective feelings. He may, for example, experience family members as intrusive or feel that the patient is pushing him beyond his level of knowledge. He may react because of his own feelings about a similar physical problem. Any of these experiences will affect the response of the caregiver and in turn affect the responses of the family member.

Implicit communications are rarely directly communicated initially, and the knowledge of this dimension of care is dependent on the established relationship of those persons involved in caring for the dying person. This dimension of care is related to the concept of legitimization which allows the person to explicitly communicate feelings and concerns that might otherwise be communicated implicitly. Legitimization is closely related to the ability of the caregiver to accept the validity of dying and death as integral parts of the life experience. Reactions to explicit and implicit content and the accompanying feelings and concerns are not always and need not always be experienced as comfortable. To the contrary, often the dying person, family members, or caregivers express feelings which may be very uncomfortable, but legitimizing expression of these feelings and concerns is a vital part of the care process and considerable benefit can be derived from their expression.

The attempt to understand the individual's need as a total person includes the attempt to understand explicit and implicit communications and the manner in which they affect the transactions. In the posture of acceptance and legitimization of both explicit and implicit content, and with the understanding of the transactions involved in the relationship, the caregiver communicates a tolerance for the feeling and content expressed and begins the important process of the validation of the person's sense of aliveness. When self-awareness and a knowledge of the experiential dimension of care is added to the process of care, the dying person and others involved in the care situation lead us to understand their responses and needs and prompt us to understand their and our most basic needs. In this process of caring, personal significance and meaningful activity in the relationship are enhanced and the sense of aliveness is increased in the persons cared for as well as the caregiver.

Care involves not only approximation but is the process of eliciting, clarifying, and assisting with the defining of the total range of communications and needs, as well as an awareness of the transactional dimensions of the care situation. The caregiver's task becomes one of assisting the individual to manage the expressed needs and concerns in the most adaptive manner. To do so is not to offer a pat theoretical framework for the person, but rather to view caring as a process and to allow the person and oneself to go through a gradual process of becoming in touch with feelings, concerns, and needs and legitimizing their expression. Care involves listening, observation, presence, and above all an ability to experience one's own participation in the caring process as a human being who, like the dying person, also has intense feelings related to dying and death. In this context, care involves the appreciation of an individual as a unique person with unique feelings, concerns, and responses.

Caring for the dying person and his family involves caregivers from a wide variety of disciplines. Because of their differences as individuals and because of their training and perception sets, the needs of the patient and others are likely to be viewed in a myriad of ways. Persons from one discipline are likely to perceive needs and be prepared to meet these needs differently from persons in other disciplines. Also, because of the discipline-related identity of a person, the ill person and his family members will respond to a person from one discipline with communications which differ significantly, dependent on the discipline of the caregiver. This phenomenon is frequently seen in the care setting and has the potential to create significant levels of disruption and confusion.

The communications and the relational patterns involving the dying person and all of those individuals approximated with that person combine in such a way as to summate the total care process. Thus, understanding the reverberating circuitry of the transactions growing out of the needs, concerns, perceptions, and responses of all involved individuals as they occur over time constitutes a vital part of caring for the dying

person and his family.[1] This series of interactions may be diagrammed as follows:

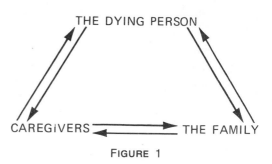

FIGURE 1

It is important to emphasize that "the family" and the "caregivers" are subgroups within the interactional triad. Importantly, just as the interactions in these subgroups are able to facilitate or impede adaptation in the patient, so are they able to assist or compromise the adaptation and support of the individuals within the subgroups. Thus the diagram may be expanded to represent these interactions.

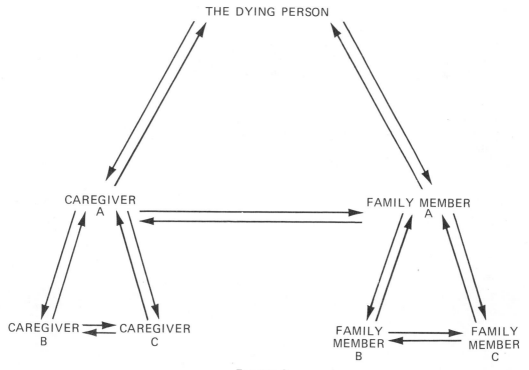

FIGURE 2

Bloom conceptualizes the doctor-patient relationship as a social system. His model points out the importance of viewing this relationship as occurring in a social "field."[6] Taking this model of caring for the dying person even further, those persons interacting also interact with the social system in which care is provided, including the medical care setting, society, and the culture at large.

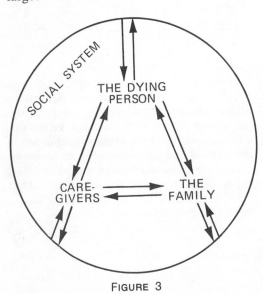

FIGURE 3

A vital dimension of providing optimal care for the dying person and his family, is that the caregivers working in this area should take as a thesis that adaptation to dying and death occurs in a dynamic, rapidly shifting series of interpersonal transactions between the patient, the family, and health-care providers. This transactional triad of care involves a series of transactions and each person participating in the care has highly individualized needs, concerns, perceptions, and responses. The expression of need, evoked responses, and the interactions in the triad, along with the interaction of the triad with the social structure represent a subtle blend of thoughts, knowledge, skills, attitudes, feelings, and behavioral responses which are capable of facilitating or impeding adaptation on the part of the persons concerned. Attaining the maximum level of adaptation and sense of aliveness for all concerned is the goal of the total process of providing care in this area. The activity that emerges in these interactions, when aimed at facilitating adaptation, provides the structure for meaning, personal significance, and the sense of aliveness for all concerned.

REFERENCES

1. Barton D: "The Dying Patient," in *Basic Psychiatry for the Primary Care Physician*, Abram HS (Ed) Little, Brown and Company, Boston, 1976
2. Weisman AD: *The Realization of Death: A Guide for the Psychological Autopsy*. Jason Aronson, New York, 1974
3. Sidle A, Moos R, Adams J, Cady P: Development of a Coping Scale. *Arch Gen Psychiat 20:*226–232, 1969
4. Verwoerdt A: *Communication With the Fatally Ill*. Charles C Thomas, Springfield, Illinois, 1966
5. Satir V: *Conjoint Family Therapy* (Rev Ed) Science and Behavior Books, Inc, Palo Alto, California, 1967
6. Bloom SW: *The Doctor and His Patient*. First Free Press Paperback Edition. The Free Press, New York, 1965

4

THE DYING PERSON

David Barton, M.D.

The care of the dying person and his family is inseparably intertwined in the complex series of interactions among the person, the family, and the caregivers, and can best be understood in terms of the complex interpersonal circuitry which occurs throughout the course of care.[1] This chapter and the two that follow focus on the needs, concerns, perceptions, and responses of the individuals in this transactional triad. Although the individuals or groups of individuals involved in the triad are presented separately, the reader is asked to visualize how the needs and adaptive maneuvers of the participating individuals serve to create reverberating interactions which give rise to subtle blends of feelings, thoughts, and behaviors that may facilitate or impede adaptation. The dying and death of an individual evokes responses and feelings within those persons participating in his care that are linked to the shared aspect of being human, of having human feelings, and of being finite. The feelings, thoughts, and behaviors of the family and caregivers are thus strikingly similar to those of the dying person.

There are a number of basic struggles that occur throughout the course of a person's dying and, for the survivors, these struggles continue after the death of the individual. Defining, clarifying, and meeting needs insofar as is possible, in the context of the process of dying and its aftermath, is viewed as the central task in providing care for the dying person and the survivors. These needs grow out of a variety of biological, psychosocial, and meaning needs. Because of the infinitely diverse needs created by dying and death, nowhere on the continuum of human behavior is the total range of responses more diverse than in the dying person and those surrounding him. Each dying person's mode of adaptation is different and unique for that person, and the individual is most unique when approximated with death. The basic force that drives the struggles of the dying person is the perceived sense of imminent loss of the self, and each loss along the way signals the progressive enlargement of the loss of the total self. No aspect of the individual's personality is spared and, depending on his personality, his interpersonal and situational circumstances, and his aspirations for the future, struggles occur in varying areas at different times. Virtually every adaptive skill of the person is called upon to a greater or lesser degree. The appreciation of the plight of the dying person thus involves the delineation of the areas of struggle for that particular individual and an appreciation of the adaptive or nonadaptive management of these struggles.

While the gradual emergence and enlargement of the awareness of nonexistence is the primary driving force in the adaptation of the dying person and those around him, two related aspects are also of great importance: the progressively damaged sense of physical, psychological, and social self, and the perception of temporal constriction accompanying the gradual loss of the future. The former generally increases as the disease progresses, and throughout the illness, the sense of the latter varies considerably in the conscious level at which it is perceived. Loss of future and temporal constriction become important forces in the adaptation of the individual, adding to the determinism of the psychological development of the past and the circumstantial happenings of the present, the whole spectrum of behaviors which are derived from a causality and determinism based on the future. This amounts to a new dimension in the individual's psychological mechanisms. Having built his life style on the development of the past and a perception of the future, the person must now integrate what has always been there—the imminent possibility of his cessation and death.

Now this more apparent constriction of the future, coupled with the recognition of progressive loss of the self, becomes a force in the adaptation of the person and those around him. Each person reacts to these forces in terms of his personality structure, in terms of the symbolic designations of loss of self, others, and social function. At the same time, the mechanisms and activities which have served to allow the person to find a sense of aliveness and to find meaning are compromised and this results in a profound experience of loss and often despair. A future that has been taken for granted is now called into question and the diffusion of time creates a form of urgency which is capable of disrupting the person's entire existence.

The attempt to establish some sense of aliveness and continuity of self in the face of these changes constitutes the adaptation of the dying person. This struggle for adaptation occurs in a number of areas, creating a wide range of maneuvers designed to maintain a sense of aliveness in the presence of the forces leading to nonexistence. Each of the experiences of the person, each concern, each response, each perception amounts to an attempt to continue living and derive a sense of living against a background of the enlarging sense of personal extinction.

THE NEEDS, CONCERNS, PERCEPTIONS, AND RESPONSES OF THE DYING PATIENT

Relief of Physical Distress—Symptom Relief, Physical Intactness, and Comfort

A primary concern for the person confronted with a life-threatening illness is the pursuit of symptom relief. Symptoms such as pain, weakness, fatigue, weight loss, and others are stark reminders of the presence of illness and the progressive change in the self. Additionally, the various forms of treatments used in the course of a life-threatening illness may include side effects that create additional symptoms and feelings of discomfort. For example, certain drugs used in the treatment of malignant illnesses may cause nausea, while radiotherapies may cause hair loss or nausea, depending upon the site irradiated. Surgical procedures, while often life saving, may be associated with relatively long recovery periods; and breast removal, colostomies, amputations, and other surgical procedures may be associated with significant changes in the individual's concept of his body and its form.

Each person has developed and incorporated into his concept of himself a mental representation of his body and its parts—its shape, the real and symbolic functions of parts or organs, and what constitutes the integrity of the total self. This representation is referred to as the "body image." Varying from person to person, parts of the body and the body image are endowed with certain real and symbolic meanings important to the individual's psychosocial adaptation. Damage to the body and the body image is thus not only a physical matter but a psychological one as well. A middle-aged woman perhaps already concerned about a sense of waning physical and sexual attractiveness is likely to be significantly more concerned about the loss of a breast than someone less invested in this direction. Similarly, a young, highly mobile, athletic man who requires the amputation of a limb quite obviously perceives a great sense of damage to his body image. The importance of a body part may well have even more unique meanings for a particular person. This was evident in the case of a sixteen-year-old woman who required leg amputation for osteogenic sarcoma. When interviewed, she said she had always dreamed of being a dancer. Her feelings of despair about the amputation were intensified because of her particular future aspirations.

The emergence of symptoms may upset the person's level of adaptive equilibrium and create considerable psychosocial unrest. Over and above the discomfort experienced in the already present physical disabilities, the person interprets the emergence of new symptoms as progression of the illness and the symptoms become a reminder of the constricted future. In the latter stages of a fatal illness, when the individual is in a lingering stage, he may have considerable difficulty achieving any level of physical comfort. Functions which have been part of the person's normal life activities such as motility, visual perception, memory, and intellectual ability may be compromised by the process of the disease. Energy is in short supply and must necessarily be conserved for those activities which he perceives most important. Physical abilities, when limited, are often associated with a compromised range of adaptive abilities and each change in physical status evokes responses in the person and in those around him.

Temporal Constriction and the Sense of Loss of Future

The marked sense of constriction of remaining time for the dying person is central to the constellation of adaptive maneuvers characterizing the person's adjustment. Having paced himself with a relatively infinite perspective of anticipated future, the person now becomes aware of a limited and uncertain temporal existence. The future is telescoped into the present, creating a sense of urgency. This leads to a form of living in the now which requires considerable rearrangement of feelings, thoughts, and behaviors. In these circumstances, the future becomes deterministic in a different manner than previously experienced. Where previously the future was experienced as a time continuum in which feelings might be resolved, thoughts might be developed toward some goal, and behaviors directed toward accomplishment, the future now becomes increasingly absent. Aspirations and goals thus must be necessarily altered.

When finiteness becomes more recognizable and more a part of awareness, the person rearranges or attempts to rearrange his life plans accordingly. Progressive signs and symptoms of an illness are further reminders of the dying person's finiteness and may heighten the sense of urgency. When the individual first becomes truly aware of his dying, the sense of urgency has a chaotic

quality to it. Depending on the person's personality organization and his life circumstances, the sense of urgency is managed in many differing ways. The initial chaotic efforts to manage this compromised futurity gradually give way to more organized approaches to the loss of the self; however, the emergence of urgency and chaotic emotions, thoughts, and behaviors can usually be expected to erupt during the course of the person's illness. This aspect of future determinism is quite likely involved in many aspects of human personality development, but it becomes most evident when a person is confronted with the implications of his dying.

Temporal constriction has a number of implications for the individual's interpersonal relationships. For those persons relating with him, the sense of constricted future is shared to a greater or lesser degree, but is never actually shared at the same level as that experienced by the dying person himself. Thus, the dying person may perceive the reflected appraisal of his situation as being incongruent with his own concept of the urgency of the situation. This may be interpreted as a lack of concern or even disregard for the person's feelings and lead to disruptive interchanges. Often there is a sense of anger directed toward those who quite obviously have a future before them. For example, a young man dying of a malignant illness found himself intensely and unexplainably angry each time a friend told him of plans he was making for the future. In discussing these feelings it became apparent that the levels of the anger were even more intense when the plans described by the friend were long-range ones such as those related to career advancement or long-range aspirations for his family life.

The Crisis in Identity

The sense of temporal constriction and its accompanying urgency lead to a subjective questioning of the sense of identity, and the dying person becomes acutely aware of who he is, who he wanted to be, and what he wanted to accomplish. In essence, against the background of a constricted temporal frame of reference, the images by which the person conceptualizes his idea of self are brought into focus and called into question.

There is a sense of fragmentation of the established self and a desire to achieve a rearrangement of the personal concept of self more in keeping with the anticipated temporal framework.

The identity previously established to provide a self concept that allowed for comfortable future-directed participation in the person's life style and personal circumstances now seems inappropriate to fulfill his goals and aspirations. Thus, at times, there is an urgent and desperate attempt on the person's part to create a new identity and a new sense of self which is congruent with the limited future. The desperate quality arises from the recognition of the sense of temporal constriction and the attempt to dispel the perceived sense of urgency and its associated anxiety. At times this creates a wide range of behaviors which may involve an intense constriction of present identity or a chaotic, urgent experimenting with a new sense of self. The person may become dissatisfied with or change his vocational activities, plunge into new acts of creativity, or become deeply absorbed in philosophical or religious matters. He may rapidly change his style of relating to others. The formation of an identity is, however, a life-long process and is never really completed; nevertheless, the desire to experience a sense of closure, to have some consolidated sense of self in line with the constricted future is sought in an active, sometimes disruptive manner.

This quest, similar in many ways to the adolescent's quest for identity, may become markedly disruptive to relationships. The individual's self-centeredness, self-absorption, the forceful quality of his search for a new identity, and his redirected activities may be incongruent with the established life styles of the persons relating with him and the concepts held of him by others. The quest to "find oneself" is more or less tolerated or culturally legitimized in some phases of the life cycle, such as adolescence, but it may be poorly tolerated in a person at other times in his life. A dying person may, for example, become intensely immersed in religious or philosophical ideas quite incongruent with those of his past. He may then feel that his family and friends should be equally devoted to the subject and interper-sonal difficulties may ensue when this does not occur.

Individual Designations of Dying and Death

The person's adaptation to dying and death is strongly colored by those individual designations that he attributes to the dying process and to death. The designations are influenced by a number of factors, including the age of the person,[2] his past psychological development,[3] his accumulated experience with other dying persons and death, the interpersonal and social contexts related to his dying and death circumstances, and the manner in which he manages his sense of continuity with the future.[4-6] The personal designation of death is also markedly affected by the course of the illness, the time involved in the dying process, and the physical discomfort, changes, and limitations imposed by the illness and treatment process.

Weisman and Hackett have outlined three dimensions of experiencing death which vary with the levels of personal involvement.[7, 8] These three dimensions are impersonal death, interpersonal death, and intrapersonal death. Impersonal death confronts death as "an impersonal event, stripped of the human element, and the dead are simply dead bodies classified or discarded according to various categories." It is the death of an individual or number of individuals treated impersonally as an "it" or "its," viewed as a number or numbers. The interpersonal dimension considers the "objective fact of death of the *other* one." Whereas impersonal death implies "it is dead," interpersonal death implies that "someone else is dead." Intrapersonal death is likely the most important of these three dimensions of experiencing death, for in this dimension, the "I" is involved. The process of dying and the fact of subjective death are included in this dimension of experience. Dying is experienced as being equivalent to dissolution, and personal death as a feared event may come to be symbolically designated as abandonment, desertion, banishment, loneliness, dependence, pain, guilt, or retaliation.

Wahl, drawing on the fear of death (thantophobia) in children, discusses the derivations of the symbolic fear of death in the context of childhood thought processes and development.[3] The anger of the child in response to frustration is strongly colored by childhood omnipotence and becomes equated with a death wish. In this formulation, the accompanying operation of the Talion Law ("an eye for an eye, a tooth for a tooth") causes the child to become fearful of his own death as punishment for his wishes. Death, for the child, may then become equated with banishment, separation from or abandonment by the parent, and lingering remnants of these repressed conflicts may come to be operant in the complex symbolism of death later in life. The imagery of death described by Lifton and Olson as separation, stasis, and disintegration, contrasted with life imagery associated with connection, movement, and integrity, may also be seen as an important aspect of the imagery and symbolism related to the dying patient.[5, 6]

Importantly, how a person conceptualizes his immortality or lack of immortality is also incorporated into the symbolic designation of his death.[4-6] The mode of immortality gained from religious or personal views is often integrated into the complex symbolism.

A distinction is often made between symbolism attached to dying and that attached to death. In clinical practice the distinctions are blurred and for the individual, often intertwined. Designations of the dying process may include retaliation and punishment, gradual disintegration, separation, a wresting away of control, increasing dependency, the threat of abandonment, isolation and desertion, helplessness, exposure, increased vulnerability, chaos, peaceful acknowledgement of reduced expectations, attack, or transition to another life. Death itself may be invested with the same or different meanings.

The symbols of aloneness and isolation appear to be most striking in the dying person, the symbols bearing close connection with the fears of interpersonal abandonment accompanying dying. The fear of aloneness tends to be sometimes concretized as the fear of abandonment or desertion by those persons most close and significant to the individual and indeed this fear is at times

partially realized through the subtle interpersonal distancing which may occur while the person is dying. For example, a young woman was terrified that her physical deterioration during the course of her illness would make her less desirable as a wife and friend. As she came closer to death her physical appearance did indeed change markedly and some of her friends were unable to tolerate spending significant periods of time with her. Having been a gregarious, outgoing person, the physical limitations imposed by her illness in its later stages further compromised her ability to continue her previous level of interpersonal involvement. In some ways, her fears of being more alone and isolated were realized.

The symbolic perceptions an individual has about his illness and his dying are also significantly shaped by those individuals relating with him. An ill person may still possess considerable abilities to care for himself, yet be approximated with a family member or caregiver who, out of his own needs, reacts in an overprotective, controlling, and all-giving manner, meeting all needs before the person is able to use his own abilities. The perception of being helpless and dependent thus becomes reinforced. Similarly, those persons relating with a dying individual may assume the planning of activities and consciously begin to take over various tasks which had been in the domain of the dying person when this does indeed become a necessity. The dying person may see this as intrusive and controlling even when it is necessary.

How the dying person reacts to these interpersonal maneuvers will depend on the degree of actual debilitation, the perception of the reflected attitudes of caregivers, and the history of the relationship in terms of established patterns of interdependency, as well as the degree to which any specific person allows himself to rely on another for his sense of self. Additionally, the reactions will depend upon the degree to which the relationship is valued as a life-affirming one. Symbolic designations, then, are not totally derived from the dying individual's internal psychological makeup, but also represent the reflected designations of those persons caring for the individual. In this regard, it should be mentioned that medical regimens and their implementation are often necessarily intrusive and controlling. Restrictions and prescribed orders may cause the person to perceive his illness as representative of his being passive and controlled and he may then respond with defiance.

The designations attributed to the dying process by the individual are significantly influenced by his personality traits. Each happening and change in the process is interpreted in terms of the predominant modes of adaptation and interaction developed in the individual prior to the onset of disease. Thus, in a person desiring order and predictable routine, the uncertainty accompanying the events related to the dying process becomes particularly threatening. The highly mobile person who uses mobility and activity to bring about a sense of well-being may be particularly threatened by bodily changes that encroach on his activity. An individual who required the use of a cane to assist with his walking, for example, came to resent the cane as a symbol of encroachment on his mobility. The resentment and self-consciousness led to his refusal to use the cane and a number of serious falls because of his unsteadiness. This same person also viewed driving as a symbol of his mobility, and was highly reluctant to stop even when physical changes made driving nearly impossible.

The individual who is insistent on a perfectionistic body image and relies heavily on this intactness for his sense of self will react most severely to disfiguring changes brought about by his illness. The gregarious, outgoing individual may be more sensitive to his perceptions of abandonment than the person who is accustomed to a more solitary existence. This was evidence in the case of a young man whose illness dictated confinement to his home. The decreased ability to actively seek out friends led to considerable despair.

All of these aspects of the symbolic attributes of the dying process and death are dealt with and markedly affected by the pre-existing personality traits of the individual. It is true that a person dies as he has lived, reacting to the changes brought about by his dying in terms of the symbolic designations of the changes as they compromise various aspects of the manner in which he has lived.

Interpersonal Continuity

The dying person searches for a sustained sense of relatedness with those around him. Implicit in this search is the need for a sense of reliability, availability, and stability in relationships. Whether these relationships be close ones or relatively distant ones, the perception of the dying person is that the relationship may become more vulnerable, easily disrupted, and more fragile. These fears are based on the gradual loss of a sense of continued participation in all relationships and the determined need to ensure a sense of ongoing, relatively unchanging participation in the usual course of relatedness. Often there is the feeling that others will desert or abandon the person, and a feeling of being easily replaced. This may be founded in the symbolic designation of dying as representing imperfection, worthlessness, and becoming devoid of any appeal. All too often, however, these feelings are validated by the sense of being abandoned which results from the distancing of other persons. Responses of the dying person may be self-modulated or altered so as not to threaten required need for interpersonal continuity; this often is accomplished at the expense of the person's emotional well-being. This was apparent when a patient feared that her friends having knowledge of her illness would result in their being more uncomfortable around her, and she then refused to share her "secret" with them. This created a strained quality in the relationships and caused her to be constantly anxious and on guard in conversations.

As dependency increases and the individual becomes less autonomous and more dependent on the environment for needs, the desire for interpersonal continuity becomes an even more urgent matter. An exquisite sensitivity may become apparent and the individual quickly recognizes or sometimes imagines even subtle hints of withdrawal of those relating to him. Complicating the situation is the process whereby increased dependency demands lead to increased inner conflict for the individual or increased conflict in his interpersonal surroundings. Resenting his dependency, a man with leukemia became increasingly hostile toward any caregiver providing care for him, including his family. At the same time, he feared aloneness and isolation. The intensity of his anger escalated and his hostility served to drive people away, reinforcing his sense of being abandoned.

The interpersonal continuity sought after and found or not found by the dying person may well have a relationship to the level of personal significance, meaning, and the sense of aliveness experienced by the individual. For many individuals the primary form of feeling alive is the sense of aliveness achieved in a relationship. The activity generated by the relationship in this case is most meaningful and necessary to provide a sense of aliveness. The intense need for a stable relationship which will be unaffected by conflict seems to be a persistent need for the person. In some circumstances, however, conflict may actually be actively created by the person in the relationship as a means of testing its strength. This affirmation of the integrity of a relationship occurred when the wife of a patient noted that he became increasingly "grouchy" during periods of debilitation in the course of his illness. She continued to state her devotion regardless of his irritable moods, thereby confirming her dedication to remaining supportive in the relationship.

While there is the intense need for the maintenance of the relationship, at the same time other factors are operant. The dying individual is beseiged with feeling. There are feelings related to the urgency generated by the temporal constriction, the anger of protest in response to loss, sadness, grief related to the loss, anticipated loss, and numerous feelings associated with helplessness, the fear of being abandoned, increasing dependency, and feelings related to bodily change. Perceiving many of these feelings as having the ability to disrupt a relationship through their being experienced negatively by the person with whom he is relating, or perceiving them as feelings which by the nature of their intensity will drive the other person away, the dying individual resorts to any number of maneuvers

to manage this high level of feeling, while at the same time protecting the relationship or the emotional integrity of those with whom he is relating. This intense need to protect a relationship may well account for the maintenance of varying levels of expressed awareness regarding the illness or varying levels of talking about one's illness. One patient stated that she felt like the "Ancient Mariner" and could understand full well why he had stopped a stranger to unburden himself of his story. She, also feeling burdened by the intensity of her emotions and the happenings of her life in connection with a malignant illness, felt that "her story" had the potential to drive away those with whom she was closely related and felt that talking with a "stranger" would be less fraught with this danger or loss of a meaningful relationship than discussing her problems with someone close to her.

This need to protect a relationship may also be seen in the way many patients interact with their physicians. Talking of feelings related to dying and death may be seen by the patient as counterproductive in a relationship where the physician is held up as a vitalist—the person concerned most with life, and the person who is viewed as possessing the life-giving force. Thus, a patient who was highly concerned about "hurting others' feelings" said he did not wish to inform his physician about the finding of newly enlarged lymph nodes which obviously represented an acceleration of his disease process. While wishing to protect himself from the acknowledgement of the progression of his illness, there was also a need to "protect" the feelings of the physician treating him. When this withholding of information was explored in depth, it became apparent that the patient fantasized that the physician, with whom he had a supportive relationship, would "give up on his case" and turn his care over to another physician. Another related form of protection of a relationship is seen in the situation where the dying person provides substantial amounts of support for those around him. Here the dying individual himself, through supportive reassurance or listening to the feelings of others, becomes the one who helps others adapt. One patient complained that he found himself having to expend considerable energy helping his friends adjust to his illness, to the extent that he preferred that many of them simply not know that he had a malignant illness.

The most extreme form of loss of interpersonal continuity extending into the social context is the actual abandonment which may occur in relationship to the dying patient. This phenomenon has been referred to by some writers as "social death."[9-11] Kastenbaum writes that a person is viewed as " . . . socially dead when there is an absence of those behaviors that we would expect to be directed toward a living person and the presence of those behaviors that we would expect when dealing with a deceased or nonexistent person." Sudnow, in an institutional and organizational frame of reference, writes of a view of the termination of life which " . . . concerns itself not with how the biological organism expresses life, or lets go of it finally, but with how the social organization deals with this personal tragedy." He writes, "Social death begins when the institution, accepting impending death, loses its interest or concern for the dying individual as a human being and treats him as a body—that is, as if he were already dead."[10] Voodoo death is perhaps an extreme type of social death in which the individual experiences himself as totally abandoned, is treated by others as dead, and for whatever reasons indeed does die.[12]

Regardless of the frame of reference, these phenomena call attention to a type of attitude toward the dying patient which can result in an extreme sense of estrangement, alienation, loneliness, and abandonment. In this form of abandonment, a context for interpersonal activity which might result in some sense of aliveness is no longer available and the suffering of the dying person is accentuated.

In summary, the dying person seeks interpersonal and social participation and continuity to affirm his aliveness. The forms of interpersonal and social interaction involved include not only the intimate circle of persons relating to the dying person but also the entire range of caregivers within the institutional framework in which care is provided. However, the unique qualities of the dying person's needs, responses, and perceptions

bring factors into play which actually may serve to make relationships more difficult to maintain. The sum total of feelings generated around the dying person may serve to create an atmosphere of discomfort and unease which may in fact further isolate him from those relating with him.

Expression of Feeling

In caring for the dying person, the whole area of the expression of feeling assumes immense importance, for the individual in his confrontation with his own nonexistence is often overwhelmed by a wide and intense variety of emotions. Additionally, the manner in which these feelings are expressed and managed is affected by the life crisis of dying. These feelings have any number of implications for the person's sense of interpersonal well-being or absence of well-being, for many of the feelings are poorly tolerated by a particular interpersonal setting. The individual has operated in a time frame in which he felt there would be a future in which to work through feelings exchanged in interpersonal relationships. Now, facing death, the individual becomes extremely cautious about the expression of intense feelings as well as new emotional commitments.

Anger, a feeling experienced frequently by the dying person, is a particularly difficult emotion to manage. Feeling dependent upon others for care and for affirmation of aliveness, the individual perceives his anger and rage as having the potential to alienate persons at a time when relationships assume even greater importance. The anger present in the dying person may be based on reality circumstances, stem from everyday interpersonal relationships, or represent the anger related to increasing dependency, helplessness or loss of control. It may exist in reaction to losses sustained throughout the illness or be a type of anger which lacks an object—the anger merely related to having a life-threatening illness.

The anger associated with the dying process may intensify hostility experienced in everyday interpersonal relationships. The anger may be directed toward those individuals who usually surround the person. It may become diffusely expressed in the form of irritability and displaced to anyone or anything available as an object for its expression. Nurses, physicians, and family members may be met with unexplained outbursts of rage and hostility which seem to them inappropriate to the circumstances. Often, however, these unexplained outbursts are in reaction to some symbolic aspect of an interchange or an event which is a reminder to the individual of his illness and its effects on his total functioning. The anger may be in response to some reminder of unacceptable dependency and loss of autonomy, the sense of helplessness, the threat of abandonment, or the loss of the potential for continued social involvement. This was illustrated by the case of a person with a malignant illness who became intensely angry with his son as he reached the age when he began to date and become more involved in extracurricular school activities. The dying person, sensing a "beginning" of these activities for his son and an "ending" of his own social activities, was continuously reminded of his loss and directed the anger caused by the feelings of loss toward the son. Another patient became extremely angry with her spouse because he was uanble to remain constantly at her side. Each separation which occurred as a result of the spouse's need to continue to maintain his vocation and carry out newly assumed household functions was a symbolic reminder of the threat of abandonment and isolation. Some persons find the anger which surges in them totally unacceptable to themselves and in other cases there is a strong reaction to the anger by those in the environment.

Expressions of sadness and depression are still other feelings which are at times suppressed by the individual. These feelings are often felt to be representative of indulging in self-pity or being maudlin or morbid. The expression of emotions through crying or simply withdrawing into sadness may not be acceptable to the individual because of his personality makeup or his interpersonal environment. The feelings may also be suppressed as a protective maneuver to spare others the recognition of the mental state of the person. As one patient said, "How long can I go on crying like this? I'll drive everyone away from me by seeming so maudlin and caught up in myself. People just can't

stand feelings that are this 'heavy'."

Aside from the range of feelings that are frequently viewed by the person as having negative connotations, the dying individual often also has difficulty with the expression of more positive feelings. Expression of tenderness, love, and intimacy may become restricted in an attempt to forestall an intensification or deepening of a relationship. This form of protectiveness is used to spare the other individual in a relationship the grief and anguish that the ill person anticipates the other person might experience. This phenomenon was apparent when a young man with a life-threatening illness became highly reluctant to involve himself in a relationship with a young woman to whom he was attracted. He felt that the development of the relationship would only hurt the other person, because after his death she would be faced with grieving his loss.

In other situations the sharing of intimacy and commitment may be constricted as a means of "stopping time" or essentially freezing a relationship where it is so as not to experience any additional sense of loss. For example, on learning that he had a malignant illness, a person immediately engaged in behaviors which brought an end to what was obviously a highly valued relationship. In discussing what had happened it was apparent that he desired to "remember the relationship as it was" without the added dimension of emotions related to his illness.

The Process of Denial and the Level of Awareness

While the amount of information given out and exchanged by caregivers and family members is an important determinant of awareness, the dying person also is heavily invested in modulating the amount of information exchanged. The psychological process of denial is an important aspect of the person's coping with the overwhelming anxiety accompanying the recognition of personal finiteness and extinction. By definition, denial is an unconscious phenomenon whereby a person does not allow the conscious perception of the reality of a situation. As a psychological process, it is involuntary and serves to modulate the knowledge and intensity of an unacceptable circumstance. Denial is seldom an all or none phenomenon and there is fluctuation in its level throughout the person's illness.[13] In effect, in talking with the dying person one becomes aware that there are times when he may act as if there were nothing wrong with him. At other times, varying degrees of knowledge of the illness along the entire spectrum of awareness and acceptance may be apparent.

In addition to denial, there appears to be another maneuver operant which may be referred to as withholding. Withholding is a more conscious coping phenomenon and is related to that material which the individual wants or does not want to communicate to the persons in his environment. Utilizing these processes, the individual appears to calibrate the level of information and awareness about his illness which he and his life circumstances are able to tolerate. Obviously the process of denial and the maneuver of withholding may have valuable coping and adaptive potential, but they may also create difficulties.

Denial and withholding must be understood not only in the subjective dimension but in terms of the individual's interpersonal relationships and the social context in which his dying occurs.[13] The level of awareness about the illness is modulated so as to protect not only the self, but also those persons with whom the ill individual is relating. Taken even further, they are at times used to protect the well-being of the care setting itself, such as a hospital ward. In considering the awareness level, what the patient tells and how he tells must be considered along with what is told the patient and how it is told. In an attempt to "protect" her family from the knowledge of the gravity of her illness, a young woman with leukemia refused to acknowledge the degree of physical debilitation she was experiencing. In so doing, she continued to try to fulfill demands her family placed upon her that were out of line with her physical abilities. She grew progressively more angry and depressed as her physical abilities waned while she continued to attempt to maintain her activities at the level they had been before her illness.

The issue of telling or not telling or how and what to tell a person about his illness is frequently discussed.[14, 15] The matter of the level of information the patient wishes to have also is important in such considerations. The answer must come out of an understanding of the individual as a unique person having unique needs. For example, a young woman with a malignancy was seen at a time when she was certain that she had only a month to live. She had assessed her prognosis on the basis of a friend's malignant illness that had resulted in death approximately one month after the onset of signs of the illness and diagnosis. It was evident that this person's illness had not progressed to the point that she only had a month to live, but when she was offered the opportunity to discuss a more accurate estimate of her prognosis with her physician, she did not want to be given any statement of probable outcome by him. She preferred to have more control over her own prognosticating, altering it as she felt necessary to the situation. Her own estimate of the time she had remaining led, however, to an intense sense of urgency that evoked incapacitating feelings.

Rather than being viewed as bad or good, denial and withholding should be recognized as part of the individual's repertoire in coping with the knowledge of his dying. These phenomena become problematic when they result in personal maladaptation, create serious difficulties in the individual's interpersonal relationships, or interfere with the treatment of the disease. Some modulation of awareness appears to be a normal process necessary to buffer the patient's and others' mental states and aid in their coping. This statement should not be taken to mean that information should necessarily be concealed; however, the manner in which information is given to the dying person and his family should be based on a knowledge of those involved and the information conveyed accordingly. To do otherwise could result in a mechanistic giving of information which may increase the suffering of the patient. It should also be pointed out that the willingness and capacity to "hear" what is told and to assimilate the information will vary considerably throughout the illness. "I heard what the doctor said, but I can't really believe it" is a theme often encountered in working with dying patients.

Response Patterns Related to Dependency and Independency and Need for Mastery and Control

It was mentioned previously that the dying person's adaptation is heavily dependent on his personality configuration. In response to the numerous crises precipitated by the dying process, struggles with dependency and independency and with mastery and control become significant parts of the adaptive process. These struggles are often present to the extent that they require special attention and therapeutic intervention.

Dying and its physical and emotional concomitants render the individual progressively less autonomous and more dependent upon the environment. Through development in the life cycle, the individual has come to manage his dependency/independency struggle in his own unique manner. He responds in certain ways to increased dependency on others or he acts in such a manner as to maintain a sense of independency and self-sufficiency. The balance achieved by the individual is disrupted by the dying process. During the course of his illness, he is likely to find himself more dependent on family, friends, physicians, and other caregiving personnel. Also, he is likely to become more dependent on the institutions of society which are geared for meeting the needs of persons in distress. Renewal of the psychosocial struggle of autonomy *vs.* shame and doubt, as described by Erikson,[16] occurs, and the individual feels shame and doubts his sense of self as his illness progressively encroaches upon his autonomy. In the usual course of adaptation to illness, a phenomenon known as regression occurs. In regression, earlier forms of adaptive behavior come into play. Thus when one is ill, he is likely to normally become more clinging, dependent, and demanding, expressing his needs in a more intense, dramatic manner to the environment. These changes may, however, cause discomfort in the person and create in-creased difficulties in the interpersonal setting, further compromising the sense of autonomy.

The recognition of this increased dependency on the environment is frequently accompanied by intense feelings of anger directed not only toward the self for the emergence of traits perceived as unacceptable, but they also may be directed toward the environment and those persons on whom the individual is dependent. Family, friends, relatives, and caregivers may become objects of the expression of this seemingly unexplained anger.

Another response frequently seen in the dying person is a drive in the direction of extreme independence and the inability to accept any form of caring behavior. This maneuver is often used to counter the recognition of the increasing dependency, as he pushes far beyond his physical capabilities and communicates a false sense of well-being to the environment. There is a kind of pretense of well-being incongruent with the actual mental or physical state. While this behavior contains elements of denial, it can also be a response to increasing dependency and the nonacceptance of this encroachment on autonomy. Thus a man with severe anemia and shortness of breath continued to engage in activities far beyond his physical capabilities. To sustain his sense of independence, autonomy, and physical stamina, he went so far as to go on a mountain climbing expedition which resulted in his developing congestive heart failure.

In the circumstances of dying, where uncertainty increases and the situation becomes progressively chaotic, the personal sense of control diminishes and a feeling of being unable to achieve mastery over the situation becomes more dominant. In most persons there are, as with dependency and independency, developed attitudes toward control and mastery; in many individuals the need for control and mastery is a particularly ingrained, important part of their personality configuration.

The sense of loss of control may be accompanied by increased anxiety, increase in the sense of helplessness, and increased anger engendered by the chaos. Also present may be feelings of an inability to bring about some sense of order and rather desperate attempts to gain control. Perfectionistic individuals may find this disorder and chaos particularly alarming. A man who suffered a myocardial infarction and was in a coronary care unit maintained accurate records of the precise times of his urinating and defecating. In this behavior, he was able to find some semblance of order at a time when he felt his surroundings to be extremely chaotic.

Some persons may attempt to bring order to the situation by insisting on knowing every detail involved in their care or trying to exert control over the care process itself. This may become an even greater problem when a person who seeks control is excluded from any participation in his care, when all decisions are made for him, and he has little or no input into the direction of his treatment. Being unable to manage the events connected with the illness, the dying person may attempt to control the people caring for him. He may resist treatment or fail to comply with directions as a means of wresting control away from others and obtaining some control for himself. Misunderstandings between care providers and the patient and his family are often in reality struggles for control.

To those who feel they must perform perfectly and always maintain the standards expected of them, the availability of various books on dying and death leads them to wonder and obsess as to whether or not they are proceeding "correctly" in their adaptation to dying. They become increasingly concerned about the acceptability or correctness of their adaptation. As one patient resentfully asked, "Am I adjusting to my illness in the best way—like the books say you should?"

During the final stages of an illness, the person may feel his autonomy to be entirely gone. At these times suicidal ideation may be expressed as if to say that he does indeed have the ultimate control over his life. In exploring his reported suicidal ruminations, one patient stated, "I can't control anything else. At least I can control when and how I die."

Response to Reality Circumstances and Concern for Future Well-Being of Family and Others

The costs of dying are high not only in terms of the person's physical and interpersonal losses. There are losses in the time left for the person to live out his life as well as substantial losses in time throughout the course of the illness, such as time lost through hospitalizations, clinic visits, and other treatment procedures. Economic costs rise and, at the same time, the ability to earn an income may be compromised. The dying individual becomes concerned about these losses related to time and finances.

In anticipating his absence from the family setting, he also becomes concerned about the survival and future of his family. Fantasies about the remarriage of a spouse become an issue and may become bothersome. Other commonly encountered preoccupations are the future financial situation of the family and such issues as how the children will be supported emotionally and economically. One patient became preoccupied with the idea that if her spouse remarried, the "new" mother might have an entirely different set of expectations and aspirations for her children. She obsessed about the possibility that all of her input into the rearing of the children would be undone following her death. The fantasy of being replaced and the recognition that this may, in some circumstances, well be a reality is bothersome and accompanied by numerous emotional responses.

Depression and Grief

Sadness and depression in response to loss characterize many phases of the dying person's adaptation to his illness. There is the depression and despair related to the recognition of personal finitude; there is also the depression and grief which occurs in response to the losses sustained and those which will be encountered in the course of the illness; there is the grief in response to the anticipated ultimate loss of the self and others.[15] All of these affectual responses are characterized by feelings of sadness, though occasionally a form of elation or euphoria may be briefly present in response to death as a relief from suffering. Elation may also be seen in some individuals whose faith in an afterlife is so strong that they view their death as merely a transition to a "better place." For example, one patient expressed her joy over the prospect of "going to heaven to be with God and the members of the family" who had died previously.

The affectual responses involved in depression, despair, and grief are often clinically indistinguishable. Generally, however, depression and despair are more sustained while grief appears to come in waves. The grief process in the dying person necessarily occurs in anticipation of the ultimate loss of self and also occurs in reaction to the sense of transience and loss present throughout the dying process. The depression and despair are in response to losses which have been sustained during the course of the illness—loss of vocation, loss of the ability to participate in usual activities, the sense of interpersonal loss, losses sustained through the process of physical deterioration, and the loss of body parts or changes in body image related to the illness. This depression may be of a mild form or reach serious proportions with agitation, loss of appetite, severe problems with sleep, marked withdrawal from any pleasurable activity, loss of all sexual interests, and suicidal ideation. Importantly, the degree of depression is likely to vary considerably over the course of the illness and is related to the degree of loss perceived at the moment. This was apparent when, on having a menstrual period after prolonged amenorrhea, a dying woman became severely depressed about her incapacity to have more children. She had wanted a larger family and secretly felt she might be pregnant. When this fantasy was dispelled by her menstrual period beginning, the realization that she would not have more children emerged.

An interpersonal problem which emerges in this area is the tendency for the depressed or grieving person to withdraw into himself. To the dismay and bewilderment of those relating with him, this withdrawal into the self may be perceived as threatening to the relationship and even a reminder of the ultimate loss of the person himself. There are times, however, in the course of the dying process, when the individual does indeed withdraw into himself in the process of quietly working through the intense feelings related to loss and other times when he simply lacks the energy to participate in an ongoing relationship. For example, a patient reported that she had so little energy that she did not even feel like talking with friends. She preferred to conserve what energy she had for interactions with her family and the few enjoyable hobbies she was still able to pursue.

The Need for Resolution of Conflict

In the face of temporal constriction, the dying person becomes concerned with resolving conflicts remaining from the past and bringing rapid resolution to any conflicts that emerge in the present. Guilt and anxiety over old unresolved issues come into awareness as difficulties with which to be dealt. A common theme is the perception on the part of the person that the disease represents a deserved punishment for some perceived misdeed in the past. A middle-aged man who had an extramarital affair years before, for example, became preoccupied with the happening and wondered if his disease was a form of punishment for his infidelity. This need to resolve conflict, to finish out one's life work in the emotional sphere, often takes on the quality of urgency and intensity similar to that seen in the dying person's search for identity.

Paradoxically, in becoming an urgent matter, the intensity may lead to additional interpersonal conflict as the person attempts to work through unsolved conflicts. In an attempt to bring resolution to remaining conflict, old issues may be brought up in the context of present relationships. For instance, a young woman felt that she had never been accepted by her in-laws. She became exquisitely sensitive to her interactions with them after she developed leukemia. Even the slightest indication of disapproval was interpreted as total rejection, and she reacted to them by being over solicitous and giving, while at the same time harboring resentment over their perceived nonacceptance. Her urgent attempts to win their approval led to further unrest.

Aspects of relationships which symbolically represent unresolved conflict may become focal points in the search for conflict resolution. For one dying individual, the struggle for control had always been present in the marriage. During the person's illness, the struggle over who would make decisions about the children's participation in activities became a central issue symbolically representing the broader struggle.

Concerns with Dying and Death

The dying person is not continually concerned with the abstract issues connected with dying and death, and this lack of concern during some phases of his illness should not necessarily be viewed as a form of denial. Many patients are most interested in talking about problems in living resulting from their confrontation with dying and death rather than engaging in abstract conversations about the meaning of dying or definitions of death. It should be emphasized that a person's deep feelings about dying and death represent an intimate and very private part of his being. The caregiver must recognize this, for it is far too easy to attend to one's own needs and insist that the individual talk about these issues when the need of the dying person is not necessarily in this direction. At the other extreme is the caregiver who is so uncomfortable with these feelings that the person for whom he is caring is disallowed any expression of thoughts and feelings about dying and death. Neither posture is appropriate and only in the context of a comfortable need-discerning relationship can the level at which the person wishes to talk be determined.

At times the person may become preoccupied with feelings and thoughts connected with the meanings related to the actual dying process and death. At these times, a caregiver should be able to relate to the person in a way which allows the individual to express his concerns and feelings, but even in these situations, the person's focus may be primarily on living and life rather than on dying and death.

In relationship to the physician, the dying person appears to engage in an interpersonal phenomenon which deserves further comment. The dying person, holding up his physician as the life force, may not choose to talk with him about issues connected with dying and death. At times this is protective for the patient in that it keeps issues connected with death out of the relationship. At other times this phenomenon may be protective for the physician, as the patient attempts to spare the doctor the feelings and thoughts connected with death rather than life. The ramifications of this phenomenon, in terms of the doctor-patient relationship, are important, for it appears that both the physician and the dying individual at times engage in a mutually protective operation to assure the "life-giving" efforts growing out of the relationship.

This mutual protection takes its toll in terms of the physician being able to discern all needs, and it often also means that the patient will at times choose to discuss the various vicissitudes of his dying and death with persons other than the doctor. Depending on the individual, the thoughts and feelings may be shared with a nurse, a clergyman, a chosen family member or friend, an aide, or even someone whose periodic clinic appointments happen to coincide with those of the patient. Different areas may be discussed piecemeal with a wide variety of persons, diffusing the thoughts and feelings. Because of this, information as to what the person is experiencing is often widely dispersed and each person providing care only has access to partial information. This has important implications for the care of the person and underlines the importance of collaboration among caregivers, for it is often only through such collaboration that needs can be accurately determined.

Stage Appropriate Coping Maneuvers

In viewing dying and death as stages in the life cycle, it must be recognized that certain responses, feelings, and behaviors observed in the dying person are "stage appropriate"; that is, for this stage in the person's life and the circumstances surrounding it, the experiences may be legitimately expected to occur as a usual and even normative part of the person's overall repertoire of responses. This concept is drawn from the psychology of childhood where certain types of behaviors may be viewed as evidence of psychopathology at other stages in the child's life, but occur as normal phenomena in this early stage of development, thus being "stage appropriate" for the child. Such behaviors are, in certain circumstances, usual and expected responses for the particular level of development.[17] A preschool child, for instance, separated from a parent in a supermarket would be expected to react with crying, fear, and even anger. This behavior would be viewed as appropriate for the child's stage of development. In effect, the child signals that he is lost, alerts the environment to his distress, and conveys the feeling he is experiencing. The response of those around him is to restore the child's continuity with his environment through seeking out the parent.

Similar situations arise with the dying person. Some of the behaviors and emotional states which may appear to be severe psychopathology, or at least may be designated as such, may actually be attempts to cope and adapt to the illness and impending death. An example of such behavior is the expression of self-destructive ideation by the lonely, dying person. The behavior is likely to bring about significant interpersonal contact for the person and also allows him to experience some sense of control. This type of behavior was evident in a person with a life-threatening illness who complained of "being dead."[18] While the complaint reached the proportion of a delusion, in viewing the person's total life circumstances, his sense of social alienation, physical disintegration and changed body image, the complaint could be better understood. In his case, the communication of "being dead" became adaptive, in that the interpersonal contact which ensued, along with the care and concern that he had been unable to obtain otherwise, served to affirm his being alive.

In another case, a person dying of leukemia engaged in hostile interactions which led to his abandonment by most of the persons with whom he had been relating. Perceiving this alienation and abandonment, he could then say that death was preferable to life and, in this position, came to accept death as a release. In the context of the terminal phase of a person's life, such re-

sponses, while not actually purposive, may be adaptive, reparative, and even appropriate. These behaviors do not necessarily come about as conscious coping efforts, although at times the behaviors appear almost contrived in their obviousness. As study of this phase of life increases, it is likely that any number of responses of the dying person will be found to be in this category of "stage appropriate" behavior.

Recognizing behavior or emotional states as "stage appropriate," however, does not mean that the responses do not require intervention. Quite often these behaviors have profound disruptive impact on the environment. The danger, however, comes when such responses are not recognized as "stage appropriate" adaptive maneuvers and there is no attempt made to understand the motivating factors. When these behaviors are viewed as "stage appropriate" behaviors, their effects on the interpersonal environment may be more amenable to intervention and acceptable as expressions of need.

Sense of Aloneness and Isolation

The gradual sense of enlargement of the part of the self which is to be nonexistent is perceived by the individual as a sense of separation from life and from those persons with whom he is closely related. Facing death is, in the final analysis, a state of being alone. This sense of separation and aloneness is present throughout the entire process of the person's dying and is all too often accentuated by the sometimes blatant and other times subtle interpersonal abandonment of the dying person. The presence of a caring person is desired by the dying individual, though the desire is not necessarily that the caring person do anything other than be present or at least demonstrate that he is available. The tendency toward the avoidance of dying persons in the past has created for the ill individual an increased sense of being "noxious" and has contributed to his sense of isolation. In many cases, the patient's inability to talk about "dying and death" or related life problems with others is viewed by him as an appraisal of his uselessness and nonworth. As one patient said, "I feel like a grotesque freak because I'm dying and no one wants to spend time with a grotesque freak . . . it makes me feel more alone."

Responses to the Non-Human Environment

Throughout various phases of care, the dying individual is approximated not only with human beings as caregivers but with all of the supportive administrative protocol accompanying the acts of the caregivers as well as the apparatus and machinery of modern medicine. The administrative protocol, procedural activities, the sometimes awesome arrays of tubing and machinery, monitors, and the actual physical environment in which care is provided are referred to as the non-human environment.* While not persons relating with the dying individual, the non-human environment forms an important part of the dying patient's existence and in effect, he "relates" to it in varying ways. The manner in which a person relates to the non-human environment varies considerably.

The patient's personality traits, the particular characteristics of the non-human environment, matters related to the person's illness such as the degree of dependency on the non-human aspects of care, and the manner in which these aspects of care are utilized and presented by caregiving personnel are among the determinants of the effects of this aspect of care on the person. Thus an individual will respond in certain ways to physical considerations such as the privacy or nonprivacy of his room, long waits for diagnostic and treatment procedures, the procedures themselves, as well as the administrative routine of the health-care setting. He is likely to notice others with the same (or the imagined same) illnesses in waiting rooms. He will relate to various types of monitors and life-support machinery in terms of his personality traits and response to illness. He will be concerned about food and the comfort of the surroundings in which his family must spend long hours.

Patients may personalize machinery and develop complex psychological feelings toward it.[19] The busy movement of the intensive care unit and all of the ramifications of the individual's responses to the apparatus and protocol play an important part in his adaptation. The isolation experienced in various treatment techniques such as those used in burn care or specialized radiotherapy techniques may engender severe emotional reactions. For example, a patient with carcinoma of the lung became panicky each time he received radiation therapy for his disease. After one treatment he refused further therapy. In discussing this with him he stated that the size and appearance of the small room in which the treatment was given and the absence of people around him led to his feeling that he was "walled off," like being in a coffin. His fears of death became accentuated by the setting and its symbolic meaning.

The impersonality and exposure experienced in the multiple bed ward become part of the stress to which the person must adapt. The disruption of the continuity of care brought about by change of personnel in the hospital setting or in teaching hospitals may be extremely stressful. In one case, a young patient who had formed a comfortable relationship with a resident physician became extremely anxious and depressed when she learned that he was to rotate to another service in the hospital. When he informed her that he would still come by to visit with her, her anxiety and depression subsided. Explanation and clear instructions about what to expect, leaving room for patients' questions and expressions of feeling can serve to provide a humanizing effect on the non-human aspects of care.

CRISIS IN MEANING—SEARCH FOR ACTIVITY THAT PROVIDES A SENSE OF ALIVENESS

Meaning, the structure of the sense of aliveness, is dependent on activities which ensure the continued sense of aliveness in the confrontation with one's dying and anticipated death. The ability to find meaning or personal significance is a requisite for a

---

* Searles stresses the importance of the role of the "nonhuman" environment in psychological development. Searles, H. R. *The Nonhuman Environment in Normal Development and Schizophrenia*. International Universities Press, New York, 1960.

continued feeling of being alive when the person is approximated with his sense of deathliness. For every person who confronts death and for the dying person in particular, the events which lead to the expanding recognition of the potential for non-existence may be seen to precipitate a crisis in living which can be referred to as the meaning crisis. In the meaning crisis, the level of meaning which can be derived from one's existence may fluctuate significantly or sharply diminish. The sense of being alive becomes blurred, dampened, and indefinite and there is a significant increase in death awareness with its accompanying feelings.

The meaning crisis may be accompanied by a feeling state characterized by extreme anxiety or terror, exquisite sensitivity to transience and loss, despair, urgency, and a sense of time diffusion. When these feelings reach a high level of intensity and become overwhelming, the person may feel numb, distant from the living, and may experience little sense of pleasurable participation in his life circumstances. There is little sense of aliveness and the person experiences the relational quality of life as fragmented. This latter feeling state is, I believe, akin to the mental state described by Lifton as "psychic numbing."[6, 20] Statements such as "This has no meaning," "I can't make any sense of this," "I feel dead already," "Why can't I go on and die?" are not only expressions of despair, but are also statements of a crisis in meaning. In effect, the person feels more dead than alive and this perception may be validated by the responses of those around him who avoid him or treat him as an object rather than as a person.

In the face of a meaning crisis, the individual moves in the direction of activity which assures a sense of aliveness. This search for meaningful activity represents an attempt to counter the force of the emergence of "nothing" with meaning. Gradually, and at times acutely, the inability to carry on activities in the biological, psychological, and social dimensions may result in a pervasive sense of meaninglessness accompanied by the sense of non-aliveness and the gradual enlargement of the sense of separation from the living. Finally, in the course of many illnesses, the reflected sense of aliveness derived from the presence of a caring individual may become the only source of meaning left for the dying person.

Dying as a process is in itself accompanied by many losses and limitations which compromise the individual's ability to engage in meaningful activity. Changes which result in loss of body parts and bodily functions that enabled the person to engage in meaningful activities, changes in the psychological state which disrupt the individual's established patterns of activity and coping, changes in relationships, and changes in the person's social context such as his job or status in society all play a part in interfering with his established sense of meaning and aliveness. In response to this impaired ability to engage in meaningful activities and in connection with the ever-growing sense of nonexistence, the meaning crisis becomes a most significant problem in the person's adaptation. There is an urgent search for meaningful activities to assure a sense of aliveness and, at the same time, a constriction of the ability to derive meaning. As meaning diminishes, the person is brought into direct confrontation with the loss brought about by the illness and the losses anticipated through death. At these times, death awareness increases, accompanied by high levels of feeling or a state of numbness.

Meaning may, for some, be obtained through activity aimed at combating the illness process. At other times, it is obtained through participation in relationships which have the qualities of assuring aliveness. Such relationships may range from being conflict-free to being extremely conflictual. In either case, the sense of relating is present and the activity allows the person to derive meaning. So long as the person views himself as alive and he is viewed as such by those persons relating with him, then the stage is set for his gaining the maximum degree of aliveness possible, even when all else falls away. The derivation of meaning extends into the social context and for many into the spiritual realm. For many persons, it is spiritual activity which enables them to continue to derive a sense of aliveness in their confrontation with death.

In this approach, no judgment can be made as to which form of meaning is the most desirable one. This should always remain the choice of the individual. It is, however, the caregivers' task to facilitate the person's ability to engage in those activities which are meaningful for that unique person and, through their presence and knowledge and skills as caring individuals, to assist the person in using whatever is left to him to obtain meaning in his living with his dying.

Thus any particular dying person's needs, concerns, responses, and perceptions grow out of highly individualized blendings of the areas discussed in this chapter. Variations of the types and intensities of the needs and responses are to be expected from person to person and from time to time in any one person. Each need and response becomes a part of the person's subjective state as well as the interpersonal interaction involved in the care of the individual. The manner in which these needs and responses are addressed have the potential to lead to a sense of relative well-being or a sense of abandonment and isolation. The need-discerning presence of those approximated with the person contributes substantially to his adaptation or maladaptation.

REFERENCES

1. Barton D: "The Dying Patient," in *Basic Psychiatry for the Primary Care Physician*. Abram HS (Ed) Little, Brown and Co, Boston, 1976
2. Nagy MH: "The Child's View of Death," in *The Meaning of Death*. Feifel H (Ed) McGraw-Hill, New York, 1959
3. Wahl CW: The Fear of Death. *Bull Menninger Clin 22:*214–223, 1958
4. Lifton RJ: On Death and Death Symbolism: The Hiroshima Disaster. *Psychiatry 27:*191–210, 1964
5. Lifton RJ, Olson E: *Living and Dying*. Praeger Publishers, New York, 1974
6. Lifton RJ: *The Life of the Self: Toward a New Psychology*. Simon and Schuster, New York, 1976
7. Weisman AD, Hackett TP: Predilection to Death: Death and Dying as a Psychiatric Problem. *Psychosom Med 23:*232–256, 1961
8. Weisman AD: "Thanatology," in *The Comprehensive Textbook of Psychiatry* 2nd Ed, Vol. II, Freedman AM, Kaplan HI, Sadock BJ (Eds) The Williams & Wilkins Co, Baltimore, 1975
9. Kastenbaum R: "Psychological Death," in *Death and Dying: Current Issues in the Treatment of the Dying Person*. Pearson L (Ed) The Press of Case Western Reserve University, Cleveland, 1969
10. Sudnow D: "Dying in a Public Hospital," in *The Dying Patient*. Brim OG, Jr, Freeman HE, Levine S, Scotch NA (Eds) Russell Sage Foundation, New York, 1970
11. Sudnow D: *Passing On: The Social Organization of Dying*. Prentice-Hall, Englewood Cliffs, New Jersey, 1967
12. Cannon WB: "Voodoo" Death. *Psychosom Med 19:*182–190, 1957
13. Weisman AD: *On Dying and Denying: A Psychiatric Study of Terminality*. Behavioral Publications, New York, 1972
14. Verwoerdt A: *Communication With the Fatally Ill*. Charles C Thomas, Springfield, Illinois, 1966
15. Kübler-Ross E: *On Death and Dying*. Macmillan, London, 1969
16. Erikson E: *Identity: Youth and Crisis*. W. W. Norton and Company, New York, 1968
17. *Psychopathological Disorders in Childhood: Theoretical Considerations and a Proposed Classification*. Vol. VI. Group for the Advancement of Psychiatry, New York, 1966
18. Barton D, Fishbein JH, Stevens FW Jr. Psychological Death: An Adaptive Response to Life-Threatening Illness. *Psychiatry Med 3:*227–236, 1972
19. Abram HS: Psychological Aspects of Intensive Care Units. *Med Ann DC 43:*59–62, 1974
20. Lifton RJ: On Death and the Continuity of Life: A Psychohistorical Perspective. *Omega, 6:*143–159, 1975

5

THE FAMILY OF THE DYING PERSON

David Barton, M.D.

The dying and death of a family member are the most intense and disruptive stresses a family can encounter. Adaptive tasks required during the dying process and the death of a family member are numerous, difficult, and themselves often extremely disruptive to the structure and function of the family unit. While providing care for the dying person and being immersed in the context of death, the family must continue to meet its members' needs, function as a social unit in society, and provide a structure for the growth and development of its members. The family must adapt to the many changes resulting from the dying person's illness, maintain its identity, and begin to provide for the adaptation to the ultimate loss of the person by reorganizing to continue its function after the family member's death.

All of these activities are accomplished against the background of a pervasive sense of loss and transition which is in itself stressful and disruptive to the intactness and integrity of the family's structure and function. Internal reorganization is the rule; renegotiation and change of the family members' internal transactions and the family's interaction with society becomes a necessity; restoration of some semblance of family structure and function following the death of the individual must be achieved. None of these tasks is easily accomplished and each progressing juncture in the process of the dying person's illness has the capacity to promote further familial disruption and dysfunction. It is not surprising, then, that family members employ denial or utilize

withholding, acting as if all is well when in reality it is not. Full recognition of this grim reality is tantamount to acknowledging a sense of disintegration and death not only of the family member, but also the existing family structure and the integrity and identity of the family itself. In this sense, an additional threat of annihilation accompanies the death of a family member and enters into the process of adaptation surrounding the death of a person in a family. There is the threat of the death of the sense of family itself and the sense of the dying and death of the family's structure, function, and identity.

Understanding the difficulties encountered by a family in adapting to the death of a family member requires a general knowledge of concepts related to family types, family structures and functions, and roles within a family. The family itself is a smaller structural and functional unit of the socity in which it lives, and as that society changes, the characteristics of the family are also subject to reorganization. These changes have important implications for the problems encountered by a family in caring for a family member who is dying.

Families may be classified as being of two general types: the extended kindred family, and the isolated nuclear family.[1] The extended kindred family is typified by the large family structure of the agrarian past. In the extended kindred family system, there were abundant, readily available, interpersonal resources with numerous relatives living in a close, supportive, familial setting. Family members, including parents, brothers and sisters, grandparents, aunts and uncles were readily available for interpersonal and other forms of support when necessary. These individuals often lived in relative proximity and the large family was far more functionally self-contained than many contemporary families. While not as socially mobile and adaptable to changes in society, the extended kindred family was a source of massive interpersonal support at times of stress. If the capabilities of smaller units within the extended kindred family became overwhelmed, other family members in the larger family unit were available to buffer stresses and assume some of the functions of the overwhelmed family or its incapacitated member.

As a result of increased societal mobility, industrialization, urbanization, and rapidly changing societal forms, the extended kindred family structure of the past has tended to become replaced by the isolated nuclear family. The isolated nuclear family is a highly mobile, smaller unit, generally consisting of a wife, husband, and their children. This type of family often lives and functions at considerable distance from its original family ties and internally has less supportive capabilities than the extended kindred family of the past. In order to meet its needs, it must delegate an increasing number of familial tasks to the society in which it lives; it must thus depend on that society for many ancillary supportive functions. Because of its limited ability to provide increased supportive functions, the isolated nuclear family is more vulnerable to stress, and its abilities to meet its members' needs may be compromised more easily than the extended kindred family. These sociological changes in family structure represent significant problems for the care of the dying person, for when a family member is ill there is significantly less support in many contemporary families than in those of the past.

In many cases the delineation of family types is not as sharply defined as presented here. Some families may exist as isolated nuclear families but still have related members who live relatively nearby. Still other relatives may live at significant distances but in times of stress may rejoin the isolated family unit to provide additional support. Isolated nuclear families also tend to de-

velop relationships with close friends or networks of friends who can assist in providing support in times of stress. In general, however, the contemporary family is less able to deal internally with the stresses created by the presence of an ill family member than was the extended kindred family of the past.

An important issue in the development of the isolated nuclear family is the need for delegation of responsibilities of care to caregivers other than family members. This often means that the medical institution must assume increasing responsibility for the care of the dying person. This, coupled with the development of technology within the medical institution and the desire that each family member receive the maximum benefits of this technology, moves the care of the dying person more in the direction of the hospital setting.

The family is in essence a small group whose structure, functions, and dynamic interactions are aimed at promoting the growth and development of its members, maintaining cohesiveness, and developing and maintaining itself as a viable social unit in relation to the society in which it lives. Within the family, certain members have roles which are associated with categories of function. One parent, for example, is likely to assume responsibility for expressive functions while the other assumes responsibility for instrumental functions. (Expressive functions relate to internal family matters such as affective needs, understanding feelings, development of self-awareness, and the manner in which feelings are communicated and exchanged. Instrumental functions of the family pertain to its interactions with society such as maintaining economic survival and the acquiring of required supplies.) Most often one or the other parent assumes the position of providing the role model for each of these functions and even as society changes and the role models in families become more blurred there remains some delineation in the assumption of these roles.[2, 3]

The family unit performs a number of functions for its members. Fleck describes these functions as: marital, nurturant, relational, communicative, emancipational, and recuperative. Marital functions refer to the provision of a setting in which the respective needs of the spouses are met and an appropriate constellation for development is established. Nurturant functions include not only feeding in the concrete sense, but also feeding in the abstract sense of making caring available and providing appropriate experiences for development and growth. Relational functions include those functions related to the development of interpersonal abilities within the intrafamilial setting which can later be used as a basis of relating to peers and others outside of the family. The family also provides communicative functions, educating family members in verbal and nonverbal skills congruent with the culture. Emancipative functions refer to those functions which equip the family member to attain physical, emotional, and economic independence and the desire and ability to begin his own family. The family also provides recuperative functions, providing a setting which allows the family member to rest, relax, and reconstitute his energies for continued participation in the larger society.[3] Depending on the family member involved, his role and contribution to the function of the family, and the degree to which his illness prevents his participation in roles and functions, each of these functions is likely in some way to become impaired as the family adapts to the impending death of a member.

Families have characteristic and in many cases established patterns of accomplishing these functions for their members. Each individual and each subsystem in the family assumes or is designated as having a set of responsibilities for certain functions. In most families, there is a coalition between the spouses which serves to provide necessary separateness of their relationship, and a unified front in child-rearing and decision-making in the family.[1, 3] There are established patterns of relating and transacting among family members and characteristic ways of meeting such needs as dependency. There are acceptable and unacceptable styles of expression of feelings. There is also a sense of family identity that includes a sense of what the family as a unit stands for as well as a sense of how the family is viewed by the society in which it lives. The family has characteristic ways of negotiating with the society in which it lives to fulfill needs viewed as necessary for preserving the intactness of the family unit. Under stress, for

example, some families will attempt to meet their own needs at any cost, allowing little assistance from outside, while others will seek considerable support externally.

A family has its own internal value system and a value system related to the societal surroundings. One family may have certain religious convictions and certain methods of meeting its meaning needs as a unit which are quite different from those of another family. The family also tends to have certain characteristic repertoires of coping with stress. In one family, emotions may be expressed openly, while in another they are suppressed. In some, one member will rush to support another, while in others stress becomes a divisive force which disperses family members in the direction of self-protection and individual survival. Any particular family also tends to have certain relatively constant levels of time and economic resources.

When a family member is dying, the time and costs involved in the care of the person, the depletion of available energy, and resulting changes in the emotional and relational atmosphere of the family affect the structure and function of the family in its adaptation to dying and death. Past experience or lack of experience managing illness, and the family's level of expectations of continued intrafamilial participation by the person who is ill affect the family's mode of adaptation. In turn, the ill individual's responses, his unacceptance or acceptance of the sick role, his strivings for dependence or independence, his expression of feeling, and his knowledge of his illness drive family adaptive maneuvers in varying directions. The awareness context (the degree to which the family openly acknowledges or does not acknowledge the facts and implications of the illness) plays a vital part in the manner in which the family adapts to an illness.[4] Importantly, the degree to which the family can delegate responsibilities for role needs or functions to peripheral family members, friends, caregivers, or societal support organizations has an important impact on the flexibility of rearranging a functional structure for the family to care for a dying member.

As structure and roles necessarily become rearranged by the dying and death of a family member, the functional abilities of the family are likely to be impaired. All of the functions of the family previously mentioned are affected and threatened to a greater or lesser degree. Instrumental roles and functions, the ability to survive, to acquire needed resources, and to support the family in the society in which it lives are often markedly disrupted. Expressive roles and functions, the feeling or affectual activities of the family and those related to self-actualization and self-awareness are also significantly affected. Coalitions must be loosened or tightened, relationships altered, tasks redefined and redelegated within the family and its subsystems. Any number of struggles and conflicts bring about new and intensified responses, needs, and concerns in relation to the dying and death of a family member.

DEPENDENCE AND INDEPENDENCE AND DISRUPTION OF ROLES AND FUNCTIONS

The increasing dependency brought about by the dying person's illness provides a highly significant stress in the family. In addition to the person's own struggle with this need, the family must also shift its attention toward meeting growing dependency needs of the person. This not only involves caring for the person in the physical sphere, but involves the diversion of large quantities of emotional support in the direction of the ill person. As a result, shifts and changes in emotional support for other family members occur. For example, a wife of a patient who spends long hours at her husband's hospital bedside is less able to meet the emotional needs of children when she returns home. At the same time, her own needs for emotional support are also intensified.

If the illness affects the member of the family who is responsible for the economic support of the family, an attempt to continue this support must be made by another family member or the support must in some way be provided by the societal system. Similarly if the illness affects a member of the family who is responsible for meeting the dependency needs of the family, this role and its associated tasks must be assumed by another member. In one such case, a husband was required to assume the care of the home and his three young children during his wife's prolonged illness.

This necessitated his losing considerable time at work and required that he learn a number of new housekeeping skills. At the same time he was required to provide care for the children. An inability or reluctance to delegate these responsibilities or allow friends to help, increased the magnitude of his emotional drain.

Quite often these changes result in what amounts to role reversal in the family setting, and this required rearrangement is not accomplished without considerable functional disruption and feeling response. A spouse, recognizing that he or she is no longer able to continue to provide economic and emotional support for the family, may make a conscious or unconscious decision to delegate this responsibility to the other spouse. At this point there is the possibility of rejection of the imposed role or resentment around the requirement of having to assume the role. At other times, the role is readily accepted only later to bring about conflict in the marital pair in response to the ill individual's resentment in having to give up the role and its related functions. When a spouse becomes ill and progressively debilitated, the interdependency and coalition maintained by the spouses in a marital pair becomes disrupted. Ultimately one or the other may by necessity be required to assume primary responsibility for presenting the common front to the children. This entails the assumption of increased and sometimes undesired responsibility.

The sometimes unconscious decision that a spouse is to "train" for independence in the anticipated absence of his or her mate can lead to a disruption of long-established patterns of relating. Competitive conflicts are often activated as the freedom, mobility, and control of the emerging independent spouse becomes a source of resentment for the ill person. The lowered self-esteem and anger of the person who must become dependent becomes subtly and sometimes blatantly involved in the relationship within the family. If the dying person is a young married adult and there are young children in the family, the other spouse may be left with tremendous increases in responsibility for the general welfare and operation of the family. Conflict in this area most often takes the form of lowered self-esteem for the person who must accept increased dependency. However, resentment and anger may be generated in those who must assume the independent role when they would prefer it to be otherwise.

The family functions of nurturing and relating are markedly affected by the shifts in dependency and independency. If the family member who is ill is a child, there is often a tremendous shift in relational and nurturing functions in the direction of the child. Here the balance of distribution of nurturing functions, emotional support, and relational continuity become significantly disturbed. Similarly, other functions such as emancipative ones may be affected, as when an adolescent who is at a stage when he or she must be able to move out into the social system is restricted by necessarily having to remain at home to care for the dying person. Recuperative functions are also affected, as the family system may be no longer able to engage in behaviors which serve to allow rest and relaxation, letting down defenses, engaging in recreation, or creative endeavors.

The isolated nuclear family is usually maintained in the direction of an independent indentity. The family as a whole has trained itself to act in a more independent fashion than the more traditional extended kindred family. Thus the family as a unit may resent its dependence on outside support and persons within the family may feel abandoned or resent their care being delegated in other directions. While the isolated nuclear family is in many ways more directly related with society in general, it is sometimes less connected with or rejects traditional societal support systems from which it might derive support. Many nuclear families continue to retain strong affiliations with their religious orientation, but others have become disengaged or dislocated from their beliefs and affiliations and no longer have this form of support. The general society may provide a large amount of support in the form of various agencies, but this support may be rejected or received with hesitancy. Public health nurses or others involved in care, for example, may find that they are initially welcomed caregivers but may encounter significant resentment as they begin to take over activities previously assumed by other family members.

DIVERSITY OF FAMILY MEMBERS AND ITS EFFECT ON CARE

The family is a group or a system in itself with its own identity, but it is important to bear in mind that each member of the family is an individual with unique needs, concerns, and responses. How each member of the family system faces the process of dying and the fact of death will play an important role in the overall adaptation of the family. The diversity of needs and responses is determined by the ages of the individuals, their individual personality configurations, the stages at which their personality development is consititued at the time of the stress, the level and quality of their relationship with the dying person, their ability to express their needs and concerns, and their roles in the overall function of the family setting. There are also diversities in the coalitions and subsystems within the family setting which require attention in understanding the reaction of the dying person's family. The diversity among the family members often results in the generation of considerable tension and disruption at critical junctures in the process of care, for individual family members react differently to change and stress. Some family members are tolerant of emotional expression while others are frightened by it, and some family members will legitimize strong feeling while others attempt to suppress it. Those family members who, because of age, are unable to appreciate the facts or implications of the illness encounter marked difficulty in understanding family changes. Some family members may become involved in the care process to the extent that their own psychological and social integrity become impaired, while others remain aloof and distant. The importance of these observations is that the heterogenicity of the responses and caring abilities of family members may cause considerable difficulty in the family's reaching a level of common purpose and shared collaboration in the care process. This was apparent in a family in which the level of the dying person's debilitation was perceived as being quite different by various family members. Varying levels of expectation for the continued participation of the dying person in family activities and functions were present. This led to considerable disagreement and conflict among the family members and a consensus could not be reached. In this disruption, various family members lost emotional support during an extremely trying period of time. Also, the dying person became more and more withdrawn as a means of avoiding conflict. In so doing, he also lost badly needed support.

THE FAMILY'S LEVEL OF AWARENESS AND NEED FOR COMMUNICATION WITH CAREGIVERS

The awareness level of the family may be defined as the degree of acknowledgment of the facts and implications of the illness and the acceptance of the ultimate loss of the dying member.* This awareness is dependent not only on the amount of communication between caregivers and the family members. Each family member tends to modulate his awareness of the gravity of the situation based on his personal needs, his place in the family setting, and his relationship with the dying family member. The individual awareness of all family members is never at the same level. In this context of varying levels of awareness, solidarity of purpose is difficult to achieve.

Like in the dying person himself, the family's level of awareness may fluctuate in a dynamic manner throughout the course of the person's illness. The subtleties of this modulation of awareness are related to the family's need to maintain its integrity, identity, and sense of continuity in the face of the presence of a dying person and death. Through these modulation of awareness, individual family members are sometimes enabled to continue with their own development and flexibly approximate the caregiving situation so as to assume the necessary roles and functions. The modulations in awareness are not, however, without drawback, for they may lead to significant interference with communication among family members. A family member who lacks an appropriate level of information about a family member's illness may continue to make unreasonable and inappropriate demands on the ill family member. On the other hand, overwhelming awareness and absorption in the process of the dying family member may be paralyzing in terms of the flexible assumption of new roles and functions in the care process and required reorganization of roles, structure, and function in the family. The difficulties in communication growing out of the varying levels of awareness may also serve to lessen the ability of a family member to derive support from another family member, a caregiver, or a person or agency outside of the family.

Whatever the level of awareness, families have an understandable and intense need to retain active lines of communication with health-care professionals. At times this need reaches urgent proportions. Paradoxically, the intensity and urgency with which information may be sought may tend to disrupt the relationship with physicians and other caregivers. Similarly, the need for clarity, structure, predictability, and certainty may also interfere with communication with caregivers. The intensity of the need for communication and the type of information requested may actually create distance between the family and the caregiver at times when approximation is most needed. Many of the issues which the family wishes clarified by caregivers are issues which simply cannot be clarified. Questions asked are often unanswerable with any level of certainty. Questions such as "How long will he or she live?" may push caregivers far beyond the limits of their capabilities in the situation. When pain, debilitation, and suffering become intense, some family members feel that not enough is being done. At other times, family members feel too much is being done to prolong life and become intensely concerned with quality of life considerations. These problems and their direct and indirect expression may lead to the caregiver's avoidance of family members. Feelings of frustration and anger are then engendered in the family members but because of their dependency on the caregivers and the fear that the relationship will be threatened, these feelings are seldom directly expressed. They smolder on and are

---

* Glaser and Strauss provide an informative discussion of the family's involvement in the awareness context surrounding patient care in Glaser BG, Strauss AL: *Awareness of Dying*. Aldine Publishing Company, Chicago, 1965.

expressed in an indirect manner or displaced to other circumstances and persons connected with care (hospital protocol, nurses, clergymen, aides, consulting physicians, social workers), the result being an increased and more complex breakdown in communication.

An additional problem is that often communications and questions are directed to the wrong caregiver, both on the basis of incorrect assumptions about the caregiver's area of competence, knowledge, or access to knowledge, and also on the basis of lack of accessibility and availability of other caregivers. The family will turn to the most accessible and available caregivers and often these persons do not have access to the information being sought. This lack of information is frequently the result of a lack of communication between the physician and other health-care professionals. Thus, nurses, clergy, and social workers as well as aides or students in training settings are often placed in the position of being asked about issues about which they have little information. The caregivers asked, may out of necessity be evasive or may even give incorrect information. When the family is unable to gain access to caregivers who might provide information they may feel a sense of isolation and separateness and become progressively bewildered, angry, and agitated.

The awareness level of the family and its members also plays an important role in communication with the caregivers. Varying degrees of denial and conscious pretending often give the caregiver the impression that the family will "hear what they want to hear." In this regard, a subject that has been previously discussed in detail may be addressed later as if it had not been discussed at all. Informational exchange thus occurs as a transactional phenomenon, with both caregivers and those cared for modulating the amount of information exchanged in the relationship.

The requests of the family regarding the conveyance of information to the dying person may also present a problem in communication. At times a family member will ask that information not be conveyed to the patient, thereby requesting the maintenance of a "secret" atmosphere. Often this protectiveness is an adaptive maneuver to protect the family member himself, and the dying person is already fully aware of the information about his illness. Rarely, this protectiveness grows out of a realistic appraisal by the family member that the ill person is unable to integrate and assimilate the level of available information at that particular time. An attempt should always be made to understand the determinants of the protectiveness, with the realization that total withholding of information from the patient is rarely indicated. It is the manner in which the information is communicated rather than the issue of telling or not telling that is of greatest importance[5]

PATTERNS OF EMOTIONAL EXPRESSION

The approximation of a family with the dying process and death of a member generates tremendous levels of emotion. Patterns of emotional expression within a family tend to continue in the same styles as prior to the person's illness; however, some feelings are intensified while others tend to be suppressed. Negative feelings or feelings considered as having negative overtones are generally softened or diverted away from the ill member or in other cases simply contained by the person experiencing them. This is particularly true of angry feelings and often is true of sadness and grief. When these feelings are expressed, even in very appropriate situations, they are often accompanied by excessive guilt and misgivings. Within the family setting there is a shifting of the expression of negative feelings and they are frequently displaced to a family member other than the one who is ill. An atmosphere characterized by irritability or general blandness may pervade the home setting.

The softening, dampening, and containment of strong emotions leads to an inability to respond in a flexible, open manner. The recuperative atmosphere of the home is markedly affected by the tensions of this emotionally strained situation. The feelings of security and warmth relating to a nurturing atmosphere are depleted for large amounts of energy are necessarily invested in the process of constantly modulating the expression of feeling, containing emotion or managing buried resentment and sadness.

Each family member becomes increasingly sensitive about the expression of feeling and watches carefully so as not to provide additional stress in what is already a stress-loaded situation. The ups and downs of the physical situation, uncertainty, frequent need to rapidly create rearrangements in time schedules, and the interference with open communication add to these difficulties. A pervasive sense of loss, sadness, and grief around the dying situation creates a distorted matrix of emotional interchange.

In the family setting, a conflict related to struggles and feelings of the patient frequently emerges in response to other family members who somehow symbolize the patient's conflict or concerns. High levels of feeling are generated in these situations. A patient who becomes acutely aware of temporal constriction may direct anger toward younger members of the family who are seen as having most of their lives before them. If the conflict concerns control and mastery, the patient may develop intense feelings related to the perceived control exerted in the care process by family members. A person who has suffered impairment in mental or physical functions from the disease process and physical deterioration may resent others who have not sustained these losses. A patient who feels trapped and confined by his home surroundings will have intense feelings about those whose motility remind him of his captivity. In one such example, a man who was paralyzed would become enraged each time his spouse left the home. Even when shopping or performing duties related to sustaining the family, her mobility was a reminder of his inability to be active as he had once been. A patient whose life plans are significantly altered by his illness may have high levels of feeling toward family members who are actively involved in constructing their life plans. These feelings further electrify the atmosphere in which care is provided, and the relational and communicative functions of the family may be seriously impaired.

Each family member, in being directly approximated with a dying person who forms an important part of his aliveness and identity, is led into a direct confrontation with his finiteness. Each family member must come to grips with the feelings related to the experience of massive loss and the potential loss of himself. In the modern society, when the dying person is treated away from the home setting in the hospital, the absence of the person becomes an important part of the family's experience. Home care can, however, be equally disruptive to the family setting. In any case, the family members' feelings may create a sensitivity to loss that increases their sense of personal vulnerability. One family member of a patient summed up those feelings by saying, "There is a feeling that the immortality balloon is definitely punctured and one has to deal with his own finiteness as well as that of the person who is dying."

ECONOMIC AND TIME DEPLETION

The dying and death of a family member brings to the everday life of the family any number of changes in life circumstances. Aside from the depletion of emotional reserve, reality circumstances in the family often result in considerable depletion of finances and time. Medical costs and costs of transportation, specialized home care, and specialized equipment frequently add to the family's financial burden. Treatment may require travel and long periods of residence away from home. Not only does this result in increased financial expense, but the family becomes dispersed and members isolated from their usual support systems. Separation from income sources such as the job of the patient or member of the family accompanying the patient occurs.

The patient may begin symbolic buying, random purchasing, or engage in costly activities to repair his sense of loss or leave behind gifts or momentos for the family. This further taxes the family's financial structure, but counter forces exerted to contain these activities are met with hostility and engender guilt in the person who tries to stop these activities. The result of these increased financial strains may be marked changes in the family's financial structure or even the depletion of life savings. Each member of the family is likely to experience these stains in varying ways and may feel resentment related to the necessity of foregoing his own needs. The resentment can lead to feelings of guilt and create more strain in the interaction.

Each family desires the best of diagnostic and treatment care for the person who is ill. This in itself may prove to be costly; however, doubting and desperation on the part of the patient or family members sometimes leads to consultation with numerous physicians or multiple trips to well-known centers for additional opinions. At times this may be warranted, but it may also represent a form of non-acceptance and denial on the part of the family or the patient, or may grow out of anger directed at the health-care facility or persons providing the original care. This phenomenon of "shopping around" may also take the person outside of recognized treatment channels in the search for "miracle cures." The dying person and his family desperately search for cure and this sometimes leads to massive expenditures of financial resources in inappropriate directions.

Time, a vital commodity for the family, is depleted. Long hours spent in home care, visits to outpatient facilities and hospitals have a significant impact on the usual time distribution patterns of the family. As the disease progresses, the time required for care and attention by the family increases and becomes less controllable or predictable. Often family members wish to remain by the bedside of the dying person during the final days and hours. In some cases, however, what are presumed to be the final days and hours extend into weeks and even months. Persons who have come from far away may leave and return many times. During this period of time, the emotional and physical resources of the individuals keeping watch may be totally exhausted and overwhelmed. With this overwhelming of resources, the ability to provide care is severely compromised.

Re-allocation of time may also cause emotional distress in other family members. When the dying person is a child, one or both parents may divert all attention toward the ill child and the needs of other children and family members go unmet. A spouse taking over the responsibilities of the other spouse must necessarily cut down on time spent with the family while at the same time gradually losing the support of the ill spouse. The depletion of time in the family setting sometimes generates feelings of ur-gency and chaos which may be a strong disruptive force to any semblance of effective family functioning.

CHILDREN IN A FAMILY WHEN A FAMILY MEMBER IS DYING

Regardless of the age of the child and other apsects of the child's relationship with the dying family member, the child is affected by the death of a family member, be it a sibling or a parent. Varying ages, stages of growth and development, patterns of closeness and relatedness, needs for dependency and nurturing, and changing needs for identification with one or the other parent enter significantly into the child's adaptation to the dying and death of a family member. Through the presence of a dying family member, the child is also brought into a confrontation with dying and death and will react at the level of his ability to understand and integrate the experience. He also responds to the loss of fulfillment of his own needs brought about by the loss.

Often, in an act of protectiveness, the child is left out of the awareness context, and there is pretense. Questions may be answered evasively or not at all. Yet, even with this pretense, the child continues to preceive the rearrangement of the family structure and functions and senses the transition and loss. Protectiveness, carried to extremes, may result in the child's having little ability to communicate his concerns, to have questions answered, or to establish the cognitive and emotional channels necessary for his own adaptation to the changes and losses. At the other end of the spectrum, the child may be inappropriately used as a confidante by siblngs or parents to manage their own feelings at a level far exceeding the child's emotional and cognitive capacity. Either extreme is likely to result in disruption of the child's well being and adaptation.

Children, too, have needs in the context of dying, but these are often overlooked by the most well-meaning of parents. The threat to nurturance, disrupted patterns of communication, changing patterns of expression of feeling, difficulties resulting from time and economic depletion, the necessity of assuming responsibilities extending beyond his abilities, the perception of loss, and the need to grieve are problems for the child as well as the adult. In response to these needs, behaviors and emotional responses of the child may require increased attention to assist with the process of adaptation. Difficulties with schoolwork, difficulties in peer relationships, excessive withdrawal, repeated angry outbursts, and involvement in repetitive, ritualistic, symbolic acts may reflect the stresses experienced by the child and require active intervention on the part of the parents or health-care professionals.

THE FAMILY'S NEED TO GRIEVE

The grief process of the family begins long before death. It may begin at the moment of recognition of the symptoms of illness or even at the moment of suspicion of a life-threatening illness. In other cases, the grief process begins at the moment of the acceptance of the implications of the illness and the recognition that the member will be progressively lost in the family setting and ultimately lost as a living person. The transition that occurs as the illness progresses and the losses experienced in reduced physical and emotional contact, diminished physical and emotional presence, and apparent changes in the member's physical intactness promote the sense of loss and grief. What has been termed anticipatory or preparatory mourning and grief in the patient is also seen in the family as a series of grief responses to each loss and the reminders of the ultimate loss to come.[5, 6] Thus the family legitimately grieves throughout the dying of the person, beginning the process of grief over the ultimate physical and emotional losses which will come at the time of death.

Various forces may deter this grief. Family members may feel that they must contain their feelings in the presence of the patient. They may also receive the subtle or open message from caregivers that they must maintain a facade of cheerfulness and well being. Some members of the family may forego their expression of grief as a maneuver to protect other members of the family, a phenomenon common in the relationship of a parent who "protects" a child. The psychological makeup of the person himself may also deter the expression of appropriate grief. At other times, circumstances resulting in actual physical separation and a lack of knowledge of happenings surrounding the dying process and death may make grieving difficult.

DYING AND DEATH IN THE ALREADY DISRUPTED FAMILY

When there are disrupted relationships in a family prior to the identification of a life-threatening illness in a family member, special problems may arise. "Already disrupted" families include families in which there is significant marital discord, those in which there are significant difficulties in family interaction already present, families in which there is a disturbed adult or child, and those where there is disruption related to separation or divorce. While it might be assumed that the threat of the death of a family member would tend to override strained relationships, often the opposite is true, for still another stress is introduced. Marital discord may be accentuated to the point that separation or divorce is considered. If the illness affects one or the other spouse, difficulties in emotional expression, role reversals, changes in patterns of dependency and independency, or matters such as the denial of the severity of the illness may disrupt relationships which are already fragile.

Should the disruption reach the point where divorce is considered, the relationship may continue only on the basis that the person is ill. Feelings generated in such situations are difficult to manage. Should the couple actually proceed with separation or divorce, ambivalence, anger, guilt, and societal pressures may complicate the separation or divorce. Difficult questions arise related to whether or not one should leave an increasingly dependent ill individual or separate from an ill person who is afraid of being isolated and abandoned. If the dying person is a child, there are increased demands on the relationship of the mother and father. These include increased time and emotional demands and may cause a shift in meeting dependency needs which upsets a delicate balance and introduces additional stresses in an already strained marital relationship.

If divorce has occurred a short time before the onset of the illness and the feelings and problems in interaction related to the divorce remain unresolved, there may be an expectation that the divorced healthy spouse participate in the caring process. The dying person, in his need to resolve past conflicts, may feel that restoration of the marital relationship is a necessary part of his conflict resolution. An ill person may also turn to that person with whom there is still some remnant of a relationship to attempt to meet the intense needs for interpersonal closeness. If the relationship is resumed at some level, it may still be fraught with the same problems and mixed feelings which led to the separation or divorce. The anger present in the separation or divorce may even increase in the re-established relationship, and issues related to the illness itself used as a means of exerting control or expressing anger. In some cases the healthy ex-spouse may be kept at a distance when he or she desires to be helpful and comforting. This results in increased guilt on the part of the healthy ex-spouse as well as denying him or her the type of access to the dying person which would allow the process of grief to proceed. Disallowing the grief of the healthy ex-spouse may be the dying person's means of expressing intense anger toward the person. It may also be a means of settling a lingering issue of control in favor of the dying person. The phenomenon was illustrated in the case of a woman whose ex-husband very much desired to participate in her care during the terminal stages of her dying. She refused to allow him to visit her and excluded him from participation in the interpersonal setting surrounding her dying. When this was dealt with as residual of the divorce, related to anger and control, she then allowed him to visit and deal with his own grief.

Children who have been involved in the separation or divorce may become involved in the struggles between the spouses which occur around the dying process. The dying parent may insist on access to the children when legal settlements have been made otherwise. Old issues related to struggles over control of children may be accentuated by the desire of the dying person to have contact with the children. Children, having feelings of their own, may be torn in their need to please one or the other parent in terms of their allegiances. Established patterns of re-latedness to one or the other parent may be forced to change in the context of the dying and death situation, thereby creating increased problems for the children in their adaptation.

FRIENDS AND RELATIVES

Those persons who are more peripherally involved in the dying and death process of a family must also be considered in the overall care of the dying person. Depending on the intensity and characteristics of the relationship with the dying person and the needs of the relative or friend himself, these persons may also be intimately involved in care. Their involvement, like that of others, has the potential to run the gamut from being constructive to destructive in the overall care process.

Persons with little understanding of the dying person's unique needs may impose their own needs on the dying person in an intrusive, nonsupportive way. Friends and relatives may possess a level of curiosity which is intrusive in terms of the intimacy of the situation. At the same time, they may have difficulty in knowing the level at which the person wishes to share his or her feelings and ideas related to the illness. In these situations, the relationship may become disrupted, uncomfortable, and strained, thereby rendering it less than supportive. In some cases, friends and relatives are not allowed access to information about the illness and must be content to relate to the person in an awareness context which differs significantly from that of others in supportive caring positions. This, coupled with the need to comfort and to provide acts of caring, frequently makes the relationship difficult and frustrating.

Close friends who themselves are brought into a confrontation with their finiteness may become overwhelmed with feelings, particularly when the person is in their age group and has similar interests and life patterns. These similarities allow a higher level of identification with the dying person and a more blatant confrontation with personal feelings about death. In his relationships with healthy friends and relatives, similarities and a high level of identification may, from the point of view of the dying person, result in an increased awareness of those aspects of living which he is losing. This may stir feelings of envy and resentment in the dying person and become a disruptive factor in the friendship. As the disease progresses and the dying and death of the person become more of a reality, visits of relatives and friends may significantly dwindle away. This is particularly true in the lingering phase when there is uncertainty as to the timing of the death of the person and the emotion surrounding the anticipated death of the person is at a high level. These phenomena may result in interpersonal distancing of varying degrees and be preceived by the dying person as further validation of his fears of abandonment and isolation.

Personality traits, patterns of expression of feeling, and the levels of friends' own comfort with dying and death are important aspects of the caring activity which may occur. Personal needs may cause the friend to reinforce the denial of the patient. Comfort may take the form of "cheer up" attitudes when indeed the need for legitimization of feeling is a more salient need. Inappropriate reassurance may replace listening to the person's feelings and suppress the expression of feelings and ideas which the dying person wishes to share. A friend may suppress his grief in the presence of the patient and the family, creating even more dysphoric feelings for himself.

Friends and relatives may, by virtue of varying needs of the dying person, be brought even closer into the circle of the family relationships and are often caught in the middle in emotionally loaded interactions. Disapproval by the friend of the family's management of some interaction or circumstances may result in interference with the friend's relationship with the dying person. Family members may subsequently attempt to move the friend further to the periphery and out of a caring position. Often a friend becomes the person with whom the most intimate aspects of the dying person's needs, concerns, and responses are shared and this person may have information that closer persons do not have. Intimate feelings about a family member may be shared with a friend instead of being expressed directly to the person. This may be helpful, but it also has the potential to place the friend in an adversary position, particularly if the shared feelings are negative ones.

Friends and relatives often have an intense need, as do health-care professionals, to do something which is tangible. At times this may take the form of lavish and inappropriate gifts. At other times it may take the form of taking over the responsibilities of family chores and emotional support at a level which becomes excessively draining for the friend or offensive to the family. Other friends may help in very constructive and supportive ways by simply offering their support when it is desired, recognizing when absence as well as presence provides a form of caring for their dying friend.

At times, the dying person and his family are placed in the role of supporting friends rather than receiving support. This may occur to protect the relationship and enable the friend to remain in a position of continuing to provide some aspect of care. Paradoxically, however, this may cause considerable drain on the patient or family members.

The support provided by relatives or friends becomes an important aspect of the overall care process, particularly in the case of the isolated nuclear family. Thus the interactions of relatives and friends with the family must be viewed as a part of the interactions of care.

DISSOLUTION OF FAMILY IDENTITY AND THREAT OF DEATH AND DISINTEGRATION OF THE FAMILY

The presence of a dying person in the family setting and the changes involved in the adaptation to the dying and death of a member provide a most serious threat to family identity and the sense of a living family unit. The pervasive sense of loss during the course of the illness and the recognition of the ultimate loss of the family member causes a sense of transition and change which is equivalent to the sense of death of the family itself. Thus, in addition to coming to grips with the recognition of the loss and finiteness of the person himself, the family must also ultimately come to grips with the death of the family unit as it has existed in the past. Changing patterns of family relationships and changes in the family itself have, prior to the presence of a dying person in the family, also provided a sense of change and transition, but there has been a sense of survival and continuity of the intact family into the future. Now this view must be changed and the family must rearrange its structure, re-delegating many of the functions which will equip it to survive in the social system and continuing to provide for the growth of the family members.

After the death of the person, the work or rearrangement of structure, and changing patterns of function must continue while the grief process proceeds. This, too, will be accompanied by a sense of loss and the presence of the family member who has died will continue to be a vital force in the psychosocial and meaning activities of the survivors. Those patterns of interaction established through the family's adaptation to the dying and death of a family member, as well as the many structural and functional changes which have accompanied the process, must now be integrated into the overall function of the family as it works toward survival. The destructive forces such as divisiveness and conflict which arose in the family's ad-

aptation, as well as the intensification of relationships and the constructive rearrangements of family responsibilities, become part of a new family identity which will emerge after the person's death. Those activities which become a response to both the death of the person and the death of the family structure as it existed must be integrated into the new family constellation and provide a sense of continuing meaning and aliveness for the family unit.

REFERENCES

1. Lidz T: *The Person: His Development Throughout the Life Cycle.* Basic Books, New York, 1968
2. Parsons T, Bales RF: *Family, Socialization and Interaction Process.* The Free Press, Glencoe, Illinois, 1955
3. Fleck S: "The Family and Psychiatry," In *The Comprehensive Textbook of Psychiatry.* 2nd Ed, Vol. I, Freedman AM, Kaplan HI, Sadock BJ (Eds) The Williams & Wilkins Co, Baltimore, 1975
4. Glaser BG, Strauss AL: *Awareness of Dying.* Aldine Publishing Company, Chicago, 1965
5. Kübler-Ross E: *On Death and Dying.* The Macmillan Company, London, 1969
6. Lindemann E: Symptomatology and Management of Acute Grief. *Amer J Psychiat 101:*141–148, 1944

6

THE CAREGIVER
David Barton, M.D.

Those who work intensively with dying persons and their families must, early in their work, recognize and begin to come to grips with the tremendous torrent of feelings stirred in them by this work. If they fail to do so, they experience a growing awareness of intense discomfort which can lead to abandonment of the work and those persons for whom care is being provided. The tendency in the past toward abandoning the area has in large part likely grown out of a failure on the part of caregivers to deal with these feelings in any way other than avoidance.

The feelings have at their base a blatant confrontation on the part of the caregiver with his own mortality. This central feeling theme is also accompanied by a profound sense of loss of control and helplessness which is stirred in the caregiver. The feelings arise from the awareness of a life, not unlike one's own, slipping away in spite of all caring efforts to the contrary. They are the feelings of standing by helpless to intervene in a process that will ultimately reduce a relationship with the person cared for to nothing, and the recognition of the ultimate possible reduction of the self to nothing. The resonance of this shared sense of humanness which occurs in this intense caring relationship grows out of the recognition of death as a basic part of living in both the dying person and the caregiver.

Involved in this caring is the process of disengagement and "letting go," a painful process which varies with the amount of involvement in the relationship. This disengagement is potentially accompanied by the experience of a loss of part of the self and often gives rise to feelings of being professionally ineffective and incompetent. This experience can jar the caregiver's own sense of fulfillment and useful participation in the caregiving process.

The feelings experienced by those caring for the dying person encompass virtually the entire range of human emotions. These feelings are not only varied, but are frequently disquieting and disruptive to the care process. At a conference during which a group of caregivers working with dying persons and their families delineated the numerous feelings evoked in those caring for the dying individual, the following feelings* were among those expressed:

Confusion, grief, helplessness, fear, anger, draining, loneliness, inadequacy, ambivalence, nameless feelings, intimacy, love, pity, needing appreciation, guilt, increased commitment, entrapment, needing release, superiority, lacking knowledge, intrusiveness, threatening, disintegration, wanting the person to live, wanting the person to die, protectiveness, abandonment, avoidance, alienation, lacking authenticity, intolerance, distance, vulnerability.

The wide variety of feelings listed here are likely experienced in many caregiving settings but the feelings experienced in the context of the death situation appear to pos-

---

* A similar list, derived from the conference, The International Convocation of Leaders in the Field of Death and Dying, held in Columbia, Maryland, November 1974, has been reported by J. Lynch in the *ARS Moriendi Newsletter* (see Ref. 1).

sess a special type of intensity. They may or may not be present in every caregiver at any given time and they vary quantitatively in different circumstances and with varying levels of involvement. The fact that they are potentially present should be recognized, for they are at least disquieting and in some cases they are potentially overwhelming. Even at the level of being disquieting they are capable of leading to levels of discomfort in the caregiver which bring about defensive maneuvers. These may include actual physical removal or the defensive position of isolating the emotions associated with the caregiving situation with intellectualized concepts. When the feelings approach a level which is threatening to the person the mechanism of denial may come into play and those areas of care which evoke the most intense feelings may be selectively ignored. In many cases these maneuvers become nontherapeutic and interfere with the caregiving process.

Any feeling evoked in a caregiver in a health-care situation relates to the personality configuration of that person, his own experiences, his perceived role in the care process, the theoretical posture of his approach, the interactional circumstances in which care is provided, and the usual means by which that person is accustomed to managing feelings. The feelings are also affected by interaction with the dying person himself and the manner in which he encourages or discourages the development of a relationship and the expression of feeling. All of these feelings and responses emerge in a dynamic ever-changing process throughout the course of the caregiving process. In the case of the dying person, these responses and interactions are couched in the intensity of the ever-present threat and anticipation of the death of a human being not unlike the caregiver.

Understanding one's personal responses to a patient and the responses of others caring for a person is a vital part of any health-care process. Because of the intensity of the emotions and the potential for them to disrupt care, understanding and management of these feelings are even more important in the area of caring for the dying person. This self-understanding places the caregiver in contact with his own feeling state and allows him to achieve greater under-

standing of the patient's emotional state. It allows him to remain approximated with the person in such a way as to recognize needs. Without this self-understanding the caregiver is likely to misperceive the patient's responses and needs and respond to the person in a mechanistic, ritualized manner, thereby reflecting only distance and technical interest to the patient. It is, however, important to mention that sometimes this distancing and technical involvement may become appropriate, for the feelings evoked in caregivers have the potential to reach overwhelming proportions which in the extreme can compromise care. At that point, the emotional integrity of the caregiver is disrupted, rendering him unable to provide the type of care required by the situation. While sensitivity to the situation must be maintained, involvement to the point that the caregiver's own integration is threatened is contraindicated. The caregiver must attain a delicate balance in achieveing a position which allows self-understanding, sensitivity, and flexibility in utilizing his skills and knowledge.

All of the feelings named in the preceding list represent important dimensions of care. All are signs of involvement and the subjective appreciation and exploration of their presence is a critical part of the care process. Some of these feelings are consistently present and deserve closer scrutiny.

IMPACT OF RECOGNITION OF PERSONAL FINITENESS

Approximation with a dying person and the entrance into a relationship with that person and those related to him is accompanied by an intensification of the caregiver's recognition of his own mortality, his own potential for the loss of self. Thus, not only is his professionalism threatened, but his presence, endurance, and continuity of the self is also threatened. The more closely the caregiver becomes involved as another human being, the more intense is the confrontation with his own mortality and his sense of personal vulnerability. There is in essence a more intense shared sense of being human and in being human, being finite. At the deepest levels of investment in the dying person and the care situation, the person is aware of a sense of fleetingness, transience, futility, estrangement, and loneliness, and an intense and often extreme sensitivity to loss. The latter may be perceived not only in the context of the relationship with the dying person, but may generalize to any area of the person's life which has a quality of loss and transience. This often gives rise to a pervading sense of despair and an urgent need for some meaningful professional activity; the validation of aliveness is sought through tangible acts of professional "doing." There may also be a drive toward an intensification of interpersonal relationships. This urgent need for interpersonal support is a maneuver for a sense of aliveness in order to overcome a sense of emptiness and despair. In his confrontation with death awareness, the caregiver may even come to perceive much of life and his usual pursuits as being mundane and of little value. There may be a turning away from living matters, a romaticizing of death, and intense investment in the abstract and philosophical aspects of dying and death, or an absorption in the intellectual aspects of the area, representing an attempt to give rational explanation to the affective component of the experience.

The importance of these feelings cannot be overemphasized. Quite often in the early involvement in this area, the zeal and desire to help are able to overcome the feelings, but the caregiver who remains approximated with the area comes to experience these emotions in their most blatant forms. They are the very basis of the intense involvement in the care area itself and drive a personal desire to come to grips with one's own finiteness. At the other extreme, the feelings may become the basis of an avoidance of the area growing out of the person's desire to hold the recognition of his being finite at a distance. In this case, the caregiver may experience what has been referred to by one student as the "I want to get the hell out of there" feeling. It is the feeling of having been touched by death — the feeling related to the enlargement of that part of the self that potentially is also dying.

Perhaps the most troublesome feelings experienced by caregivers who work in this area are those feelings designated as being "nameless." These are feelings which are closely related to the subjective experience of the personal confrontation with death. These feelings are indeed often nameless as there is a lack of words or symbolic designations in language for feelings of this magnitude and quality.* They are the feelings which are experienced as a sense of fleetingness, transience, futility, estrangement, and the loss of the sense of futurity. They may be experienced as feelings of fragmentation, feeling disintegrated, coming apart, or not being whole. The feelings are vast and are closely related to words in our vocabulary such as cosmic, oceanic, uncanny, and "heavy." They are the feelings which at bottom are connected with the resonance with the part of the self and the part of the person being cared for which is potentially absent and nothing. The multitude of emotions surrounding these very basic feelings often assume immense proportions. Collectively these feelings are related to that part of the person that knowns his death will become a reality. The basic constellation of feeling grows out of what has been referred to as *death awareness*.

Death awareness characteristically gives rise to activity and this activity can reach a frenzied state. The activity is looked to as a source of meaning a personal significance to generate and structure a sense of aliveness for the caregiver. The activity may be channeled into caring, to promote a sense of meaning and aliveness in the one being cared for, and thus becomes a source of meaning for the caregiver as well. But its random nature, particularly when unrecognized as a response to death awareness, may lead the caregiver away from its source and out of a caring position, leaving the dying person in a state of meaningless despair. Thus the management of this death awareness becomes a central issue in the care of the dying person, as the concern for the dying person is also the concern for ourselves as caregivers.

---

* One can relate these consideration to Lifton's concept of "psychic numbing," the process whereby there is interference with the ability of the mental apparatus to elaborate meaningful images and symbols related to life and the continuity of life. More specifically the person is unable to develop imagery related to connection, movement, and integration (see also Chapter 2).

CAREGIVER'S CONCEPTUAL AND SYMBOLIC DESIGNATIONS OF DYING AND DEATH

Like the patient and members of the family, each caregiver brings his own beliefs, concepts, and symbolic designations related to dying and death to the care process. Influenced by the caregiver's age, his psychological development, his experience with dying and death, his belief and value system, his religious concepts, and his professional identity, these concepts and symbolic designations are brought to the care setting and become significantly involved in the caregiver's transactions with those for whom he is providing care.

The caregiver's concepts are heavily influenced by his professional identity and the means through which his education, knowledge, and skills equip him to think, feel, and respond in the context of dying and death. Nurses, physicians, clergy, social workers, and others caring for the dying person have varying knowledge and skill sets which allow them to place the process of dying and death in certain conceptual frameworks related to their disciplines, and to provide care accordingly. These designations are blended with personal beliefs and attitudes and form the basis of a large part of the person's approach to care. Individual caregivers also have their individual designations of the dying process and the events surrounding death. These designations, often symbolic, are changing, complex, and multifaceted, and endow varying stages of the dying process and the occurrence of death with varying symbolic attributes. Conceptual frameworks and symbolic designations of dying and death form important bases of many of the caregiver's interactional responses in the care setting.

The differences in concepts and the varying forms of imagery brought to the care setting become strinkingly obvious in a classroom experience related to learning more about one's personal imagery of dying and death. Using a method suggested by Robert Neale to explore feelings, attitudes, and designations about dying and death, students from a number of disciplines learning about the area drew their images of death on large blank sheets of paper[2] These drawings were used as a basis of understanding individual designations of dying and death which may enter into the interactional process of care, and reflected a wide variety of such personal symbolic designations. The exercise produced drawings such as an atomic bomb blast at Hiroshima destroying buildings and people; a body with its parts disconnected; lightning striking an amorphous form surrounded by the words "zap" and "pow"; chaotic scrawlings; a ship on a peaceful sea sailing into a swirling sky engulfing a person's body; a person isolated in a cage-like room; two hands unable to touch; an electrocardiogram beginning with a normal representation of a heart beat, fading into a dysfunctional arrythmia and then becoming a flat line; a picture of heaven with numerous crosses placed about the picture; a delicate, fragile, disconnected array of net-like webs scattered about the paper; a stick-like figure standing in front of a cave, the entrance to the cave darkened and filled with question marks; a wilting flower; and many other symbolic representations of the caregivers' views of dying and death. One student left the paper blank, saying that there were no appropriate images that he might draw to represent his feelings. The caregiving individual brings his feelings, these complicated representations of his images of death, and his concepts related to dying and death to the caregiving process. Personal understanding of this imagery and the individual's personal concepts can be helpful in understanding the person's interaction with the dying patient and his family.

THREAT TO MASTERY AND CONTROL

Authors writing in this area frequently refer to the health-care professional's struggle with death. Physicians and other health-care professionals are viewed as doing combat with an essentially personified "Death," and the conclusion is reached that the goal of the health-providing professions is to prolong life at any cost. The death of a patient, according to some authors, may threaten the personal and professional goals of the physician and the belief that every patient should get well.[3–5] Death in this sense is seen as a failure and a contradiction of professional purpose. The observed striving of professionals toward bringing about cure raises the possibility that some health-care professionals themselves have entered the profession because of an above average fear of their own deaths.[3, 4] A choice of profession based on such a fear would be perhaps termed counterphobic — an attempt to overcome or master a fear through confronting the situation and experiencing oneself as having mastery through curing all illness rather than seeing any illness lead to death. While it may be that some physicians have a greater than average fear of death and that their work is designed to overcome this fear, there are likely other matters involved.

Many persons entering medical and related professions are persons who are heavily invested in achieving a sense of mastery, order, and control over the happenings in their lives. The majority of medical students, for example, have been shown to have obsessive-compulsive personality organizations and manifest traits such as concern with detail and perfectionistic strivings.[6] Predictability, order, and organization are sought after as means of gaining control and avoiding anxiety. The process of education in medicine is exacting and leans toward an ethic of knowing all and achieving percision and perfection. Mistakes are poorly tolerated and any sense of omnipotence that was present in the individual's personality configuration which led him toward the health-care professions is reinforced by the expectations of both the profession and society. The need for training for uncertainty in medical education in order that students may recognize that many medical situations are indeed uncertain and unpredictable has been noted.[6, 7] Even so, health-care professionals are often led to believe through their studies and the subtle and blatant reflected attitudes of their instructors that the practice of medicine is an orderly, certain, and precise process. The ethic of medical education promotes a feeling that there is always an answer if only the correct source can be found. The dream of a medical student a few weeks into his first year of medical school illustrates that indeed if not consciously, unconsciously this is believed to be the case.

There was a wreck and someone was seriously hurt. I though I could save the person but then I was only a first-year student. A second-year stu-dent came by and couldn't help either. Then a fourth-year student tried to help. He couldn't save the person and he died. I was sure by then he would know how to save him and felt depressed when I learned that he couldn't.

It is only after extensive clinical experience that the student recognizes that numerous situations arise in which there is ultimately little or nothing that can be done to stop physical deterioration and death. Even when this point is reached, the individual is still likely to engage in considerable painful self-doubting, self-questioning, guilty self-incrimination, and agonizing over what might have been done differently. This process is, however, not without its positive aspects, for the individual's expectations of himself are held at a high level and there is little room allowed for error. Nevertheless, those situations which are reminders of the loss of control and the inability to achieve mastery are likely to be avoided unless the person comes to appreciate what he may reasonably expect of himself.

Thus while there are undoubtedly tremendous personality variations among persons entering the health-care professions, the desire for control and mastery is a commonly seen characteristic. But nowhere in medicine is this need for control more threatened than in the context of caring for dying persons and their families. Each situation which involves a dying person represents a care situation where ultimately order will become disrupted and certainty will dissolve. While this is most apparent in the physical dimension, the multitude of responses and feelings involved in the dying and death of another human being are likely to have unpredictable, intense, spontaneous, chaotic, incomprehensible, and even disorderly qualities. The caregiver not only is forced to view his control over the physical condition reduced, but also must confront the chaotic feelings associated with helplessness, anger, loneliness, and other feelings experienced by the patient, himself, the family, and other caregivers. The interactional dimensions of the feelings, the results of the interchanges among those involved, become even more incomprehensible and chaotic. The sense of loss of control potentially leads to intense anxiety in the caregiver and evokes an intense need to bring some sense of order to the situation. The intensity generated by the death situation and the encounter with the dying person may intensify the sense of loss of control, total comprehension, and mastery.

Varying maneuvers designed to bring some sense of order to the care situation may be employed. The first line of defense is actual physical distancing. Another is emotional distancing. Another form of distancing may occur in the individual's attempt to apply a specific inflexible conceptual framework to the situation. Others attempt to bring order to the chaos through intellectualizing or the use of discipline-related ritual, for in caring for the dying person each caregiver's discipline may provide some framework or set of rituals to which they may retreat for some sense of order. The physician may take refuge in his cognitive understanding of the disease process and his technical skills, and in so doing he may come to view the person purely in terms of the physical dimension. The nurse may use a busy, routinized administrative schedule to avoid encounters with the patient and thus provide a sense of order. The clergyman may relate to the person and his family only in theological terms, using religious ritual to provide a sense of mastery.

Importantly, it should be emphasized that such discipline-related care operations are not in themselves to be judged as being negative in terms of care, for they are often indicated and vital. At times they are not only necessary, but they may actually be adaptive and protective of the caregiver's role and integrity as a provider of care. It is only when they are used inappropriately from a position of reduced sensitivity to the true and varied needs of the patient that they affect care adversely. Furthermore, a total retreat into the framework or set of any one discipline may lead to a form of control and insensitivity which disallows the participation of other caregivers who may contribute significantly to the caregiving process. Control in this case is achieved and defensively maintained through viewing any approach or attitudes other than one's own as being unacceptable. Some gain control through attempting to control other persons with whom they are relating. The interventions of other caregivers are viewed as increasing chaos and undermining control,

and thus others are excluded from the care process.

The need to maintain control may lead to postures in care which can be described as intolerance. In this case, the caregiver maintains a rigid position and feels that the dying person should adapt as the caregiver would have him adapt. A rigid intolerance toward the approaches of other caregivers may also become problematic and lead to conflict and intense feeling states. As the feelings surrounding the death situation and the adaptive maneuvers used by each individual are unique and dynamically changing, the mode of adaptation of the person or family members may come in conflict with the caregiver's perception of the desired means of coping. For example, religious views of the patient and the caregiver may be entirely different and this sharp divergence may lead to conflict. Patients may not react in a manner which fits the cognitive conceptual framework held by the caregiver and may not proceed through orderly sequences in adapting to their impending death as he would have them do.

At the other end of the spectrum is a posture that also has the potential to render the caregiver ineffective. In this position, the caregiver begins to value and even seek out a sense of chaos and disorder. Feeling responses and the experiential dimensions are always emphasized without any attention to the practical matters involved in the care of the person; *i.e.,* the caregiver develops an extreme sensitivity to the feeling dimension and ignores the skill and knowledge related to his or her discipline. This maneuver leads to disenchantment with one's discipline and an abandonment of attempts at any form of control, providing still another form of distraction from the realities of a grim, uncontrollable circumstance. The caregiver becomes sensitive not only to issues related to the patient, but feels emotionally drained and intensely sensitive to loss in any other area of his life. He becomes increasingly gloomy and feels a sense of utter futility and despair. At times he may experience brief periods of inability to pull his thoughts together, and a sense of fear of fragmentation arises. Concern with professional purpose may become excessive and one's professional identity, commitment, and efforts seem meaningless and ineffective. There is an all-pervasive sense of death awareness which colors not only his work with dying persons but other aspects of his life as well. This posture represents an extreme of a normally experienced feeling in the care of the dying person and his family, and the perception of these feelings should serve to remind him of the need to calibrate his level of involvement.

POLARIZATION AND DICHOTOMY OF COGNITIVE-TECHNICAL AND EMOTIONAL EXPERIENTIAL

The intensity of the feelings generated by the death situation has the potential to move caregiving persons in the direction of firmly entrenched polarized positions.[1, 8] Often the position assumed are either cognitive-technical or emotional-experiential. In the cognitive-technical mode, individuals engage in a constant search for intellectual structure or the utilization of technical skills to assist in their management of the situation. There is a constant attempt to understand or to perform in tangible, objective ways. At the other end of the spectrum, the caregiver involves himself in the emotional-experiential happenings of the moment. In truth, the caregiver needs the flexibility to engage in both modes of functioning and to use that mode which is most appropriate for the discerned need at any particular time. It would, for example, be inappropriate for a surgeon to be so intimately involved in the feeling dimension as to be unable to utilize his technical skills. On the other hand, to insist that an individual follow an orderly progression through his adaptation to dying or to impose a series of theorectical stages on someone grieving the loss of a significant person may discourage the expression and management of important emotional responses. While flexibility is important, the attitudinal mode adopted by individual caregivers will depend largely on their own personality style and may be closely related to their caregiving specialty. The caregiver must always bear in mind that at differing times in the overall care process one or the other or a blend of both may not only be appropriate but vitally necessary. Also, while one caregiver provides care in the cognitive-technical mode, care in the emotional-experiential mode may also be required. The need in any specific part of the

care process is dictated by the situation. If this tendency toward polarization can be recognized and understood as a usual and expected part of caregivers' responses to working with the dying person, then the conflicts resulting from this polarization may be avoided. Rather than focusing on the conflict resulting from the polarization, a useful and constructive approach which blends various attitudes can be developed.

CAREGIVER'S REACTIONS TO FEELINGS AND CONFLICT

In caring for the dying person and his family, a particular caregiver may find his own emotional experiences and reactions to conflict personally painful or unacceptable. These feelings and responses may be personally unacceptable because of the individual's personality structure, his feeling related to certain kinds of interpersonal needs and conflicts, or his value system. They may also be unacceptable because they lack legitimization in the individual's particular health-care discipline or the care setting. While these feelings are intensified by other feelings evoked by working specifically in the context of dying and death, the reactions may be experienced in other areas of care as well. In causing unrest in the caregiver, they significantly affect the total care process.

A patient's expressions of a strong emotion such as anger may threaten a caregiver who has difficulty in expressing and experiencing intense feelings or is frightened by his own anger. In providing care, he may suppress the anger of the patient and family members when these feelings are appropriate and even part of the person's adaptation. Similarly, expressions of sadness and grief are also often discouraged by caregivers. This is particularly true in the caregiver who is unable to face and effectively deal with losses within his own life. The loss experienced by another becomes a reminder of personal losses and renews the numerous painful feelings connected with that loss. While no person can be totally accepting of another person's entire range of feeling, the recognition of non-acceptance is an important aspect of care.

Varying feelings and responses stemming from relationships may also cause difficulty. The intense interpersonal needs of the dying patient may create significant anxiety in a caregiver who himself has the need to maintain interpersonal distance in his relationships. A verbal, gregarious, outgoing caregiver may find his attitudes incongruent with the needs of the patient when a patient wishes to withdraw into himself and be alone. An individual who constantly seeks approval may be severely threatened by any evidence of dissaproval by the patient, his family, or other caregivers. Refusal of certain forms of treatment may engender unacceptable feelings of anger toward the patient and his family or be perceived as a painful form of rejection. Demands placed on the caregiver by the patient and his family may severely tax a caregiver who is unable to set limits around dependency needs. Rejection of the dependent role by the patient may be seen by the caregiver as a rejection of care and a personal rejection of the individual providing that care. The behaviors of a patient or family member who is insistent on maintaining control may create uneasy feelings in a caregiver who feels that he must always maintain control.

Many of the feelings, responses, and adaptive struggles involved in a person's adaptation to dying are only intense variations of basic conflicts which occur in any life crisis. Thus, the caregiver is likely to experience a strong personal sense of identification with various aspects of the dying person's adaptation. The caregiver may unknowingly project himself into the patient's situation and feel intense discomfort related to the adaptive struggles of the person. The level of personal involvement may blur the distinction between the feelings and responses of the patient and those of the caregiver. This phenomenon is particularly likely to occur in those areas in which the caregiver himself experiences some sense of personal conflict or vulnerability. Thus struggles with dependency, the expression of strong feelings, mastery and control, or identity may threaten the caregiver who personally has difficulty managing these areas and unconsciously identifies with the patient's struggles.

Feeling trapped in a painful relationship and desiring release and distance may run counter to the person's concept of the manner in which he conceptulizes medical care. Fantasies and thoughts about wanting the person's death to occur may be particularly upsetting, for this feeling tends to contradict much of that for which the health-care profession stands. The caregiver is confronted with the myriad of feelings emanating from the perceived human suffering and knows that the patient has reached a stage of irretrievable anguish beyond the application of medical knowledge, but still experiences this feeling as an alien or unacceptable one. Even though the dying person or the family may openly express this feeling, for many in the health-care professions, the acceptance of such a feeling approaches being impossible.

Feelings related to personal vulnerability, helplessness, or the need for emotional support are infrequently expressed openly in caregiving settings. Very often such feelings are viewed as being "nonprofessional" or arising because one is simply "overly involved." One might expect to experience helplessness, fear, anger, sadness, grief, and emotional drain as normal responses in this care area. These responses are intensified in the context of the death situation. These feelings are not often legitimized in caregiving settings and the acceptance of their appropriateness and expression is not a part of the usual open interpersonal interchange among caregivers. Because of this the individual is likely to contain these feelings and experience them as a kind of weakness kept out of awareness. When there is no setting in which the feelings may be dealt with in an open manner, they become even more unacceptable.

NEED FOR SELF-AWARENESS

Self-awareness and the ongoing management of personal feelings on the part of the caregiver are vital aspects of caring for the dying person and his family. Not only must the caregiver understand and manage feelings related to his confrontation with his own finiteness and inability to maintain control and a sense of mastery, but he must also appreciate how other feelings and responses enter into the process of care. To accomplish this he must develop an ability to accept his feelings as his own and to understand the source of these feelings, whether they are internal ones or they develop in response to the feelings and responses of others. He must also understand the basis for the non-acceptability of certain categories of feelings. Without this self-awareness, the caregiver is likely to respond in ways which severely compromise care.

In varying psychotherapy and counseling processes, it is an established principle that self-awareness and self-understanding are necessary parts of the care process itself. Self-understanding implies that the individual recognizes the broad spectrum of feelings and responses experienced in working with the person and the interactions from which they stem. The caregiver utilizes these feelings as a means of further understanding the needs of the person and the circumstances, and responds appropriately. When this is accomplished the caregiver may then act on the need basis of the patient rather than acting only on the basis of his own needs. The recognition of a particular feeling may yield clues to the type of interaction occurring. For example, if one experiences anger in working with a person, the anger may be in response to intense dependency or an inability on the part of the caregiver to perform to his own expectations.

When the caregiver is unaware of his personal involvement in the emotions and responses of the dying person, he may use the patient's feelings and struggles in an attempt to resolve his own personal conflicts or to fulfill his own needs. The caregiver who fears dependency, for example, may project his own conflicts into the patient's management of his illness, encouraging autonomy and self-sufficiency when regression and dependency are appropriate responses. Similarly, the caregiver who has an intense need to take responsibilities for others may encourage dependency and resist any movement on the patient's part to retain control and a sense of independence. In so doing, the caregiver attempts to deal with his own feelings rather than the patient's. In other situations the conflict may be one which is so painful to the caregiver that even the perception of the conflict is denied. Caregivers may also encourage persons to express feelings growing out of their own needs rather than those of the patient. This phenomenon is evident in the following vignette.

A caregiver who was required to work with dying patients as part of his training stated that the most important aspect of caring for these patients was to get them to express their anger. He felt that this was true of all of his patients and as he addressed the teaching conference about patients' need to express their anger, he banged his fist repeatedly on the table. Later, in a group discussion exploring the feelings of persons working in this area, he came to realize that he was furious about being required to work with patients who were dying, as they made him most uncomfortable. His means of managing his own anger was to insist that the patients expressed theirs whether they felt it or not.

To provide an atmosphere of optimal acceptance the caregiver must continually remind himself that adaptation to dying and death is a unique human experience. While there are shared affective components which remind the individual of his finiteness and basic human struggles, the manner in which the person copes with these issues is a complex and unique blend that is different in each situation. Differing responses are the rule rather than the exception.

When the caregiver finds himself experiencing intense or painful emotions in the context of caring for a dying patient, he should ask himself, "What needs of the person are resulting in my experiencing this feeling?" If one feels continually emotionally drained, the caregiver should ask, "Am I attempting to give too much, or failing to delegate responsibility as a means of ensuring control, or failing to allow the patient or family to assume some of the responsibility of care?" "Is a feeling of anger, sadness, or helplessness appropriate to the situation?" "Is this a time that I should express my limitations both personally and professionally?"

Another category of identification with the dying person's feelings deserves comment. In this case, the caregiver may find himself experiencing many of the same feelings experienced by the dying person. Here, the caregiver may be accurately perceiving the feelings of the patient. This category of feelings also grows out of a shared sense of humanness and the relationship established in the caring process. Self-awareness in this aspect of caring may also be used as a means of improving care, for when the caregiver is aware of his own feelings, this may provide insights into the needs and concerns of the patient. This resonance of feelings which occurs in an approximated caring relationship in the context of dying and death may be used to better understand the feeling dimension of the person's responses. In order to do this the caregiver must be able to appreciate his feelings and understand them as related to the care situation. Feelings of helplessness and loss of control in the caregiver may be akin to the feelings of the patient. Feeling personally vulnerable may signal to the caregiver that the patient or the family also feels vulnerable. Feeling anger or sadness may relate to the patient's experience. Feeling loneliness and isolation in caring may indicate that the patient also feels isolated from other caregivers or members of the family who might provide support. The caregiver must, however, be certain that his feelings are indeed those of the patient and this can be accomplished only by a knowledge of the patient's feeling state through perceptive awareness of both one's own feeling state and that of the patient. Subjectivity is combined with objectivity and used for the well-being of the patient and the caregiver rather than to resolve the caregiver's conflicts.

CONFLICT BETWEEN CAREGIVERS

An important determinant of unrest for the care situation and the caregiver himself is the conflict present among caregivers from the many disciplines working with the dying patient. This conflict and the resultant divisiveness and isolation of caregivers is one of the most important deterrents to the provision of adequate care for the dying person. The conflict results from preconceived sterotypes held by various caregivers about one another, varying sets and levels of knowledge, differences in language, role conflict resulting from overlap in areas of care and institutional hierarchy, tradition and routine, differing approaches of the disciplines, poor communication patterns, and the lack of effective settings for overcoming this conflict.

The result of this divisiveness is not only the failure to develop effective means of collaboration and cooperation, but also an interference with the therapeutic use of an individual's knowledge, skills, and attitudes. Importantly, the conflict leads to the failure to develop a mutually supportive setting in

which the intense feelings and emotional drain related to the death situation can be effectively managed. Thus self-awareness in relationship to interactions with other caregivers also assumes an important place in the care process.

THE CAREGIVER'S GRIEF

The loss of a relationship evokes some level of grief in anyone relating with that person. Multiple contacts through repeated outpatient visits and frequent and prolonged hospitalizations mean that the caregiver often has extensive contact with the patient and comes to know the dying person intimately as a person. This can result in a highly personal concern and a significant relationship. Grief, then, is to be expected as a normal process in the patient, in the family, and in such cases, in the caregiver as well. Grief in the caregiver does not necessarily begin with the death of the person. The process referred to as anticipatory grief, mourning before the fact of death, may occur in the caregiver prior to the death of the person, just as in the family and the dying person himself. For the caregiver, it may begin with fleeting feelings of sadness and guilt. The caregiver becomes preoccupies with what he might have done differently or feels guilt over interactions which might have been unpleasant. The sense of grief may be transient but it becomes particularly apparent in the presence of the person. At the same time the caregiver is involved in the development of a caring relationship, he is cognizant at some level of the ultimate loss of that relationship. As the person becomes increasingly ill, the caregiver experiences this grief as the sense of losing a significant person and must begin the process of "letting go." This "letting go" process not only involves the actual management of the loss of the relationship, but simultaneously involves the recognition and personal acceptance of the transient state of self and the potential loss of the self. The individual must come to grips with the fact that he will be left with memories of the experience of the relationship and that his ultimate recognition of finiteness as a fact of life will be reinforced.

When death itself occurs, the caregiver must return to his work and be involved in establishing similar relationships, but now with the more experienced recognition that new relationships also ultimately will be lost. Except for brief exchanges of sorrow following the death of the person, the caregiver is in most cases denied the opportunity to continue his grief process in the social context of the grieving process of the family and friends. Most often, the persons with whom he might share his grief are other caregivers. All too frequently, however, the grief of the caregiver, like other feeling states of the caregiver in this area, is not legitimized and the person is left to grieve in an isolated position. In many situations, a person intimately involved in the care of the person contains his grief and is not allowed the comfort brought about from the sharing of the experience in the interpersonal setting.

A young student nurse who had been assigned to work with a young woman with Hodgkins' disease sought out another caregiver approximately two weeks after the death of the patient. She had worked intensively with the patient and was severely distressed by the patient's death. She reported having recurrent dreams in which the patient appeared, again alive. She was alarmed by her sadness and the recurrent dreams. In talking with this nurse, it became apparent that she was experiencing normal grief. She was considerably relieved to be able to express her feelings about the loss of a person whom she had come to know well during a prolonged hospitalization. Her status as a student had, however, created reluctance about sharing her feelings of distress, as she viewed such feelings as unacceptable in the training setting.

In this case example, legitimization of feelings was lacking and this acceptance and similar forms of legitimization of caregiver responses are lacking in relationship to many other feelings evoked in caring for the dying person. This failure to legitimize the grief of the caregiver may have the additional adverse effect of causing the caregiver to fail to accept the grief of the person and his family.

During the care process itself, the caregiver constantly becomes aware of the series of losses of the patient and potential losses for himself. These losses not only include the recognition of the loss of part of or the total biological, physical self, but also the loss of the interpersonal self, the social self, and the potential loss of meaning derived from the relationship. This reaction to loss and the sense of transience is at the very core of human existence, for in each true encounter and its loss there is a loss of part of the sense of self held by the person prior to the loss. Grief in such circumstances is not only a human response, but an appropriate response and a measure of the intensity of the dyadic encounter with another being.

NEED FOR MUTUAL SUPPORT IN CAREGIVING MILIEU

The feelings elicited in the caregiver working in the area are at least discomforting and often are capable of rendering the caregiver utterly incapable of providing effective care. The overwhelming nature of the feelings experienced can contribute to an inflexibility and a paralysis of shifting postures of care which lead to an excruciating sensitivity or a mechanistic, insensitive, rigid approach to the patient. The lack of shared support and a setting for the expression of feelings in the caregiving milieu may lead to a painful state of isolation, meaninglessness, and despair. In this state, the caregiver may experience a sense of alienation and estrangement from other caregivers, which is in itself emotionally upsetting. He is left to deal with his feelings with a sense of being separate and alone. The caregiver in effect lacks affirmation of the validity of his feelings and the support which may be derived from knowing that others share similar feelings. The divisiveness present in the caregiving setting, the failure of the caregivers to exchange feelings of helplessness, emotional drain, dependency, grief, and the very questioning of their professional competency in the face of death leads to interpersonal isolation and nonsupport.

In caring for the dying person, the ability to recognize the legitimacy of one's feelings, the ability to confirm a shared sense of purpose with other caregiving persons, and the ability to recognize shared affectual responses in the context of death may be major means of available support. At bottom, all caring, be it for the patient and his family or for other caregivers, has as its purpose the provision of an atmosphere in which meaning and a sense of aliveness can be derived. In the caregiving process the meaning and the sense of aliveness is derived from the activity surrounding the sharing of feelings related to the human aspects of providing care. The activity of the relationships with other caregivers, the validation by another of the legitimacy of human feeling, is the affirmation of one's status as being alive and human and is as important for caregivers as for patients, particularly when the caregiver's task is to assist the patient in continuing to find meaning, to find a sense of aliveness, and to retain his dignity as a human being to the greatest extent possible. There is thus a vital need for the development of support systems for the caregiver in this area. Only on the basis of this support and in the knowledge of the availability of this support can the process of care effectively occur.

The feelings engendered in working with the dying person and his family are at times indeed awesome. They are the feelings of the dying self or at least the feeling of the potentially dying self, and in approximation with the death situation, the validation of aliveness is as important for the caregiver as for the dying person and his family. The strengths derived from relationship are the key to this validation of being alive, for like the dying person, the caregiver may also feel lonely and abandoned.

The person who is dying and the family of the patient are often overlooked as sources of support for caregivers working in this area. This occurs because of the isolation brought about by the intense feelings generated in the caregiving triad, traditional stereotypes of professional roles, the feeling that including patients and family in the supportive aspects of the care process may lead to interference with the busy system of providing health care, and the general reluctance of caregivers to express to families and patients their need for support. This may lead to a failure on the part of caregivers to bring the patient and his family into a mutually reciprocal supportive position in the care process. In the context of a developed relationship, however, this support, through communication and expression of feeling, is not only available but aids in the development of a therapeutic posture for all concerned.

At times, it becomes appropriate to draw on the views of the family to provide additional insight into the overall needs involved in the process of care. Family members may be far more in touch with varying needs of the circumstances. Family members and patients themselves at times recognize the limitations of medical treatment and care before they are actually acknowledged by the physician and other health-care personnel. Sometimes members of the family are actually in a position which allows them to be more objective about certain aspects of care than is the caregiver. Only through the inclusion of these persons in the care process can their input and support be obtained. The practice of isolating the input and support of the family from the caregiving process can only serve to increase the caregiver's feelings of being burdened.

In working with dying patients, the caregiver often feels an intense sense of personal responsibility. This may indicate that the caregiver is taking more than the necessary amount of responsibility for the situation and not dividing or delegating the responsibility in a manner conducive to best care. The feeling or perception of being emotionally drained or being too responsible may serve as an indicator that he is failing to appropriately share aspects of care — that he is closing out supportive interchanges with the patient, the family, and other caregivers. Team meetings with other caregivers often provide an effective setting in which this aspect of care may be evaluated. Similarly, it is often a helpful therapeutic maneuver to see the members of the family most involved in the caregiving process together in order to assure an effective and continuous form of communication and to establish to posture of working together toward more effective care.

DISENGAGEMENT

The caregiver must maintain presence when it is indicated, and also recognize those times in the care of the person and his family when he must disengage himself from the person and allow a highly personal, internal, and subjective process to occur. There are times in the care process when the patient prefers to withdraw into himself in a quiet, subjective, working-through process.

During these times, the caregiver who has been intensively involved with the patient is likely to feel unneeded and indeed must temporarily disengage from the caregiving process and allow the person the solitude to deal with his feelings. The patient may, during these times, find his own feelings "nameless" and simply have the need to quietly experience his feelings without talking. The need for solitude and dwelling in a subjective state may be expressed very directly, thereby adding to the caregiver's discomfort, or it may be expressed indirectly through passivity and reluctance to talk, or in subtle nonverbal ways. An abrupt physical crisis may rapidly precipitate the need for disengagement. Where the relationship has been a deep, intensive, emotional and verbal relationship, the person may now simply be unable to continue with this form of relationship. His energies are directed in different directions. Although the caregiver may himself feel abandoned, his task is to remain available to meet developing needs of the patient. In such circumstances the caregiver must develop the ability to recognize when he must change directions in the relationship so as not to interfere with the process of adaptation. In these circumstances family or other caregivers may need the presence and support of the caregiver. At other times, however, the caregiver must, in the interest of effective care, simply move to a peripheral position. If the caregiver is set on maintaining control and constantly feels that he must always be an active participant in the caregiving process, this type of disengagement may be particularly difficult.

Disengagement may also become necessary when, during the care process, the caregiver must step aside and turn over various aspects of care to members of the family or other caregivers. In these circumstances possessiveness, the intense need on the part of the caregiver to maintain continuity and presence in the relationship, the desire to be needed, or traits such as competitiveness may interfere with the process of transferring a phase of care to someone else.

The process of disengagement is experienced as a loss or death of part of the total relationship. It is in essence a "partial death."[9] This act of "letting go" or disengaging from the dying patient is a symbolic reminder of the anticipated ultimate necessity of disengagement from the individual as he comes closer to death. As such, the feelings associated with disengagement are feelings of loss and grief. Disengagement therefore is symbolic of the finiteness of the relationship and must be recognized as such. As physical decline occurs and the dying person comes closer to death, the caregiver is faced with the final disengagement. At this point, even stronger feelings related to loss may be experienced and the relationship enters a realm which Kübler-Ross has called *"the silence that goes beyond words."* [10]

CONTROLLED DISTANCING—A VITAL PART OF CARING

Having recognized the tremendous potential for the care of the dying person and his family to result in a withdrawal, avoidance phenomenon, and the tendency for the intense feelings evoked by the care situation to drive the caregiver away, the caregiver is now in a position to integrate this knowledge into the care process rather than acting it out in actual withdrawal and abandonment of the person and his family. When, in the process of caring for the dying person and his family, the feelings evoked by the process do indeed become overwhelming, this is the time during which the caregiver's effectiveness may be compromised.

At certain junctures in the care process, there is the opportunity to engage in activities which are still directed toward caring but provide some diminution of the emotional intensity of the care situation. These junctures may serve to aid the caregiver to dilute or diminish feelings which approach awesome, overwhelming levels. Sharing the load of a responsibility with another caregiver in some situations may allow the caregiver to remain approximated with the care process while allowing enough distance to dilute the total experience, Attempting to understand objectively what is happening is another activity which may reduce emotional intensity. Recognizing when the patient and the family are able to carry the care process along by themselves and realizing when one is "present" only through habit rather than actual need may also furnish some therapeutic distance. Requesting consultation with another caregiver or discussing one's feelings with another caregiver may serve to bring some objectivity to the care process and aid with the emotional intensity involved. During a particularly tumultuous time in the care of a dying patient, a caregiver was experiencing overwhelming, bothersome emotions. In discussing the situation with another caregiver, he stated that the patient seemed too aware of her impending death and questioned how he might "increase her denial." The consultant pointed out that perhaps the caregiver was concerned as to how he might increase his own denial as he was experiencing extremely painful feelings. This insight caused him to look more closely at his level of involvement and calibrate it so as to be able to provide more effective care. Explicitly stating one's limits may become necessary. The task is to select those junctures and circumstances in care during which distance remains compatible with the care process and to be flexibly able to utilize that distance to manage one's own feeling level in a recuperative manner.

Controlled distancing is a therapeutic maneuver designed to allow the caregiver to maintain his own emotional integrity in the face of a continuous care process which involves the evoking of high feeling levels. It should not be confused with an attempt to develop insensitivity. Sensitivity and involvement continue but the caregiver develops the ability to flexibly use appropriate forms of distancing as a means of caring rather than engaging in total distancing which compromises care. In an interdisciplinary approach, the primary care physician may be intimately involved in a dialogue with the person and then, when the need occurs, have to move into a position in which he utilizes technical skills. At that point, rather than abandoning the interpersonal needs of the patient, another person in the care team should be able to take over the responsibility for providing the sense of interpersonal dialogue for the person involved. This requires a great deal of communication and interpersonal sensitivity on the part of all persons involved, but it serves the important purpose of protecting the caregiver against his ability to care becoming overwhelmed.

DISRUPTION OF PROFESSIONAL MEANING FOR CAREGIVER IN CONTEXT OF DYING

As many health-care professionals find their personal significance and meaning in that activity which is aimed at ensuring biological or physical aliveness in their patients, the dying person's care contains a dimension which may not only threaten the caregiver himself in terms of his personal finiteness, but also threaten the very meaning of his professional activities. If the caregiver limits his caring to ensuring survival and hope only in the biological and physical dimensions, he may feel unable to generate professionally meaningful activities in the context of dying and death, and the very validity of the profession as a viable activity for obtaining meaning for the caregiver is encroached upon. At these times, the individual may engage in serious questioning of the effectiveness of his profession as a caregiving profession. In the care of a dying person the caregiver is finally led into a confrontation with those aspects of any caring process which fall in some way short of the total expectations that he places upon himself. The caregiver is in this context quickly aware of professional limitations, and limits in skills and knowledge.

This phenomenon has the capacity to cause the caregiver to feel helpless, powerless, and frustrated. It has the capacity to divert his caring to more certain areas, to divert his caring away from those professional areas where there is a limit to knowledge. More specifically, the whole area of working with dying patients may be avoided because of this phenomenon. Meaning for the health-care professional is a far broader matter than providing a sense of aliveness for the patient only in the biological dimension. Broadening one's goals to provide meaning and a sense of aliveness in the psychosocial sense will serve to substantially increase the potential of a health-care professional to engage in meaningful activity and need not supplant maximizing the person's biological or physical comfort or sense of being alive.

REFERENCES

1. Lynch J: Reflections. *ARS Moriendi Newsletter* 2:3–4, 6–7, 1975
2. Neale RE: *The Art of Dying.* Harper and Row,

New York, 1971

3. Feifel H, Hanson RJ, Edwards L: Physicians Consider Death. *Proceedings*. 75th Annual Convention, American Psychological Association, 1967

4. Feifel H: "The Function of Attitudes Toward Death," in *Death and Dying: Attitudes of Patient and Doctor*. Vol. V. Group for the Advancement of Psychiatry, New York, 1965

5. Kasper AM: "The Doctor and Death," in *The Meaning of Death,* Feifel H (Ed), 1st McGraw-Hill Paperback Ed, McGraw-Hill, New York, 1959

6. Knight JA: *Medical Student: Doctor in the Making.*

Appleton-Century-Crofts, New York, 1973

7. Fox RC: "Training for Uncertainty," in *The Student-Physician,* Merton RK, Reader GG, Kendall PL (Eds) Harvard University Press, Cambridge, Massachusetts, 1957

8. Barton D: On Caring for the Caregiver in the Context of Dying and Death. Unpublished manuscript

9. Shneidman ES: *Deaths of Man.* Penguin Books, Baltimore, 1974

10. Kübler-Ross E: *On Death and Dying.* Macmillan, London, 1969

7

APPROACHES TO THE CLINICAL CARE OF THE DYING PERSON

David Barton, M.D.

When encountering the threat of dying and death, a person adapts in a highly individualized manner. Similarly, those persons interacting with the dying individual also manifest a wide variety of responses. The variations encountered by caregivers working in this area are virtually unlimited in number. Not only does the individual's uniqueness become an important determinant in the difficulties encountered, but the involvement and reactions of family members and caregivers from many disciplines further compound the complexity of the care situation.

A preplanned, definitive set of actions, reactions, and interventions in the care of the dying person and his family is virtually impossible to elaborate; no other care situation in medical practice requires such flexibility, sensitivity, versatility, wide variety of knowledge and skills, and the collaborative participation of caregivers from so many disciplines. Care in this area also involves intense feelings and requires a level of self-awareness far above that required in many other treatment situations. These factors have contributed to the difficulties in developing effective means of caring for the dying. The caregiver is denied an orderly set of happenings to which he might apply an unchanging, inflexible series of methods and interventions. Shifting needs and changing patterns of interaction dictate that responses be developed out of the dynamic process of care itself. While disconcerting and often frustrating, this concept is basic in caring for the dying person. In accepting this, the care-

giver can work toward developing an approach which allows him to perceive and respond to the unique constellation of needs of the dying person and to retain the highest level of flexibility in providing optimal care.

In working with dying persons and their families, the caregiver often wants a set protocol, a definitive approach, and ironclad methods. However, he quickly learns that the uniqueness of the individual and the circumstances involved defy the use of a rigid approach and that care provided in this way may serve to meet the needs of the caregiver rather than the patient and his family. Persons beginning to work in this area often ask, "What do I say to a dying person?"; "What can I do for someone who is dying?"; "How do I get to their feelings about death?" or "What do I say to the family?" While it would be comforting to have definite answers to these questions, they become answerable only through the process of care. The caregiver must struggle with the situation, coming up with answers as he proceeds through the process of care.

This chapter is designed to provide the caregiver with an approach to the *process* of care. Because of the uniqueness of the individual approximated with his dying and death, care can proceed only when caregivers possess an ability to discern the needs of the person, remain approximated, continue to perceptively gather data, and elaborate sets of need-meeting interventions ecompassing the biological, psychosocial, and meaning dimensions. The process of care must meet the explicit and implicit needs of the person and his family as perceived in the context of an ongoing relationship.

CHARACTERISTICS OF RELATIONSHIP WITH DYING PERSON AND HIS FAMILY

The relationship between the health-care professional and the patient and his family is unquestionably a key factor in caring and assisting all concerned to reach a reasonable level of adaptation in the process of dying. Thus, the caregiver should look closely at the characteristics of this relationship. Eissler suggests that establishing a relationship with a dying person which " . . . reawakens the primordial feeling of being protected by a mother . . . " can significantly reduce the pain and suffering of dying.[1] He is referring here to an important aspect of the patient's feelings toward the caregiver in which the person feels the protection, security, and trust which he felt in the early relationship with a mothering person. This "primordial feeling of being protected by a mother" represents a recapturing and reverting to an earlier mode of relating in the context of the patient's relationship with the physician. Eissler views another aspect of the relationship with the dying patient as central in his care. He believes that the treatment of the dying patient centers around what he refers to as "the gift situation." In this formulation, the "gift" attains, in the therapeutic relationship, an important positive symbolic meaning for the dying patient. The gift is in essence, " . . . experienced by the patient as the physician's giving him part of his own life, . . . " thereby overcoming the sense of isolation and creating a symbolic sense of dying together."[1]

Norton's treatment of a dying person provides additional insights into the characteristics of the relationship with a caregiver.[2] In her work with her patient, Norton notes, legitimizes, and interacts appropriately through the patient's stages of progressive regression. In relating to the patient's regressive response to her illness, Norton responded by assuming certain functions much as the mother would do for the developing child. During the last phases of the treatment of the patient she allowed the regression to proceed unashamedly so as to stir minimal anxiety in the patient, appropri-ately meeting needs as they emerged in the process of the patient's dying. She maintained presence in order to overcome the patient's sense of interpersonal loss. Mourning and the giving up of investments in the persons with whom she had related, as well as mourning the loss of her own health, productivity, and future, were noted to be prominent features of the patient's last months of life. Identification with the therapist and the act of introjection (a primitive taking in of aspects of the therapist) were integral parts of the therapeutic relationship which allowed the patient a sense of living despite her dying. Commenting on Eissler's concept of "the gift situation" Norton states that her case report " . . . would suggest that the really crucial gift the therapist can give is that of himself as an available object [person]." Availability, reliability, empathy, and appropriate responses to the patient's needs are viewed as the important therapeutic tools of the therapist in the treatment of the dying person.[2]

Kübler-Ross views attending the dying patient's needs as they arise in her five stages of terminal illness—denial, anger, bargaining, depression, and acceptance—as a central part of care.[3, 4] In the passage through these five stages, the therapist may encourage the patient's expression of dismay over his dilemma, allow him to ventilate his anger, or legitimize his grief. He may change his mode of relating from active participation to silent companionship as the needs of the circumstances demand. In commenting on facilitating the stage of acceptance, she writes, "If we can help them express both their anger and their grief without feeling ashamed, bad, or guilty, we can facilitate their last stage, the stage of acceptance. This is the time when they express few needs except for the companionship of a loved one. They have to be physically cared for like an infant in many ways. They need some fluids, a little food, warmth, and the awareness of a caring person. It is the time when everything has been said—the moment of silent companionship that will last until the person actually dies."[4]*

Weisman, in his writings, speaks of "safe

---

* Reprinted by permission of Grune & Stratton and E. Kübler-Ross (see Ref. 4).

conduct" as an important goal in caring for the terminally ill patient.[5, 6] He writes, " . . . it is safe conduct that the doctor and other concerned professionals must promise, even pledge to those patients who are obliged to surrender their autonomy as time goes on and must yield essential control to someone else. After all, the difference between a healthy dependency and a sick victim is entirely a problem of being able to trust and to be trusted."[5] Providing and ensuring safe conduct, then, involves the process of the caregiver's facilitating the patient's progress through the events of his illness with a sense of safety, security, and trust in those caring for them. The process of providing safe conduct for the dying person refers both to the caregiver's behavior toward the patient and to the feelings of security and safety generated in the person.[6] Weisman also identifies "dignified dying" as a goal of care. He writes, "Dignified dying is not an exotic concept; it simply means that one continues to regard a dying patient as a responsible person, capable of clear perceptions, honest relationships, and purposeful behavior, consistent with the inroads of physical decline and disability."[6]

Common to all of these approaches is the establishment of a relationship which respects and meets the needs of the dying person's regression in the face of his illness, the presence of the caregiver, the use of oneself as a therapeutic facilitator in maintaining the ability of the patient to adapt, to express thoughts and feelings, and the protection of the person's rights of being human. The relationship itself is used to ensure the patient's sense of security and safety in the face of progressive loss of autonomy, and to ensure that his death will approximate his ideal in living. In short, the caregiver enables the dying person to find meaning and an enduring sense of aliveness even while dying.

Considerable emphasis is often placed on the need for the dying person to "talk" about his difficulties, but the caregiver must assess and appreciate the ability and the level of desire of the dying person and his family to talk in depth about their plight. The caregiver must bear in mind that the need to talk about various issues and the content expressed may be strongly related to the dying patient's perception of the caring person's role in the care process. Denial, withholding, and the fluctuating modulation of awareness also affect the ability and desire to communicate.

The patient and the family may or may not wish to talk about certain feelings. They may express these feelings at a superficial level or in great depth. The relationship, however, should be maintained at a level which allows the patient to talk about what he wishes and about feelings he wants to express. The caregiver must be particularly careful not to be intrusive, especially in the sense of forcing the patient or family to talk about feelings which the caregiver has the need to deal with rather than the patient. The patient should be allowed to set the pace; talking with the dying person and his family should proceed in a gentle but open manner. In an effectively established and maintained relationship, there is a constant need to calibrate the level at which the patient wishes to communicate his thoughts and feelings. When talking with the dying person and his family, the caregiver must pay attention to the content, the accompanying feeling, and the nonverbal behavior, and he must listen carefully for the symbolic communication behind the spoken word.

The characteristics of the relationship with the dying person and his family which meet the needs of all concerned requires a need-discerning presence and the capability of "being there." Being there is an interpersonal phenomenon closely related to interpersonal process, especially the mutual affirmation of the viability and continuity of the relationship. It depends heavily on the caregiver's self-awareness, commitment to understanding the subtle and implicit issues of care, and his ability to remain approximated with the care situation.

Being there does not necessarily mean engaging in tangible acts of doing something. Caregivers tend to underestimate the effectiveness and positive value of simple presence in a relationship as a therapeutic act. In fact, in some phases of caring for the dying, "doing" becomes impossible, inane, or simply diversionary. There is simply nothing that can be done or said, and even maintaining presence becomes extremely difficult or even painful. If the caregiver is able to maintain presence at this point, he recognizes that he, like the person for whom he is caring, is also human and cannot always make the incomprehensible comprehensible and bring certainty to an uncertain situation. This is particularly true of the very terminal phase of the person's illness when he is actually approaching death. Participation in care at this point means the caregiver is able to engage in what Kübler-Ross refers to as the *"silence that goes beyond words."*[3] In these transactions with the dying person, the caregiver realizes that he is relating with a living person who is dying and that human presence may, at times, be the highest form of caring one can provide.[7]

The triad of providing an interpersonal setting for the expression of feelings by the patient and family members, the acknowledgment of those feelings by another, and appropriate legitimization is a vital part of the process of caring for the dying person. The caregiver may expect discomfort in response to many of the dying person's feelings but must develop the ability to tolerate the full expression of these feelings. A patient's crying, the expression of desperation, intense frustration, or anger may make the caregiver particularly uncomfortable, but the ventilation of these feelings is often necessary for the person. While the outward expression of intense feelings often is characteristic of a person, at times the caregiver may encounter him or members of the family in a more withdrawn state. During these periods, the person has difficulty in expressing words or feelings. Often, the feelings go beyond symbolic designation in language and it is not uncommon for the patient to report that he has no names for his feelings or words with which to describe them. These withdrawn states are often simply related to the person's quietly and internally "working through" his feelings. At other times the withdrawn state represents a form of self-imposed separation from the living world and a preparatory withdrawal into the self. The following example illustrates this concept.

A young woman with a far advanced malignant illness was visited regularly in a home care setting. During one visit she stopped abruptly during a conversation and asked that the care-giver please leave. She later reported that she was unable to describe her feelings at that time and wanted time to herself to try to deal with the feelings which she said "lacked names." She perceived the presence of the caregiver as a demand to relate at a time when she felt the need to withdraw into herself. Her wishes were acknowledged as legitimate and she was told that she should communicate this need during any visit with her. She was also reassured that the caregiver's presence did not constitute a demand to talk.

While these feeling states are often most apparent in the dying person, they may also be present in family members and in the caregiver. The disquieting and uncomfortable nature of the feelings in the caregiver is an important issue if the dysphoria reaches a level which causes him to withdraw from the care situation, thereby isolating the patient. When this occurs, it is often in response to feelings which cannot be made totally comprehensible. These feelings are those associated with what has been referred to as death awareness in Chapter 2. They are shared feelings of being human and are experienced when the caregiver is approximated with one who is dying. These feelings are best managed through mutual support and with the collaboration of other caregivers. Mutuality among caregivers thus becomes a most important aspect of assuring effective care.

While at times the caregiver may focus primarily on the feeling dimensions of dying and death, conversations with the dying person and his family should also be directed toward gathering important data in other areas. As the dying person and his family are in the midst of a very real life crisis, it is important for the caregiver to have access to a wide variety of information related to the person and the social context in which he lives. This information is best gathered in the context of an effective relationship and most often is obtained over time. The caregiver is cautioned against following a definite outline or confining himself to a single theoretical construct in a rigid, reductionistic, and overly structured fashion.

Caregiver's inquires should be designed to let the individual reply at the level he wishes. Much of the information has the quality of being private and an intimate part of the person's life. Intrusive questions which go beyond the level of the person's desire to communicate will frequently evoke negative reactions in the patient. The caregiver should be attuned to such responses and when this occurs, recognize that he has failed to accurately calibrate the level at which the interview should proceed.

Rather than rigidly adhering to a specific outline, the caregiver asks what the patient wishes to discusss and about his feelings. Questions are posed in a way which discourage a "yes or no" answer, encouraging the person to circumscribe his own areas of concern, and allowing him to respond at his own level. For example, the question, "Are you feeling sad about your illness?" may only draw a "yes or no" answer or an evasive response; whereas a question worded, "How do you feel about your illness?" allows the person latitude to respond in a more personalized manner. Continuing reassessment is necessary to remain in touch with the changing aspects and fluctuation of needs and attitudes throughout the course of the person's illness, especially since the needs, concerns, and responses of the individual will change dramatically over time.

Inquiry about the same areas may elicit different material, depending upon the time in the course of the illness at which the question is asked, the area being investigated, who is asked, and who is asking the question. Rarely can the data base or full body of information about a particular dying person be obtained by one caregiver without consulting others as to what information they may have, might provide, or obtain. This means that there must be an ongoing process of dialogue among caregivers, patient, and family.

The following outline is presented to delineate significant areas of information which may assume importance in the care of the dying person and his family. It should be altered depending on such variables as the patient's age, the type and course of the illness, the time the caregiver begins working with the patient, and the discipline, style, and methods of the caregiver. The areas are not as discrete and clear as presented here, and there is significant overlap in the material. The topics cannot be expected necessarily to be covered in the same order as they are outlined. Also, talking about many of the topics depends on the presence of an established, trusting relationship and the caregiver cannot expect to explore these with the person or the family until considerable rapport has been developed. The caregiver should not use this outline to rigidly structure an interview in a manner which would discourage spontaneous and individualized presentations of problems or concerns; rather it should be viewed only as a guide to that information which may be useful in the overall assessment in the process of care.

I. The Biological Dimension
   A. Onset of illness—how signs or symptoms initially came to the person's attention
   B. Current forms and level of physical discomfort (pain, nausea, weakness, etc.)
   C. The person's immediate reaction to recognition of illness
      1. Time lapse between onset of initial signs and symptoms and first consultation with health-care profession
      2. Time and place of initial contact with health-care system and informational exchange at that time
   D. Diagnostic procedures utilized
   E. Informational exchange regarding illness
      1. Information received (including diagnosis, if given)
      2. Manner in which information conveyed
      3. How and what was communicated
      4. Who conveyed the information
      5. To whom information conveyed (patient, family members, parent, child)
   F. Perceived concept of outcome based on information received
      1. Nonverbal data perceived by person
   G. Type and place of treatment received
   H. Response to treatment

I. Current treatment methods being employed

J. Limitations imposed by physical condition (motility, physical self-sufficiency, mental capabilities, level of debilitation)

K. Previous history of illness, surgical procedures, and responses

L. Body parts involved as a result of illness and treatment

M. Evident changes or distortions of body image, disfigurement, and responses to these changes

N. Mechanical devices and prostheses required for care
   1. Effectiveness of these devices

O. Forms of recurrent or sustained physical discomfort

P. Ongoing assessment of patient's and family's knowledge of physical status and effects of disease process

II. Psychosocial Dimension

A. Subjective data
   1. Concepts and feelings about previous illness or surgical procedures involving self or others
      a. Previous experiences with illness in general or deaths of others
   2. Previous associations with similar illnesses and related feelings
   3. Responses to previous stresses, particularly illnesses and interpersonal losses
   4. Assessment of general personality traits and life style
   5. Emotional precedents of the illness
   6. Recent losses
   7. Self-esteem mechanisms and interference with these mechanisms by disease process
   8. Current or unsolved conflicts
   9. Characteristic coping styles likely to be interfered with by the disease and treatment process
   10. Expected areas of internal conflict (dependency and independency, mastery and control, management of strong feelings, identity)
   11. Fantasies about illness and its effect on the self and the interpersonal environment
   12. Level of desire for knowledge about illness
   13. Perceived threats to sense of self evoked by illness
   14. Attitudes toward participation in the care process (activity, passivity, dependency, independency, need for control)
   15. Personal significance of dying and death
   16. Perceived primary supportive persons in environment
   17. Current emotional status (anxiety, anger, depression, grief)
   18. Estimate of person's ability to deal with feelings associated with illness
   19. Individual's perception of interpersonal environment's ability to deal with illness and associated feelings
   20. Reaction to treatment settings (clinic, hospital, extended care facilities)
   21. Ethical value system toward illness, prolongation of life, quality of life
   22. Person's fantasies and concerns about the family or others after his death
   23. Personal religious convictions
   24. Attitudes about immortality

B. Interpersonal and Social Context
   1. Person's characteristic manner of relating interpersonally (tendency to withdraw from others, tendency to seek out others, verbal, quiet, etc.)
   2. Changes in interpersonal style following onset of illness
   3. Needs of person characteristically met in relationships (overt approval and admiration, attentiveness, and support)
      a. Ability of environment to meet these needs
   4. Family structure
   5. Effect on family structure of person's illness
   6. Identifiable strong coalitions in family involving patient or others

7. Communication patterns
8. Delegation of responsibilities within family (roles, function, patterns of dependency and independency)
9. Current family conflict
10. Personality traits of various family members
11. Awareness of family members regarding severity of illness
12. Attitudes of family about person's illness and differences in attitudes among various family members
13. Available external support system for family
14. Family's willingness to seek out or allow support from outside family constellation
15. Degree of family's isolation from or involvement in social environment
16. Caregivers designated by person and family members as responsible for various needs
17. Attitudes and feelings of person and family toward physician, other caregivers, and health-care system
18. Family's feelings about access to caregivers
19. Family's feeling about informational exchange with caregivers
20. Depletion of resources by illness (time, economic, physical, emotional)
21. Financial position of family
22. Family vocational involvement and work patterns
23. Effects of illness on vocational involvement
24. Communication patterns with persons in health-care system
25. Family's desire and ability to participate in care, including special abilities available to assume specific care functions
26. Responses of children in the family and their involvement in the care process
27. Family plans for adaptation to the illness
28. Community support systems available

29. Friends' involvement in illness
30. Difficulties involved in reaching health-care facilities
31. Disruption of usual time schedules
32. Dislocation of person or family from support systems
33. Family religious convictions
34. Persons outside of family available for support
35. Desire for home *vs.* hospital care
36. Person and family's reaction to non-human environment
37. Assessment of family capabilities for enduring stress over time
38. Ethical value system of interpersonal environment
39. Legitimization of responses and feelings in interpersonal and social context
40. Anticipated adjustment patterns of family after death
41. Estimate of interpersonal environment as being conducive to grief process after person's death

III. Meaning Dimension

This category relates to those activities utilized by the individual to attain meaning, personal significance, and a sense of aliveness. Because the aspects of a person's life that provide meaning are unique to him, it is somewhat difficult to delineate clearly the exact areas to be included in this dimension. The caregiver may, however, ask questions such as "What in your life provides meaning for you?"; "What has been the source of meaning in your life?"; "What makes you feel really alive?"; "What do you do to help you feel alive?" or "What activities in your life provide you with a sense of vitality?" General areas which may be explored are:
A. Meaning derived from physical function (motility, bodily intactness, intellectual pursuits, sensations, physical activity)
B. Meaning derived from subjective sense of well being
C. Meaning derived from interpersonal relationships (significant persons,

style and intensity of relationships, interpersonal activities)

D. Meaning derived from participation in the social environment (work, social pastimes, community activities)

E. Meaning derived from spiritual life (concepts of religion, faith, immortality)

F. Manner in which illness interferes with usual ways of attaining meaning (compromised motility, disrupted relationships, vocational impairment)

G. New meaning modes and activities developed as a result of being ill

H. Future aspirations and the effect of the illness on these aspirations

I. Quality of life considerations as conceptualized by the individual

J. Appraisal of the process of care as continuing to validate or invalidate the individual's sense of aliveness

K. Changes in activity levels throughout illness

L. Redirection of activity throughout illness

INDIVIDUALIZED DYSFUNCTION AND MALADAPTIVE RESPONSES

The dysfunctions and types of maladaptation which occur in the care of the dying patient and his family are difficult to categorize specifically. Our present knowledge prohibits the elaboration of firm diagnostic categories which represent specific constellations of dysfunction to which one may respond accordingly. While such might be in keeping with a medical approach to problems, it would obscure the unique constellations in which the problems of the dying patient fall. On the other hand, it seems reasonable to delineate the presence of such phenomena as denial, depression, grief, anxiety, and in some cases, the occurrence of frank psychiatric disorders in association with a life-threatening illness.

In this approach, rather than circumscribing definite and specific categories of dysfunction which are generally applicable to every individual, I conceptualize the care of the dying person as a series of biological, intrapersonal, interpersonal, social, and meaning responses or transactions which occur as a process over time (see Chapter 3). Many of these responses and transactions

are adaptive and result in successful coping. They may for a particular person, however, result in various constellations of dysfunction or forms of maladaptation. To assist the patient, his family, and other caregivers in managing the potential difficulties which may arise as a result of this process, the caregiver should have at his disposal a wide variety of interventions to be employed in response to the individualized dysfunction perceived to be operant. The following categories of intervention presented here thus assume varying priorities. Throughout the process of care one or many of these categories of intervention may assume increased importance in the care of the patient.

Expressive-communicative Interventions

These interventions involve activities aimed at fostering the expression of feelings associated with the threat of dying and death and the maintenance of a setting in which communications related to these feelings can occur. The primary task of the caregiver is to create an atmosphere in which feelings may be freely expressed, maintaining presence during their expression and attempt to understand the communications even when they are at a symbolic level.

The infant perceives that the expression of feelings moves the environment toward action and change. As the person develops, feelings remain powerful interpersonal tools, capable of bringing about movement and activity in relationships. Later in life the expression of feeling is, in itself, often important to the person's sense of well-being. For this reason ventilation and catharsis of strong feelings are important aspects of the caregiving process. At times in the care of the dying person the expression of feeling appropriately moves the environment toward action, but at other times the feelings need only to be accepted and legitimized.

In the dying patient feelings are frequently suppressed, and their expression guarded both by the patient and by others in the environment. Patients, family members, and caregivers attempt to contain feelings which may cause them or others discomfort. Statements such as "You shouldn't be angry; they are doing all they can" or the ever-present "cheer up" along with any number of other subtle communications cause the patient to suppress feelings. Even when suppressed by the caregiver or the patient himself, they often continue to be expressed in nonverbal or covert ways. The following case examples are illustrative:

When a family pet died, a young woman with cancer became preoccupied and depressed about the animal's death. She dwelled on the details of how much the animal meant to her and her family and the resulting sadness of other family members. She became very upset when the children wanted to replace the pet immediately. The death of the animal, her reactions, and those of the family evoked feelings in her related to her own impending death. She became fearful that she would also be replaced immediately. These events were discussed at length and she was subsequently able to express many of her feelings of sadness about her illness as well as her concerns about the reactions of her family.

Lacking access to his ex-wife, a man with far-advanced lymphoma would appear, completely intoxicated, and make a scene outside her front door while she was entertaining guests in her home. The expression of anger toward his ex-wife, whom he felt should not have "deserted" him, represented "unfinished business" for this man who anticipated his death to occur shortly. When a situation was provided in which he was more directly able to express his anger and the divorced wife was helped to see the basis of his anger in relationship to his illness, the hostile outbursts and the drinking behavior subsided.

A man with a far-advanced malignancy brought a cartoon sequence to his session which showed a physician reporting his findings to a patient, stating that he found "nothing wrong" with the patient. Further in the cartoon, the character was shown with a fantasy of a gravestone with his name on it. The man obviously was extremely concerned about his illness and felt that his death was more imminent than he was being led to believe. When inquiry about his feelings was made regarding his perception of his physician's communications with him about his illness, he felt the physician was not responding at an appropriate level and was extremely angry about what he considered to be a lack of concern. A conference for the man and his physician was arranged in order to clarify their communication and allow for the direct expression of feelings.

A woman with a virilizing adrenal tumor which had caused her face to become moon shaped, her voice to deepen, and hair to grow profusely on her face reported that she had great difficulty looking in the mirror and seeing her changed face. She was anxious and saddened about these changes but initially denied any feelings, only reporting her reactions to looking in the mirror. Later she was able to acknowledge her feelings about the losses related to her body image.

The caregiver engages in expressive-communicative interventions when he perceives feelings which are associated with blocked or distorted communication. The patient should not, however, be coerced to express feeling; rather, he should be allowed to move at his own pace. In situations where the distorted expression of feeling is disruptive and maladaptive, more active measures are often necessary to encourage expression in a more adaptive manner.

In relation to the expression of feeling, one frequently hears, "Of course he (the dying patient) is angry; he has every reason to be so" or "Why shouldn't he be depressed; he's got a right to be sad." The individual making these statements may be so accepting of the feeling that he fails to allow the patient room to explore the basis for these emotions or even fails to interact with the individual. Merely saying that someone has a right to be depressed is no substitute for talking with him about his depression and/or tolerating the acceptance of the expression of anger, sadness, or other emotions in the context of an ongoing relationship.

A psychiatric consultation was requested on a patient whose demanding and angry behavior had alienated the entire ward staff. It became clear that he was very depressed and was using his behavior not only as a means of expressing his anger and sense of worthlessness but also as a means of seeking retaliation from his environment as punishment for these feelings. Interpersonal contact with the patient had decreased substantially. When his physician was informed that he was depressed, he remarked "Damn it, he's got a right to be angry and depressed; he's dying." The consultant explained that the patient's depression had created an isolated state in which there was no provision for the exploration of his feelings. When his physician talked with him about his depression rather than simply ignoring it, further intervention was unnecessary. His angry outbursts stopped shortly thereafter.

At times, a patient may feel uncomfortable about discussing his feelings with a specific caregiver or one from a particular discipline. At other times, the caregiver himself may feel unable to help the patient express his feelings. Caregivers should be attuned to this possibility and simply say, "You seem to have a lot of feelings. Is there someone with whom you'd feel more comfortable discussing them?" The patient may then say that it is his minister, a relative, or someone else with whom there is an ongoing relationship.

Fostering the expression of appropriate feelings may be accomplished by nonverbal as well as verbal behavior. Immediately after the death of a family member, the caregiver, recognizing that emotions may well be suppressed in a busy hospital corridor, might simply say to the family, "Perhaps you would like some time to be alone . . . There is a room down the hall you might use if you'd like." Thus members of the family are given the opportunity to have an appropriate place to deal with their feelings if they so desire. Sitting at the bedside of a patient rather than standing, similarly nonverbally communicates a willingness to listen.

Subjective Insight-oriented Interventions

These involve the caregiver's efforts to assist the dying patient, family members, and others in gaining insight into their feelings, thoughts, attitudes, and behaviors as they facilitate or impede adaptation. Through the process of self-scrutiny and gaining increased awareness, one is helped to understand his plight. The person may be helped to see how his increasing dependency leads to anger or encouraged to understand how his need for control is anxiety evoking in the face of a highly unpredictable situation. He may be encouraged to look at his reaction to loss and the damaged sense of body image or sexual identity. He may be helped to be accepting of a dependent state with the development of trust that the environment will meet his needs in the face of regression. He may be helped to consolidate his sense of identity in the face of losses and the sense of temporal constriction through the realistic evaluation of those options which continue to be available. What he wishes to become (the ego ideal) may be explored and attempts made to assist the individual in approaching this ideal to the extent possible.

An important intervention designed to assist the dying person manage loss and continue to feel a sense of intactness of the self involves helping him find a psychological prosthesis to repair his sense of loss.[8] While some patients find a psychological prosthesis on their own, assistance in this direction can be an effective therapeutic maneuver. Developing a psychological prosthesis involves utilizing creative activities or employing some tangible supportive element in the environment to replace symbolically or compensate for some of the sustained or anticipated losses during the process of living with a life-threatening illness. The person is called upon to rely on creative abilities, skills, or interests which were present prior to the onset of the illness or helped to develop new activites during the course of the illness. The following examples illustrate the use of this intervention.

A young woman with leukemia, prior to the debilitating stages of her illness, was gregarious and outgoing. Her high level of interpersonal involvement served to foster her sense of self-esteem, and she maintained this behavior during the earlier phases of her illness, busily visiting friends and relatives. As she became increasingly ill and finally bed-ridden, her interpersonal contact diminished sharply, her self-esteem fell, and she became increasingly depressed. She became interested in a citizen's band radio system, using this to facilitate and renew her high level of interpersonal involvement, and her depression diminished.

A middle-aged man with lymphoma whose life interests prior to the onset of his illness had been characterized by a love of nature and hiking in the woods was severely limited in these endeavors by anemia and shortness of breath associated with his illness. He had also enjoyed a sense of freedom and motility and was an avid horseback rider. Because his disease also led to a bleeding tendency, he was advised to give up the horseback riding for fear he might be thrown from the horse and develop serious bleeding difficulties. The loss of motility, sense of freedom, and gratification from the riding led to increased depression. He subsequently acquired a motor vehicle which had the capability of going through the woods and placing him in contact with unexplored places off conventional roads. The vehicle helped to restore his sense of loss and in essence served as a psychological prosthesis, symbolically compensating for his losses.

A young man with a far-advanced malignancy had throughout his life wanted to travel in Africa. When he recognized that this goal would be impossible to fulfill, he was encouraged instead to collect artifacts from that continent and also to begin a correspondence course in African art. Thus an attempt was made to assist him in fulfilling his wish to the extent possible in a manner compatible with the disability of his illness.

Even in the later stages of a life-threatening illness, a psychological prosthesis may compensate in some symbolic manner for the losses sustained. It may be a simple or more complex activity that enables the person to continue to experience a sense of aliveness and to deal with these losses.

Interactional and Relational Interventions

These interventions involve the caregiver's attempt to reduce the dying person's interpersonal conflict to a minimal level, thereby assuring maximal support and continuity of relationships with significant persons in the environment. Any number of interpersonal conflicts arise in the course of a dying patient's adaptation as a result of the reverberating interpersonal circuitry discussed in previous chapters. The presence of significant caring persons is a crucial part of maximizing the dying individual's sense of aliveness and continued participation in living activities.

Interpersonal conflict tends to drive people apart and to decrease the effectiveness of communication which may lead to its resolution. Facilitating communication is frequently the key to the effective resolution of interpersonal difficulties, but restoring it is often not enough. The caregiver must have a knowledge of the needs, concerns, perceptions, and responses of the dying person, his family, and other caregivers in order to effectively manage interpersonal conflicts as they arise.

Clarification of normal phenomena such as stage appropriate behavior associated with the dying process and death is often helpful in restoring interpersonal well being. At times, the caregiver might talk with the patient, the patient and other family members, or the family alone in an attempt to restore effective communication, explaining the disruptive interpersonal phenomena and dealing with the feelings driving the conflict and engendered by it. This may involve dealing with the patient's and the family's deeper feelings about dying and death in order to clarify and overcome the protec-

tiveness and avoidance present in the situation. At other times, the caregiver may find it necessary to assist with the modulation of the awareness related to the amount of information exchanged about the status of the person's illness. The following examples illustrate interactional interventions.

A woman with metastatic carcinoma of the breast who had recently undergone surgery made demands upon her husband which he considered excessive in terms of her degree of recuperation. He felt considerable resentment in being asked to constantly wait on her. Rather than assuming household duties as she continued to recover, she remained regressed, withdrawn, and demanding. In intervening in the resultant conflicts and increasing hostility, a caregiver talked with the couple to clarify realistic limitations of her illness but encouraged her to reassume activities compatible with her strengths. This led to the couple's defining together their expectations of one another and brought their communication to a more effective level.

A middle-aged man in the midst of a stage appropriate sadness about his illness withdrew from all social interaction and participation in pleasurable activities. His wife felt that he should "keep going, no matter what" and pushed him to resume his previous levels of activity. He became irritable and hostile with her and their relationship deteriorated. When it was explained to her that his sadness and grief were appropriate, she was able to assume a more supportive and understanding posture.

Interactional interventions should also be preventive and aimed toward averting interpersonal crisis. When an individual or family is dependent on the person who becomes ill, the caregiver may anticipate difficulties in the relationship. As the healthy party assumes a more independent position, the ill one becomes increasingly dependent and regressed. In such a case, providing increased support for the healthy person becomes an important means of averting a crisis.

One of the major means of validating a person's aliveness is through the presence of others and the continuation of meaningful relationships regardless of the stage of illness. The caregiver assures the viability of relationships which becomes increasingly important with the dying person's gradual sense of loss of self, lowered self-esteem, the sense of impending isolation, fears of abandonment, and the emerging awareness of death. Through the knowledge and sense of constancy in interpersonal relationships, the dying patient is enabled to experience an increased sense of meaning and hope.

An innovative intervention employed by a young student nurse in the care of her patient is notable in demonstrating an attempt to maintain a patient's desired level of interpersonal contact during the final stages of illness. A young woman with leukemia had markedly deteriorated physically, laying quietly in her hospital bed with oxygen administered by face mask. When her visitors entered her room, they were overwhelmed by her deteriorated appearance and would either leave immediately or feel so uncomfortable as to be totally unable to interact with her. Knowing that the person relied heavily on relationships for her continued sense of aliveness, the student nurse pinned a large "motto" button on her pillow which stated, "I'm Refreshingly Different." When visitors and others entered the room, they saw the button and it allowed them a starting point for conversation and interaction with the patient. Though seemingly a small gesture on the part of the student nurse, this act proved to be one of the most important parts of the patient's terminal care.

Social Context Interventions

Interventions of this type consist of efforts made to negotiate with and maximally utilize the social environment to aid in facilitating the adaptation of the patient and his family to dying and death. In this category of intervention, the caregiver asks such questions as: How might the social system better meet the needs of the patient and his family?; What support systems are available to facilitate adaptation?; At what points in the interface between the social system and the patient and his family might I effectively utilize my knowledge and skills to facilitate overall adaptation?; On what aspects of the social system do the patient and his family rely most heavily and how might these supports be effectively increased during the process of the patient's dying and death?; How might the social system provide for the needs of the survivors after death?

The answers to these questions will vary considerably depending upon the person's illness and its effects, his age, his vocation, his financial state, the family constellation, the health-care facility where care is pro-

vided, and the availability of support systems within a given community. Interventions include aiding the individual in maintaining vocational stability to the extent possible, securing financial aid, assisting with school adjustment or re-entry difficulties in the case of children, locating appropriate support facilities and organizations in the community, communicating with and effectively utilizing public nursing services, coordinating community agency assistance, facilitating the use of extended-care facilities for sick and elderly persons, and developing support systems for persons receiving care at great distances from their homes.

Social scientists have pointed out the relationship between societal values and attitudes and the management of dying and death within society.[9, 10] All too often, however, we fail to see an individual's and his family's adaptation to dying, death, and bereavement in terms of societal designations or in relation to the provisions made by society for assisting with the management of these life crises. "Safe conduct" for the dying person is a concept of care which should not only be applied to those who work in the social institution of medicine but also needs to be addressed by the society in which the individual lives.

The provision of adequate social services and societal resources for dying persons and their families and the coordination of these services and resources at the community level is generally lacking. To effectively care for the dying patient and his family, education and re-education along with the development and coordination of community services and resources will be required. The caregiver, however, should look closely at those points in the patient's adaptation where social context interventions may be effected with currently available resources, such as self-help organizations, public health services, and services provided by national and local disease-related organizations.

Physical Comfort Interventions

This category includes those efforts on the part of the caregiver aimed at maintaining the maximum sense of physical well-being in the dying patient. This category of interventions includes pain relief and the relief of other discomforting symptoms such as nausea and respiratory distress. Physical therapy to ensure maintenance or restoration of physical movement, the use of mechanical devices to assist in overcoming physical disabilities, the maintenance of comfortable physical surroundings, assuring privacy where it is desired, attention to the patient's body aimed at minimizing deterioration which would result in further discomfort, disfigurement, and change in body image, attention to cleanliness, maintenance of maximal physical appearance, attention to proper diet and cleanliness, maintenance of excretory functions, and proper instruction and care regarding the use and maintenance of devices (such as ileostomies and catheters) are among the physical comfort interventions necessary for the dying person.

Many of these interventions have important implications for the psychological and social needs of the patient and family members. In the terminal stages of illness, the level of responsiveness of the patient may be such that some of these interventions may seem unnecessary and even perfunctory in terms of the patient, but they continue to be of great importance to the family. For example, attention to cleanliness, particularly in regard to excretory functions, assures the family that the patient is continuing to be treated as a living human being.

The question is often raised whether a dying patient would be more comfortable in a hospital or a home care situation. As each setting has its advantages and disadvantages, the question must be resolved in dialogue with the patient and family. In making this determination, consideration should be given to the requirement of the medical situation, the desires of the patient and the family members, the emotional, physical, and mechanical support and comfort-providing facilities available in the home *versus* the institutional setting, and the ability of the family to adapt to and withstand the tremendous stresses of home care. While dying and the concomitant regression that occurs may be more comfortable in familiar surroundings, the physical and emotional strain placed on the family and its members may outweigh the advantages. Home care may be even more demanding, or even im-

possible, for the nuclear family who has little support from numerous family members. Complex medical regimens and the necessity of complicated means of administering medications and fluids may be difficult in a home setting. Physical movement of the patient may be a problem; and mechanical devices, such as lifting apparatus or electrically operated beds, may be necessary for maximal comfort, but unavailable. Thus while the institutional setting may have disadvantages in terms of the patient and his family's comfort, it may also provide services which are unavailable at home. Even when home care is embarked upon, a time may be reached when hospital care becomes a necessity, either to allow the employment of medical and comfort measures available only in the hospital or to provide the family some degree of relief from the taxing stresses of home care.

The development in England of a therapeutic community for the care of dying patients by Dr. Cicely Saunders represents an intriguing movement to address not only the physical comfort needs of the dying patient, but also a myriad of other needs of both the patient and his family.[11-14] The care facility is called a "Hospice," the term relating back to the Middle Ages when housing was made available for those crossing Europe en route to various pilgrimage sites. The concept also relates to the medieval hospitals which were along the pilgrims' routes and to the care facilities developed by the Irish Sisters of Charity.

According to Leigner, "The principal orientation at St. Christopher's [Hospice] is that the total care of the dying patient refers not only to the medical-symptomatic management, but, more importantly, to the concept that anything that produces distress or pain for the dying patient or the family is the concern of the Hospice. Hence, the total psychosocial impact of the dying patient is treated, including the psychic and social pain of the bereaved family up to and subsequent to the death of the patient."[14] The facility is designed for the comfort of the patient and family visitors; personal belongings are brought by the patient; liberal visiting hours are employed; and the privacy of the patient is given attention. "Polypharmacy," the use of adequate medications for pain relief and other symptoms, is employed by the staff of St. Christopher's Hospice ". . . to maintain an integrated functioning individual who is neither in pain, nor symptomatic in any other area and who, if able, is alert to his surroundings and to the people about." The event of death is managed with dignity and respect, and there is follow-up contact with the family to aid in individualized matters of bereavement.

Importantly, staff attitudes are a vital contribution to the effectiveness of the Hospice care of the dying patient and his family. The Hospice provides a setting which maintains a high standard of care for the terminally ill patient. Currently, there is movement toward establishing similar facilities in this country.[15]

Spiritual Interventions

The clergy and religious institutions have been involved in providing aspects of care for dying persons and their families long before others turned their attention to this area. For many, this important area of care assumes a central position in their adaptation to their dying and death; yet the clergy, who might be included more directly in the care process and provide substantial support for the individual and his family, often must perform their functions on the periphery of the medical care effort. Frequently, they are not provided with access to medical information and thus may be handicapped in providing maximal care for the patient and his family. If access to dialogue with primary physicians is lacking, they may be unable to provide those caregivers with important information they have obtained which might serve to facilitate adaptation in the dying process. A dying person or a family member may express his concerns and feelings in the language of his religious beliefs. When this occurs, the clergy may be able to bring these issues into the total care considerations, thereby providing a far broader perspective of the person's needs and concerns.

Often through traditional ties based on religious identity or based on years of association with the person and his family in the community, the clergyman is in a central position to assist the patient and his family

in coping with illness and death. Traditionally, the clergyman has participated in assisting the family in the mourning process after death and in many cases is the one individual who provides continuity by virtue of long-standing relationships before and after a family member's death. Also, many clergy possess skills in counseling in addition to their abilities to deal with theological and spiritual issues. All caregivers, regardless of personal religious convictions, should be attuned to the needs of their patients in this area; and when the patient and his family are desirous of this care, facilitate the clergy's approximation with the total care process.

Quality of Life Interventions

In working with dying patients and their families, increasing attention is being given to issues related to the quality of life. These issues encompass a wide variety of considerations, including ethical issues, the continued productivity and creativity of the dying person, the general level of the person's ability to continue to participate in the living activities of his environment, patient rights, and matters connected with the participation of the patient and his family in the formulation and implementation of treatment plans.

Outcome of treatment may be appraised not only by considering the effect of treatment on the disease process, but also by evaluating the quality of life after treatment. In this regard, Patterson lists a number of components involved in appraising the "quality" of clinical response to treatment. They include "(1) health, the prospect of cure *vs.* failure; (2) function, the ability to work and the quality of performance; (3) comfort, the freedom from pain and the limitations to activity; (4) emotional response, self-acceptance, anxiety about the future, and social adjustment; and (5) economics, the impact of costs and earning capacity."[16] He suggests that subjective as well as objective response should enter into the assessment of overall response if the quality of survival is to be given importance.

Literature, debate, and studies* related to patient rights, medical ethics and euthan-

---

* For additional material on bioethics, the reader is referred to *The Hastings Center Report*, published as a periodical by The Institute of Society, Ethics and the Life Sciences, Hastings-on-Hudson, New York.

asia should be reviewed by the caregiver interested in working in this area.[17-31] Quality of life considerations cannot be viewed as the province of the medical profession alone, for these issues are intimately intertwined with theology, ethics, philosophy, law, and other disciplines. They also develop out of the ongoing transactions between the medical profession and the society at large. Importantly, they often involve matters which are highly subjective and individualized in that the patient's and his family's concepts of quality of life can only be determined through an ongoing dialogue between the caregivers and the patient and his family. Establishing a dialogue aimed at arriving at what constitutes quality of life for an individual is often more effective than the attempt to establish definite criteria which may be applied to every patient regardless of his wishes.

The increasing desire of individuals to participate in determinations regarding their treatment and considerations of "quality of life" is illustrated by the text of the "Living Will," a document prepared by the Euthanasia Educational Council, which expresses the wishes of a person in relation to his treatment during the terminal stages of his dying:

To my Family, my Physician, my Lawyer, my Clergyman:
To any Medical Facility in Whose Care I Happen to Be:
To any Individual Who May Become Responsible for my Health, Welfare or Affairs:
 . . . If the time comes when I, _____, can no longer take part in decisions for my own future, let this statement stand as an expression of my wishes, while I am still of sound mind.
If the situation should arise in which there is no reasonable expectation of my recovery from physical or mental disability, I request that I be allowed to die and not be kept alive by artificial means or "heroic measures". I do not fear death itself as much as the indignities of deterioration, dependence and hopeless pain. I, therefore, ask that medication be mercifully administered to me to alleviate suffering even though this may hasten the moment of death.
This request is made after careful consideration. I hope you who care for me will feel morally bound to follow its mandate. I recognize that this appears to place a heavy responsibility upon you, but it is with the intention of relieving you of such responsibility and of placing it upon myself in accordance with my strong convictions, that this statement is made.[32]

The caregiver engages in quality of life interventions when he considers these issues and establishes a dialogue with the patient and his family which permits the open exchange of views on the subject. Resolution and closure related to these considerations may be difficult or even impossible to achieve, but in many cases they are a vital aspect of care.

Process of Care Interventions

These interventions represent efforts on the part of caregivers to insure that the overall caregiving milieu provides maximal utilization of discipline-related skills, knowledge, and attitudes, to facilitate adaptation and to manage interactional matters in a manner conducive to the provision of the highest levels of therapeutic care. Attention to the non-human environment (those aspects of the caregiving milieu such as the physical setting, medical technology, administrative protocol, and procedural matters) also falls into this category.

Communication among caregivers must be facilitated and conflicts stemming from traditional hierarchy and role stereotypes managed as part of the interactional component of patient care. This requires ongoing scrutiny of interactions in the caregiving milieu and rapid management of disruption. Discussions and decisions as to which caregivers may best meet the needs of a person and his family at any one time in their care is an ongoing process. As these decisions are reached, the way must be cleared for the caregivers to have access to the patient, and they must be provided with categories of information required to carry out their interventions effectively. Mutual support for caregivers to ensure that they are encouraged and psychologically able to remain approximated with the patient and his family must be provided by other caregivers working in the setting.

If the care process becomes excessively disrupted, consultation with a mental health professional outside of the group intimately involved in care may be helpful in assisting with problems which arise in the interaction in the caregiving milieu. The person may be asked to participate as an objective observer of the interactions involved in the process of care. Utilizing knowledge of group process, the consultant may help to restore a level of adaptation and facilitate the overcoming of a disrupted interpersonal, nontherapeutic environment.

In teaching institutions, where there is rapid turnover of personnel due to the requirements imposed by changing rotations of students and housestaff, the issue of continuity of care becomes an important consideration. Therapeutic relationships are formed only to end as the student or trainee moves on to another position. The same is true outside of teaching institutions when longstanding relationships with family physicians and familiar medical care surroundings are disrupted by the necessary referral of the patient to other more specialized treatment facilities. In-depth communication with those persons who will assume the care of the patient, along with management of the individual's feelings and thoughts related to the transition, represent important efforts to facilitate adaptation to the encroachments on continuity. Revisiting the patient and his family after transfer or making rounds with the person to whom care is transferred is an effective means of communicating the intention to provide continuity. These transitions are not only stress-producing for the patient and his family, but they may also be difficult for caregivers who must deal with the loss of a significant relationship in which they have had considerable investment. The following example is illustrative:

A young woman with Hodgkins' disease became agitated, anxious, and depressed first when an intern who had been involved in her medical care completed his rotation on her ward and was transferred to another service, and again when the same circumstances occurred with a student nurse assigned to her care. Arrangements were made whereby both of these trainees could continue to participate in her care at a limited, but effective, level. When she learned that she would continue to have contact with these caregivers, her mental state improved significantly. These trainees perceptively recognized the need for this arrangement from the patient's point of view and their own.

A thorough knowledge of the psychosocial effects of the non-human environment on the patient's adaptation is important in providing effective care. Specialized units, procedures which require isolation or long periods of waiting, machinery used for survival, the physical arrangement of the care setting, necessary conformity to hospital and clinic routine, compliance with administrative protocol, and long delays in waiting rooms with patients in varying stages of relative distress, while necessary, may contribute substantially to the problems in adaptation of the patient and his family.

Delirium may be precipitated by the sensory deprivation involved in isolation techniques or by the patient's being placed in a totally strange surrounding with unfamiliar persons. This is particularly likely to occur in the elderly or in individuals whose perception is already compromised by disease. In some isolation techniques caregivers and others wear face masks and gowns as precautionary measures. While such measures are often imperative, they diminish interpersonal contact by reducing the communication which occurs through nonverbal behaviors such as facial expressions.

Simple therapeutic efforts to avoid the development of delirium may be employed. A television set or radio, a soft light on at night, and the continuation of an adequate amount of comforting interpersonal contact to provide orientation stimuli may serve to prevent the development of disorientation, confusion, agitation, and fear. Clear and explicit explanations about procedure and administrative protocol are also helpful in overcoming the patient's anxiety-producing fantasies.

Knowing when to provide education and information for the patient and his family is still another important aspect of facilitating the process of care. Left to his own devices, a patient or family member will often turn to literature sources which are out of date or inaccurate in his particular case or listen to nonprofessional persons who may give incorrect information. In the desperate search for certainty, this information often becomes an entrenched part of the individual's response to his illness. The caregiver then, throughout the process of care, should not only attempt to anticipate those questions which might arise, but should repeatedly inquire as to whether or not the patient or his family has questions regarding the illness. When the question is unanswerable, patients are often far better able to accept a statement such as, "We don't really have an answer to that question just now," than they are able to accept evasiveness or answers which are only attempts to make certain that which is obviously uncertain.

Interventions for Recognized States of Emotional Dysfunction

During the process of dying and death, individuals may manifest psychological difficulties which reach the proportions of dysfunctional emotional states requiring more active intervention. At times emotional reactions may reach levels which impair the individual's ability to function or become so disruptive to the interpersonal environment as to require management as an established emotional disorder.

Some individuals may show levels of depression which reach the proportions of intense, prolonged, and severe reactions, severely compromising the person's ability to function effectively. These depressive states are more disabling and disruptive than the depressive responses one would expect to encounter during the person's adaptation to his illness. The usual signs and symptoms of depression may be present, including feelings of sustained sadness and despair, withdrawal from pleasurable activities, loss of appetite, insomnia, loss of sexual interest, and, at times, suicidal ideation. While some depression may respond to the person's talking about the losses incurred in his life circumstances, sustained and profound levels of these symptoms require more active treatment. In such cases, psychiatric consultation may become necessary. The following brief history illustrates such a case.

A patient with an advanced malignant illness developed severe depression characterized by sustained and deep sadness, loss of appetite, and weight loss far in excess of that which would be expected in her illness. She had severe insomnia with early morning awakening, became disinterested in keeping up her physical appearance, lost all sexual interest, and expressed self-destructive ideation. In the course of a psychiatric evaluation, she expressed feelings of worthlessness related to her debilitated state and her compromised ability to interact with her children as she desired. She felt she was no longer a good mother and had fantasies that her children would be taken away from her and placed in a foster home. Because of physical changes related to her illness, she also felt that she was no longer attractive or sexually pleasing and feared that her husband would search out the company of other women to replace her. At night, she ruminated about her feelings and concerns and had great difficulty falling asleep. During one session, she reported a dream in which her husband and another woman were in church singing hymns at a funeral service. While she had milder depressive episodes earlier in the course of her illness, this deep depression began shortly after the death of a person in the community who died of a similar disease.

Her fears of being a "good mother and wife" related back to conflicts present long before the onset of her illness. She had always seen her own mother as an "ideal" person and felt that she had never lived up to this standard. As a child, she also felt that her father would love her only if she were "perfect." She thus maintained intense perfectionistic strivings and always attempted to please others, feeling "unloved" when she was unable to accomplish this in every relationship. Therapy involved not only dealing with the conflicts and feelings related to her illness, but also involved deeper exploration of earlier conflicts. On two occasions, she and her husband were seen together. During these sessions, he reassured her that he was devoted to her regardless of whether she was ill or not. As she came to grips with her limitations and gained insights into her conflicts, she improved significantly, recognizing that she could be loved and cared for without being "perfect" and always pleasing others. When her depression diminished, she was able to do more for her children than she had been able to do in her saddened state and began to again enjoy being with her husband and children even with the limitations imposed by her illness.

Self-destructive ideation or behavior may occur in the context of a life-threatening illness. As with any person, this ideation or intent is a sign of intense emotional unrest. Although there are few studies in this area, it appears likely that the stressful factors involved in adapting to a life-threatening illness may increase the likelihood of suicidal behavior. Abram, for example, has found that the risk for suicide among patients in chronic renal dialysis programs exceeds that of the general population, and that suicides occur at a rate approximately 200 times greater than that of the general population.[33] Another study suggests that suicidal risk is higher in patients with certain personality traits, such as those who are excessively demanding, show strong needs for attention and reassurance, and have a strong need to maintain control and direct their situation.[34] A dying person strongly feels the loss of control, feeling controlled instead by his disease or other individuals in his environment. In such circumstances self-destructive behavior may be viewed as a means of regaining control over his life (or death), symbolically wresting control away from the disease process and those involved in his care.

The expression of self-destructive intent by the dying patient also has important interpersonal implications, for the mere expression of such intent evokes the response of increased interpersonal contact on the part of the environment. The expression of suicidal ideation or intent must be evaluated in terms of the risk involved and the motivations driving the ideation or behavior. The maintenance of the desired level of interpersonal contact is a vital part of preventing self-destructive behavior, for hopelessness and lowered self-esteem in dying persons is often closely related to the level of perceived interpersonal disruption and the sense of abandonment and isolation.

Severe anxiety states often develop as a salient feature of a person's response to a life-threatening illness. Through interviews and discussions an attempt should be made to determine what preoccupations and conflicts are giving rise to the anxiety in order to aid the individual in coping more effectively. At times, minor tranquilizers in adequate dosages are useful in helping a patient through a particularly trying phase of his illness. Pharmacological agents may be effective in reducing the level of anxiety to a point where the individual can employ his usual coping mechanisms. Minor tranquilizers may be prescribed on a regular dosage schedule. However, their use on an "as necessary" basis with prescribed minimal time intervals between doses and dosages, not to exceed a specified amount per day, may be useful diagnostically. Prescribed in this manner, one can inquire as to when the medication was used and determine the association of the anxiety with certain thoughts, events in the person's daily life, or types of interactions which are stressful. When these connections are established, they may then be discussed in more depth to try to clarify the causes of stress and anxiety. Because patients with life-threatening illnesses may be on numerous medications or have varying physical problems associated with their illness, careful considerations should be given to side-effects and drug interactions which may cause difficulties when prescribing psychotrophic drugs.

Psychotic reactions with gross distortions of reality or severe impairment of mental faculties may also occur in association with a life-threatening illness, particularly when the disease is complicated by compromised brain function. When such reactions occur they are often associated with multiple etiological factors including the psychological stresses of the disease process, interpersonal disruption, or impaired mentation. The evaluation and treatment of these disorders must take the possibility of multiple causative factors into consideration. The following case example illustrates the multiple factors involved in one case.

A highly mobile and independent man with a malignant illness developed brain metastasis which resulted in paralysis of his legs. His motility became markedly impaired and he was confined to a wheelchair. Having been highly independent and always in control of his life circumstances, he now perceived others as "controlling his life." Subsequently he began to accuse his wife of trying to kill him by giving him too much medicine and became highly suspicious of all persons in the household, feeling that they were plotting ways to harm him or force him into total submission. He developed outbursts of intense anger which occurred without provocation. As his disease progressed, he became increasingly confused and disoriented and began to hear persons "talking about him" when no one was present. The patient was treated with small dosages of antipsychotic medications in order to control the psychotic symptoms. The family was encouraged to include him in planning activities of the household so as to increase his sense of control and participation. His wife also became involved in counseling to assist her in coping with the behavior.

Psychiatric consultation is indicated in the treatment of some dying patients when anxiety or depression is incapacitating, suicidal ideation or intent is expressed, or a psychotic reaction occurs. When pre-existing conflicts are markedly increased in the context of a life-threatening illness or when personality traits lead to exceptionally disruptive behavior, consultation or treatment may be helpful in averting the occurrence of insoluble interpersonal conflict. A psychiatrist may also be helpful in dealing with distorted or delayed grief reactions characterized by extreme and prolonged interpersonal withdrawal, excessive and unresolved identification with the lost person, and bizarre variations of grief in which the individual presents a psychotic variation of the grief response. A psychiatric consultation should not be used to avoid interaction with the dying patient and his family or as a substitute for the development of a collaborative and cooperative approach to care.[8]

A psychiatric consultation was received which read, "Please inform these parents and their four-year-old child that he is to have his leg amputated for the treatment of a malignant bone lesion." In talking with the physician who had requested the consultation, it was apparent that he was experiencing overwhelming feelings about the situation and was using the consultation to assist with his reaction to the situation. In this case, it first became necessary to help the referring physician deal with his own feelings and evolve a means whereby he could feel more comfortable in talking with the parents and the child.

Postvention

Shneidman uses this term which encompasses ". . . those activities that serve to reduce the aftereffects of a traumatic event in the lives of the survivors. Its purpose is to help survivors live longer, more productively, and less stressfully than they are likely to do otherwise."[35] Professionals, busily involved in the ongoing care of patients, are likely to view the death of the individual as a signal for the ending of their efforts. While Chapter 8 is devoted specifically to the problems and issues associated with grief and bereavement, the subject of postvention is mentioned here as much of the groundwork for the caregivers' efforts after death are potentially laid down in the period of time when care is provided prior to death. For example, the intervention of legitimizing grief before death is an important aspect

of postvention. The need for caregivers to provide continuing services for the survivors following the death of a person is becoming increasingly apparent as there is the potential for considerable mental and physical morbidity during this time.[36] This need is still another reminder that caring for the dying person and his family is a process extending over time.

Meaning-oriented Interventions

Meaning has been defined as the structure of a sense of aliveness. It is found in those activities which enable the unique individual, while in the moment of approximation with the threat of his death, to continue to experience himself as being alive. Meaning interventions encompass all of the activities of the caregiver included in his caring, as this activity itself is an affirmation of the person as a living individual even when dying. When the caregiver is no longer able to remain approximated with the dying person, the potential for meaning and the sense of aliveness is reduced. In this state, the despair connected with death awareness, the sense of being more dead than alive, overwhelms the sense of being alive and participating in life as a living human being. Because of the diverse constellations of activities in which any one person finds meaning, the most important intervention in which the caregiver can involve himself is to maintain a form of flexibility in his caring which maximizes the individual's activities in the most meaningful direction. This then becomes the most vital and hopeful aspect of the caring process.

REFERENCES

1. Eissler KR: *The Psychiatrist and the Dying Patient.* First Paperback Ed. International Universities Press, New York, 1969
2. Norton J: Treatment of a Dying Patient. *Psychoanal Study Child 18:*541–560, 1963
3. Kübler-Ross E: *On Death and Dying.* Macmillan, London, 1969
4. Kübler-Ross E: "Psychotherapy for the Dying Patient," in *Current Psychiatric Therapies,* Vol. 10, Masserman JH (Ed.) Grune and Stratton, New York, 1970
5. Weisman AD: "Psychosocial Considerations in Terminal Care," in *Psychosocial Aspects of Terminal Care,* Schoenberg B, Carr AC, Peretz D, Kutscher AH (Eds) Columbia University Press, New York, 1972

6. Weisman AD: "Thanatology," in *The Comprehensive Textbook of Psychiatry,* 2nd Ed, Vol. II, Freedman AM, Kaplan HI, Sadock BJ (Eds) The Williams & Wilkins Co, Baltimore, 1975

7. Barton D: The Dying Patient: Intimations of Your Own Mortality. *Med Dimen 2:*14–15, 20, 1973

8. Barton D: "The Dying Patient," in *Psychiatry for the Primary Care Physician,* Abram HS, (Ed) Little, Brown and Company, Boston, 1976

9. Fulton R, Geis G: "Death and Social Values," in *Death and Identity,* Fulton R (Ed) John Wiley and Sons, Inc., New York, 1965

10. Parsons T, Lidz V: "Death in American Society," in *Essays in Self-Destruction*, Shneidman ES (Ed) Science House, Inc., New York, 1967

11. Saunders C: "St. Christopher's Hospice," in *Death: Current Perspectives,* Shneidman ES (Ed) Mayfield Publishing Company, Palo Alto, California, 1976

12. Saunders C: "A Therapeutic Community: St. Christopher's Hospice," in *Psychosocial Aspects of Terminal Care,* Schoenberg B, Carr AC, Peretz D, Kutscher AH (Eds) Columbia University Press, New York, 1972

13. Ingles T: St. Christopher's Hospice. *Nurs Outlook 22:*759–763, 1974

14. Liegner LM: St. Christopher's Hospice, 1974: Care of the Dying Patient. *JAMA 234:*1047–1048, © 1975, American Medical Association

15. Kron J: Designing a Better Place to Die. *New York Magazine 9:*43–49, March 1, 1976

16. Patterson WB: The Quality of Survival in Response to Treatment. *JAMA 233:*280–281, © 1975, American Medical Association

17. Annas GJ: *The Rights of Hospital Patients: The Basic American Civil Liberties Union (ACLU) Guide to a Hospital Patient's Rights.* Avon Books, New York, 1975

18. Proceedings of The American Cancer Society's National Conference on Human Values and Cancer, Atlanta, Georgia, June 22–24, 1972. American Cancer Society, Inc., 1973

19. Ramsey P: *The Patient as Person: Explorations in Medical Ethics.* Yale University Press, New Haven, Connecticut, 1970

20. *The Dilemmas of Euthanasia.* Behnke JA, Bok S (Eds) Anchor Press/Doubleday Anchor Books Ed., Garden City, New York, 1975

21. *The Right to Die: Decision and Decision Makers,* Vol. VIII, Symposium No. 12. Group for the Advancement of Psychiatry, New York, 1973

22. McCormick RA: To Save or Let Die: The Dilemma of Modern Medicine. *JAMA 229:*172–176, 1974

23. Travis TA, Noyes R Jr, Brightwell DR: The Attitudes of Physicians Toward Prolonging Life. *Inter J Psychiat Med 5:*17–26, 1974

24. Brown NK, Bulger RJ, Laws EH, Thompson DJ: The Preservation of Life. *JAMA 211:*76–82, 1970

25. Laws EH, Bulger RJ, Boyce TR, Thompson DJ, Brown NK: Views on Euthanasia. *J Med Ed 46:*540–542, 1971

26. Brown NK, Thompson DJ, Bulger RJ, Laws EH: How Do Nurses Feel About Euthanasia and Abortion? *Amer J Nurs 71:*1413–1416, 1971

27. Dilemmas of Euthanasia: Excerpts from Papers and Discussion at the Fourth Euthanasia Conference, New York Academy of Medicine, December 4, 1971. The Euthanasia Educational Council, Inc., New York, 1971

28. Euthanasia, Rights and Realities: Excerpts from Papers and Discussion at the Fifth Euthanasia Conference, New York Academy of Medicine, December 2, 1972. The Euthanasia Educational Council, New York, 1972

29. Gustafson JM: Mongolism, Parental Desires, and the Right to Life. *Pers Biol Med* pp 529–557, Summer 1973

30. The Right to Die With Dignity: A Discussion of the Medical, Legal, Social and Ethical Aspects of Euthanasia. Fourth Printing. The Euthanasia Educational Council, New York, 1974

31. Fletcher J: *Situation Ethics: The New Morality.* Westminster Press, Philadelphia, 1966

32. A Living Will. Euthanasia Educational Council, New York

33. Abram HS, Moore GL, Westervelt FB, Jr: Suicidal Behavior in Chronic Dialysis Patients. *Amer J Psychiat 127:*119–124, 1971

34. Farberow NL, Shneidman ES, Leonard C: Suicide Among General Medical and Surgical Hospital Patients with Malignant Neoplasms. *Medical Bulletin MB-9,* Department of Medicine and Surgery, Veterans Administration, Washington, D.C., February 25, 1963.

35. Shneidman ES: *Deaths of Man.* Penguin Books, Inc., Baltimore, 1974

36. Parkes CM: *Bereavement: Studies of Grief in Adult Life.* International Universities Press, Inc., New York, 1972

8

THE PROCESS OF GRIEF

David Barton, M.D.

The grieving process is a normal and universal reaction to loss inherent in being human. While its manifestations differ from person to person, from family to family, and in differing social and cultural contexts, the process of grieving is a necessary part of the reaction to all levels of loss, including death. Through the process of grieving, a person comes to recognize the finality of the loss and psychologically and socially integrates the thoughts, feelings, and behaviors related to the loss. Gradually, the person comes to continue living with a sense of meaning, personal significance, aliveness, and participation in the living community. When the process of grief is accomplished effectively, the survivor is able to disengage from the lost person and reinvest in other activities and people. The extent to which this disengagement and reinvestment is accomplished is relative rather than absolute, for the impact of one person's life on another, the sense of loss created, and the recollections of the relationship continue at some level in the survivors' existence. The entire course of the grief process does not possess the painful qualities which immediately surround the loss. However, dependent on factors such as the effectiveness of the grief process and the relationship between the survivor and the lost person, the sense of loss is likely to continue at some level indefinitely.

The manifestations of grief are likely to be highly variable and individualized dependent on the characteristics of the survivor, the lost relationship, the survivor's social environment, and the culture in which he lives. This assumes major importance in the consideraion of what is normal or abnormal grief. It precludes a view of the grief process as one which in any particular individual will follow a definitely prescribed course. A person's grief does not conform to a certain time frame, nor is its expression limited to definite thoughts, feelings, and behaviors. One cannot establish a definite level of disengagement from the lost person for the survivor. In the process of grieving there are, however, certain phenomena which are likely to achieve expression in most people. But it is the manner in which these phenomena are expressed and managed along with their effect on the person's changing intrapersonal, interpersonal, sociocultural, and meaning needs that determines the ultimate adaptive or maladaptive quality of the outcome of the grief process.

Grieving is not confined to those persons who are directly related to the dying person, though it is most apparent in those persons. The dying person grieves, family members grieve, friends grieve, caregivers grieve, and in some cases communities and the society at large grieve. Perceived differences in these persons relate to determinants such as the intensity and qualities of the relationship with the lost person, the level at which grief is communicated or is visible, the legitimization of the expression of feelings in the interpersonal context, the manner in which a specific person or group grieves, and the time period prior to death available for preparatory grief. Also, social, cultural, and religious mores dictating appropriate expression and circumstances in which grief is allowed, encouraged or discouraged, bear heavily on the visibility of the grief process in those experiencing the loss.

Grief occurs not only after the loss of the person. It also occurs in preparation for and with the anticipation of loss. The process begins when there is recognition of the potential loss of some part of a person such as a valued aspect of the relationship. It intensifies as recognition of the potential loss of the total person is approached. Grief which occurs prior to or in preparation for the loss is referred to as preparatory or anticipatory grief.[1, 2] Anticipatory grief is experienced by the dying person, the family, and in many cases, caregivers. While grief is necessarily anticipatory in the dying person, for the survivor it begins as preparatory and extends into the period of time after the loss.

Grieving occurs not only in response to the anticipation or recognition of the total and final losses related to death. Grief also occurs in response to partial losses and significant changes—the "partial deaths" or "psychosocial transitions" which occur along the course of an illness.[3-5] The term "psychosocial transitions" is used by Parkes to designate a type of relatively rapid change such as one in which " . . . a person is forced by illness or accident, to give up one view of his world and himself in it and replace it with another."[4, 5] The dying person grieves not only in response to the anticipated loss of his total self, but also in reaction to the loss of parts of this total self and the rearrangement of his world. He may grieve the loss of valued aspects of his relationships with others, such as his ability to continue his usual style of relating in the family setting. He may grieve the loss or change of a body part brought about by surgical removal or the disease process itself. He may grieve in response to changes in his body image or the loss of physical and mental abilities resulting from deterioration.

The family and others associated with the dying person respond in a similar manner. Each perceived loss or sign of potential loss along the course of the illness is in effect a prelude and reminder of the person's impending death and precipitates feelings of loss and grief. They, too, respond to the loss of parts of the person such as gradual physical or mental deterioration or the loss of valued aspects of the relationship. Each anticipated or perceived loss along the course of the person's dying accentuates the sense of grief related to the anticipation of the person's death. The family may, for example, have difficulty looking at the person when physical deterioration is significantly advanced. Removal of a cherished person from the home for the purpose of hospitalization is often experienced as loss accompanied by grief. As a disease progresses, the reduction of the potential for interaction leads to a perception of loss and in turn, grief. Grief, then, occurs not only in reaction to death itself but, in a broader sense, is a response to transience and change—to the awareness that what was is not to be or actually is no more.

THE PHENOMENA OF GRIEF

While the phenomena associated with grief are numerous and variable, a number of writers have made significant contributions in describing these phenomena. Lindemann, who derived his observations from interviews with 101 patients who had suffered losses, described acute grief as a definite syndrome characterized by psychological and somatic symptoms. Lindemann pointed out that after a loss the grief syndrome may appear immediately or be delayed. The grief syndrome may be exaggerated or absent, or may appear in distorted forms. Appropriate methods may be utilized to transform the distorted variants of grief into more normal grief reactions which may then move toward resolution.[1] Lindemann found the symptoms shown by those acutely grieving persons he studied to be "remarkably uniform," but it is important in this regard to point out that Lindemann's classic paper was primarily descriptive and concerned with the *symptoms* and *signs* of the phenomena of grief. It did not describe the multitude of ways in which these signs and symptoms might be manifested in any one particular individual or in varying interpersonal and cultural settings.

Lindemann's description of the symptomatology of acute grief included: (1) Sensations of somatic distress that occur in waves, including respiratory distress such as sighing respirations, lack of strength, exhaustion, digestive symptoms and appetite disturbance, and an intense subjective type of distress referred to as "tension or mental pain." The waves of somatic discomfort are precipitated by various reminders of the lost person such as references to the dead person or the expression of sympathy by others. (2) A mild sense of unreality, a sense of emotional distance from others and marked absorption in images of the lost person. (3) Guilt feelings and obsessional searching related to the time before death in an attempt to discover evidence of failure and wrongdoing in relationship to the lost person—the survivor's engaging in many forms of self-blame. (4) A sense of a loss of warmth in relationships and a tendency to be irritable, angry, with the wish not to be bothered by others. (5) A sense of loss or significant changes in established life patterns, characterized by responses such as restlessness, continual searching for something to do, and an inability to sit still. There is a feeling of being unable to begin and maintain organized routines of activity, a lack of zest, a sense of merely going through the motions of living, and a sense of having to exert great effort to maintain and carry on life activities which previously were done more automatically. Each part of an activity requires great effort and appears to be a formidable task. The bereaved person finds that a large part of his customary life activities were done in some meaningful association with the deceased person and they now seem insignificant without him. Social interaction seems particularly difficult.

In addition to these five areas which Lindemann described as characteristic of grief, another manifestation was noted in persons having more significant difficulty with the grief process. This phenomenon is " . . . the appearance of traits of the deceased in the behavior of the bereaved, especially symptoms shown during the last illness, or behavior which may have been shown at the time of the tragedy." This phenomenon is indeed frequently observed in grieving individuals. It may be blatantly obvious, as in a patient who developed headaches for which no or-

ganic etiology could be determined, after her mother died from a stroke. During the final days of her illness, the grieving person's mother continually complained of severe headache. Another patient persistently complained of a "lump in her throat" after her daughter's death. During the terminal phase of her illness, the daughter had developed an intracranial hemorrhage which resulted in a paralysis of the muscles in her throat involved in swallowing. At other times it may be more subtle, as in the case of a person who inappropriately fancied himself a knowledgeable person in business matters after the death of his father, a successful businessman. Still another subtle form of this phenomenon was seen in a man who began to express his anger in a smiling, caustic, and sarcastic manner which had been the characteristic manner of expression of anger by his dead wife.

Using systematic interviews, Clayton et al. interviewed 40 survivors 2 to 26 days after the deaths of relatives. Twenty-seven of these 40 persons were again interviewed one to four months after the death. It was found that three symptoms, depressed mood, sleep disturbance, and crying, occurred in more than half of the subjects. Other symptoms, including difficulty in concentrating, loss of interest in television and news, and anorexia and/or weight loss occurred frequently but in less than half of the persons interviewed. In their follow-up interviews, 81% of these persons were improved and 4% were worse. The improved subjects noted their improvement to have occurred six to ten weeks after the death.[6] In a later study of 109 widows and widowers Clayton et al. again confirmed crying, depressed mood, and sleep disturbance as the cardinal symptoms of the bereavement period.[7] Another study related to these patients demonstrated that 35% of the widows and widowers manifested a collection of depressive symptoms not unlike those seen in psychiatrically depressed patients.[8]

Parkes lists seven features common to many bereavement reactions. These are:

"1. A process of realization, i.e., the way in which the bereaved person moves from denial or avoidance of recognition of the loss toward acceptance.

2. An alarm reaction—anxiety, restless-

ness, and the psychological accompaniments of fear.

3. An urge to search for and to find the lost person in some form.

4. Anger and guilt, including outbursts directed against those who press the bereaved person toward premature acceptance of his loss.

5. Feelings of internal loss of self or mutilation.

6. Identification phenomena — the adoption of traits, mannerisms, or symptoms of the lost person, with or without a sense of his presence within the self.

7. Pathological variants of grief, *i.e.,* the reaction may be excessive and prolonged or inhibited and inclined to emerge in distorted form."[9]

Of considerable importance in considerations related to the phenomena of grief is the anniversary reaction. On or about the time which marks or is associated with the loss, an individual may experience a reawakening of the responses associated with the original loss. The anniversary reaction is an example of the tendency of certain individuals to react to symbolic links with the original loss. For example, on the anniversary of his father's death, a young man experienced considerable anxiety and chest pain. His father had died one year previously, from a heart attack. No organic cause could be demonstrated to account for the son's chest pain and it was only after a number of interviews that he was able to associate his mental state and the "pain" with the reminder of his father's death brought about by the anniversary. When this occurred he became aware of considerable sadness and grief. In some circumstances, the anniversary reaction may be a more intense reaction than that associated with the original loss. Similarly, a later loss may precipitate the grief process associated with an earlier loss, the original grief process having been suppressed, dampened, or delayed. In one such case, a woman experienced little grief when her daughter died because of her own tendency to suppress her feelings and the nonacceptance of her feelings by her family. Some months later when a young relative was killed in an automobile accident, she began to experience the full impact of the feelings associated with her daughter's death. While she had less association with the relative, the similarity in age and the knowledge that the daughter had been close to the relative provided a link which precipitated her grief about the loss of her daughter. A renewed grief experience may occur not only in reaction to a temporal connection, but also in response to life happenings or combinations of circumstances which serve to remind the survivor of the loss. For instance, visiting the same hospital where the person died may serve to renew feelings of grief.

Clearly there are any number of symptoms, signs, and reactions seen in the grief process. The precise manner in which these phenomena are manifested will demonstrate considerable variation, but their painfulness is an apparent part of the response to loss. Depressed mood, sleep problems, weeping, anger, longing for the lost person, guilt over perceived omissions, disruption of interpersonal relationships, loss of interest in life activities, restlessness, preoccupation with imagery related to the lost person, fatigue and exhaustion, varying levels of recognition and acceptance of the loss, a sense of disordered life circumstances, and feeling of emptiness are among the phenomena likely to be seen in the grieving person. These symptoms appear also to have a wave-like quality and may not be present constantly. This wave-like quality and the sudden emergence of the phenomena, sometimes without clear explanation, appear to be characteristic of the grief process. Often, however, the occurrence of the phenomena is associated with a symbolic reminder of the original loss.

GRIEF: THEORY AND FORMULATIONS

A number of psychoanalytic formulations have been advanced to clarify and conceptualize the psychological phenomena associated with grief and mourning. Generally, in psychoanalytic thought, the process of mourning is viewed as a series of mental operations through which the bereaved person gradually loosens the ties with the lost person, accepts the loss, and reinvests in the living world as it exists in the absence of the person.[10-12] According to Fenichel. "The tie to the lost object [dead person] is represented by hundreds of separate memories; for each of these memories the dissolution of the tie is carried through separately and this takes time."[11] This process was designated by Freud as the "work of mourning."[10, 11] To control the overwhelming flood of painful feelings stirred by the loss, the survivor tends to attempt to maintain the many memories of the person, and even to maintain the illusion that the person still lives by creating within the mental apparatus representations of the lost person. This later phenomenon occurs through various internalization processes such as introjection and identification. The survivor in essence creates substitute representations of memories linked to the lost person within the psychic apparatus through the processes of introjection and identification. A delaying of the impact of the loss is thus brought about through the maintenance of psychological representations of the deceased person within the mourner. Once the representations of the individual are incorporated in the survivor's mental apparatus, the attachments to the incorporated memories and identifications are gradually loosened through the process of mourning and the investments in the internalized representations of the lost person are withdrawn. They then are again available for relationships and activities outside of the person.

During this process, the survivor had and has a number of feelings about the person, and these feelings now are aimed toward the internalized representations of the lost person. Mourning becomes complicated when the relationship of the survivor to the lost person was a highly ambivalent one — that is, there were feelings of both love and hate for the deceased individual. In this case, feelings of both love and hate would be aimed toward the person in his psychologically internalized form. The internalized representations of the lost person are invested with the same feelings associated with him in life, along with the feelings of anger at being abandoned associated with the person's death. Thus not only are the feelings of love turned toward the internalized lost person but also the feelings of hate and rage are also aimed at the representa-

tions within the survivor. The rage toward the internalized representation is experienced by the grieving person as dislike for the self, self-depreciation, and sadness. Also the perception of the hostility toward the lost person engenders guilt and self-punitiveness in the survivor. Thus the feelings are turned upon the self and aimed at internalized representations and there is both the attempt to preserve the person and to destroy the hated person within as well. In some situations the grief process is likely to be more intense and to approach frank depression. This occurs when the lost person has been loved in an immature manner and has been used primarily as a person to fulfill and gratify, the survivor's own narcissistic needs, when the relationship has been extremely ambivalent, and when the grieved person is extremely dependent on external sources for his sense of self-esteem.[11, 12]

Identification with certain aspects of the dead person plays an important role in maintaining the illusion of the continued existence of the lost person, and a maintenance of a symbolic connection with the lost person. In the bereavement process, varying levels and types of identification phenomena are manifested. Identification with the lost person or aspects of the person may be constructive or it may lead to considerable disruption of the person's overall function.[13] Constructive identifications may occur in such circumstances as the survivors identifying with and successfully taking on the rewarding interests or activities of the deceased. In one such case, a young widow who identified with her dead husband's professional interests subsequently entered medical school and became a successful physician. On the other hand, symptomatic identifications such as identifications with actual physical symptoms of the deceased person's illness may cause considerable problems. Parkes distinguishes between "identification phenomena" and a type of these phenomena referred to as "identification symptoms." The latter he reserves for various types of hypochondriacal symptoms in the survivor related to the illness of the dead relative.[9] For example, a young man whose father's fatal illness began with chest pain and shortness of breath became preoccupied with the possibility of his having a heart attack. He noted vague chest pain and even experienced shortness of breath though no physical cause for his symptoms could be determined.

In bereavement the grieving person may successfully identify with components of the lost person, do the work of mourning, and emerge as a separate person with successful resolution of his grief. However, another level of identification termed "merging" is a more pathological form of identification which may lead to severe difficulties in resolving the grief process. In this situation, the bereaved person no longer has an awareness of himself as separate from the lost person but regards the lost person and himself as essentially one and the same.[14-16] This occurred in the case of a middle-aged woman whose daughter had died of leukemia. The mother reacted as if she herself were also dead. She complained of feeling cold, numb, and lifeless. She reported that she and her daughter were like "two peas in the same pod" in that they were so similar in their personality makeup and likes and dislikes. Intermittently she was able to differentiate herself from her daughter, but for the most part she stated that she felt that *all* of her had also died when her daughter's death occurred. Another patient whose husband was killed abruptly and unexpectedly in an automobile accident spoke of herself and her husband as being like two trees, so entangled and intertwined as to really seem as if there was only one tree instead of two. She had great difficulty in seeing herself as having any identity separate from her husband.

According to Bowlby, " . . . mourning is best regarded as the whole complex sequence of psychological processes and their overt manifestations, beginning with craving, angry efforts at recovery, and appeals for help, proceeding through apathy and disorganization of behavior, and ending when some form of more or less stable reorganization is beginning to develop."[17]

Bowlby[17] views many of the phenomena of mourning as attempts to adapt to the loss and means of attempting to achieve reunion with the lost person. He delineates three phases of the mourning process. In phase one, there is the urge to recover the lost object. This phase is characterized by weeping and anger, both of which represent responses which earlier in the life of the person adaptively served to bring about the reunion of the person with the lost object. When the infant misses his mother, his first response is to cry and the mother usually responds by rejoining him. Thus, " . . . when he weeps the bereaved adult is responding to loss as a child does to the temporary absence of his mother." Similarly, the anger of mourning may be viewed as a reaction which served adapatively in the child's relationship with the mother, the aggressive behavior having earlier in life been useful and serving as a reproachment to discourage the mother's leaving him again. In the second phase of mourning, disorganization occurs. The despair and depression associated with this phase arise " . . . as a result of the disorganization of behaviour patterns which is consequent on loss of significant object or goal in the external world." This phase represents a breaking down of the patterns of behavior which are associated with the lost object and is necessary and even adaptive in order that the person may reorganize his life patterns in the absence of the lost person. Old patterns are painfully broken down to be used again in establishing new patterns and goals. Thus " . . . so must the individual each time he is bereaved or relinquishes a major goal accept the destruction of a part of his personality before he can organize it afresh toward a new object or goal." In this phase, the process of becoming disorganized which accompanies the disruption of familiar patterns of behavior is painful and alarming. In the third phase of mourning, reorganization occurs and there is " . . . discrimination between patterns that are clearly no longer appropriate and those that can reasonably be retained . . . " The individual maintains values and pursues " . . . goals which, having been developed in association with the lost person, remain linked with him and can without falsification of reality continue to be maintained and pursued in reference to the memory of him. It is in this way, indeed, that an effective and loving relationship with the lost person can be built afresh." These three phases are also equally applicable to infants and young children over six months of age. The phases correlate with the designation of the first stage as one of protest, the second as one of despair, and the third stage as one of detachment. Bowlby's considerations of mourning lead him to think " . . . that the painfulness of mourning is to be accounted for by the long persistence of yearning for the lost object and the constant repetition of bitter disappointment on not finding it." He suggests that " . . . the persistent seeking of reunion with a permanently lost object is the main motivation present in pathological mourning, although it appears in forms which, because of repression and splitting have become disguised and distorted."[17] These phases as described by Bowlby are presented in a revised classification by Parkes.[18] Bowlby's original three phases relate to the second, third, and fourth phases of the following classifications:

First Phase – Phase of Numbness – during which the fact of loss is partially disregarded.

Second Phase – Phase of Yearning – during which the urge to recover the lost object predominates and searching takes place. In this phase it is the permanence rather than the fact of loss which is disregarded.

Third Phase – Phase of Disorganization and Despair – during which both the permanence and the fact of loss are accepted and attempts to recover the lost object are given up.

Fourth Phase – Phase of Reorganization of Behavior."

Parkes designates "searching" as a principal component of the grief process.[9, 18] Supporting Bowlby's hypothesis that the urge to recover the lost object is an important and often frustrating part of the mourning process, he views this attempt at recovery of the lost object as being manifested in the survivor's "searching behavior." Searching behavior includes: "Motor restlessness, preoccupation with a clear visual memory of the lost person, development of a perceptual 'set' for the lost person, direction of attention toward those parts of the environment in which the person is most likely to be found, and calling to him. . . . "[18] Searching thus is goal-directed in the sense that it is aimed at recovery of the lost person, but the behavior obviously results in the survivor's

experiencing considerable frustration. With repeated unrewarded searching behavior and the failure to bring about reunion, searching behavior diminishes, the person unlearns his attachment to the lost person, and the work of grief is accomplished. A form of this behavior was apparent in a young widow who was used to receiving numerous telephone calls from her husband each day, and continued to have the feeling that the phone would ring and it would be he calling. Each time she received a call from someone she felt disappointed, frustrated, and saddened that it was not he. She recognized the irrational nature of her expectations and after a few weeks, they ceased. A pathological variant of this searching behavior was apparent in the case of a woman who made frequent trips to the cemetery to visit her daughter's grave to be near her. In an effort to be close to her, she repeatedly returned to the gravesite, sometimes several times a day and at times in the middle of the night. She would lie down beside the grave in order to be nearer her daughter and verbally begged her to return and be with her. Despite the protestations of her family, she continued this behavior for a period of months. Her searching took other forms such as her forming a close relationship with a friend of her daughter whom she felt had many characteristics similar to those of her daughter. The searching behaviors did not, however, diminish with time and she subsequently required psychiatric hospitalization when she began expressing a desire to kill herself in order to rejoin her daughter.

Lifton has noted psychological patterns characteristic of survivors who have been immersed in a death experience. Included in these characteristics are a "death imprint" which is often associated with an increased sense of vulnerability, the guilt of the survivor who inwardly concludes that he has lived on at the expense of the death of others (a phenomenon often observed in a grieving person who asks, "Why couldn't I have died instead of he or she?" or states, "I wish I had been the one to die so he or she could have lived."), and "psychic numbing," a type of desensitization or decreased ability to feel. These characteristics of survivors assume importance in the phenomena of the grief experience and are manifested in varied ways.[19, 20]

The mourning process may then be viewed as a disorder of meaning and personal significance, for the bereaved person is often unable to engage in activities from which meaning may be structured and a sense of aliveness obtained. In response to the loss of a person significant in his life, the survivor's own awareness of death is intensified. This intensification relates not only to his awareness of death as it relates to the lost person, but also to an awareness of his own finiteness and his awareness of transience in general. Because of this, there is the development of an extreme sensitivity to loss and even the smallest loss or potential loss may be distorted out of proportion and seem to threaten his very existence. Commitment to activity which may be potentially lost becomes extremely difficult. This increased sense of death awareness may cause a temporary paralysis of engagement in the usual activities in which the person normally finds his personal significance, meaning, and sense of aliveness.

The survivor is particularly disoriented by the loss of the activity and meaning generated by and derived from the relationship. That activity related to the lost person that generated meaning is no longer available in the repertoire of activities which would provide a sense of aliveness and meaning. Because the primary and central loss of meaning for many individuals who have lost a loved one is associated with the lost activity of the relationship, other relationships are feared. Thus this method of achieving meaning and a sense of aliveness is temporarily blocked for the person. The feelings related to death awareness become overwhelming and the person withdraws from living, viewing life as threatening and providing only an increased chance of loss of other relationships and the self. As one patient stated, "I am terrified of the future. There may be other losses and I have had such problems managing the death of my wife that I feel paralyzed to make a commitment to anything or anyone."

As was previously pointed out, grief and mourning are not restricted to the survivors but are also experienced by the patient who is dying. The dying person's anticipatory grief occurs in response to the anticipated loss of parts of the self, of the total self through gradual deterioration and debilitation, of activities which allow a sense of aliveness and, importantly, of relationships which have become a vital part of his sense of aliveness. The dying person must gradually give up the meanings attached to the parts of the self which are lost and the meanings involved in the relationships with family, relatives, friends, and caregivers. Aldrich, in writing of the dying person's grief, points out that the acceptance of loss may be particularly hard on the individual who has a marked capacity for meaningful human relationships. "The more personality resources a person has, the more friends he has and the closer are his relationships with them; the more friends and close relationships, the more grief; and all things being equal, the more suffering."[21]

In addition to the loss of relationships, there are the reactions and grief of the patient and others to the loss of body parts. Surgical procedures such as mastectomies or amputations may be a necessary part of the treatment of a life-threatening illness. For example, in the case of a mastectomy, in addition to the anxiety associated with the surgical procedure itself, there is likely to be concern about sexual desirability, sexual relationships, and feelings related to the sense of damage to the image of the self. A marital relationship may be felt to be endangered. Also accompanying these anxieties is the fear of death.[22–24]

The person who loses a body part reacts to the loss of biological function of that organ, its symbolic attributes, its place in the person's interpersonal and social functions and its role in those activities which allow the person to find meaning and a sense of aliveness. The sense of loss is directly related to the degree the body part or function is part of the individual's identity. At bottom, the reaction represents a response to threatened loss not only of part of the self, but of the entire self. Again, death awareness is increased and the person is further led to a confrontation with his finiteness. In one case, a young man who was an artist developed an illness which caused progressive blindness. When one eye became affected, he became extremely agitated and experienced many of the phenomena of grief. While not dying, the threatened loss of a significantly invested sensory function precipitated a severe grief reaction. Further exploration of this reaction revealed an intense confrontation with his mortality as well. The treatment of this reaction required essentially the same methods utilized in the management of any grief process.

The theoretical constructs and observations derived from studies of grief and separation form an important basis for the caregiver's understanding and facilitation of the effective resolution of the grief process in any one person. This understanding is also necessary in order to comprehend phenomena related to variants of the grief process which reach pathological proportions.

PATHOLOGICAL VARIANTS OF GRIEF

The distinction between what is sometimes referred to as "normal grief" and what is designated as "pathological grief" remains obscure. In the current state of our knowledge, characteristics of "normal" grief and those of atypical, morbid, or pathological grief are so intertwined as to make any discussion of these states or the processes involved in them as separate and discrete entities most difficult. It is apparent that there is a fine line between "normal" and "pathological" grief and that many of the phenomena seen in pathological grief stages are abberations, intensifications, prolongations, or distortions of the usual and expected mourning process. Engel's use of the term "uncomplicated" grief rather than "normal" grief may be a useful way of approaching the issue.[25] Uncomplicated grief refers to a process which runs a reasonably consistent course and has as its outcome adaptation to the trauma of the loss and the restoration of a reasonable level of mental and physical well-being.

Grief, however, may certainly become complicated. There is sufficient data to indicate that the process is often associated with dysfunctional physical and mental states, and that its outcome may be disruptive, disabling, or even fatal.

Engel describes a psychological state which occurs in response to significant loss and may contribute to the subsequent development of illness.[26, 27] He proposes that in this state the capacity of the organism to deal with potentially pathogenic factors is diminished. This condition, designated as the "Giving-up — Given-up complex," includes the following characteristics: "(1) the giving-up affects of helplessness or hopelessness; (2) a depreciated image of oneself; (3) a loss of gratification from relationships or roles in life; (4) a disruption of the sense of continuity between past, present, and future; and (5) a reactivation of memories of earlier periods of giving-up."[27] This state was observed to be present in a man who developed lymphoma following a six-month period during which his only brother was accidentally shot in a hunting accident and his father suddenly died from a heart attack. During the period preceding the development of his illness, he was deeply grieved, felt overwhelmed, quit his work, stopped all pleasurable activities, and became extremely withdrawn. When his illness was diagnosed, he showed minimal interest in being treated and continued to feel helplessness and hopelessness. His coping abilities had diminished sharply and he remained in a severely depressed, withdrawn state.

Parkes and others have engaged in a number of studies of various aspects of the outcome of the grief process. These studies have demonstrated significant morbidity in terms of mental and physical health as well as an increased mortality rate in bereavement.[9, 28-32] Clearly, in some cases the process proceeds in the direction of frank psychiatric disturbance. One must conclude that in the grief process there is definitely the potential for considerable disruption of the survivor's overall functioning.

Lindemann described a number of forms of "morbid grief reactions" which represent distorted variants of normal grief. These include: (1) Delayed or postponed grief reactions, the delay or postponement ranging from a brief period of time to years. (2) Distorted grief reactions such as hyperactivity without the sense of loss, the development of symptoms symbolically associated with the deceased person's last illness, a recognized medical illness, changes in interpersonal relationships with increasing social isolation, intense rage toward specific persons, schizophreniform disorders, persisting disruption and loss of patterns of social interaction, activities which are detrimental to the mourner's social and economic existence such as uncalled-for generosity, and frank agitated depression with depressive symptoms including suicidal ideation. Lindemann noted that, "The duration of a grief reaction seems to depend on the success with which a person does the *grief work,* namely, emancipation from the bondage to the deceased, readjustment to the environment in which the deceased is missing, and the formation of new relationships." He further noted that, "One of the big obstacles to this work seems to be the fact that many patients try to avoid the intense distress connected with the grief experience and to avoid the expression of emotion necessary for it."[1]

Parkes concludes that " . . . among the various mental illnesses that can be precipitated by bereavement the most frequent are likely to comprise atypical forms of grief. Although these atypical forms differ in intensity and duration from the more usual reactions to bereavement, certain aspects of which may be exaggerated or distorted, they do not differ in kind." He further states that "There are no symptoms that are peculiar to pathological grief although it seems reasonable to view extreme expressions of guilt, identification symptoms (as opposed to other phenomena of identification), and delay in the onset of grief of more than two weeks' duration as indicators that the reaction to bereavement may take a pathological course."[9]

Volkan feels that the clinical diagnosis of "established pathologic mourning" is justified when there is a persistence of an ambivalent yearning to recover the lost person six months or more after a death. The survivor both desires and dreads the recovery of the lost object. The " . . . established pathological mourner is that person who became fixated in the initial reactions to death and is caught in the struggle of loss and restitution without coming to resolution."[33-35]

In a pathological grief state, one may encounter a depressed and saddened mood, prolongation and intensification of the grieving process, difficulties related to identification phenomena, the urge to rejoin the lost person, marked disturbances in socialization and vocational function, or blatant suppression of feelings. This state often arises due to some form of delay or disruption in the normal grief process and results in the individual's failure to accept the loss of the dead person and to reorganize his life in the face of this loss.

POSSIBLE COMPLICATING FACTORS IN GRIEF PROCESS

Any number of factors may combine in a particular individual to act as deterrants to the process of grief. The following is a listing of possible complicating factors which may lead to difficulties in the grief process.[1, 9-18, 31, 33-40] The caregiver should not expect to encounter all of these in any one individual. The list is offered as a guide to those complicating factors which *may* be found to be operant in persons who are encountering difficulty in the grieving process or are likely to have difficulty in resolving their grief.

1. Complicating Factors Related to the Death Itself

Suddenness of death without adequate time for psychological preparation.

Death considered exceptionally untimely, as in the death of a child or young adult.

Mode of death considered incomprehensible, as in suicides.

Ambiguity and unsureness about the death, with questioning of its actual occurrence; *e.g.,* marked deterioration or mutilation of the dead person to the point that there is the feeling that it is not actually the person who has died.

Absence or isolation from the occurrences surrounding the death resulting in inadequate sensory perceptions for the acknowledgment of its reality.

A sense of having "participated" in the actual event causing the death accompanied by excessive guilt; *e.g.,* the driver of an automobile involved in a wreck in which someone else is killed.

2. Complicating Factors Related to the Survivor's Psychological Traits

Unresolved feelings and conflict related to earlier losses in the person's life.

Tendencies toward depression or established difficulty in managing loss.

Difficulties in expressing and managing feelings of sadness and anger.

Extreme dependency on the reflected appraisals of others and the need for excessive approval by others, especially in the expression of feelings.

A tendency toward assuming inappropriate levels of responsibility and the presence of excessive guilt over perceived failure related to the death.

Excessive dependency on others to meet needs based on actual limited personal resources.

A tendency to form markedly ambivalent relationships with others characterized by both loving and hating those persons.

Survivor too young to conceptualize and integrate the finality of the loss.

Limited options in terms of developing new life styles separate from those shared with the lost person.

Failure to establish independent existence due to undermining of independence by others with whom the survivor relates — forced dependency.

3. Complicating Factors Related to the Survivor's Relationship With the Lost Person

Extreme levels of identification with the lost person.

The presence of intensely ambivalent feelings toward the deceased.

Intensely close relationship with the lost person to the exclusion of any close relationship with others.

Excessive and continued reliance on established life patterns with the pretense of a continued relationship with the dead person.

The presence of unresolved conflict involving the lost person.

Extreme dependency on the lost person for validation of self, identity, and meaning-related activities — an inability to see oneself as a separate person.

The deceased individual having been excessively dependent on the survivor.

Excessive guilt related to the life events and death of the deceased accompanied by an intense sense of personal responsibility.

Excessive and prolonged survivor's guilt.

4. Complicating Factors Related to the Inability to Express Feelings Related to the Loss

Inability of the survivor to be accepting of the high level of feelings surrounding the loss of the person.

Suppression of the expression of feelings as an act of protectiveness toward others.

Inability of other family members to legitimize the feelings related to grief.

Failure of caregivers to legitimize the feelings surrounding the grief process.

Other intense and extreme losses or compounded losses occurring at the same time.

Interpersonal disruption in the individual's environment which disallows the grief process.

Survivor unable to participate in the grief process during the established grief period due to his own physical incapacitation.

Lack of access to usual rituals or belief systems employed in the management of loss and the grief process.

Insistence by others that the survivor's grief be managed in a specific manner; *i.e.*, intolerance.

Dislocation of the person from the usual interpersonal context which is important and supportive in his expression of feelings.

Dislocation from the usual sociocultural and religious context for the expression of grief.

Excessive use of drugs or alcohol to suppress feelings connected with grief.

Conversion of the expression of grief feelings to unrecognized symbolic expressions (as in identification symptoms involving physical symptoms).

Extreme interpersonal isolation with an inability to establish other supportive relationships after the death of a significant person.

Concurrent development of physical illness in the survivor, making it difficult to deal both with feelings related to the loss of others and the self.

"Religious conflict" which leads to suppression of feelings.

The dead person having extracted a "promise" that the survivor will not be sad or grieve after his death.

Excessive attachment and maintenance of close proximity to possessions of the deceased individual, allowing the survivor to maintain a sense that the deceased is still alive.

Excessive and premature involvement in life activities to the point that the loss is not acknowledged.

MANAGEMENT OF GRIEF STATES

Ideally the management of grief states associated with life-threatening illness should begin before the actual loss occurs. It is then that the caregiver is able to lay the groundwork for the open expression of feelings related to the loss, to establish the legitimacy of the processes which occur in grief, and demonstrate to the bereaved the effectiveness of a caring relationship in assisting with the adaptation to the loss. In a culture where the containment and suppression of feelings is often reinforced, the caregiver can be highly effective in facilitating and legitimizing the process of anticipatory grief, thereby preparing dying persons and their families to begin the process of mourning and grief. When this occurs before the actual loss, these persons may proceed more naturally with their grief after the loss has occurred.

Individuals from different disciplines may play varying roles in assisting with the grief process. The nurse who is present throughout much of the care process may facilitate the expression of grief and provide a setting in which grieving is legitimized rather than swept aside;[41] the clergyman who may well have a long-standing relationship with the family because of personal or symbolic identifications may help monitor and facilitate the process of grief; and the physician may provide solace in times when the family has questions about possible omissions in care by his presence and consoling statements, such as "you and we have done all we could do."

Throughout the grieving process, the caregiver encounters phenomena which deter the person's expression of feeling related to loss and preclude involvement in a setting which allows talking about the death. Prior to death, the level of denial may be such that the individual is unable to allow feelings associated with the loss to surface. This is not a time to attempt to forcefully break through the person's denial or to insist on his dealing with his feelings; rather, it is a time to make oneself available should these feelings reach awareness and their expression be desired. In time, the knowledge of a caring, listening, and available person will often comfort and reassure the person suffering the loss so that he can allow feelings to surface. Then the relationship itself serves to provide a sense of safety and security which will encourage the expression of feelings which would otherwise seem overwhelming and devastating.

Immediately after the loss, the person sustaining the loss is likely to be in a state of overwhelming emotions. During this period, availability, gentle support, legitimization of feelings, the provision of a place where the person may express his feelings, and affirmation rather than active or forceful inquiry may be most effective in facilitating the expression of feelings. The caregiver should also recognize that the phenomena of protectiveness and withholding are often operant both in the preparatory phases of mourning and during the period of time after the loss. When in the presence of the patient or other family members considered to require protection, the individual will often withhold feelings. When, however, the person is spoken with alone, he may welcome the opportunity to express his feelings. This protectiveness sometimes isolates children from the happenings around a death and may separate them from the mainstream of the family's grief. It is important to remember that they also have a need to grieve and should be assisted with their grief in a manner compatible with their age.[42]

Great resentment may be stirred when efforts are made by the caregiver to dislodge the mourner's investment in the lost person. Such maneuvers amount to an interference with the survivor's maintaining an illusion of the lost person's continued presence and his attempt to achieve reunion.[17] Premature attempts at focusing the person's attention on other pursuits, social interaction, or attempts at forcing the individual to "forget and go on" are likely to be met with anger and may well interfere with the therapeutic potential of the relationship. Attempts, then, to move the survivor in the direction of pursuits unrelated to the lost person must be gentle and timely. Again, simple presence and "being there" as a receptive listener may be a more effective and therapeutic approach in facilitating the bereavement process.

Caregivers' attitudes toward grief, toward the expression of feelings in general, and their feelings about the individual's particular style of expression and management of his grief can play an important role in facilitating or impeding the grief process. Outbursts of hostility, anger, and intense expressions of sadness in the form of weeping are upsetting to those who themselves feel uncomfortable with these feelings. Yet for many they are a very normal part of the bereavement process. Feeling uncomfortable with the intensity of the feelings, some caregivers will not only withdraw, but may actually attempt to suppress these important feelings to avoid the discomfort they create. On the other hand, not all grieving persons will express their feelings with great intensity; some express them more quietly. A caregiver may, however, feel that relief is brought about only through the intense expression of feeling and attempt to force the individual to express his feelings more intensely than is appropriate at the time. The caregiver may find some forms of ritual employed by the survivor or involvement in religious ideas foreign and even unacceptable in his own frame of reference. In reaction to this, he may attempt to suppress the use of these important aspects of the person's life style and means of adaptation. This form of intolerance may reinforce the survivor's tendency to avoid utilizing these means of adaptation and severely impede the grief process. In those circumstances in which a caregiver finds himself unable to allow or tolerate the survivor's usual means of coping with loss, he should allow someone else who is more comfortable with the situation to assist the individual.

Earlier in this chapter it was pointed out that the loss of a relationship and all that the relationship means increases "death awareness" and leads to a heightened sensitivity to threatened loss. This may seriously interfere with the individual's investment in other relationships and create a guarded, cautious posture toward relating with anyone. For many people, their sense of meaning and personal significance is largely derived from a relationship. While the lost person can never be replaced, a meaningful relationship in which there is a freedom of expression of thoughts and feelings and an affirmation of aliveness may be the best setting in which the process of grief may be accomplished. The anger, sadness, and the ambivalent feelings around any new relationship, however, make this a difficult endeavor and the caregiver should not be discouraged when the mourning person feels the need to temporarily withdraw from a helping relationship. He should affirm his availability and willingness to be in a helping position should the bereaved person so choose.

Intolerance which may occur in caregivers in relationship to the expression of feelings, styles of coping, or the use of ritual or belief systems may seriously interfere with the establishing of a therapeutic relationship. This intolerance results in reflected appraisals of disapproval in the interpersonal context and may cause the person to become even more pessimistic about the development of any sense of restoration of relatedness. Grieving seems to be best accomplished in the context of a relationship, for that relationship is a transitional promise of the restoration of relatedness not only with the caregiver, but with others as well. It yields a promise of a continued sense of participation in the community of the living. Even so, it should be recognized that there are times when a grieving person desires to be alone, quietly going over his feelings, memories, and recollections about the lost person. Caregivers must recognize this need and legitimize it when appropriate.

The grief process relies on the presence of established forms of societally approved belief systems and ritual, including those related to the persons's religion and culture. The use of these means of adaptation should be viewed for many as not only necessary, but an important part of their usual means of dealing with loss. For some, however, life styles and belief systems dictate against certain aspects of societal ritual and in these cases the individual's desire should be respected. If, for example, a person desires to see and spend time with the dead person, this should be allowed, but it should not be forced upon someone who feels that it is unacceptable or inappropriate. It should be recognized that the forcing of a confrontation with the awareness of death may for some be difficult, untimely, and even inappropriate and that these individuals may have other means of accepting and integrating the reality of the loss. In some situations, the survivor may obviously avoid acknowledgment of the death or the use of ritual and reliance on his belief system. When these behaviors appear to represent an obvious deviation from his usual style of adapting, the caregiver may choose to gently explore the basis of this change in attitude. In so doing the individual may be helped to consider what is best for him in his usual style of coping.

For many persons, the funeral serves a vital function in assisting the individual to grieve in a societally acceptable manner. Pine, in comparing funeral practices around the world, demonstrates that funeral practices are designed as socially sanctioned means of managing important needs occurring at the time of bereavement. In comparing the funeral practices he notes similarities that appear in a social context in response to needs of the bereaved individual. Funeral practices tend to offer social and group support for the bereaved individual; they usually involve the use of religious ritual; they generally involve material expenditure and offer a tangible material communication to society of the bereaved person's investment in the lost person; they provide a health function; they generally employ a visual confrontation with the dead body; and they tend to end in a procession which may well have the symbolic value of a "final journey." These similarities would seem to represent, for many, important components of the "rites of passage" involved in the mourner's acknowledgment and integration of the death of a loved person.[43]

The use of medications in the management of the grief process remains a questionable matter, for drugs may allow the individual to avoid or suppress the normative pain of grief, interfere with the grief work, and possibly prolong the mourning process.[9] The judicious use of small amounts of tranquilizers and sleeping medi-cations may at times be indicated during the early phases of the grief process, but the provider of these medications should maintain the utmost vigilance in their use. He must be sure that they are used only when they would facilitate the individual's reorganization, assist with overall coping, and with disturbances in such functions as sleep. They should not be used in any way that would suppress the normative grief process but only as an adjunctive means of facilitating the individual's restorative processes. The possibility of habituation as a means of forestalling the pain of grief must also be considered. All too often, it is easier to prescribe a drug to manage a feeling state than it is to utilize therapeutic dialogue as a means of assisting the person in expressing and coping with his feelings. The caregiver should also be aware that in prescribing medications for an intense feeling state there is often the implicit communication that the feeling state should not be present and this may work against legitimizing the expression of feelings and the acceptance of grief as a normal process. The use of appropriate medications may, however, become necessary in some stages of the grief process.*

The management of pathological or complicated variants of the grief state frequently becomes a matter of importance in the overall management of grief. As there is likely an increased risk of developing physical difficulties during the bereavement period, the caregiver should ensure that the grieving individual receives adequate preventive medical care during this period and that attention be given to physical symptoms which develop. This is particularly important in view of the fact that many bereaved persons are likely to have depressive feelings and pay less than optimal attention to the development of physical distress. The failure to attend one's own needs is characteristic of depressive symptoms and is operant in many grief states. This should be borne in mind as the bereaved person is assisted with his grief.

Lindemann's principle that distorted grief

---

* For a further discussion of the use of medication in bereavement and complicated mourning states, see Klein DF and Davis JM: *Diagnosis and Drug Treatment of Psychiatric Disorders.* The Williams & Wilkins Co., Baltimore, 1969.

responses can successfully be transformed into more normal grief processes with resolution remains the cornerstone of treatment goals in most forms of pathological grief.[1] Transformation of pathological grief states to forms of mourning which proceed to resolution is most frequently accomplished through the use of the usual techniques involved in psychotherapy. This involves a process whereby the expression of previously repressed or suppressed feeling is encouraged and attempts are made to deal with those factors which hinder the progression and resolution of the grief process.[9] There are times, however, when pathological grief reactions reach severe proportions and other forms of intervention such as psychiatric hospitalization or the use of medications in connection with psychotherapeutic efforts must be employed. This is particularly likely to be necessary when personal or environmental forces lead to suppression of feeling or the individual has severely limited resources to reorganize as a separate person. In working with persons with pathological grief responses, the list of factors which may complicate the grief process should be reviewed and an attempt made to ascertain which deterrents may be operant in any particular person. It should be pointed out that the management of pathological grief states may be a slow and tedious process. As with the dying patient, presence, the encouragement of expression of feeling, and acceptance and legitimization of the feeling states are usually effective therapeutic methods. Volkan and Showalter have described a type of psychotherapy for individuals suffering from complicated and pathological grief states which they refer to as "re-grief work." The reader is referred to their writings for an in-depth and systematic presentation of the techniques.[16, 34, 35, 37, 38]

Facilitating and managing the process of grieving represents a vital part of caring for the dying person and his family. It is a further indication of the need for the process of care to be viewed as a longitudinal one in which caregivers must continue to participate even after the death of the individual. Furthermore, it points to the necessity for a flexible, cooperative, and collaborative posture among caregivers and the necessity for maintaining approximation. This will provide a sense of interpersonal continuity which will result in the outcome of the survivor's feeling alive and participating in the community of the living.

REFERENCES

1. Lindemann E: Symptomatology and Management of Acute Grief. *Amer J Psychiat 101:*141–148, © 1944, The American Psychiatric Association
2. Kübler-Ross E: *On Death and Dying.* The Macmillan Company, London, 1969
3. Shneidman ES: *Deaths of Man.* Penguin Books, Inc., Baltimore, 1974
4. Parkes CM: Psycho-social Transitions: A Field for Study. *Social Sci Med 5:*101–115, 1971
5. Parkes CM: Psycho-social Transitions: Comparison Between Reactions to Loss of a Limb and Loss of a Spouse. *Brit J Psychiat 127:*204–210, 1975
6. Clayton P, Desmaris L, Winokur G: A Study of Normal Bereavement. *Amer J Psychiat 125:*168–178, 1968
7. Clayton P, Halikes JA, Maurice WL: The Bereavement of the Widowed. *Dis Nerv Sys 32:*597–604, 1971
8. Clayton P, Halikes JA, Maurice WL: The Depression of Widowhood. *Brit J Psychiat 120:*71–78, 1972
9. Parkes CM: *Bereavement: Studies of Grief in Adult Life.* International Universities Press, New York, 1972
10. Freud S: "Mourning and Melancholia," in *The Complete Psychological Works of Sigmund Freud,* Standard Edition, Strachey J (Trans. and Ed.) The Hogarth Press, London, 1963
11. Fenichel O: *The Psychoanalytic Theory of Neurosis.* W.W. Norton and Company, Inc., New York, 1945
12. Volkan V: Normal and Pathological Grief Reactions: A Guide for the Family Physician. *Virg Med Mon 93:*651–656, 1966
13. Krupp GR: Identification as a Defense Against Anxiety in Coping with Loss. *Inter J PsychoAnal 46:*303–314, 1965
14. Schafer R: *Aspects of Internalization.* International Universities Press, New York, 1968
15. Volkan V: Typical Findings in Pathological Grief. *Psychiatr Quar 44:*231–250, 1970
16. Volkan V: The Linking Objects of Pathological Mourners. *Arch Gen Psychiat 27:*215–221, 1972
17. Bowlby J: Processes of Mourning. *Inter J PsychoAnal 42:*317–340, 1961
18. Parkes CM: "Seeking" and "Finding" a Lost Object: Evidence from Recent Studies of the Reaction to Bereavement. *Soc Sci Med 4:*187–201, 1970
19. Lifton RJ: On Death and Death Symbolism: The Hiroshima Disaster. *Psychiatry 27:*191–210, 1964
20. Lifton RJ: *The Life of the Self: Toward a New Psychology.* Simon and Schuster, New York, 1976
21. Aldrich CK: The Dying Patient's Grief. *JAMA 184:*329–331, 1963
22. Goldsmith HS, Alday ES: Role of the Surgeon in the Rehabilitation of the Breast Cancer Patient. *Cancer 28:*1672–1675, 1971

23. Asken MJ: Psychoemotional Aspects of Mastectomy: A Review of Recent Literature. *Amer J Psychiat 132:*56–59, 1975

24. Caplan LM, Hackett TP: Emotional Effects of Lower-Limb Amputations in the Aged. *N Engl J Med 269:*1166–1171, 1963

25. Engel GL: Is Grief a Disease? A Challenge for Medical Research. *Psychosom Med 23:*18–22, 1961

26. Engel GL: A Psychological Setting of Somatic Disease: The "Giving Up-Given Up" Complex. *Proc Royal Soc Med 60:*553–555, 1967

27. Engel GL: A Life Setting Conducive to Illness: The Giving-Up—Given-Up Complex. *Bull Menninger Clin 32:*355–365, 1968

28. Parkes CM: Effects of Bereavement on Physical and Mental Health—A Study of the Medical Records of Widows. *Brit Med J 2:*274–279, 1964

29. Parkes CM: Recent Bereavement as a Cause of Mental Illness. *Brit J Psychiat 110:*198–204, 1964

30. Parkes CM, Benjamin B, Fitzgerald RG: Broken Heart: A Statistical Study of Increased Mortality Among Widowers. *Brit Med J 1:*740–743, 1969

31. Parkes CM: The First Year of Bereavement: A Longitudinal Study of the Reaction of London Widows to the Death of Their Husbands. *Psychiatry 33:*444–467, 1970

32. Parkes CM, Brown RJ: Health After Bereavement: A Controlled Study of Young Boston Widows and Widowers. *Psychosom Med 34:*449–461, 1972

33. Volkan V: "Death, Divorce and the Physician," in *Marital and Sexual Counseling in Medical Practice,* Abse DW, Nash EM, Louden LMR (Eds) Harper and Row, Hagerstown, Maryland, 1974

34. Volkan V, Cilluffo AF, Sarvay TL: "Re-Grief Therapy and the Function of the Linking Object as a Key to Stimulate Emotionality," in *Emotional Flooding,* Vol. 1 of New Directions in Psychotherapy Series, Olsen P (Ed) Human Sciences Press, New York, 1975

35. Volkan V: More on "Re-Grief" Therapy. *J Thanatol 3:*77–91, 1975

36. Deutsch H: Absence of Grief. *Psychoanal Quar 6:*12–22, 1937

37. Volkan V, Showalter CR: Known Object Loss, Disturbance in Reality Testing and "Re-Grief Work" as a Method of Brief Psychotherapy. *Psychiat Quar 42:*358–374, 1968

38. Volkan V: A Study of a Patient's "Re-Grief Work" Through Dreams: Psychological Tests and Psychoanalysis. *Psychiat Quar 45:*255–273, 1971

39. Levinson P: On Sudden Death. *Psychiatry 35:*160–173, 1972

40. Weisman AD: Coping with Untimely Death. *Psychiatry 36:*366–377, 1973

41. Engel GL: Grief and Grieving. *Amer J Nurs 64:*93–98, 1964

42. Wessel MA: A Death in the Family: The Impact on Children. *JAMA 234:*865–866, 1975

43. Pine VR: Comparative Funeral Practices. *Prac Anthropol 16:*49–62, 1969.

part **II**

PERSPECTIVES

9

THE THOUGHTS, FEELINGS, AND REFLECTIONS OF A PERSON WITH A LIFE-THREATENING ILLNESS — Linda N. Cummings

Linda N. Cummings died from malignant melanoma. Her chapter was prepared approximately one year before her death. Seven months before her death, the spread of the disease resulted in paralysis of both of her legs and her right arm. While her mobility was severely compromised, she remained alert until almost a week before her death. She desired to die at home and was treated in home care with the assistance of home nursing and medical care. She remained at home and died there as she desired. She was 34 years old at the time of her death. This chapter is based on a series of recorded interviews and was prepared by the editor in collaboration with Linda N. Cummings. (*Editor's Note*)

I do like to live and I really feel that I've been kind of lucky in life. That's silly in some ways because I'm not real happy about this illness . . . but I guess I feel I've been lucky. I've had a lot of good things happen to me. I think I'm feeling more fulfilled all the time . . . that's why I hate to die now. Since I've turned thirty, I've really started liking myself more and liking what I'm doing. I really think that I'm just a happy person by nature, even though I have a nasty streak, a bad disposition at times, and a wretched temper . . . but I basically just like living and I enjoy being alive . . . I don't feel like I've been cheated in life. That's what I feel makes people bitter. I don't feel like I've been cheated . . . I'd like a little more of life, but so far I don't think I've been cheated.

I think I changed a lot, eleven years ago, when I first had the mole removed. Starting then, I thought more in terms of living each day. I tried to just enjoy each day — just to be happy and look around me. I never had been a person who felt that my responsibilities always included keeping the house spotlessly clean and serving a good meal. I was fairly free from those things that catch up most women when they're first married, and make their lives miserable. But I think having that mole made me really see that my philosophy was right for me. You can't live for decorating your house and all those silly things! I felt freed from the pettiness that most people's lives seem to consist of, like worrying about the cracked ceilings, the carpets, and the drapes. It was the kind of change in perspective that I think comes when you see your mortality. I began to do things pretty much because I wanted to do them, rather than feeling like they were things I should do. I'm not talking about a total lack of responsibility, but being freed from the imaginary things that you feel you have to do.

I remember once when we lived in an apartment complex and one of the men we knew there had some sort of growth removed from his back. One day, I went up to him and said something like, "It certainly does change your perspective, doesn't it?" And he said, "Yes, it means that from now on, I'll go to the doctor about everything!" Somehow, that wasn't exactly what I had in mind.

About twelve years ago, I had had the mole on my back for a while and had worried about it. Finally I went to a dermatologist about it. He said it looked all right. He just took it off. The day I was to go back to have the stitches out, it was very cold and I called him and said that I would come in for my appointment in a few days. He said, "No, come down today. It's rather important." He just said that there were some things in it that didn't look good and he thought that perhaps a larger section should be taken out. After that was done, I later went back to the dermatologist. That day he appeared nervous and said something like, "Do I make you nervous?" And I said, "Yes." He said, "Well, we don't know with things like this." "We don't know if it will come back or when." But then he said, "How old is your youngest child?" They always bring up these maudlin things. I said, "Two," and he made a gesture that expressed a blend of hopelessness and inadequacy. And then I wandered out into the street and almost fainted halfway down the block because I realized that he was really worried about it.

I really wasn't aware of the seriousness of it at the time and yet subconsciously, I knew something from his parting statement . . . but I didn't really know. I would see magazine articles about malignancies and I wouldn't want to read them, but I would read them anyway.

I think I should have been told about it in relatively full detail . . . or at least enough that I could understand it was malignant. It probably would have happened the same way anyway, but I would have had more information. I wasn't really aware of the seriousness of it at the time. I don't like to think back on that experience because it really makes me angry. I don't know . . . I don't think the ultimate outcome would have been different . . . but I don't know that there may not have been some difference.

Last year, when I found these new tumors — three things that turned out to be tumors — two on my hip and one on my stomach — my doctor advised surgery and set up an appointment with a surgeon. Neither one of them was saying anything to me about what they thought it may or may not be . . . but you can feel when they are concerned . . . or maybe you imagine it. When I was in the recovery room, I asked the surgeon, "Well, what was it?" and he said, "It will take 36 hours to tell." I know that with breast cancer they can tell right away so I didn't know whether that was true or not. So I felt it was an evasion. Whether it was or not, I don't know.

Then there was a period of time — ten days — when they were waiting for the information from the first operation. Things were going through my mind like, "Am I really having a recurrence?" I had worried for so many years and I had gotten to the point where I didn't think I had to worry anymore about that. I thought about it, but I didn't feel I needed to worry. I just kind of floated from day to day while they were waiting for the information. I could just hope that it wasn't really a recurrence. If they don't know, I thought, it left other possibilities open. But I figured that if they were waiting for the information obviously there was something more . . . it wasn't a benign tumor because they could tell me that right away. That's just the way my mind works. Logically, if there were nothing wrong, then they would tell me.

We finally went in for a conference. The doctor was very serious looking and said that they thought it was a melanoma. He more or less said that's it. I was half in a state of shock . . . I didn't cry . . . I sort of sat there when he said it was a melanoma. And I said, "Well, if it took ten years to recur, why can't it take another ten years before I have my next recurrence?" And he kind of just shook his head "No" and said, "I won't give you percentages, because everybody is an individual," which, of course, let me know immediately that the percentage of the people who live is low.

The doctor to whom he referred me for treatment seemed more direct. I'd rather somebody deal rather directly with me. It's you and it's your business as much as it is theirs; it is you and you're the one who's most concerned. I think it's something that's better off being handled matter-of-factly, then you can cope with it better and it doesn't have this hidden horror that you get from those little awful looks and little side remarks. It's less horrifying. It's almost like you need to kind of rely on somebody and you feel like if they can handle it, then you can handle it. It's something within the realm of human handling, but when you find a doctor who can't handle it then you think . . . well . . . this is really awful. Of course, I don't know what would happen if the doctor doesn't have the ability to face it himself . . . I don't know what you do about that.

The doctor I'm seeing now offers hope and yet withholds it at the same time and that's not a bad approach. He's very realistic about your chances of dying and yet he'll say, "Don't give up hope yet, we've got a few more things to try." You kind of realize that part of this is that he's hoping and also, he's talking in terms of time rather than life and death. Where you're talking about and thinking about life and death, he may be talking about giving you a few extra months. But the important thing is that he doesn't make you feel just totally deserted and despondent. Yet he doesn't lie about it.

I think a lot of things can be faced if you are realistic about it. At least, with me that's true and besides, I don't like people talking about me behind my back. I think that I have a right to know what's wrong with my body. I don't mean totally – I don't want to know all the details by any means, but I don't think they should be making decisions if I haven't been told the true situation. Maybe that's my need to have control, but if they don't tell you, then you don't really know and you can't make decisions. You really only have a moderate amount of choice, because obviously you are going to pretty much do what they recommend, but at least you feel like you know what's going on.

While we were waiting for the information from the previous surgery, it was kind of a time out of time. I felt sad . . . my husband took a lot of time off from work. I cried a lot and he cried a lot and we sort of consoled each other. We just sat and talked. I remember it was sunny, which means it had to have been a happy time in some ways . . . a sad, happy time because I wouldn't remember it as sunny otherwise. It was sort of a limbo period . . . when I just kind of floated along and didn't have touch with reality. It was like I would die, but I would still be here. It was like unreal, happening to somebody else more than to me. In the background, I guess there must have been some hope.

I think you almost experience certain feelings of joy. It's not quite joy, because that would be sick to be happy, but there's a difference between joy and happiness. We went down to the park and walked around and looked at the flowers and the trees and each minute just kind of expanded and became an entity in itself. It's almost a timelessness, but you can't keep it at that level too long. We'd just sit on the sofa and look at the sunshine or we'd walk up the hill across the street and pick flowers. Dumb things that really make you happy. But you can't sustain that for too long . . . you have to get back to your day-to-day routine. I liked the joyful feelings better, and that's the way I would have lived my whole life, but that's impossible.

When I finally got to see the doctor who is now treating me, it was very late in the day. I was tired, nervous, and upset. I started crying in front of one of the residents and he left the room. He just kind of excused himself quickly. I think it kind of embarrassed him. I said to the nurse, "I know I'm dying. Will the doctor have time to talk to me?" She answered, "I don't know if he'll have time but I hope so. He's awfully busy, but I hope so." When he came in, I kind of forgot about dying just for a little while. I was able to forget, because he is a very vital man. He's positive . . . a sort of positive force. I felt like something concrete was going to be done.

He began treatment after that. I would spend most of my time lying in the sunshine thinking. I did that for the next two or three months. I thought about everything . . . not concrete thoughts. Thoughts would just kind of drift through my head and I didn't analyze them. I just let them flow through. It was kind of nice, you know . . . memories came back, mostly pleasant ones, mostly all pleasant, but they wouldn't really come back in concrete form . . . just fleeting images . . . and then I'd feel very peaceful. That peaceful feeling is what I can't regain now. I guess that's your immediate reaction because you are almost in a state of shock. It takes a while. You think you accept it, but it takes a while to really accept it.

The sun got too hot for me to lie out in the backyard. It got too hot and I couldn't go outside. Then I began feeling more depressed. I used to wake up in the morning and cry, just feel like crying and then I'd pull myself together, get out and go about my business and I'd feel better. But my immediate reaction would be to cry. I started summer school, and that got me up and out each day. Otherwise, I would just lie in bed and feel depressed. So I started going to summer school, and I would get up each morning and get dressed and go to summer school and see people and have a reason for the day and that was about all I did. That was enough, though.

Eleven years before was when I saw my mortality, but this time, I think I got a little frenzied. When you see your death really right there, I think you become a little frenzied, and try quickly to shove it all in the last few days. You can't do that.

At times, though, the panic would close in on me. It was almost like waves of nausea . . . but not really nausea. It comes in waves. It just floods you. It's like shudders coming from the outside and getting you and they're dark. It's hard to describe. It comes in surges and then it lets up a little for a minute and then comes in another surge. It's almost as if it starts away from you and comes into you and then you can end up with actual physical shaking. It comes from the outside and then you take it on yourself. And then there is an absolute despondency. It lasts fifteen or twenty seconds, and usually you have it again. The feeling itself is rather quick, but I may have the shakes for five or ten minutes afterwards. I always have to pull myself out of it, because you just can't dwell in it. It can just kill you. You just have to say that things really aren't that bad. Whatever it is that's so horrible is always nameless . . . there's always something nameless . . . but you just have to really fight against it.

But I still get the feelings of joy. It feels good . . . this timelessness. If I were religious, I would say it's a religious experience. It only happens on sunny days. It's like there's a universality in everything and that's as close as I can come to what I guess is a religious experience. It's like everything is one and everything is great . . . over and under all this bad stuff that happens, there is almost this eternal joy and you're a part of it. It's like what happens to me is just part of

the whole thing and it doesn't really matter that much. It's too bad that I can't just summon the feeling up at will.

Usually I'll be thinking about dying and worrying about it and then this feeling of peace comes over me and I feel happy . . . not happy, but joyous. This is just a feeling of being part of the whole, so yes, you don't feel bad all of the time. At least I don't feel bad all the time. I have happy moments. But I don't think you ever forget about the fact that you are dying. I don't think that leaves your mind for a minute. But it's kind of like an acceptance thing . . . you kind of don't really believe it at times. It's there but you don't really believe it.

Things began to get urgent and frenzied. Then I realized that I was not just going to drop over dead. I realized that you don't die that fast. Sometimes, I think it would be tempting to know exactly when. It would be . . . if you did know then you could arrange everything so it would come to a completion right at that point. Some people might like to know exactly when, but I just figure what you don't know won't hurt you so much.

Some times, it's sort of difficult to start new things and yet that's really the secret of life . . . starting new things and meeting new people. I've already done most of the things in life I really wanted to do, but I had always thought that I would like to scuba dive, ride a motorcycle, and go to China. I feel that if those are the only three things that I haven't done that I really wanted to do, then I haven't missed too much. It's endless, though, the list of things I'd really like to do. A few months back, I did buy a motorcycle. I think it was a need to do something that made me feel alive. I had always wanted one. Getting one was something I had always wanted to do and I let people talk me out of it. I guess that the motorcycle was something I could take a stand on. I've been thinking of taking up some new hobbies. I may start collecting Chinese stamps.

I just consider death as non-existence . . . I mean it's nothing. Now the act of dying . . . I don't know about. Death itself doesn't frighten me, because I think when you're dead, you're dead. I'm saying that now but as it gets closer, I may change my mind. I'm not really physically disabled yet. I may sing a whole different tune when I'm lying there with tubes and all . . . that's the part I hate to think about. But at some point you have to come to terms with it . . . it occupies your mind fully until you come to some sort of terms with it. You can't think of anything else. I don't see death as frightening itself . . . it's all the things that you have to give up to die. All the good things. I don't want to die and I really sometimes wonder if I really believe it or if I'm just talking to myself.

I worry about the pain and just lying there and dying slowly. It seems so dumb . . . so pointless. If you're going to die, that's one thing . . . but why should you suffer so much in the end? I can't see any point in that and that's what frightens me. I mean you don't die when you're healthy. I'll be deteriorating and I worry about being physically repulsive. I don't want to be a subject of pity. I can't conceive of myself as being that sick because I've never been sick very much. I don't want to be a bother. I guess I want to die graciously. I mean there are socially acceptable patterns of behavior for everything else. I don't want to make it a big scene.

When you go into the hospital and you're going to die, I mean when you go in for the final time . . . how do you say goodbye to your children? When you leave . . . who wants to go out screaming and crying? What if I can't walk? I don't know how this kills you. I mean I don't know what it does to you as it progresses, and I guess it depends on where it progresses . . . but I don't know . . . and I don't know if I want to know. What if I'm in a wheelchair for a while? What if I lose control of my body functions and somebody has to take care of me? Who would you want to take care of you? I don't think it's humiliating on an intellectual level, but emotionally . . . on a personal level . . . I would hate that.

At one point, I was worried about people abandoning me. It's not really me they would be trying to get away from . . . they try to get away from anything that's unpleasant. And I think, too, that it reminds them of their own mortality. But I don't think I'll be abandoned. I think even more than the fear of being abandoned, it worries me to have to be that intimate with people. Like I have a tremendous sense of privacy. Part of

it is that we were raised to be so inhibited about our bodies. There are people I just wouldn't want to see me naked . . . I wouldn't want judgmental people to see me exposed or naked. I have a hard time taking care of sick people myself, so if I'm not sympathetic to sick people, how can I expect them to be sympathetic to me? So when I'm sick, there will be certain chores that will be unpleasant. Nobody wants to do them and if they don't want to do them, then I don't want them to do them. But then they have to be done. But I'll worry about that when the time comes . . . I can't worry about it yet.

There have been some people that I haven't wanted to talk with about my illness. Sometimes, I've wondered if I've done that because I don't really want to face it myself yet. Maybe I'm not really ready and I don't feel like other people are ready to deal with my dying very well. It's a touchy subject with some of my friends, and I feel that a lot of people feel sorry for me or don't want to be near me because it reminds them that this could happen to them. It's like . . . BANGO! . . . if it can happen to me then it can happen to them. I don't want people to feel sorry for me. Feeling sorry for someone to me connotes condescension . . . of a sort. I don't feel sorry for myself and I just think these things happen in life . . . I think it's a matter of happenstance . . . either it does or it doesn't. You've got enough problems to deal with . . . you just can't deal with everyone else's problems. Sometimes, you feel like you're becoming others' crutch and they need to be reassured.

People react differently. Some of them think I lean too much on other people . . . that I'm too dependent on my husband or them or talking to a psychiatrist. They think I should be able to do it more by myself. Others feel they can be of help to me and sometimes seem overly solicitous. I think some people have a need to be needed and they seem to try to put me in the position of needing them, whether I do or not. But the day may come when I do need them.

Some have had experiences with dying people and think they can help me because of their experience. One of my friends told me that she had thought about how she would feel if this happened to her . . . how she would feel if she had found out that she was dying. She thought she could then talk to me and be helpful. I don't think you can possibly envision it. It's not like anything else . . . it's so confused. Sometimes, I feel I'm helping some of my friends deal with their feelings about dying instead of being helped. I think, sometimes, that they are just uncomfortable about it.

One friend is ideal. She's not squeamish about it. She doesn't ever ask questions. She doesn't act like she feels sorry for me. She treats me as normal, but she's not ignoring it because she'll go out of her way to do small things. I think it's probably because she has more of an acceptance of life in general and doesn't have too many personal problems and she treats me like she did before only slightly with a little more care . . . but not too much.

It was particularly hard for me to let some people know and now that they do, I don't like them knowing. With some people it was like if you didn't tell, it wouldn't be true. Keeping the secret, I could conjure up this feeling of bliss within myself. In a way it was like maintaining my privacy and my independence. I didn't want them to share in my dying . . . to tell me how to do it or to be judgmental. I wanted to be independent of them. Also, I think I felt I would have to support them at a time when I really needed support. My dying isn't something I would have had happen on purpose. They will just have to handle it. It's not my responsibility. I can't say I'm not going to die just to make them happy. I can say it, but I can't do anything about it. I guess I felt responsible for them and at the same time felt that I would be letting them down and they would blame me.

I think I've always felt really close to my husband. I think because we got married so young that I almost think of him as my total family. I think I can always rely on him, no matter what I do. He's the only person I've ever known that no matter what I do, he likes me. He doesn't like what I do always, but he always likes me. He even likes me when I'm dying . . . and he doesn't blame me . . . I have had times when I've blamed myself, but he doesn't blame me.

Sometimes when he is irritable and I don't

understand why, I get puzzled . . . I know it's not directed at me. But I ask myself, "How can he be angry when I'm dying? How can he do that when he has so little time left with me?" But then I'm very sensitive. Sometimes my dying creates distance. I guess that these are just those times that he can't accept the fact and likes to try to pretend that it's not happening. Once, I felt angry with him because he was distant, and in my anger said, "I wish you were dying just for a day so you could see what it feels like." And he said, "I feel like I am." I had knowingly made him feel bad and that was selfish but I think it was a really nice thing for him to say and to feel. That convinced me that he had a lot of feeling for what was happening and almost felt as bad as I do about it.

A great part of my acceptance of my dying . . . one of the most important things is love . . . having somebody love you . . . I think that does a world of good for you . . . just to have that reassurance. And that's what my husband has done . . . he's always there. I believe in love . . . I think it's a very important factor. I just think I'm lucky to have him . . . the real factor is love . . . and acceptance.

My dying has brought about changes in the family. My husband and children have had to take over more of the housework. I feel more selfish and placing more of the burden on them bothers me. I can convince myself by saying that I'm training them to carry on when I'm gone. And that is true to a certain extent. They have to stop being so reliant on me and be able to take care of themselves a little more. Some of dying has to do with shifting the burden . . . shifting the burden physically, mentally, and emotionally. You have to . . . because you did take up a certain space and others have to come in and fill up that space . . . and that's a shifting of the burden.

I don't think the children really realize what is happening, but I am trying to make the older one more aware of it. The other day one of them was talking about cooking something . . . she likes to cook. It was one of those days when I wasn't feeling well so she said she would wait until I was feeling better or more hungry. I just said to her, "I may never feel better or be more hungry," which was really kind of finally saying something. I keep thinking . . . here we have this little bit of time and it should be special. It bothers me in situations when I get angry with them.

I wonder if ultimately you don't face dying and death alone. Sometimes the people close to me can't really support me because they are having difficulty coping with it and they need support also. But most people must face it alone. That you do face it alone is what's so frightening about it. I think no matter what, the dying person just has to do a lot of thinking and feeling bad. But it does help to talk with someone . . . it's a traumatic situation. You begin to deal with some problems you've had all your life . . . problems that normally don't bother you. But when you find out you're dying and you just have such a short time, you want to get yourself straight.

I think that people in the medical profession can help by reaching their own conclusions about death and not trying to force their conclusions on you. I think the people who handle dying patients well have almost had to come to terms with dying themselves. If they can accept death as a matter of life and aren't frightened about it, then they can allow the dying person to find his own way of handling it. If they are comfortable with dying and death, that comes across to the patient and it makes it easier for the person to come to some acceptance of his own. The physician who is the main one taking care of you is your tie with life . . . you don't want to talk with him about dying too much. But you do want to be able to talk about it when you feel like it. I have this feeling . . . sometimes I don't like to talk with my physician about my dying because I feel that I might be disappointing him.

I think that the doctor who doesn't have his own ideas together should stay away from the dying patient. Because if medical people are disturbed about the subject, that can have an effect on the patient. Of course, if the doctor is brilliant in his field and has a chance of saving a life then maybe the dying person can put up with it, but it could have a terribly devastating effect to be around a doctor who did not really have his feelings

straight about dying. Some doctors may not be able to get their feelings straight and would come up with pat little death speeches. The death speech would be a little speil meant to reassure the patient, but would have little meaning and convey little understanding.

Some doctors don't seem to be able to handle the emotional discomfort in the dying person. Once, in the clinic, I expressed concern about something . . . it was a very minor statement . . . I made some comment about the discomfort and a resident said something to the effect that it was better that I was uncomfortable than dying, and I should be glad they had something to do for me. I felt that he was being too hard on me for what I had said. I was expressing emotional discomfort, too, in this statement, and he insinuated that I was being a baby about it. I didn't feel that was true. I hadn't meant the complaint so much as a physical complaint as an emotional one. It was a plea for emotional support and he so much as told me I'd better shape up. I thought he had a total lack of compassion. And I just feel that he shouldn't be working with people if he has that much of a lack of compassion, at least not with people who are sick and dying. Sometimes, these funny little statements come out of your mouth when you don't expect them to. You don't always necessarily feel brave and there's no reason why somebody should always expect you to feel brave. I just think there are some people who aren't compassionate, and that's tricky, because that's something you can't teach. Even if you tried to teach them this, they would be the type that would come up with the pat death speech.

I guess the main trait I would like to see in people who work with dying people is compassion and having a zest for life themselves . . . people I would like for friends. I think they should have their minds somewhat straight about their feelings. I think that's important because the main thing is when you're dying you're very much different from the way you were before, but you're really very much the same. You want to be treated like you were before. I think that they should have their ideas straight about dying and just be happy, joyful people. No sad sacks, but not that awful cheeriness either.

I think the dying patient needs honesty. It may make the patient uncomfortable for a few moments if someone taking care of him becomes tearful, but that's all right. I don't see anything wrong with it. But if people went around weeping every time they came into your room, that would be hard to take. But I am a person who values honesty in all relationships. Sometimes, I believe that the dying person gets to the point where they are supportive . . . that they become the supportive ones. I don't think the illness is as bad, once you get into it. Once you can cope with it . . . it isn't as bad when you're into it as it seems from the outside.

I'm not a particularly religious person. I don't believe in an afterlife. There was this woman who was able to explain poor attendance at a church meeting as an act of God. It would have been her way to have things turn out one way . . . but she accepted that God's way was different. I think that would almost be too easy for me, but it would be nice to think that everything that happened, happened because it was God's way. There is such a tremendous yen to make it all so neat. I don't think a real religious person would help me, because I'm not really in doubt about my beliefs. I may not know exactly what they are, but it's because I've reached the point where I just don't think I can know . . . and reaching that point is not from indecision.

I've struggled with my feelings about immortality. I guess I've come to the conclusion that it is important that life goes on. If you're part of the life process itself, a part of the whole, then there is a continuity. I guess that's what I'm coming to. There doesn't have to be as direct an immortality as living on through my children. But that may not be the answer for anybody else. But it takes a lot of pressure off when you come up with some sort of answer. A while back, I was hassling with my children, trying to put them in shape real quick so that they could be my immortality. Why should they bear that responsibility?

People will remember me. Last Christmas, a man at work was telling me about a relationship he had with a woman when he was much younger. The relationship was just a memory. We were talking and all of a sudden he said, "I don't know what brought that to my mind." That's the way I'll be to a bunch of people. All of a sudden . . . I'll be a little memory here and there, big memories to my family, but just little memories to most people. That's part of the life process.

Lately, I've felt a sort of need to change myself psychologically, to withdraw to some extent. Some of that is to keep from being hurt and some of that is to conserve my energies. You just don't have the physical or mental energy for those things that aren't really important to you—the things that aren't worth your time. I find myself withdrawing from my peripheral friends . . . really choosing those people that I prefer to spend time with. Maybe that's too much for those people because they don't have the same need that I have. I don't mind meeting new people to a certain extent, but I'm not really that anxious to start new things because I feel that I won't have time to get good at them or accomplish them. I feel like you kind of have to prepare yourself. I guess it's setting your own mind at ease. Part of that is when you just lie there and let things go through your mind—that's a kind of withdrawal and setting your mind at ease. It's kind of disassociating yourself from events and relationships, or at least disassociating yourself emotionally.

One of my friends feels that I am too accepting of my dying. I don't think that by accepting it you're saying you're going to quit here and now. There are really two aspects to acceptance. I accept the fact that I'm dying, and there's very little chance that I won't. But that is the acceptance of the fact that this is a good probability. I don't accept it from the standpoint of giving in to it. I don't quit living and say, "I'm going to die so I'm not going to do anything." There's something rather grotesque about denying the fact that you're dying. I always leave the possibility open that I may not, but not much room. It's fatalistic to say, "I'm definitely going to die," but I think its more realistic to realize that you are or that you probably will than to pretend that you're not or to hope that you're not. I always leave a little room emotionally. Intellectually no, but emotionally—I do leave some room. But then you have to be careful or that gets too big. I think that dying does complete a life cycle and that is almost creative, but I'm not ready for my life cycle to be over. Right now, I'm in a hopeful mood. If I had died ten years ago it would have been a tragedy. I'm not going to like it when the time comes. I'm not going to like it . . . I don't like it already. But it is just a part of life.

10

THE THOUGHTS, FEELINGS, AND REFLECTIONS OF A PERSON WITH A LIFE-THREATENING ILLNESS — John W. Gattis

John W. Gattis was diagnosed as having chronic myelogenous leukemia five years prior to his death. Six months before he died, he developed the acute or blastic stage of the disease. His chapter was prepared three months before his death. He was 43 years old at the time of his death. This chapter is based on a series of recorded interviews and was prepared by the editor in collaboration with John W. Gattis. (*Editor's Note*)

About five years ago, while on my way to an out-of-town conference, I became aware of a pain in my back between my shoulder blades, and the pain continued to intensify. After I arrived at the conference the pain became even worse and finally, at two in the morning, I asked a friend to take me to a local hospital. The doctor did a blood test, gave me some pain and sleeping medication, and said that I would have to be seen the next day by another doctor. The next day the doctor had the lab technician do blood tests and when the results came, he looked at them and was disbelieving and irritated. Obviously, the technician had made a mistake because she was reporting a white count of about 70,000, so he sent the technician back to do the tests over again. The second report came back 65,000 and he was still incredulous and still not believing the results. He sent me over to a hospital where he thought they would do a more careful and accurate job. It was as if it just couldn't be true. When I saw him the next day, at that point he said that my counts had the characteristics of leukemia, but it was likely what he called a leukemoid type of reaction to something and therefore probably was not dangerous. He thought it was unlikely that it was leukemia but felt that I should go into the hospital for further tests. I asked to go home to have these done and turned the training conference over to someone else for its completion.

People don't want to believe that the worst may be possible. The same sort of thing happened again when the leukemia became acute. This time, the differential cell count was high and my doctor, feeling that there was obviously an error in the results, sent it back to have another test done. But doctors are dealing with this kind of thing all the time—hoping for the best and hating to see the worst kind of news coming along. When it does, in a way it means that the doctor has to deliver bad news.

The diagnostic stage is not a comfortable one. As a minister, I have called on enough patients who are in that stage who will latch onto the worst possible alternatives, acting as though that is the one that it is before they really know. I knew that it would be a period of time before any kind of answer could be given, so I got two or three good books that I had needed to read and just stayed in my hospital room and read them. After a few days they came in and said, "We've done every test we can; we've eliminated all the other possibilities and it is leukemia that you have." That was a shock . . . it was a surprise, but it was not the end. It was said in a way that I knew that there would be some time. There was that kind of feeling communicated — that it was leukemia in the chronic stage and that meant it would not take its toll right away. I can't remember the exact words, but there was that kind of feeling communicated. I guess I felt that there was nothing immediate to worry about. I had the feeling that I didn't know exactly what this would mean . . . ultimately it would mean death . . . it would mean some radical adjustments . . . I didn't know what . . . and that I would have to learn. I felt sadness and an awesome sort of mystery about it, a strange kind of feeling that this happens to other people but it wouldn't happen to me. But now it really had happened.

I was referred to a hematologist and my first session with him was an important one. He was very direct and forthright. He answered any questions that I had and didn't hold anything back from me. We even talked about costs and he said that he had one patient who had recently died whose bill had run to $40,000. It had been necessary to write off part of the expenses. In terms of time he said my future had been taken away from me and what I had left was the present. He mentioned a friend of his who had been riding a motorcycle the previous weekend, had run off the road and had been killed instantly. He felt I was more fortunate than he because I had some time to do the things I wanted to do. I asked him about estimates of time and he said that the national average was a 50–50 chance for my living three to five years. Somehow or other, I latched onto that very quickly and I felt I could count on at least that much time. He said that because the disease had been found early and was in the stage it was, I would probably be on the better side of a 50–50 chance for the three to five years statistics.

He felt that the focus that he had seen in other patients that seemed most destructive was when they dwelled on thoughts like, "I might not get to see next spring." The focus he felt to be most important and helpful was to enjoy this spring and that was very timely advice. Another thing that my doctor said was, "Don't think about what you won't get to do, but experience to the fullest the things that you do get to do." I found that to be extremely helpful. I tried to put that into some kind of meaningful form. I talked with

my family and told them that when I was in the hospital they found that I had a disease that meant that in the future I wouldn't be able to do as much as I could then do, so it was important to make the most of the present and then we would just see what the future would hold. They listened and understood. . . .

Shortly after that, I presided over a meeting in New York. The place for the meeting was in a church and my chair was situated in a place where I could look out windows into a very large old burial ground. I was very much aware of that, and during one of the breaks, I asked one of my colleagues to walk with me through the burial ground. It was the first weekend in May and leaves were not yet beginning to burst their buds on the trees. As we walked I noticed the barks on the trees and the wide variety of textures of the barks. I commented about that to my colleague and he remarked that I must be more aware of that kind of thing than before. That was true. During the past five years when I was in the chronic stage of leukemia, my sensitivity seemed heightened. I've seen things that I don't believe I would have seen otherwise. I was very much aware of being some place and having the desire to come back but not knowing if I could count on that. So I would make the most of my being there that time.

But there were times, though, when I thought about the future. For example, I had thoughts that I would not live to see my daughter married. On one trip I had seen the play, *Fiddler on the Roof.* As I sat in the dark and they came to the wedding scene and Tevye and his wife sang, "Is this the little girl I carried?", for the first time, tears came streaming down my cheeks. I again tried to focus on the present and what I needed to do in the now . . . and to try to do that.

I began to feel a sense of urgency. I felt a realization as though I was suddenly converted. I became aware of the pattern of my life . . . of going and doing a lot of things. Converted is a Greek word that literally means to turn around and go the other way.

Shortly before the onset of my illness, I heard a talk by a church leader. In his introductory remarks he told how he had taken a month to spend time to decide how he would like to use the next ten years of his life. I placed that away in the back of my mind as something that would be nice to do sometime if I ever found time. After the diagnosis of leukemia was made it came back to me clearly that now, if ever, was the time to do just that, and I was able to arrange to have an entire week for myself to do this. I spent three days talking with various people who knew me rather well — friends at church, my wife, and people with whom I worked, just collecting their impressions about me. Then for two days I listed everything that I was presently doing or had thought I wanted to do in regard to my family, the community in which I lived, the church to which I belonged, and my responsibilities on my job. Having made separate listings in each of these categories, I then arranged each list in terms of priorities so that I could see what I would eliminate then and as time passed and my energy and time diminished. I found it to be a very helpful thing for me to look at my life in that way while I had full energy and somehow knew that I could count on three years. My priority list was designed in such a way that it would cover those three years.

Down in the bottom right hand corner of the page of the priority list, I can still envision a statement I wrote at the time. It was quite a change for me. I indicated that anything that I would undertake during this period of time had to be done in such a way that others could step in and carry on the work. Nothing could be done in a way that required my continued presence throughout the whole period of time the effort required. In each of the decisions that I made this would have to be an important consideration as to what and how I would plan and do a task. I not only included tasks, but I included people I wanted to get to know and places I would like to go. There were books I wanted to read and people with whom I wanted to have contact. I wanted to go and watch the sun set and rise in the Grand Canyon, out in the Far West — a part of the country that I love so very much.

I noted changes in some of my relationships with people, for in talking about my illness I sometimes developed a sense of their being unsure of what to say to me, and found that usually I had to open up the whole question of the disease. They would make a kind of cautious statement and then I would have to reply by saying, "You're talking about my leukemia?" and that would bring a kind of relief. Then it was all right to talk about . . . they recognized that there was nothing that they could say that would shatter me, which they undoubtedly wanted to avoid doing. Conversations have seemed to tend to follow three steps. First, what it was like for me, what I was feeling; second, if they wished to go in that direction, how did that make them feel, and then into whatever was a third mutual kind of concern that would have brought us together in the first place.

I've found that while people were concerned about providing some kind of comfort for me, often they didn't know how. They seemed appalled and it often turned out that I had to be the source of strength in the situation. I've talked with others with terminal illnesses who have reported a similar kind of thing; that instead of their necessarily receiving comfort and care, they themselves had to provide comfort and care for others. There are some who are able to make it a reciprocal, mutual kind of give-and-take, but that takes much more development of the relationship.

There are also people who come as comforters. I've found three categories. The first one says, "Well, life is very unsure and I could die from an accident this afternoon." When I try to point out that I, too, have the same odds of dying from an accident "this afternoon" as the person, they look at me rather quizically. Not once in five years has anyone said, "Well, I could get leukemia also." So this comforter in essence says, "Don't take it seriously, I could die at any time also." The second kind of comforter is the one who says, "Well, they're doing so much in research nowadays that by the time your disease progresses they will probably have come up with something that will be a cure." But I haven't been able to count on that. The third comforter is one who says, "Well, I have an 'Aunt Sally' who lived to be 81 with leukemia." That's fine — but what kind did she have and what were the conditions? I can't have any kind of promise. My doctor has said that from time to time he has seen patients with this illness go on for 15, 16, 17, or 18 years, and I would say, "That's fine — you're going to promise me one of those?" But there have been no promises . . . no promises whatsoever. Such things offer encouragement, but they aren't a sign of a promise and a promise was what I would have preferred.

What has provided true comfort is a few friends, some time with my family, feeling unlimited in terms of life and feeling unrestricted in what I've been able to do. I've tried to take on tasks I could finish, knowing that the importance for me is what happens before death and not what happens after death. I was surprised that I did not focus on life after death. My concern has been for the quality of living for people, for me and for others. And there are ways that I have seen that I could contribute something that would begin to bring about some changes in the character of life and also influence institutions for those who would directly participate; hopefully changing and influencing in new and better directions and being life-giving so that I could take some pride and pleasure in knowing that I was able to do something that would make a difference for me, for people in my own family, and for people in the communities. These changes would not depend on my presence and would not necessarily carry my name afterwards, but when they came about, I could say that I had been able to do that . . . that I helped to fill a need and to give life through my actions.

Comfort comes from knowing that there are persons who will come and be nearby . . . come just to be here. People need to understand that the need is to reach out not only to the patient himself, but also to reach out to those that are also closely affected by the situation — children, spouses, or parents — to be available to those people as well so that they can find relief with the matters that are pressing them most deeply, and they then can become more accessible to the patient.

Some people seem very interested in the disease — where the blood counts are, how I'm feeling physically. A few people pursue it further and say, "Okay, that's how your disease is, now how are you? How are you feeling?" and those are the people who become important. These people, friends, doctors, and nurses who are able to move into that level of a relationship beyond the disease attached to the person are the ones who have been the most helpful. There have been some who, when I have felt low, have attempted to be reassuring . . . to be reassuring about the disease itself rather than just responding to the feelings about the person whom the disease is affecting. But others cared about me in a different way — they were aware of what was happening to my body, but they were caring for my needs and in some way their needs, just by being there. They cared for me as a person and they were somehow caring for their needs also just by being there. What was happening to me was happening to them, too. The direction and the dimensions of the disease would have continuing effect upon them and not just me.

Soon after I found out that I was in the acute stage of the leukemia, a friend came in and sat down. I was just right on the verge of tears. I had no way to deal with my feelings . . . and I could not speak. I said to the friend, "Hold my hand," and we just sat there. After a while my friend said, "Would it help to talk?" I said, "No, not now," and we just sat there quietly for at least an hour. Later my minister came and I was able to talk, but the person who just sat with me was most helpful when I needed that kind of care. The same was true when I was treated with the asparaginase. It's a kind of chemotherapy and I reacted to it so very strongly with deep, heavy nausea. The first afternoon there was six hours of nausea and I couldn't talk with anyone. A friend came in, and I was able to open my eyes and see that she was there. She sat on the edge of the bed and took my hand and I could sense her weeping, but all I could do was say, "Thanks for your tears and thanks for being here." And that was it . . . but just the person's presence and her being there was helpful. Being present is very important. There has been a great deal of concern that visitors were draining on me, but it hasn't been. I've felt no drain of energy but a mutual give-and-take. I felt that I gained as well as gave during that time.

I believe that when someone is giving care, it's okay for them to show that they are upset. I've seen tears in my doctor's, my pastor's, and others' eyes. That's really okay because I've got them, too. It helps me and them to express the feelings. Rather than blocking them and trying to avoid the feelings and the area . . . it's okay to talk about dying. It's not to be avoided, it's not taboo. They give exactly the wrong instructions on the visitor's information at hospitals. It says just to be pleasant. It's more important to be real than to try to be pleasant. If you are feeling sad, it's important to be able to say that.

I found that some people came in extremely nervous because they didn't know how to come into a room where there was a patient with a known terminal illness. They wanted to be able to say something that would be really important to me, as if they had a feeling that if they only knew the right kind of words, it would become some sort of profound statement that could be posted on the wall. It seemed as if there was almost an obligation for some people to dc that. I noticed it most often the first time that a person was there — that I needed to let them have the clues that it was okay just to be there and to encourage them, even at times to say, "Are you feeling kind of nervous?" I needed to help them to express that and then to relieve them of the obligation of having to be astute and profound.

I've found it important to experience my illness, to find out what it's like . . . knowing that it's something that cannot be avoided or pretended about. Pretending that it cannot be there would be useless and sharing it with others has been important. I learned that right from the very start — that others would come and seek me out when they were ready. Or if I gave them permission to do so, they would kind of anxiously watch to see what it was like . . . to know if it was okay to ask a question about my illness.

It's also important that people let me say how I am really feeling and hear me; to hear me say my feelings and to respond on the same plane; to let me know that it's okay to feel that way. I was talking with one of the floor nurses the other evening and said I was feeling pretty low and I got reassurance. It was on a different plane for rather than hearing, it was just listening. It's okay when

I feel some way that is easier for them to accept. If I'm feeling joyful or something like that then they'll rejoice in that, but if I am feeling blue, that's difficult for them to deal with. Once, I asked about a patient who had been in the next room and one of the nurses spent a long time walking around the truth — "Well, it was really pretty sad," and such things — and I finally said, "Did the patient die?" and she said, "Yes," and went out. But there are some who can respond, who can listen and respond directly, one to one.

I believe that there are several ways that the best medical care can be given a dying person. One important way is through what I have experienced with my physicians in their being totally open and honest with the diagnoses as they were developing . . . no sense of withholding any information but helping me to have that information and to be able to interpret that. I don't know whether this kind of openness in giving information would work for everybody, but I know it's been very important for me. It's made it possible for me to know what to deal with rather than to leave me with any kind of wonderings through the night or questioning what does he mean by that or asking myself what is not being told me. Another kind of thing that the doctors have done has been to come in and to sit down with a sense of "I really care . . . I am really present." And when necessary they have been open with me about their feelings. Being a real person means showing feelings.

There were some things I was afraid of. One was to be alone, being isolated, dying alone, just being cared for by impersonal nurses and doctors doing things to perpetuate the living as long as possible, being competent, but not being persons that I could share with. During one of my hospitalizations, it was extremely reassuring that people gathered around and there were those from whom I gained strength, but I don't know where they'll be when I actually am dying. I have lost a certain degree of that fear of being actually alone. Now I know there will be people there when I die. There will be medical people who are there, not just in a professional role, but in a personal role as well.

At times, I fear that every attempt may be made to extend my life longer than necessary. I don't want to overstay, I don't want to be delayed. I've seen that with some patients and there is the expense and there is the wear and tear upon others. Where death is certain, its occurrence is prevented and the quality of the time is unuseable. At that point, there is nothing that I or anybody else can do that would amount to a meaningful relationship. I know it's difficult to be the person to pull out the plug, whether it's on a machine plugged into the wall or whatever is the life-giving force. It's extremely difficult. But to just be able to count that more days happen and nothing has actually occurred — I don't know that that would be worthwhile. From the start, I've been able to have great confidence in my doctor and from the start, I have said of him that he is one who would help me to have a good life . . . and a good death . . . and those things . . . I still want. I want to know that is happening and to share in its happening.

Before this last admission to the hospital, when things began to get worse, I began to have a sense of finality. My physical condition was deteriorating. I felt very weak and felt a sense of urgency to get some things cleared out and thrown out or given away. I talked with my pastor to give him some material that I thought might be considered for a memorial service to clear those arrangements and get that out of the way. I went through a lot of material deciding what to do with it. I noticed that the mood at home changed from a sense of hilarity and wit, a sense of ease and lightness, to one of remorse and grief. The materials I was going through had represented important parts of me . . . contributions to who I am. Some of the things I felt could be thrown away . . . some of them could be used by somebody else, and some I had a feeling of importance for and felt that there ought to be somebody in the world to take care of them . . . they ought not just be disposed of. I gave some memorabilia to my children. I cleared my desk and threw away all the unimportant things that I had been saving. All of that material on my desk was out of the past, and if I could get rid of that then the past would be gone, and I would really be in the now

and I would like that . . . that would feel good.

A lot got thrown away. Each of the kids wanted some of the things and took them. It was good to be able to do that . . . again that feeling of I won't be able to take care of these things or give them as much attention as I had given to them . . . but they represented important events and times and people earlier in my life, and now I didn't want to just dump them out. I'd like for somebody to know about them. I guess those things would represent a physical reminder of me that might continue to help to bring forth the feelings of sadness and happiness . . . to draw out some of the good feelings and some of the bad feelings . . . there might be something to physically touch and be alone with and allow others to explore their own feelings. I'd like people to experience the full range of emotions in their grief — not just sadness, nor attempts at expressions of celebration for this life in order to avoid expressions of sadness. I want people to be able to cry and to laugh and even to be able to deal with some of their anger about the kind of person I was.

I'm aware that eventually things have to be put in place and done away with. I'm aware that eventually there will be a time that my doctor will say, "I can't treat you." I think I really kind of expected that to come already. The time will come when he will say, "I can't treat you but I'll help to make it the best for you." I need to be ready for that. I had a sense of maybe that would happen soon and then it would be too late to get things cleared away. Maybe I wouldn't be able to leave the hospital again to go home to sort out the books. Maybe I wouldn't be able to go home to clear off the desk, so I had better do it then, when I was sure I could. It was all a tangible way of saying . . . it's final.

It's here, it's real. I'm getting blood, and there's no way of denying that it's happening. I've had the whole range of infections; I had the low counts; I've had things happening to my body that I've never seen before. I cannot help me nor can others help me if I just pretend it's not here. Acceptance is saying, okay, it's something that I need to go through, and I'll go through with it. The choice is not whether I am going to go through it or not, the choice is how I'm going to go through it. I have no options at this point. I know what the termination of this is. I do not know what's going to happen at the end, but I'll find out. Of course there are times when I'd like to escape it . . . when I would just as soon not have to go through this. I don't know if there is anything special that allows me to accept it. I just realize that no life is eternal and my condition is real.

11

HEALING AND DYING

Charles E. Scott, Ph.D.

"For in the immediate world, everything is to be discerned, for him who can discern it, and centrally and simply, without either dissection into science, or digestion into art, but with the whole of consciousness, seeking to perceive it as it stands: so that the aspect of a street in sunlight can roar in the heart of itself as a symphony, perhaps as no symphony can: and all of consciousness is shifted from the imagined, the revisive, to the effort to perceive simply the cruel radiance of what is."

James Agee
*Let Us Now Praise Famous men**

When I was asked to write this piece, I thought of including thumbnail sketches of what five or so philosophers have said on the topic of death and dying. That could conceivably have been distracting and perhaps interesting for those of you who like ideas and are curious. That would also have been a silly thing for me to have done — particularly on this topic. Philosophy is not a thumbnail sketch of anything. It is reflective activity which has as its goal an interpretation of realities, an interpretation that is most aware of what it itself is doing.

The realities before us are dying and death. In this chapter, our goal is to be philosophers for awhile. To do so is not to be able to be erudite about what others have said, but so that we shall know our own existence. For how shall a person be a physi-

cian with another dying person if he mistakes the reality of dying and death?

THINKING ABOUT DYING

Most people most of the time fear death in a natural way without thinking about it. Or so it seems. Walking happily off a curb, one is seized with a moment of terror as a car bears down on him and only narrowly misses him. He does not want to die. Or a person with a temperature of 105°, emaciated from weeks of pain sets her jaw and eyes and "holds on" because she does not want to die. Or we plan our canoeing trip with care because we want adventure but not death. We are often threatened by a cool and well-planned suicide because our own desire to live is relativized by this event of planned death. We want to want to live.

Our desire to live, our will to be, is so natural and so strong that protection from death and from the power of our fear of death can be a major barrier when our professions have to do with people who are especially or obviously close to death. And death as a possibility is so pervasive of our lives that our fear relating to death can be a major barrier to accepting the finite openness of our own existence.

e.e. cummings[1] sees, however, that the experiences of growth and joy and freeing immediacy all involve also at once dying and death.

We can never be born enough . . . birth is a supremely welcome mystery, the mystery of

* Reprinted by permission, Houghton Mifflin Company.

growing: the mystery which happens . . . whenever we are faithful to ourselves. . . . Life, . . . is now; and now is much too busy being a little more than everything to seem anything, catastrophic included.

The 'now' says, as it were, 'impermanence.' And our impermanence is our never being tied down finally to how we were or to how we are now. But possible catastrophe is also part of the meaning of impermanence. Dying and death are an essential part of the ". . . mystery of growing: the mystery that happens . . . whenever we are faithful to ourselves." We turn with impermanence to ourselves and discover, in being true to ourselves, the meaning of being impermanent and aware. Rilke[2] said in a letter, "even in the most-coming wind we breathe parting." Coming and going, growing and dying, all seem involved with each other. Being here now already bespeaks dying in the very impermanence of the moment — and in the impermanence of ourselves as the moment.

Because dying and death are so central a part of our being as well as of our communal, personal, and professional lives, and because we fear and turn away from it, thinking about it is important. One kind of thinking can be part of our escape: we think away from death by dealing with it in rigid, conceptual categories, or we merely "examine" what important people have said on the topic. That is bad thinking as well as bad psychology because it deals with the reality of death largely by denying and distancing us from the reality of death.

Another way of dealing with death is to think toward it. "Thinking towards death" does not mean that one's thinking culminates with his death. It means that one reflects his experiences of death and dying and interprets those experiences. That process involves a descriptive recognition of the experiences, a search for the words that give most vividness to the way the experiences occur, and the development of judgments or interpretations that relate these experiences to other experiences, i.e., the reflection of experiences of death and dying with other experiential reflections.

By this process we *uncover* prereflective experiences — that is the opposite of hiding from them — and we integrate them in rela-

tion to other parts of our lives. Our aim in this case is to bring together the experiences related to death and dying with all the basic experiences of our life so that we do not need to protect ourselves from death and the fear of death. Nietzsche[3] phrased this aim in his own way:

"From love of *life*, one should desire a different death: free, conscious, without accident, without ambush."

THE EXPERIENCE OF DYING AND DEATH

For convenience in this section I want to use the words *dying* and *death* to name different kinds of events. e.e. cummings[4] made the distinction in one way. He found dying to be "fine," he says. It is a natural and utterly lively part of life. For cummings, dying means birth and creation and new beginning. But death, he says, is evil. It is something at a distance from being alive, an absence of life, a rigid determination that can be defined, but not lived. He is grateful for dying and finds death to be a sin against life.

Cummings is right in seeing that *dying* names an experience of one dimension of our living, whereas *death* names an objective 'thing' that is not immediate in our lives. We often think of dying and death as something we can only go through once, unless we are brought back to life after our hearts have stopped beating. One result of this way of thinking is that we actually separate dying from living, and the idea of the experience of dying seems strange to us. I want to show that the experience of dying, as distinct to death, is very much an aspect of our living and that consequently the meaning of living and the meaning of dying need not be antithetical to each other.

The experience of death, as I think of it, is seeing someone stop breathing or imagining myself as not here. To imagine myself as totally absent is possible only as a leap into a non-imaged state of feeling, an experience that is quite different from imagining my funeral, although the latter may be a step toward the profound sense of my own non-being. These experiences can be highly significant, particularly before we have thoroughly realized and experienced the meaning of our finiteness. But we shall concentrate now on the immediate experience of dying. I stress this latter experience because it is, I believe, the one most difficult to interpret and the one most important for understanding ourselves in relation to our mortality.

I want to emphasize two of the dominant ways of experiencing dying which I shall call the experience of transition and the experience of lapse of meaningful direction.

The Experience of Transition

The experience of transition happens as the loss of some aspect of my existence and as the emergence of some aspect of my existence that is new for me. I experience dying, for example, when my child, or spouse, mother, or father dies. I do not experience his or her death. I experience the loss of a living relationship. *I* am changed. I am *bereaved*—that word, *bereaved*, comes from the Anglo-Saxon word which means *to be deprived* or *to be dispossessed*. The loss is not under my control. I *am* deprived. I am changed. I undergo a deep change of relationship. In that sense a part of my reality dies and a new way of being replaces that other aspect of my existence—in this case my relation to someone permanently absent replaces my relation to that person as alive.

Another kind of dying occurs when a person himself changes significantly; when, for example, I become free of an illusion that has dominated my relation to people. Part of me dies in losing that illusion, and I may grieve a loss over which I am also happy. Or I experience dying when I discover, against all my expectations, that some people are not trustworthy, or as I move from childishness to responsibility and independence.

The experience of dying happens as we lose some aspect of the way we are—a relationship, a factor of our identity, a fundamental direction of choice, an ideal. A part of us ceases to be. Such experiences seem to mean that nothing that I am is final and free from radical change. They seem to mean that I am myself a process of changing, that *I* occur as dying and as being reborn. These experiences of dying are themselves the experience of the pre-reflective awareness that my own being is always in question and fundamentally uncertain. I am aware of myself pre-reflectively as a state of transition.

That awareness, although it is one way we are immediately aware of ourselves, can be frightening. It is our nonreflective sense that our best and strongest *control* of ourselves and of our environment does not define our existence. Our own existence is deeply outside of our control. Our experience of dying is our living out that insight. It means that when our professional work and our personal lives are strongest and most integrated, we are a living process that is not defined finally by our work or our personality. It is defined also as a process of changing—growing, declining, transisting—which is lived as an experience of dying that is not within one's control.

The fear or anxiety that can accompany our sense of being outside of our own control may be expressed in attempts to maximize the importance and meaning of what we feel we can control. I may resist knowing deeply and thoroughly that my living is also a process of dying. I may not want to understand what I clearly sense: that all that I love and want and count on is subject to transition, to the process of dying. I may well want more stability and firmness than the dying process of my living allows. The consequence is that I turn away from this central part of my own existence and focus chiefly on what I can keep at my disposal, as though these situations, things, and people were not mortal.

In turning away from my own experiences of dying in the form of transitions, I may avoid, as well as I can, all depth reminders of my own transitoriness. I may avoid people who are experiencing the pain of radical transitions. I may even deny that such transitions are going on. Or I may develop an attitude of distance, perhaps an air of superiority regarding those who suffer radical changes in their lives—a rigid moralism, a secure professionalism, a set of beliefs absolutized into rigidity.

In such cases of denial I reject a significant dimension of my own existence—the experience of transition—and I am consequently inclined to reject people who remind me of that aspect of myself. In refusing this experience of dying I refuse an important part of human living.

If one learns how " . . . to take . . . leave

and to commence afresh . . . "[5] he will have accepted one central way in which we experience dying. As we hold on to what is over as though it were not over, and we refuse the emerging parts of our lives as though they were not genuinely new and emerging, we deny our own experience of dying. And we very likely will turn away from those who remind us of our own denial.

Experiencing a Lapse of Meaningful Direction

We begin with a situation: You find yourself with nothing to do. You feel strange or ignored and deeply lonely. You don't want to do anything in particular. The options are:

1. Start doing something — anything — go out and find someone. Think about your work. Wash your hair. Pick up something to read. Find an activity.

2. Feel blue, depressed. Sit and stare. Sleep. Think hateful thoughts about the people outside who are laughing.

3. Draw conclusions about reality from your feelings at this moment. Some conclusions that can be drawn: (a) The universe is a crock of shit. (b) Mother and Daddy hate me. (c) My wife is unfaithful to me. (d) No one really appreciates me. (e) I'm the only one who understands the way things really are. (f) I'm a bad person, etc.

4. Feel sympathy for the loneliness which other people experience. Want to help in some way. Want to serve somehow.

5. Ask yourself what is missing, wait for an answer, affirm the directions of meaning that appear in this sense of emptiness, affirm the sense of emptiness to be valuable.

What has happened in this passing moment? A direction of meaning was not apparent. Without such direction we may experience ourselves, if only for a fleeting moment, disconnected from reality in general. Feeling disconnected is a dying experience. We experience a closure of meaning, separation from the world, an absence of meaningful dialogue. Though alive, we experience a loss of a sense of aliveness and vitality.

In the first situation in which I find just anything to do, I distract myself from my situation by some activity or by something that takes my attention. My fear of dissociation, or my unease with it, happens as my scurrying around to find something to do. I am immediately aware of the emptiness of living without a direction of meanings and of the absence of the direction which I need in order to feel deeply and thoroughly alive. I run around anxiously.

In the second situation of sitting and sleeping, I fall prey, at least momentarily to my sense of emptiness. I am deactivated. I am overcome by a sense of detachment and indifference. I feel like I am dying for a while.

In the third situation, as I draw conclusions about things in general, I pull away from the immediacy of my feelings enough to think, instead of sitting and staring, but not enough to grasp the relative place of my feelings. So I absolutize them for awhile with mementos of thought writ on marble, little tombstones of reflection.

When I feel close to the loneliness of other people, I discover the relation, the commonness of us all, in the experience of dissociation. I find a basis for hope for relation in my sense of deathliness, my experience of too little meaning for life. In this case, caring for others in our common pain is a dominant way of finding release from the sense of meaninglessness.

In the final instance, when I wait with my sense of emptiness, I attempt to discover who and how I want to be, allowing my loneliness and meaninglessness to be, grieving if need be, hoping for an option, a direction, that I can make mine, being prepared to choose a way for living, but being open now in the absence of something to choose.

In these observations, I have made the experience of meaningful direction a counter pole to the experience of meaninglessness. I have said in effect that the experience of deep loneliness and dissociation is natural, a common kind of happening, and that it is one of our contacts with our contingency and deathliness. I have also said that human living is experienced, as we say, as *really* living according to the directions with which we identify ourselves. Those directions have to be appropriated, chosen in some sense of the word. If we choose them with intensity and if we live out our directions of choice with vigor, we live intensely.

Being overcome by a sense of meaninglessness is an experience of dying — a common experience. As our meanings die away, as they lose their directional force, we experience an absence, sometimes for a moment, sometimes for extended periods, and such an experience is an experience of dying. By *dwelling* with that experience — by *letting it be*, by hearing my own being in the passing away of directions of meaning, I live that *openness*, that *region for hearing*, where *birth* of direction can occur. Letting the experience of meaninglessness happen, but not falling prey to it, just letting it occur, is a painful experience of openness for the future. That is an experience of contingency, of deathliness, which is also *freedom* for possibility, for growth, as well as freedom for death, or for absence.

MEANING AND OPENNESS IN HUMAN EXISTENCE

The *experience* of dying points out that human existence is an experiential process. Our existence does not happen like an object of investigation happens. It happens as a conscious occurrence, as an event of meanings that is alert and subject to pain and fulfillment. When we forget our human reality, we may treat ourselves as mere objects and assume that *dying* refers to no more than physical processes.

Three ordinary occurrences on ward rounds follow:

(1) A young man eighteen years old, in the final stages of leukemia. It has come on quickly. His body is still strong and developed. His black skin glistens as the light plays off his sweat. Very low white count. His feet twitch. Danger of dehydration. The attending physician calls for an I.V. His eyes widen. "Am I goin' a die, Doctor? I don't wan' a die! God, I don't wan' a die!"

(2) Eighty years old. Fever of unknown origin. Chronic diarrhea. Now unable to keep food in his stomach. So sunken into his bed that he hardly looks present. Skeletal head. Cheeks sink into his toothless mouth. A wisp of white hair standing straight up on his otherwise bald pate. Small, wizened, staring at the wall. His wife, white-headed, healthy, worried, tired, stands by his bed.
Dr: "How is he today, Mrs. R.?"
Mrs. R: "Oh, he's no good, Doctor. Nothing we do works. He vomits everything up."
Dr: "How's his bowels?"

Mrs. R: "He had two little dabs, but they was bloody lookin'."
Dr: (after a pause, with a sympathetic and worried look) "What are we going to do with him, Mrs. R.?"
Mrs. R: "All we can do is keep on loving him I reckon, Doctor."

(3) Thirty-five year old mother of three. Final days. Her fair skin splotched from a body-covering rash that drove her wild with itching for days. Fever, 105°. As the nurse applies the cold washrag, she yields to the movement of the rag, a quick, almost defiant, yet fully cooperative movement. Her eyes, like a flogged animal's eyes, show anger, pain, deep hurt, quiet determination. She lies on her back. Her arms are on the pillow by her head, so that her armpits can be swabbed. But she looks like she has been strapped down and is undergoing, without crying out, some torture.
Dr: "Well, Judy, how are you today?"
J: (looks at him long and slow, fully alert; her eyes tell of no comprehension of her disease, of a life of yielding to forces greater than she) "O.K., I guess."
Dr: "I don't know what to do with you next, Judy. Every time we put you on something you break out like this. Every time we take you off, you don't have enough resistance to fight whatever germs come along. I don't know what to do." (after a long pause) "Do you ever wonder why this happens, Judy?"
J: "No, I don't. Maybe it's because I'm a very bad person."
Dr: "I don't think that's the reason. I don't think that you are a bad person."
J: "Well . . . why then?"
Dr: "Did you ever hear the hymn that begins, 'Courage, brother, do not stumble, though thy path be dark as night.'?"
J: "No. I never heard that." (She turns away. The doctor is dismissed.)

I note these three occurrences, which are nonfictional and which are quite ordinary, in order to recall in a focused way the fact that human illness and even the physical process of dying are events of meaning which cannot be understood by physical descriptions only. Fear, desire, etc., are all events of meaning, just as suffering is too. We surely die of physical causes. But dying is itself, in its human reality, a process of meaning that is communicated in words, gestures, eyes, attitudes, and silences. Relation with a person who is dying with some physical malady is never merely a clinical matter. It is a *relation*, an occurrence of meaning, and one possible way to relate is to be clinical about the whole thing: to relate to the person as though he or she were primarily a sick body-object. Relation with the sick, like any relation, is an occurrence of meaning in which the health professional's own relation to himself as well as how he relates with the other person are a central part of the medical situation. To ignore the relationship is to dehumanize, to sicken the situation, even when physical healing is going on. To relate as though the healer's task is primarily with a body-object is to live a deep and dangerous ignorance of human being.

I state the point so starkly in order to underscore that our concern must be with *how* one lives his or her sickness and final days or hours. The *how* is where *human* dying occurs. In order to place this emphasis accurately, we must attend to our existence as a finite, self-aware event of meaning. Short of that point of attention, we very likely will think of dying as something that an inarticulate system of organs undergoes. The person can seem almost extra, vaguely in the way, when our intuitions are centered on such a physical system.

If we are persuaded that human existence is a meaning event, we are prepared to see that *how* we experience dying will be the fundamental structure for how we approach our death. Our death occurs for us as something final, something we cannot live through. Regardless of our beliefs about immortality, death itself, in *its* time, usually means *loss* of life, *loss* of everything familiar, the most radical transition. It means an eradication of our experience of meaning, a radical separation from all that we value, a loss of direction, an emptying out and giving up.

If I have feared the inevitability of loss, *i.e.*, the transitoriness of my existence, I shall find the specific prospect of death particularly fearful. If I have maximized control in order to turn away from my sense of the uncontrolableness of my being, I shall prob-ably try to control everything up to my death and maybe my funeral as well. If frenzy has accompanied my experience of the loss of meaning, how I shall approach my death is reasonably certain. And if I have been free for loss, for uncontrolled openness, for the absence of direction, and so forth, I shall most likely be free for my fear of my death or for my desire for my death. And I shall probably be free also for my death. My experience of dying has already let me know that death, the final loss of my earthly life, is not outside my life, but a culmination for my life.

The living relation between living and dying is discovered by attention to how human existence is intrinsically a process of transition and how it involves both meaningful relations and lapses of meaning. That living relation is experienced as a kind of openness: no moment in life is final; each moment opens out into another moment and is left behind. Our meanings and values structure our openness and closedness with things. And this very openness of human being, which we find in a radical way when we experience lapses of meaning and losses of aspects of our own existence, is the way we encounter our mortality, our deathliness. When we are open to our experiences of dying, we are open to our own deathliness. We are then prepared for that most important insight of self-awareness: that we are never finally objects of control or even controlling subjects. We, in our deathliness, are not defined finally by how we control ourselves or by how we are controlled by others. And when we do not resist our experiences of dying, we are attuned to our uncontrolled openness for the world. That is at once most threatening, if we have made control central for our lives' meaning, and also most freeing if we have felt the misery of believing that our lives depended on our control of most nearly everything.

So we may say that human living is how we relate meaningfully with ourselves and with other people and things. Human existence is a self-aware, meaning-structured process. This process is characterized by profound self-alteration and by lapses of meaning. Dying is apparent in these experiences. We discover, when we do not resist the experiences of dying, that *control* can never be a *finally* appropriate relation with ourselves and with others. Release to our own nonobjectivity is the experience of being free for our dying. In that freedom, the end of our lives may appear as both a threat to our meanings and as the fulfillment of our finiteness. We become free for our existence when we do not have to hide from what we dread.

THE DIFFERENCE BETWEEN BEING AND HAVING

Gabriel Marcel[6] has developed the difference between having something at one's disposal and being undisposable. *Having* is an experience of keeping, holding, legally owning, using, and so forth. My yard, my house, my profession. But my child? My life? We certainly speak of having children, parents, lovers, and lives. Our language leads us astray in such instances to the extent that we come to think of lives and children (and patients, too) as things defined by how we dispose of them.

We know by common sense that everything we own exceeds our ownership. There is a sense, certainly, in which I have a profession. I choose it. I develop it in certain ways. I use it for certain goals. But there is also a sense in which my profession has me. I am molded by it. It fits me into a history and a future that are not under my control. My yard and my instruments also exceed me. Although I own them, they never fall fully under my possession. They have an independence that is fundamentally different from *my* ownership. I see this independence particularly when my yard will not grow what I want it to grow or when it makes me work for it. And when my instruments break or will not do what I want them to, I know that there is a sense in which I shall never own them.

When we view things in relation to being able to dispose and not being able to dispose, we find ourselves dealing with two dimensions of reality: one dimension is defined by its availability to us (*e.g.*, we can use this hammer or that person for our own purposes); another dimension is outside of our grasp (*e.g.*, the hammer and the person are not totally defined by our use of them). When we deal with caring and with dying, we are concerned by the unpossessable, *i.e.*, the nondisposable dimension of human reality.

That dimension of reality which never is the same as my relation to it, that excessiveness of my intentions, is mysterious, as Marcel describes it. A mystery, by definition, can never fall into a conceptual scheme. It is not the same as my thinking of it or my intuitions regarding it, or my uses of it. Mystery is what is present as never fitting my categories and as never the same as the reality of my thinking and willing processes.

Marcel gives the nonpossessable, *i.e.*, the mysterious, the name of *being*. Being cannot be had. It never happens as an object. It is what is independent of whatever I might do regarding it. And our own being is, of course, a nonpossessable reality. Our being, our living reality, lives and dies.

That means that to *be* ourselves is a matter of living out the immediacy of whatever we might be *in* – desire, pain, ambition, love, awe, hatred, whatever. Being ourselves human, not being only objects to ourselves, not trying to possess our futures, even when we are planning. It means being open with our aims, not trying to keep who we are. Releasing ourselves as we run ahead toward whatever we have chosen to seek or toward whatever lies ahead unchosen. Being released is being free for our unpossessableness, even when we are tied into a work-a-day world that makes us live by a clock.

And the unpossessable other? Not an object. A being. Encounterable, but not possessable. Not kept. But known. He is to be helped, served, perhaps, when we are healers. But he is not to be treated primarily as an object, not as a sick thing, but as someone living and dying. As a mystery.

Ted Rosenthal wrote *How Could I Not Be Among You?*[7] during his terminal illness. He discovered and says in this poem that the meaning of death is to be found in openness in living:

I stand before you all aching with truth
Trembling with desire to make you know.
Eat, sleep, and be simple about life.
To be serious is to be simple;
to be simple is to love.
Don't wait another minute, make tracks, go
   home.
Admit you have some place to return to.

The bugs are crawling over the earth,
 the sun is shining over everyone.
Get tickled by the tall cattails.
Kick crazily into the burrs and prickles
Rub your back against the bark, and go
 ahead, peel it.
Adore the sun.
O people, you are dying. Live while you can.

Openness for living, which means a deep willingness to live through transitions, losses, lapses of meanings, not to forget our mortality, but to live it out with full awareness, this living while we can, impresses me as an opposite of the desire to possess. I am certain that I seek to possess parts of my own life and of the lives of people around me. I often want things to be exact and predictable. Such a desire is often appropriate, but not as a controlling attitude toward myself and other people. I suspect that many people in health professions also attempt, unwittingly, to possess and control the lives of "their" patients. I recall one of so many examples: a physician telling a woman that she would either do what he told her to do or she would have to find another doctor. On the one hand, this person was deeply frustrated by "his" patient's resistances. On the other hand, he felt that he needed to be in total control in order to work his healing techniques. (He had not yet learned the art of healing.) The total control factor is witness to a kind of possessive rigidity, a closure to the frustrating, often maddening nonobjectivity of other people and of ourselves. It is also closure to whatever does not fit the grasp of our demands.

When we teach or heal or administer without giving dominance to possessing — when we live at ease with the nonobjective mystery of being, to use Marcel's language, we find ourselves free for dying. That freedom creates attitudes toward death which are revolutionary in possession-dominated situations, but which never confuse human life and death with facts or objects. We find in this quiet freedom for dying the feelings and values which will not allow us to oppress life in the name of healing or to deny dying in the name of living.

ENDING

I have pointed out that dying is a part of living, as distinct to death, which is the end of living. Some of our experiences of dying occur when relations and aspects of our lives change and when we undergo loss of meaning. How we relate to such transitions and losses reflects to us how we are related to our death. When denial is dominant in our self-relation, for example, denial of the other person in his mortality is highly likely. I have stated further that openness to the inevitability of transition and loss is at the same time openness to birth and regeneration, that we are closed to our mortality at the expense of closure to significant dimensions of possibility of creation. And finally I have suggested that the delivery of health care will reflect the dominance of openness or of possessiveness in our attitudes, that good health care (the art of the healing use of certain techniques) is dependent on our own release to our own mortality. That release will suggest to us that how we die is as important as whether we die. In medical practice the lives of the professional and the patient are always equally in question.

If our thinking about death and dying is 'right,' we shall be more open to our own dying, and that of other people, and we shall be attuned to our uncertainty, which we recognize as inevitable, concerning the meaning of death and dying. We allow that uncertainty because the 'place' of meaning, the context of meaning, itself changes, and thereby all meanings shift as constantly and as inevitably as the sea, without rest and without a final justification. In thinking this inevitability, in accepting uncertainty in our self-image and in our view of our work and our relations with others, we come to a strange peace with death: we may fear it, but we do not need to reject it; we turn toward it as we accept our lives in their mortality; we find freedom for living as we accept the inevitability of dying. And accepting that strange inevitability, we find an attunement with dying and living people which allows us to be free, nonprotective, life-affirming, and conversant with our own anxieties in their presence and in their service as healers.

REFERENCES

1. cummings ee: *Collected Poems*. Harcourt, Brace & World, Inc, New York, 1963
2. Rilke RM: *Selected Letters of Rainer Maria Rilke*. Macmillan, London, 1946

3. Nietzsche F: *Twilight of the Idols*, in *The Portable Nietzsche*. Kaufman W (Trans and Ed), The Viking Press, New York, 1968

4. cummings ee: dying is fine) but Death, in *XAIPE seventy-one poems by ee cummings*. Oxford University Press, New York, 1944

5. Hesse H: *Magister Ludi*. Bantam Books, New York, 1969

6. Marcel G: *Being and Having*. Collins, New York, 1965

7. Rosenthal T: *How Could I Not Be Among You*. George Braziller, New York, 1973

12

CARING FOR THE DYING PERSON— ETHICAL ISSUES AT STAKE

Robert M. Veatch, Ph.D.

Caring for the dying raises not only critical psychological and social questions, but basic philosophical questions of the meaning of human life and suffering. Between these practical and abstract extremes are a number of crucial ethical questions, which are both practical in the sense that everyone rendering care for the dying must face them on a daily basis, and philosophical in that they cannot be answered simply by gathering medical or psychological data. They require consideration of questions such as: What ought the dying patient be told? When is a patient in extremis really dead? When, if ever, is it acceptable to allow or to assist a dying patient to die? And what are the limits of human freedom in choosing, for oneself or for those for whom one is responsible, to change the natural course of the dying process? These are the ethical questions posed for us by the dying patient. Some possible answers will be the subject matter for this chapter.

WHAT TO TELL THE DYING PATIENT

In caring for the dying, the question of what the patient should be told is the most common, the most controversial, and the most difficult to resolve. From the standpoint of ethics, it is fascinating to ask why this most common of ethical questions remains so opaque to resolution. In asking that question we shall be able to form a framework for analyzing some of the other ethical problems in the care of the dying.

Many physicians,[1] and probably to a somewhat lesser extent other health-care professionals,[2] have a tendency to resist telling dying patients the nature of their illness, especially when the prognosis is bleak, such as in the case of the dying cancer patient. Oken found, for instance, that 88% of physicians tended not to tell their patients of a terminal cancer diagnosis. Fitts and Ravdin found that 3% "always tell" their patients and 28% usually do, while 57% "usually do not tell" and 12% "never do." Although there may be strong psychological reasons to avoid discussing such matters with patients, many tend not to tell on moral grounds, believing it is wrong, at least in many cases, to transmit the full implication of the diagnosis and prognosis. Yet studies have indicated that cancer patients, non-cancer patients, and those at a cancer detection clinic say overwhelmingly that they want to be told.[3] Our task is to see what the foundations of these positions are and what moral reasons might be given for alternative ethical stances taken by those more inclined to disclosure or non-disclosure.

At least three reasons may explain this ethical disagreement about what to tell the dying patient. Those engaged in the debate may disagree about what ethical norms or principles are relevant to the decision; they may agree on the principles (such as the principle that the health care professional's duty is to do what he or she thinks will be most beneficial to the patient), but disagree about what consequences of telling are relevant; or finally they may agree on the principles and the relevant consequences, but disagree on how the relevant consequences are to be evaluated. Let us examine these grounds in order.

Ethical Principles for Deciding What to Do

A number of classical systems in ethics (what philosophers sometimes call "normative ethics") provide a small list of principles by which one can evaluate alternative actions to decide what action is right — or the nearest to being right — in a particular case. These principles are necessarily quite general and often create serious problems in application to specific problems. Some ethical debates, however, such as what to tell the dying patient, may be understood in great part as disputes about the principles themselves. Several principles are often appealed to in the debate about what to tell a patient.

The Hippocratic or Patient-benefiting Principle

Probably the most central and dominant principle in the ethics of medicine is that the health-care professional ought to do what he or she thinks will benefit the patient. In the language of this volume, the goal ought to be to attempt to care for the patient. This is the principle at the core of the Hippocratic Oath, and, more important, is probably the principle most 20th Century health-care professionals would cite if they thoughtfully reflected on the question, "In general terms, what do you consider to be your basic ethical duty in medicine?"

The Hippocratic ethic of attempting to do what will benefit the patient sometimes seems so platitudinous as to be beyond controversy. To be sure, it is readily recognized that not every decision made by the health-care professional is in fact made on that basis. But this is only to say that health-care professionals, like other humans, are not ethically perfect.

There are, however, serious objections to adopting this principle to resolve moral problems in medicine. In fact I think it is a mistake which may account for much of the ethical confusion in medicine in general today and in problems of the dying in particular. While challenging the principle of attempting to benefit the patient may in fact be challenging the presumed goal of this volume (care of the patient), the principle may actually be incompatible with the classical systems of ethics. The problems can be seen by examining some of the competing ethical principles from other systems of ethics, principles which patients, policymakers, and some health-care professionals may hold to be fundamental.

The Classical or Social-benefiting Principle

One of the classic principles of ethics outside of the medical context is that that action is right which produces the greatest net good, the most benefit when harms are subtracted. This view, often called utilitarianism, is rooted in the nineteenth-century views of Bentham[4] and Mill[5] and is the basis of classical Western economics. The problem posed by utilitarianism for the patient-benefiting ethic is why some consequences ought to be considered as relevant (those related to the patient) while others are excluded as morally irrelevant. The consequences of telling a dying patient about his condition do not relate only to the patient himself. Failure to inform the patient of his imminent death could mean unnecessarily squandering of the resources needed to put a son through school. Disclosure might produce psychological harm for a patient's elderly mother bedridden with a weak heart. The challenge to the patient-benefitting ethic of the utilitarian position is to justify limiting relevant consequences to those related to the patient. There are several responses to this challenge. One is to maintain that the overall consequences will actually be better if health-care professionals limit their attention to patients' interests rather than broader social interests. That, however, is to say that the real principle relevant to health-care decisions is after all the general social consequences. If social consequences are the basis of the decision, the health-care professional must accept that in some cases the consequences to others are so serious that the patient's interests must be abandoned for the good of society or others within society.

This, however, leads to serious ethical problems. Justifying the sacrifice of the individual to the good of society has never been fully accepted as an ethical principle in

Western thought. It would justify the Nazi medical experiments – provided the potential benefits were thought great enough. It would justify abandoning the dying patient simply because more good might come in the end. Nevertheless, we must realize that the patient-benefiting principle, understood strictly, rules out all non-patient consequences – the trauma of family members as well as consequences for the rest of society.

Non-consequentialist Principles

If the defender of the Hippocratic principle responds to the challenge of the social utilitarians by arguing that there is a special moral obligation to the patient which requires that particular if not total weight be given to the patient's interest, then we need to ask where that obligation comes from. To say that health-care professionals have taken it upon themselves or that it is a duty they acquire when they become members of the profession would not be sufficient basis for it to be binding upon health-care consumers – those who are not members of the professional group. One normally cannot say that he takes on a binding special duty to another unless the other person approves or consents to being so cared for. It might be said that health-care professionals have a special duty to do what they think will benefit the patient because it is simply right, not because of any specific consequences but rather because there are certain characteristics of actions which tend to make them right. This is not to say that they will always be right if these characteristics are present. There may be other, competing right or wrongmaking characteristics related to alternative courses. Some characteristics of actions, according to this view, can tend to make those actions right or wrong independent of the consequences.[6] Some examples of such characteristics might be contract-keeping, truth-telling, self-determination, and justice or fairness in distribution of goods.

The Contract Principle. One explanation of the felt duty to do what will benefit the patient could be that health-care professionals are seen as having a special contractual obligation to their patients. In the case of the dying patient this could be a special implied contract to serve the patient's inter-

est, including the duty to protect the patient from bad news or at least to inform him in a sensitive way.

The ethics of contract-keeping, however, is a special example of the ethics of promise-keeping. Many people hold that there is a special ethical duty to do some things like keep contracts, simply because it is right to do so, rather than because of any specific consequences of keeping such contracts. To be sure, it is usually beneficial to some extent to keep contracts. At least if contracts or promises were not generally kept the world would be worse off. But the special feature of the ethic of promise-keeping is that, at least according to some ethical theories, it is simply a right-making feature of actions when promises are kept. This right-making feature might, of course, be overridden by other right-making features of the same act, but in so far as a promise or a contract is involved, there is a "pull" in the direction of keeping the promise – at least according to those holding this ethical position.

This presents two problems for the ethic of always attempting to care for the patient. First, it must be asked whether the contract with the dying patient is really one where the health-care professional and patient agree (even implicitly) that the health-care professional is committed to doing what he or she thinks will benefit the patient. Second, it is the very logic of the ethic of promise-keeping that there *is* something else which is morally relevant other than attempting to benefit the patient: *i.e.,* the moral obligation to keep the contract. Each problem needs some explication.

First, it is not clear that patients, especially those in life and death situations, really do contract with health-care providers to bind them to do what they think would be beneficial to the patient, or that patients really do expect their health-care providers always to attempt to care for them. There are at least three problems. First, some patients may doubt that the physician or health-care provider is the best judge about what will be beneficial to them. Thus a patient may desire that the physician explain to him everything that is potentially meaningful and significant, leaving it to the patient to choose which plausible course of action is more likely to be in his own particular interest. In other words, there is a difference between doing what one thinks will benefit the patient and really benefiting him. Second, some patients may wish to contract for the inclusion of other consequences as relevant. The dying patient may prefer that the physician consider consequences to his family. In this case, including consequences not directly related to the patient might be justifiable. Third, perhaps most critically, the patient may consider other factors relevant as well as consequences. He may hold that even though it might conceivably be more beneficial for him not to know something about his case, he still has the moral reason to know it. He might hold that he simply has a right and a duty to know the truth and to exercise self-determination about his case.

That leads us to the second problem of the ethic of always attempting to care for the patient. If such an ethic is rooted in a contract then the real ethical principle underlying this felt duty is not ultimately to benefit the patient at all. It is rather to keep the contract. The duty to do what one thinks will benefit the patient is simply derived from a particular promise. The ethical principle which underlies the duty is really one of contract-keeping. If this is the case, the health-care professional has moved a great distance from a fundamental commitment to patient-benefiting consequences as the foundation of his or her moral duty. The health-care professional recognizes that there are some features of actions which simply tend to make them right even if they may not always lead to the best consequences.

In fact, even if the patient-benefiting principle is *not* rooted in a notion of contract, those who hold this principle have already decided that there is something morally relevant besides consequences, else how could they have excluded all the consequences not related to the patient? They must hold that there is at least one right-making feature beyond simply looking at the consequences of one's action: the principle which permits excluding some consequences (those not related to the patient) but not others. But once one concedes that there must be some morally relevant features of actions besides

the full consequences—such as limiting the consequences to those with whom one is interacting, or promise-keeping, then it becomes much easier to understand why some may consider additional features as morally right-making even though they do not bear directly on the consequences. Two of these features are the principles of truth-telling and self-determination.

The Principles of Truth-telling and Self-determination. This brings us to a major cluster of ethical principles by which we might resolve the moral debate about what to tell the dying patient. Some hold that there is a moral right, even a duty, to have the truth and to make use of the freedom to determine what happens medically to one's own body. The point is not that the consequences will be necessarily better if the patient controls his own information and treatment, although it might be the case that the consequences will tend to be better if one does know and exercise self-determination. It is rather that truth-telling and self-determination are features of actions that tend to make them right independent of the consequences. This view may make little sense to one who holds that the only significant feature of an action is its consequences. It is nevertheless a widely held ethical position. It is inherent in the ethic of contract-keeping and limiting relevant consequences to those related to the patient that there are ethical features of actions other than consequences which are relevant. Unless one is a classical utilitarian—and very few, especially in medicine, really are—one must concede the relevance of other right-making characteristics. Truth-telling and self-determination are two of the most central. Others, such as justice or fairness in distribution and the principles of gratitude for benefits received and reparation for harms done are usually less relevant to the moral question at hand, what to tell the dying patient.

Thus far we have explored one major reason why reasonable people may disagree morally about what to tell the dying patient: some begin with the ethical principle of trying to benefit the patient while others begin on radically different ground they attempt to produce the most overall benefits, they attempt to keep contracts, or they hold that it is simply right-making to tell the truth or promote self-determination. If truth-telling is a right of the patient and a duty of the health-care professional, then arguments based on consequences are either completely irrelevant (if one excludes consequences as completely irrelevant to moral judgment, as Kant would) or at least compromised (if one is willing to combine consequentialist and other right-making considerations). If it is the case that health-care professionals are uniquely oriented to attempting to benefit the patient and that other groups — lawyers, clergymen, perhaps the layperson in general — are more willing to recognize that there are inherent right-making characteristics such as truth-telling and self-determination, this would help explain the basis for continual moral disagreement about what to tell the patient. It would also imply that it is not sufficient to be convinced that telling or not telling would be most beneficial to the patient in order to decide that it is right or wrong to tell. The patient may hold a radically different ethical principle.

Disagreements About Relevant Consequences

There is a second reason why there may be disagreement about what to tell the dying patient even among those who can agree in principle that the relevant considerations should be limited to what the health-care professional believes would be most beneficial to the patient. There may be disagreement on precisely which consequences are to be taken into account. The physician who is particularly oriented to the medical consequences may feel that informing a patient of his condition might induce him to consent to surgery or to follow a prescribed regimen. On the other hand, the psychiatrist may be uniquely oriented to psychiatric consequences. The social worker may be attuned to the effect on the patient of his relationship with the family. The nurse may see dimensions of social and psychological suffering unavailable to other members of the health-care team. The chaplain may be concerned about religious consequences such as the opportunity to prepare spiritually for death. Even if all these individuals in their roles agree that patient-centered consequences are in principle what is morally relevant to deciding what to tell the patient, they may still radically disagree on the list of which consequences are to be taken into account. What is needed is a formula for assigning ideal weights to the various kinds of consequences being considered, but this is practically impossible to establish.

Disagreements About Quantifying Particular Consequences

There is a third reason why there may be disagreement about what to tell a dying patient. Even those who agree that patient-centered consequences are important, which consequences are relevant in principle, and how those consequences are to be weighted, may quantify a particular consequence very differently. Psychological consequences are especially controversial. The extent of psychological suffering produced by telling or not telling, and the physical side-effects of these psychological consequences, including psychosomatic reactions and even the potential risk of suicide, must be seriously considered. The most important factor in the physician's decision not to tell a dying patient the diagnosis is often his belief that the psychological consequences will be bad for the patient. While there is little solid empirical data about the psychological harms of transmission of bad news, some interesting and provocative data are available.

Feifel *et al.*, in a study of the psychiatric reactions of physicians to death, found that physicians have uniquely high anxiety in the face of death.[7] Such a physician might give excessive weight to the potential psychological harm that could ensue from transmitting a diagnosis of imminent death. On the other hand, those with relatively low anxiety in the face of death would give a radically different answer. We have much less data on the typical psychological responses of other health-care professionals to death. In the 1975 survey of 15,430 nurses conducted by *Nursing 75* only 20% reported that they had come to terms with fear of their own death.[8] No direct comparisons with physicians or patients were made, however. Nurses or social workers or any other health-care professional group may or may not have higher (or lower) anxiety in the face of death than their patients. The point really must be made with regard to individual health-care professionals. If one has uniquely high or low personal anxiety in the face of death, he or she is likely to read that anxiety into judgments about the impact of bad news on the patient.

It is also difficult to develop solid empirical data about such risks as suicide in the face of bad news. Most physicians will cite an anecdote to the effect that once they knew someone whose patient committed suicide after being told of a cancer diagnosis. There are no data currently available however that compare the suicide rates of those who have been recently told of a cancer diagnosis with more normal suicide rates in the population or, what would be an even more significant comparison, the suicide rates of those who in fact have been diagnosed as having cancer but have not been told. These patients with symptoms sufficient to involve medical personnel to make the diagnosis may have anxiety which would produce a higher suicide rate than normal. Guesses about such empirical data are helpful in quantifying psychological consequences of choosing to tell or not to tell the dying patient, though less relevant if one holds that psychological consequences are not in principle as important to the decision as, say, social, medical, or economic consequences. Such data are even less significant if one holds that truth-telling and self-determination are simply the inherent right of the patient, independent of whether the consequences are good or bad.

In practice, disagreements about what to tell the dying patient may be accounted for by some or all of these factors. Many hold that both consequences and inherent right-making characteristics such as truth-telling, self-determination and contract-keeping are significant to the decision. The fact remains, however, that people emphasizing different ethical principles, making use of different kinds of consequences, and quantifying those consequences differently, many reach radically different conclusions about what to tell a particular dying patient. Unless one holds rigidly to the view that health-care professionals should always do what they

think will benefit the dying patient, the moral choice cannot be made by using the simple formula of the Hippocratic Oath. If other considerations are relevant, such as what others including the patient think will benefit the patient, benefits to others, or rights of the patient independent of benefits, then the choice will be a more complex one. Since limiting the relevant consequences to the patient itself requires a recognition that individuals have special moral claims independent of the total social consequences, the recognition of other rights including the right to contract, to know the truth, and to self-determination are also plausible moral considerations. If so it will be necessary to resolve the question, what should the patient be told, by dealing with the patient's rights and obligations as well as possible benefits.

THE DEFINITION OF DEATH DEBATE

A second major issue in caring for the dying patient bridges the gap from the practical bedside problems of clinical care to the most theoretical, abstract philosophical questions. The new-found capacity of partially successful modern biomedical technology to maintain the life of a patient in irreversible coma for long periods of time without the ability to carry out any mental or other brain functions, has given rise to several proposals for a "redefinition of death" focusing on concepts of death more directly linked to brain function. The evolution of organ transplantation and the need of cadaver organs for transplant has contributed to the need for a new definition. The debate, begun in earnest in the mid-1960's, is confusing partly because the definition of death issue has become intertwined with separate but related issues such as when to let a dying patient die, euthanasia, and mercy killing. In this section we shall focus exclusively on the definition of death debate, postponing until later the related questions.

The Reasons for Adopting a New Definition of Death

The definition of death debate is further complicated by the confusion about what constitutes a legitimate reason for adopting a new definition of death. Historically it is clear that the debate grew out of our new capacities to transplant organs, particularly the heart. The Report of the Harvard Ad Hoc Committee to Examine the Definition of Brain Death gives two reasons for taking up the question.[9] First, "improvements in resuscitative and supportive measures have led to increased efforts to save those who are desperately injured. Sometimes these efforts have only partial success so that the result is an individual whose heart continues to beat but whose brain is irreversibly damaged. The burden is great on patients who suffer permanent loss of intellect, on their families, on the hospitals, and on those in need of hospital beds already occupied by these comatose patients." Second, the Harvard Committee says it takes up the definition of death question because "obsolete criteria for the definition of death can lead to controversy in obtaining organs for transplantation."

There appears to be a mixture of motives. The first reason includes the possibility of burden to the patient—the only factor which would be relevant to health-care professionals who hold that they should resolve medical ethical dilemmas according to the Hippocratic principle, that is, that they should do solely what they think would benefit the patient. It is difficult to imagine, however, how remaining comatose is a "burden" to the patient, though it might be argued that it is an indignity, an assault on the patient's memory, or a burden on the future comatose to worry about being kept in a so-called vegetative state.

The other reasons are more relevant to the second ethical principle which some may decide is appropriate for resolving moral dilemmas in medicine, the principle of maximizing total social benefits. The report refers to the interests of families, hospitals, those in need of hospital beds, and, especially, those in need of the organs of the comatose. Such considerations would be relevant only to those who hold that social benefits (as opposed to patient benefits) are decisive in determining what is right. It is especially dangerous to argue that the need for organs for transplant justifies changing the definition of death, as that might conceivably justify defining any socially unwanted class as dead so that even more organs could be obtained.[10]

This has led to arguments that the definition of death must be kept radically separate from the transplantation question. If some people who are really dead are mistakenly treated as if they were alive, that is reason enough to clarify the definition of death. In fact, there may be many in this ambiguous state who are not being considered as organ "donors" at all. Their dignity and their memories require clarity even if no organs are transplanted.

This brings us to the third major way of resolving medical ethical dilemmas: by looking toward a set of characteristics which tend to make an action right whether or not the action serves the interests of the patient or serves the interests of others. It does not seem reasonable that patient interest alone can settle the question. On the other hand it seems crass, really dangerous, to say that we should call someone dead because it would on balance be useful to others to do so. It is wrong not only morally but linguistically. When we say that a person is dead, it means that there is been a fundamental change. It is simply inherently wrong to treat the person as if he were still alive.

A final point about the connection of transplants to the definition of death debate is that while it is wrong to adopt a particular definition of death *because* it will facilitate obtaining organs for transplant, this does not mean that the possibility of obtaining organs for transplant is totally irrelevant. The fact that other lives are at stake is certainly one legitimate reason for taking up the discussion of the redefinition of death. It would be a pity—indeed immoral—to fail to save the lives of candidates for transplantation simply because of a philosophical imprecision about what it means to be dead. If we believe the potential donor is still alive, of course there can be no complaint. But it is a legitimate concern if organs are lost only because we are muddled in our thinking.

Concepts and Criteria for Death

Some may raise the objection that a definition of death could not be *philosophically* imprecise, since the question of life and death is a biological one based on scientific evidence. I would argue that there are two radically different questions at stake in the debate, one scientific, the other purely philosophical or evaluative. Let us call the former the question of the criteria for death; the latter, the question of the concept of death. By the concept of death I mean the answer to the question "What is it about human nature which is so significant or essential that when it is lost we ought to treat a person as if he were dead?" We are clearly in the realm of values here. We are speaking about what is *significant* and what we *ought* to do. We are being asked to classify the functions and characteristics of the human according to their importance. This is a philosophical or theological question which, in principle, no scientific research can answer. On the other hand, when we ask what are the criteria for pronouncing death we are asking an empirical question: "What tests or measures should we use to determine if those essential functions have ceased or ceased irreversibly?" That is a scientific question which can be answered through normal scientific methods.

The confusion between the two questions permeates the definition of death debate. Both neurologists and theologians are called to testify in court proceedings to answer the same questions, questions upon which both could hardly be expected to be experts. It arises early in the Harvard Committee Report. The title of the report is "The Definition of Irreversible Coma."[11] From the text it is apparent that the committee set out to state definitive empirical measures of an irreversible coma. The famous four criteria were developed and defended.[12] But then in the first sentence of the report the committee begins by saying that their "primary purpose is to define irreversible coma as a new criterion for death." While developing empirical measures of irreversible coma is a task appropriate for a medical school committee, it is inappropriate for the theologian, the lawyer, and the historian on the committee. And trying to establish that irreversible coma is synonymous with death is a task for which the medical majority on the committee have no special expertise. In fact nowhere in the report was any argument given that irreversible coma ought to be considered equivalent to death. There could not be any scientific evidence for that claim,

although there might be a philosophical argument that the human essence requires the presence of certain brain capacities which are excluded in the case of irreversible coma. When the question is raised at the conceptual level one must turn to a system of values and beliefs. Several plausible answers emerge.

Irreversible Loss of the Soul from the Body

For the Greek, the animating force of human life was the possession of the soul. At death the soul left the body. In fact that was what it meant to die. While such a notion is foreign to modern Western thought (the Greek notion of the soul was quite alien to the Judeo-Christian tradition from ancient times), we can see how it might be taken to be what it means to die. The criteria question would then be, "What do we measure to see if the soul has left the body?" Descartes thought that the pineal body was the seat of the soul. He might have devised a test to see what had happened to that small structure at the center of the brain. While the Greeks looked, much as we have done, at the functioning of the heart and the lungs, they must have thought it was a sign of the soul's departure, rather than a direct evidence of death.

Irreversible Loss of the Flow of Vital Fluids

When we now look at the functioning of the heart and the lungs it is for a different reason. Some hold that the essential functions of the human are the flowing of the blood and the breath — the vital fluids of the animal species. That is the clear meaning of the term "vital fluids," and it is a very biological notion of what is essential to human nature. It sees the human as quite similar to other animals. As long as the fluids are flowing the essence is still present. That is a controversial view of the essential characteristics of human species. What is important, however, is that whether one accepts or rejects this controversial formulation, it is a philosophical or theological question, not fundamentally a scientific one. We can easily think of a patient lying in bed with heart beating and on a respirator, but with absolutely no brain function. We can all agree that the patient is in irreversible coma according to the Harvard criteria, but there is no way that we can prove scientifically that he is alive or dead. It is just not that kind of a question.

Irreversible Loss of the Capacity For Body Integration

Another concept of life and correlative concept of death focuses more on the functions we presume to relate to the brain. The brain is a complex neurological mechanism which integrates our bodily activity—our moving and breathing as well as our feeling, thinking, perceiving, and reasoning. One might hold that these are the really essential functions in the human, that when they are irreversibly gone the person ought to be treated as if dead. This might have been the concept which moved the Harvard Committee although they never claim it is. It is a concept which sees the human as a complex integrated whole, more than a set of pumps and tubes for gas and nutrient exchange. It sees the human as a complex of mental as well as physiological processes. Many have become convinced that this is philosophically a more sound concept of the essence of the human than the concept oriented to the flow of bodily fluids.

If one opts for this concept, empirical criteria are still needed to decide when a patient has irreversibly lost these capacities. While the Harvard criteria appear to be winning acceptance as good measures of the loss of brain activity, the states which have adopted laws specifying a "definition of death" have wisely limited their attention to the conceptual level. They say that a person shall be pronounced dead in cases where artificial life support devices preclude using traditional heart- and lung-oriented criteria, if the functions related to the brain have irreversibly ceased. They do not specify what empirical tests should be used, however, leaving this to the current standard of medical practice, a standard which may change from time to time based on new empirical evidence, upon which the legislature should have no expertise. It is legally and morally dangerous to use any criteria oriented to brain function for pronouncing death in jurisdictions which have *not* adopted authorizing legislation. It means that those using such criteria take it upon themselves to change the common law concept of what society means by death.

Irreversible Loss of Capacity For Consciousness Or Social Interaction

It appeared that the concepts related to brain function were winning the day, that everyone would eventually abandon concepts related to fluid flow as being too animalistic and adopt a concept related to bodily integrating capacity. Then things began to fall apart. We began to ask a different set of questions. "Is it really all the functions of the brain which are essential to human nature or only certain ones?" Specifically, should a patient be considered alive if he is respiring *spontaneously* but has no higher brain function, including capacity for consciousness or social interaction?[13]

Henry Beecher, the chairman of the Harvard Committee, has said in defense of the Harvard criteria that "The individual's personality, his consciousness, his capacity for remembering, judging, reasoning, acting, enjoying, worrying and so on . . . , these reside in the brain and when the brain no longer functions the individual is dead."[14] While it is true that these functions do seem to reside in the brain, they do not reside in the *whole* brain. Could it not be possible that some other parts of the brain could be alive—parts responsible for brain-mediated reflexes or respiration, for example—while these crucial centers are destroyed? If so, would not the person be dead?

If the concept of death is really the irreversible loss of those complex integrating mechanisms of the human body, then perhaps we should stick with empirical criteria which measure the destruction of the functioning of the entire brain. This seems to be what the Harvard criteria are measuring—not simply irreversible coma. It is apparently possible for a person to be in irreversible coma and still not meet the Harvard criteria.[15] If, on the other hand, we really believe that it is the higher functions which are essential, we may be using a different concept of death, perhaps the irreversible loss of the capacity for consciousness and/or social interaction. If that is our concept of what it means to die, then we need to know what parts of the body are directly responsible for these functions and what measure can be used to determine if they have been irreversibly lost. Apparently these functions reside in the higher brain centers, the cortical areas of the cerebrum and perhaps the diencephelon. If that is the case maybe the electroencephalogram alone, only a confirmatory measure for the Harvard committee, might become the primary criterion for pronouncing death. It apparently measures cortical activity, which would be the critical function independent of whether the lower respiratory and reflex areas are still functional. Determining the precise measures which should be used to predict irreversible loss of consciousness is, of course, an empirical question which cannot be answered in a chapter on the ethics of death and dying. But the question of whether a person ought to be considered dead when there is an irreversible loss of consciousness, but spontaneous respiration, is an ethical question, one which empirical medical science cannot answer. Choosing among the concepts of death will require answers to the philosophical questions raised here.

EUTHANASIA AND ALLOWING TO DIE

Even if we answer the question of when a person ought to be considered dead, we are still left with one of the most serious and common dilemmas in medical ethics: is it ever permissible to let a person die who is still alive according to our definition of death? This leads to the issue of euthanasia and related moral controversies. Euthanasia is a terribly troubling word, meaning according to some literally "a good death," but according to others a morally outrageous death. To some it means any steps to hasten the dying process, whether actively (such as injecting an air bubble) or simply the decision to not start or to stop a medical treatment so that the dying process can continue. To some certain omissions are considered the same as euthanasia, while to others they are not. When one term can mean so many things to so many people, it is better that it be abandoned for more precise language; hence we will not use it again in this chapter.

Three Necessary Distinctions

A complex of moral problems surrounds decisions about the care of the still living but perhaps dying patient. If there is to be moral clarity as well as clarity in personal, hospital, and public policy, three distinctions are particularly crucial.

Inevitable Dying vs. Life Of Insufficient Quality

First, we should distinguish between the decision to let a person die who already is inevitably dying, and one who could go on living indefinitely, but with a life seen by the decision-maker as of insufficient quality. Both decisions lead to the death of the person, but with a quite different logic. The person who is inevitably dying, the person's parents, the courts, or hospital personnel might decide to let the dying process continue unhindered by medical interventions. To understand such cases requires a definition of what it means to be dying (as well as a definition of what it means to be dead). Although a precise definition is difficult, let us use the term to refer to persons who are suffering from a specific, progressive condition which will lead more or less irreversibly to death within a short period of time. Of course, words like "more or less irreversibly" and "short period" are vague, but this definition would distinguish those who are hospitalized with advanced cancer or a fatal genetic disease such as Trisomy 18 (where the patient is inevitably dying) from those with spina bifida, Down's Syndrome with accompanying atresia, or chronic renal failure (who will live indefinitely if treated).

While refusal of treatment might be seen as ethical in either case, it seems much easier to justify in the case of the person who is inevitably dying, when there is simply nothing more that medical science can do to serve the interests of the patient. To continue the treatment in some cases will impose a useless burden on the patient while not serving that person's interests in any significant way.

In the other cases, however, the judgment involved is much more qualitative. Any one of the three basic principles of medical ethics could lead to a decision either to treat or refuse treatment in cases where the patient will live if treated. The arguments look different, however, depending upon which principle is used. Using the Hippocratic principle, the emphasis would be on doing what is thought to serve the interests of the patient. Of course, if the parent, the judge or the patient himself, is the decision-maker, then there is no particular reason to use the Hippocratic ethic, a principle which is uniquely grounded in the medical profession and not generally recognized as an ethical principle by those in society more generally. But if the Hippocratic principle were used, the decision would rest on whether on balance the decision-maker thought the patient would benefit more by having the treatment stopped or by having it continue. In the case of a mongoloid child, life would not be particularly unpleasant, although intellectual ability is compromised. Mongoloids may actually be happier than many with greater intellectual abilities. So it would be difficult to argue that such a child would suffer because of this condition. If in addition to an intestinal blockage, the mongoloid infant also had a serious heart malformation which would require repeated surgery over many years, the burden to the patient to continue the treatment might be more severe. This could be the case in certain spina bifida infants who might face lives of continual surgery as well as severe mental and physical handicaps. In both these cases, however, the judgment must be made that the burden resulting from the treatment would be greater to the patient than the burden of letting the patient die. The judgment that some lives are not worth living is a grave one, one which must be made with fear and trembling.

The patient on chronic dialysis is similar, but may be competent to make the treatment refusal decision himself. The choice is still the same: although life could continue, would it be of insufficient quality? We shall see below that both the courts and various ethical traditions have been open to permitting such decisions on the part of competent patients.

If the principle of maximizing social benefits is used, the choice for such patients is more troublesome. One of the primary features as well as dangers of the utilitarian social-benefiting principle is that it permits the interests of one to be traded off against the interests of another. According to this principle, the burdens to the family, the hospital, the medical staff, and society become relevant. We might justifiably let a baby die if the harm done was outweighed by the good to society — the money for institutional care for the retarded child, the other uses which could be made of medical

staff time and hospital beds, and the benefits to other children of the family who would suffer if the parents had to devote an extraordinary amount of time to the afflicted child. A true utilitarian would say that, crass as it may sound, we should let patients die if the benefits to society are sufficient. They would recognize that the cost of letting the child die might be very great. The threat to others who feared they might be the next to be abandoned would have to be taken into consideration. But in the end the total social consequences are what would count.

The third major approach to resolving medical ethical problems is the examination of inherent right-making characteristics which would tend to make the decision right or wrong regardless of the consequences to the society. Here some would argue that there is an inherent right to life (this would carry more weight in cases where the person was not inevitably dying). Holders of this general view that certain characteristics of actions will tend to make them inherently right might, of course, reject the specific claim of a right to life, looking to other general characteristics such as the justice or reasonableness of the decisions. Those arguments we shall take up later, when we examine what would constitute a reasonable refusal of treatment.

Active Killing vs. Letting Die

A second major distinction in decisions in this area is that of actively hastening the death of the dying patient on the one hand and passively letting the patient die on the other. Many would hold that this is a distinction without a difference. Joseph Fletcher, for instance, argues:

. . . this seems a cloudy and tenuous distinction. Either way the intention is the same, the same end is willed and sought. And the means used do not justify the end in one case if not the other, nor are the means used anything that can be justified or "made sense of" except in relation to the gracious purpose in view.[16]

This is an argument which presupposes that the critical feature of ethical choices is the consequences; he is using the second of the three major approaches to solving medical ethical dilemmas. He is looking at social consequences.

Whether it is moral to actively kill the dying patient for mercy, there is a clear legal distinction between active killing and simply letting die. Active killing is clearly illegal in the United States.[17] Every acquittal has either been on the grounds of insanity or on the grounds that the cause of death could not be determined. The two most recent active killing cases confirm this pattern. In June 1973, Dr. Montemorano was indicted for wilfully murdering a patient with cancer of the pharynx who had been given at most two days to live. It was alleged that the doctor administered an injection of potassium chloride, which is lethal but which leaves no trace in the body. He was acquitted because there was not found to be convincing evidence that he caused the death.[18] In the same month, Lester Zygmanik was indicted for shooting his brother to death. The brother had been irreversibly paralyzed from the neck down and reportedly begged to be killed. He was acquitted on grounds of temporary insanity.[19]

Letting the dying process continue by not starting a treatment, however, is legally acceptable, at least in certain circumstances. Although there have been many cases taken to court, no competent person has ever been forced by a court to undergo medical treatment for his own good against his will. For incompetent patients, the law is much more confused, an issue we will explore further later.

The morality of the distinction between active killing and letting die has been debated for centuries.[20] Against the more apparent arguments that this is a distinction without a difference, there are a number of arguments that the moral distinction ought to be maintained. First, many argue there is a psychological difference between actively injecting something like potassium and simply letting the patient die. That there is such a felt difference cannot be denied. In one study 59% of physicians said they would act upon a request to withdraw treatment if they were sure it was legal, while only 27% would positively hasten death if it were legal.[21] Laypeople also feel the same difference. In a Louis Harris poll in 1973, in answer to the question "Do you think a patient with a terminal disease ought to be able to tell his doctor to let him die rather

than to extend his life when no cure is in sight, or do you think this is wrong?," 62% thought it ought to be allowed while only 28% thought it was wrong. When the question was asked, "Do you think the patient who is terminally ill, with no cure in sight, ought to have the right to tell his doctor to put him out of his misery, or do you think this is wrong?," only 37% thought it ought to be allowed while 53% thought it was wrong.

That there is a felt difference, however, cannot be used to prove there is a moral difference without an independent argument. It may simply be that we feel a difference because we have been taught (perhaps wrongly) that there is a moral difference.

A second reason given for the difference is that permitting active killing would change the role of the medical professional. That argument is open to debate as well. First, it might be that the role of medical professionals *ought* to be changed so that they could actively kill for mercy when appropriately authorized (presumably by the patient or the patient's agent, and perhaps by the court as well). Second, while we may decide it is important to keep the medical professional's role isolated from any anti-life activities such as mercy killing, perhaps someone else not connected with any medical role could take on the task.

These points do not necessarily lead to the conclusion that there must be a moral difference, but there are others which might. Ramsey has maintained that it is morally significant that the cause of death is different in what he calls "only caring for the dying" (that is not providing dying-prolonging treatments) and active killing (which he calls euthanasia):

The difference between only caring for the dying and acts of euthanasia . . . is the important choice between doing something and doing nothing, or (better said) ceasing to do something that was begun in order to do something that is better because now more fitting. In omission no human agent causes the patient's death, directly or indirectly. He dies his own death . . .[22]

We do know that in the law actions are treated differently from omissions. When one acts to cause harm he is invariably responsible for the consequences. If, however, one omits an action and the omission leads to harm, whether one will be held responsible is a much more complicated question. It will depend upon the relationship between the parties and whether one had an affirmative duty to act.[23]

Active killing and omissions may also be different in intent. Although Fletcher says the intention in the two cases is the same, it may not always be so. For instance, one may withdraw a treatment not specifically to hasten death, but rather to see if the patient can sustain life without medical interventions. One may withdraw support at least according to a contract theory of medical ethics not because one intends the death of the patient but rather because one feels obligated to follow a patient's instructions. While the contract, unless it is open-ended, might well permit the patient or the patient's agent to terminate the relationship or refuse authorization for a particular kind of treatment, it is unlikely that it would include the right of the patient or his agent to order the medical professional to give life-taking injections upon demand.

Finally, there may be a significant difference in the long-term consequences of the action and the omission. If we permit only omissions, the patient will die only in cases where he has a condition which if not treated will lead to his death. If, on the other hand, we permit active killing, there is no end to the number who could be "killed for mercy." Leo Alexander, the physician who played a key role in the Nuremberg trials, has made the argument that the German mass murders:

started with the acceptance of that attitude, basic in the euthanasia movement, that there is such a thing as a life not worthy to be lived. This attitude in its early stages concerned itself merely with the severely and chronically sick. Gradually the sphere of those to be included in this category was enlarged to include the socially unproductive, the racially unwanted, and finally all non-Germans. But it is important to realize that the infinitely small wedged-in lever from which this entire trend of mind received its impetus was the attitude toward the nonrehabilitable sick.[24]

One way of stopping this slide down the slippery slope is to hold firm to the distinction between actions causing the death of the sick and omissions which result from refusals by patients or patients' agents. There may be a few who would wrongly die through improper omissions (that is the question we will take up next), but there are many who simply would not die if medical personnel were instructed to omit treatments, but who would certainly die if actions were taken to end the person's life.

In addition to these ethical arguments, there are some practical reasons why we might want to maintain the distinction. It could be argued that we desperately need public policy clarification about instructions for omissions given by parents or guardians for incompetent patients. On the other hand some claim[25] that virtually no patient need be actively killed to relieve physical suffering. Adequate pain medication can give relief so that simple omissions of death-prolonging interventions would be all that was necessary. If, however, we do not need active killing, but do need clarification of the refusal of treatment, it is impractical to insist that the issues of active killing be resolved. If the majority of the population favor some sort of legal treatment refusal but oppose active killing, we would be inflicting needless burden on real patients for the sake of nothing more than philosophical clarity regarding active killing.

One might conclude that under rare circumstances, active killing might in theory be moral. An example might be a case of extreme suffering (physical or mental) which could not be relieved by any kind of intervention known to man where, in addition, the patient would not die quickly if treatment were simply stopped. While I might in theory consider such active killing moral, that does not mean that it should be legal or tolerated in hospitals. All it would require to lead to the conclusion that it could be moral but should remain illegal would be the conviction that more moral wrong would actually ensue if it were made legal — by mistakenly believing that a case was exceptional by failing to do all one could to relieve suffering, or by creating a trend in society to look more favorably on killing the unwanted.

Reasonable vs. Unreasonable Refusals

This brings us to a third distinction. If we limit our attention to cases of omissions, we still must ask the question, "When is an omission morally acceptable?" To deal with this question we must finally confront what I see as a major problem in the entire discussion of the ethics of death and dying. All too often the discussion, particularly when it is carried on in the context of a hospital setting among medical professionals, is framed in terms of what should we, as medical professionals, do with regard to the patient who is lying in our hospital bed. Should we treat; should we stop the respirator; should we discuss the matter with the family; should we mercifully inject the air bubble? I believe that as long as we keep asking the question as if we were standing above the patient — figuratively and literally — trying to decide what is best for him, we will never be able to reach any satisfactory conclusion. Only by shifting to the patient's perspective can we move any further in the direction of clarity. The question then becomes "When should I, as a competent patient, justifiably accept or refuse a particular medical treatment?" In the case of the incompetent patient, the question shifts slightly, but it has the same structure: "When should I, as agent for the patient, accept or refuse a treatment for the one for whom I am responsible?"

The question thus shifts from "When is an omission acceptable?" to "When is a treatment refusal acceptable?" The answer is still complex. It will require separating the case of the competent patient and the incompetent patient.

The Competent Patient. From the standpoint of the competent patient the Hippocratic principle that the health care professional should do what he or she thinks will benefit the patient does not make much sense. While a patient might instruct a medical professional to do whatever that professional thinks would be beneficial, if the patient really understands the situation it would be a strange instruction. What is at stake is the ethical choice about which among several treatment options is most nearly right for his particular circumstances. It makes little sense from the patient perspective to say that the medical professional's own particular value system should be used in deciding what ought to be done. While that professional might well contribute important suggestions about treatment

alternatives and prognoses under the various alternatives, once that information is presented the value choice among those alternatives could be resolved according to several sets of values: the patient's, the patient's family's, those of the church of which he is a member, of the society, of the hospital, or of the particular health-care professional with whom the patient is interacting. While there might be reason for the patient to turn to his family or his church and there might be reason for society to override the patient's values, it seems strange that the patient would want to rely on the values of a particular medical professional.

If one stands in the third major tradition of medical ethics — that which recognizes inherent rights which would tend to make a choice right or wrong — then the competent patient's right of self-determination would appear to be critical. This may produce a real conflict for the medical professional who stands in the Hippocratic or social utilitarian traditions. He may believe that there is a duty to do what he thinks to be beneficial, while at the same time others in society recognize the patient's right of self-determination.

Self-determination is very important at least at the legal level. We have already seen that the law has never required a competent patient to undergo a medical treatment for his own good against his wishes. The crime of treating such a patient against instructions is assault and battery. While self-determination is important legally and morally, however, it does not answer the patient-centered question: What treatments ought I to refuse? Nor does it answer the question of the patient's agent when the patient is incompetent. To deal with those questions, we must analyze more directly the question of what treatment refusals are acceptable.

The Incompetent Patient. For the agent of the incompetent patient (as well as for the competent patient himself) the possible refusals must be divided into ethically acceptable and ethically unacceptable. Some guidelines begin to emerge. Both in law and in ethics it seems that the refusal of a parent or guardian (I shall use the simpler term "agent") should not be tolerated if a simple treatment would restore the incompetent to normal health. We cannot permit Jehovah's

Witness parents to refuse a life-saving blood transfusion for their child who has been injured in an automobile accident even though we recognize that their motives are the highest. Based upon interpretation of Biblical texts they believe that the blood transfusion will cost their child eternal salvation. It is a prudent judgment on their part to trade a few score years of worldly existence for something eternal. Society, however, is sufficiently sure they are wrong that it feels it must override their judgment. On the other hand, if a treatment offers a relatively trivial prospect for good it may be expendable. The courts will permit parents to refuse trivial medical treatments or treatments which can be postponed without serious consequences. It might, but has not yet permitted refusal of painful high-risk procedures when there is little hope that even with the procedure the patient's life could be saved. In between these two extremes, when there is everything to be gained by the procedure and very little to be gained from the perspective of the patient, is a very murky ground where there is as of now little legal or ethical clarity.

There are some general guidelines upon which to base a decision, however. Perhaps the most significant comes from the tradition of Roman Catholic moral theology which over centuries has developed a sophisticated position. As exemplified by the statement of Pope Pius XII on "Prolonging Life" it holds that:

. . . normally one is held to use only ordinary means — according to circumstances of persons, places, times, and culture — that is to say, means that do not involve any grave burden for oneself or another.[26]

Thus Catholic moral theology, while it opposes all active killing, permits substantial latitude regarding omission of treatments which it considers extraordinary. The question remains, what treatments are extraordinary? Ramsey has astutely observed that medical professionals tend to define an extraordinary treatment with reference to the technological intervention involved.[27] The classification on this basis would hinge upon how common the particular device or procedure might be: a heart transplant would be extraordinary while a IV drip would be ordinary; an experimental cancer drug would be extraordinary; penicillin for pneumonia would (by now) be ordinary. On the other hand, Ramsey argues, theologians and others not oriented to actual delivery of the techniques for intervention focus more on the extraordinariness for the particular patient, not of the technique in isolation from the patient. Even if we recognize that the moral judgment about the appropriateness of the treatment is dependent on what is appropriate for a particular patient, we still need to know what the standards ought to be. Three meanings of "ordinary" and "extraordinary" have been proposed:

Usual vs. Unusual. First, following the most obvious meaning of the words, a treatment can be seen as ordinary (and therefore required) or extraordinary (and therefore not required) according to how usual it is. The point can be made either with regard to the treatment itself or with regard to treatments for patients in particular circumstances. But, despite what seems to be the plain meaning of the terms, treatments cannot be separated into morally required and morally expendable ones on the basis of how common they are. The status quo cannot determine what is ethically required, for if it did primary health care in most urban ghettoes would not be "required" but abortion for unwanted pregnancy might be. Some treatments unusual in a particular circumstance *are* morally required, and some which are usually given may be expendable. To hold otherwise would be to say that current practice will determine the answer to the moral question — until such time as, through what logically would be a series of immoral acts, current practice changes.

Useful vs. Useless. A second distinction could be between useful and useless treatments. But many treatments which are useless for preserving life may still be required — pain medication for instance. Other treatments which may be useful in preserving life may be morally expendable because they impose burdens too grave. Many, including Catholic moral theologians, would consider chronic dialysis for an adult patient to be expendable, if it inflicts a grave burden on the patient even though it could continue his life indefinitely. It seems, then, that these two categories do not provide a satisfactory standard.

Reasonable vs. Unreasonable Refusals. We may have to appeal to the concept of reasonableness. Those who believe that patient self-determination is critical, may hold that in the case of competent patients a "reasonable" refusal can simply be one for which a reason is given. But *some* reason must be given—it might be on grounds of religious objection, of physical or psychological suffering, or of financial cost to the family. No one should have the power to override that decision, although others might have an obligation to discuss the reason with the patient if they thought it was inadequate.

In the case of the incompetent patient, however, the agent's refusal must be supported by something more than *any* reason; it must be a *good* reason. How do we define a good reason? In the Pope's view, it could be that the treatment inflicts a grave burden on oneself (presumably the patient) or another. We would presumably require that the agent for the patient be able to sustain his judgment that the treatment would inflict a grave burden. This is a perplexing question. While the agent cannot simply believe that it would inflict grave burden (that would justify the refusal of Jehovah's Witness parents), it need not necessarily mean that society as a whole need agree completely. Society gives to parents and other agents some discretion in making value judgments about minors and other incompetents. It permits choice of a school system, while not necessarily agreeing that a particular private school is most likely to be in the child's interest. The standard seems to be that the agent must make a judgment sufficiently in accord with society's judgment that society can accept the judgment as reasonable (although not necessarily the one it would have made). So perhaps agent refusals must be close to, but not necessarily the same judgment society would have made.

We still must ask what is a sufficient reason for refusal. The papal statement emphasizes burden to the patient or another. But how can burden to another alone be an adequate reason? Does the burden to the

taxpayer or the hospital staff justify stopping treatment? Only those standing in the ethical tradition of social utilitarianism could accept this view. We may have to modify the guideline to limit the relevant concern to burden to the patient or "patient-centered burden." The latter phrase would permit including burdens the patient feels which have impact on others as well (for instance, consuming the family's resources put away for the childrens' education) but not the direct interest of others without the patient's concern.

That still leaves us with the problem of the comatose but living patient, or the treatment which imposes no real burden but does not help the patient at all. Perhaps we have to reintroduce the notion of uselessness. Uselessness for the patient's condition might be a sufficient reason for classifying the treatment as expendable, even if it presents no grave burden to the patient. Otherwise, out of concern for the patient, we could insist that a treatment continue because it inflicts no grave burden, even if it did no good. Adding uselessness as a criterion for making a treatment expendable we are led to the conclusion that with regard to decisions made by agents for incompetents, *a treatment is expendable if it is within reason to see it as useless or to see in it any significant patient-centered moral objections including severe physical or mental burden.*

This principle would permit treatment refusals by agents for patients even if the medical professional in his judgment would not consider the refusal reasonable—even if that medical professional believed the patient would benefit from the continued treatment. This is therefore not a principle which is compatible with the Hippocratic ethic—but then neither is any resolution which permits self-determination on the part of the patient or the patient's agent or which accepts judgments of courts or other social agencies about reasonableness.

Hospital and Public Policy Implications

This chapter has examined a number of ethical problems related to the care of the dying. The implications for hospital and public policy in the possible resolution of these problems are very great. Although it is not the primary objective of this chapter to explore the policy alternatives, let me note briefly some possible policies and their ethical implications.

We should first put to rest the claim that to make any decisions about letting patients die would be to "play God." The fact of the matter is that in every hospital, every day of the year decisions are made about patient care which affect the patient's living and dying. It is literally impossible to run a hospital without having someone make such decisions. We could charter a plane to fly a patient to Bethesda for the latest research procedures; we could perform the fifth operation on a patient's facial cancer even if he is in his nineties, semi-comatose, in heart failure, and even if the surgery would remove half his face. Someone often chooses not to do these things and rightly so. If the patient gives us long enough, he, his agents, or someone must make such decisions. There are several alternatives.

Ad Hoc Medical Professional Decision-making

The status quo is really what could be called ad hoc, individual physician decision-making. It is decision-making by the medical professional, normally the physician, at the bedside at the time of crisis. Hospital personnel, the patient, or the family may or may not be brought into the decision. From the point of view of the Hippocratic ethic this is the only acceptable method of decision-making. If the medical professional's job is to do what he thinks will benefit the patient then he must proceed.

There are real problems with this policy from the point of view of other principles of medical ethics, however. If the objective is to maximize the benefits for society (a principle I have not defended at any point in this chapter) the individual medical professional is in a particularly bad position to make such judgments. They at least ought to be left to the hospital administrator, who can better allocate resources, or perhaps to a government panel or to legislative instruction.

If the basis for the decision is to be a group of ethical principles, including the duty to keep the contract between the medical professional and the patient, the right and duty of self-determination, the duty to tell the truth, to promote justice, etc., then this method of decision-making would also seem unacceptable. It can hardly promote patient self-determination. It would not, except under special circumstances, fulfill any contract between physician and patient. If the duty to keep promises made to the patient (which is the foundation of the contract model of medical ethics) and the right and the duty to self-determination are to be determinative, then we must find another basis of medical decision-making about these matters.

The Medical Professional Decision-making Committee

A second type of decision-making is beginning to emerge in many hospitals. Committees are being established to determine which patients should have treatment continued and for which patients it ought to cease. This has the advantage of neutralizing the random biases which individual physicians might have. If such committees include nurses, social workers, and other health professionals, new and relevant perspectives may be added. Yet it still seems to me to be the worst possible decision-making mechanism. It eliminates the one virtue of the individual physician's decision-making: he may, in rare circumstances, know the values of the patient and be able to serve them. In principle, the committee cannot know these unless it learns them indirectly. At the same time the committee solves none of the other difficulties with the medical professional decision-making mechanism. It would still incorporate any special interpretations of the consequences or special norms which might be shared by medical professionals. It would in no way recover the sense of self-determination and dignity lacking in the individual medical professional decision-making mechanism. It would still be built on the false belief that the decision is basically a technical one which can be made on the basis of adequate medical skills. At the very least it would fail to see the choice as one fundamentally rooted in philosophical and other value choices, value choices which ought to be rooted in the patient's own values.

The Informal Letter

Several mechanisms which bring the patient more directly into the decision-making have been proposed. The Living Will is a model letter which can be written by the patient to "my family, my physician, my clergyman, my lawyer." It says, "If there is no reasonable expectation of my recovery from physical or mental disability, I, _____ _____, request that I be allowed to die and not be kept alive by artificial or heroic measures."

The model letter makes use of several distinctions we have discussed. It authorizes only withdrawing of treatment, not active killing. It eliminates only "artificial or heroic" treatments, terms meaning approximately the same as "extraordinary" treatments with all the problems of definition we have encountered. Further, it explicitly authorizes that "medication be mercifully administered to me for terminal suffering even if it hastens the moment of death." Here the letter is consistent with traditions which have long recognized that giving of pain medication such as narcotic analgesics is acceptable even if the respiratory depression, which is one side-effect, could shorten life.

There are some problems with the Living Will. For one, the document is prospective as opposed to the ad hoc decision-making done at the bedside. As such it is necessarily quite general and raises the problem of how we can know if the patient would have changed his or her mind in the time of crisis.

The most significant problem is that the document is only permissive. It specifically says it is not legally binding. Yet we have seen that only 59% of physicians would follow such instructions even if they were sure it were legal. That means that the writer of the Living Will would have four chances in ten of not having his wishes followed.

To overcome these problems we might consider a legally binding power of attorney in which an individual, while of sound mind and body, could grant to another (next of kin or anyone trusted to respect the values of the writer) could designate someone as an agent for purposes of making treatment-refusal decisions. This would, if upheld in court, be a legally binding document and would permit decisions to be made at the time of crisis — albeit by someone other than the patient. For those who have someone they would trust with such a decision and who fear that their wishes would not be carried out otherwise, the power of attorney may be a suitable substitute for the Living Will.

Legislative Proposals

There is a fourth set of policy alternatives. Many pieces of legislation have been introduced into state legislatures to facilitate the "right to die" or "death with dignity." Several states, beginning with California in 1976, have passed bills. Legislation proposed falls into three major groups. First, there are bills which would make legal not only the decision to stop treatment, but also active killing upon request. These bills, such as those introduced into the state legislatures in Idaho in 1969 and Oregon in 1973, do not maintain the distinction between active killing and letting die. Because of that, they do not address the problem of the incompetent patient who cannot authorize active killing for mercy. These seem to have little chance of passage and would resolve very few of our problems if they were passed since they would not help us deal with the dilemma of the incompetent patient.

The second kind of bill would make clearly legal a letter such as the Living Will. Bills introduced into Florida in 1973 and Massachusetts the same year follow this pattern. While these bills would make sure the medical professional who followed such instructions would not be guilty of a crime, they do not even make clear that such a professional would have to follow the instructions. They also do not handle the problem of incompetent patients who have not filled out such instructions. Since it is already clear that the competent patient can refuse medical treatment and the real problem is with the incompetent ones, this legislation would appear to serve very limited purposes.

The third kind of legislation, such as the bill introduced into the state of West Virginia in 1972, would not only make a patient's refusal instructions binding, it would establish a line of authority for others to serve as agents for the patient for purposes of making treatment refusal decisions. Since we already presume that someone must serve as the agent for purposes of medical consent for medical treatment, this is not a terribly radical departure. It does, however, systematize the procedure and make clear the legal rights and obligations of those involved. We might want to consider having a person designated by the patient as the first in line of authority, even over the next of kin. That would permit the individual to designate someone else, if he did not want to place the burden on the next of kin or did not feel the next of kin could be trusted to share his own values. As is presently the case, such bills would retain as a safeguard the possibility that the courts would intervene to override the agent's judgment in situations where it appeared the agent was acting foolishly or maliciously.

While none of the policy options will perfectly resolve the ethical dilemmas in the care of the dying, certain of them may be preferrable to others depending upon the basic ethical principles one holds. While the Hippocratic principle might be most in accord with the individual physician ad hoc decision-making, the principles of contract and self-determination may lead one more toward the patient-centered decision-making mechanisms such as the informal letter and legislation to clarify the decison-making roles.

REFERENCES

1. Oken D: What to tell cancer patients: A study of medical attitudes. *JAMA 175:*1120–1128, 1961; Fitts WT Jr, Ravdin IS: What Philadelphia physicians tell patients with cancer. *JAMA 153:*901–904, 1953.
2. Data on other health care professionals are difficult to find. With regard to nurses there are several reports that they themselves would want to be told about a terminal illness, but physicians also report that *they* would want to be told in spite of their lack of willingness to tell patients. For data on nurses attitudes see Feifel H, et al: Physicians consider death. Proceedings of the 75th Annual Convention of the American Psychological Association, 1967, pp 201–202; Quint JC: *Nurse and the Dying Patient.* New York, Macmillan, 1967, p 252; and Golub S, Reznikoff M: Attitudes toward death: a comparison of nursing students and graduate nurses, *Nursing Res 20:*504, 1971. A group of 15,430 nurses responding to a questionnaire in the November 1974 issue of *Nursing 75* indicated that

the nurse's dilemma may often be not that he or she would not want to tell the patient—60% thought the patient should be told as soon as possible after diagnosis and another 21% thought he should be told when he asks. The problem for the nurse may arise when the patient asks but the physician does not want him to know. In that case only one percent responded "Tell him the truth." Another 14% responded "Tell him that only the physician can answer the question." Eighty-one percent said, "Ask why he brought up the question, try to get him to talk about his feelings," a response which seems to avoid the necessity of directly responding to the question. See Popoff D: What are your feelings about death and dying? *Nursing 75 5:*23–24, 1975.
3. See Samp RJ, Curreri AR: A questionnaire survey on public cancer education obtained from cancer patients and their families. *Cancer 10:*382–384, 1957; Branch CH: Psychiatric aspects of malignant disease. *CA: Bull Can Prog 6:*102–104, 1956; Kelly WD, Friesen SR: Do cancer patients want to be told? *Surg 27:*822–826, 1950.
4. Bentham J: *An Introduction to the Principles of Morals and Legislation.* Edited by Lafleur J. New York, Hafner Press, 1948 (originally published 1789).
5. Mill JS: *Utilitarianism and Other Writings.* Cleveland, Ohio, Meridian, 1962 (originally published 1863).
6. See Ross ED: *The Right and the Good.* Oxford, Oxford University Press, 1939, Chapter 2, for a classical defense of this view of promise-keeping.
7. Feifel. See note 2, above.
8. Popoff D, *Nursing 75,* in consultation with Funkhouser GR: What are your feelings about death and dying? *Nursing 75 5:*44, 1975.
9. Harvard Medical School, Ad Hoc Committee of the Harvard Medical School to Examine the Definition of Brain Death: A definition of irreversible coma. *JAMA 205:*337–340, 1968.
10. See Paul Ramsey's attack on updating the definition of death for the purposes of obtaining organs in *The Patient As Person.* New Haven, Yale University Press, 1970, p 103. Also Kennedy IM: The Kansas statute on death—an appraisal. *N Engl J Med 285:*946–950, 1971.
11. Harvard Medical School, Ad Hoc Committee, *op. cit.*
12. (1) Unreceptivity and unresponsitivity, (2) No movements or breathing, (3) No reflexes, and (4) Flat electroencephalogram.
13. Brierley JB, et al: Neocortical death after cardiac arrest. *Lancet 2:*560–565, 1971.
14. Beecher H: The new definition of death: some opposing views. Paper presented at the AAAS meeting, Dec. 29, 1970, Chicago, Illinois.
15. Brierley JB, et al, *op. cit.*
16. Fletcher J: "Elective death," in *Ethical Issues in Medicine.* E. Fuller Torrey (Ed.) Boston, Little Brown, 1968, p 148.
17. Baughman WH, Bruha JC, Gould FJ: Euthanasia: criminal tort, constitutional and legislative considerations. *Notre Dame Lawyer 48* (June 1973), pp 1213–1214.
18. Andelman DA: Doctor's alleged mercy killing stirs

debate. *The New York Times,* (June 29, 1973), p
42; Euthanasia: did the surgeon do it? *Medical
World News* (July 20, 1973), pp 5–6; Euthanasia
questions stir new debate. *Medical World News*
(September 14, 1973), pp 73–81.

19. Brother held in apparent mercy killing. *The New
York Times* (June 23, 1973), p 35.

20. See Ramsey P: On (only) caring for the dying, in
The Patient as Person. New Haven, Yale University Press, 1970, pp 151–152; Kelly G: The duty of
using artificial means of preserving life. *Theological Studies 11:*204, 1950; Kelly G: *Medico-Moral
Problems.* St. Louis, the Catholic Hospital Association, 1958, p 129; Baughman WH, et al, *op. cit.,*
pp 1213–1214.

21. Brown NK, Balger R, Laws H, Thompson DJ:
The preservation of life. *JAMA 211:*76–82, 1970.
See also the views of physicians as found by Crane
D: Physicians' attitudes toward the treatment of
critically ill patients. *Bio Sci* (August, 1973), pp
471–474; and Williams RH: Propagation, modification and termination of life: contraception,
abortion, suicide, euthanasia, in *To Live and Die.*
Edited by Williams RH, New York, Springer-Ver-
lag, 1973, pp 90–91.

22. Ramsey, *op. cit.,* pp 151–152.

23. See Fletcher G: Prolonging life, *Washington Law
Review* 42, 1967, p 1009.

24. Alexander L: Medical science under dictatorship.
Reprinted by permission. *N Engl J Med 241:*39–
47, 1949.

25. See Addison PH, Secretary of the medical defense
union in London, in Good pain relief cuts chances
of euthanasia law in Britain. *Med Trib* (October
10, 1973), p 4.

26. Pope Pius XII: Prolongation of life. *The Pope
Speaks 4:*393–98, 1958.

27. Ramsey, *op. cit.,* p 120.

13

DYING, DEATH, AND THE "FRONT-LINE" PHYSICIAN

John M. Flexner, M.D.

We are presently witnessing what has been called the "Death Renaissance."[1] The publications in this area appearing recently have become legion, and include such titles as "The Distress of Dying,"[2] "Where to Die,"[3] "The Right to Die,"[4] "Learning to Die,"[5] and on and on. Not only articles in our standard medical journals but also those in the many "throw away" journals that come across the physician's desk are replete with "helpful hints" in dealing with dying patients. The authors come not only from the medical profession but also from philosophy, ethics, sociology, theology, and other fields. This outpouring of literature related to dying, death, and bereavement has stimulated Dr. Vaisrub to editoralize in the *Journal of the American Medical Association* that "Dying is Worked to Death." Dr. Vaisrub observed, "It is much too easy to write about death. There is no need for statistical evidence and for lengthy references. And no one can claim to have more direct information on the subject than from high-up. Perhaps because it is so easy to write about dying, so much is written about it without saying anything new."[6] These are sobering words as one prepares a chapter in a book dealing with the subject.

The intent of this chapter and the views presented concern those aspects of dying, death, and bereavement which I consider important from the point of view of the "front-line" physician. It is important, however, to state that the approaches I have learned and use in managing and assisting dying patients with their adaptation have come from first-hand experience in the care of dying persons and their families, for I personally have derived little of practical value from the countless articles I have read. One wonders how many who write extensively about the many moral and ethical decisions one encounters in dealing with these patients have actually "gotten their feet wet" with the actual care of dying patients. The "action" is not to be found solely in texts such as this, rather it is found on the wards in direct work with the patients, their families, friends, the resident staff, nurses, chaplains, social workers, and the entire care-giving team. It is for this reason that I have encouraged my friends in philosophy, theology, psychiatry, and social work to accompany me on my daily ward rounds to become an integral part of the many facets of patient care. It has been of immense help to me and to them. As will be outlined later in the chapter, it certainly has been influential in how I now conceptualize the over-all delivery of care to these patients.

In regard to being intimately involved in this area of patient care, I would further state that the views expressed in this chapter represent my personal views; these methods may *not work* or be entirely applicable to what another person does or how he cares for his patients. Caring in this area is largely determined by the traits and attitudes of the caregiver. "Different strokes for different folks," is a contemporary but applicable phrase to describe the wide variation of approaches available to the caregiver in this area.

THE ROLE OF SCIENCE

What does the physician bring into the clinical arena to battle with Death? First and foremost, he brings Science. By Science, I mean his training in general medicine, in specialties such as internal medicine, surgery, or one of the cancer-related fields (hematology, oncology, or the other aspects of internal medicine — cardiology, gastroenterology, nephrology, endocrinology, and infectious or pulmonary diseases). I certainly do not plan to enter into a discourse on contemporary training for the delivery of health care. Suffice it to say, however, today most physicians training in internal medicine *do* choose a specialty fellowship of one to two years. (My personal experience is in hematology-oncology, and most of my observations relate to patients with terminal lymphomas and leukemias.) In addition to training, the application of science also means keeping abreast of recent developments in one's specialty. We do this through our journals, through local, regional, and national meetings, and through our contact with colleagues who share similar interests. Self-education is a must in helping to train our resident staffs and medical students, for we further the use of science as attending physicians in our role as teachers. I feel strongly that the teaching of medical students and house officers in caring for (dying) patients is an integral part of the physician's attending role.

So often we concern ourselves with diseases and not the people who have the diseases. Physicians have been justly criticized as being too scientific and too insensitive. A familiar phrase is that physicians are trained *to cure not to comfort*. We understand our patient's illness but don't know our patients! However, the reasons for this image are usually oversimplified. Doctors are accused of not coming to grips with terminally ill or incurably ill patients because they cannot face the prospect of failure. Or it is said that physicians are so terrified of their own death that they cannot face it in their patients. We are depicted as "medical vitalists" who go to great extremes to preserve life *at all costs*. The image of the dying patient in our intensive care units with tubes in all orifices, monitors beeping, intravenous units in both arms, strapped to his bed in grim isolation, and unable to communicate with family or caregiver has been used repeatedly to illustrate the inhumanity or depersonalization of care rendered by physicians.

Problems related to a totally vitalistic posture are painfully driven home in two articles, one entitled, "Dying in Academe,"[7] the other, "Dying in a System of 'Good Care': Case Report and Analysis."[8] The first author's opening sentence alludes to this philosophy: "A patient can commit no more grievous offense in a university hospital than to die. We tolerate any other lapse in propriety — vomiting, incontinence, hemorrhage, seizure, and even behavioral aberrations. . . . But to die is an unforgivable breach of faith with the entire hospital staff, an outrage against doctors, nurses, technicians, orderlies, dieticians, housekeeping maids, and all the other major and minor functionaries of that peculiar institution called a hospital." This author further indicates that because of our modern technology, death no longer is tolerated as a natural process, " . . . an inevitable consequence of living." She refers to the 20th century as "The Age of Arrogance," possibly a very apt phrase. She then relates a moving case study of a 78-year-old terminally ill patient with colonic cancer who wished to die. Despite his feelings, when he developed respiratory distress, he was placed on a ventilator against his will. He finally succeeded in cheating his caretakers by switching off his ventilator. He left his doctors and us a very moving final message: "Death is not the enemy, doctor, inhumanity is!"

In the second article, written by a physician interested in neuropathology, we are told of his frustrations and anguishes which are the result of the impersonal treatment received in a "teaching hospital." His mother's life is needlessly prolonged simply because interns, residents, and an elusive attending physician knew no other course. The dictum seems to be preserve life at all costs. The costs are very dear to the author, his family, and to the patient herself. Communication is virtually nonexistent between these factions and the care-givers. The author stresses how our very language is impersonal and isolated from the patient as an individual. We catch ourselves talking about "beautiful leukemic cells" or "a great case of lymphosarcoma" when those "cells" and that "case" represent a human life with all its values.

These dramatic examples serve to demonstrate our dilemma. On the one hand we are asked to assure death with dignity and on the other hand we see ourselves pitted against death. This struggle was graphically represented in a lithograph I recall in a medical school library in my medical school days. In this picture, the physician with his scrub cap, mask, rubber gloves, and gown was interposed between a naked, young, healthy girl and death—depicted in the usual macabre manner—as a skeleton. This image survives today, for if the outcome of a patient's illness is a fatal one, it still represents failure to many of us. It is for this reason that those of us dealing with incurable diseases where an outcome of death is inevitable, find no shortage of referrals. We become cancer doctors by default. In the course of this presentation, I hope to outline what I consider to be a more moderate approach to this problem. I believe we must strive to preserve life with all our technology, yet the absoluteness of this endeavor can lead to folly. It is important to at least know when to back off, when to compromise, and when we have reached the limit of our capabilities. This decision, as we shall see, should not be left to physicians alone, but should include our patients, their families, and all members of the care-giving team in this process.

THE PHYSICIAN AS HUMANITARIAN

The second component in caring for the terminal patient I shall classify under the broad heading of Humanitarian virtues. Science deals with treating the patient's illness in an up-to-date fashion through present knowledge, protocols, and methods. The Humanitarian approach deals primarily with the patient's problems of adjusting to his illness and its therapy. This may be termed the personal aspect of care-giving. Here we are using "The Art" as opposed to "The Science." In addition to our roles as "healers," we must attend to other features of patient care. To do this, we must bring to bear all those personal characteristics as caregivers that make us effective in this dimension of care. The following is a tentative list of some of the characteristics I find helpful to those of us dealing with dying patients. Some of this may sound trite—an oft played tune! However, I believe that the following traits of the physician are vital to caring for the dying patient.

1. Compassion—real empathy, not feigned or counterfeit feelings.

2. Genuine concern—the ability to identify patient needs.

3. Warmth—the ability to develop meaningful interpersonal relationships with patients.

4. A sense of humor—the ability to laugh at the absurdity of a situation, even in tragic surroundings.

5. Communication skills—the ability to communicate with patients on their terms or level—not circumlocution in scientific terms—to master "lay parlance."

6. Integrity—honesty in dealing with our patient's situation and our successes as well as our failures. Not to be afraid of failure or saying, "I don't know," or "There is nothing else I can do."

7. Forthrightness—even outspokenness—the ability to "tell it as it is," not to be timid about shock words—death, dying, leukemia, cancer, and others.

8. Patience—the ability to stop and listen—to give adequate time to problem-solving.

9. Generosity—giving time, effort and if necessary the ability to muster "missionary zeal!"

10. Unconcern with one's self-image—the willingness to learn and be corrected by others. Not fearful of being displaced from one's role.

11. Attentiveness—a heartfelt concern and attention to the matters of everyday care delivery.

There are some who preach that we must totally come to grips with our own death in order to care for those of our patients who are dying. This view is interpreted as a spiritual or emotional settlement of some nature or a personal inner resolution of our own dying and ultimate death. I say nonsense! I am no more secure about my own death than my patients. I fear my own dying just as they do. I want to live just as they do. This posture makes one better able to deal with his problems, not less able as has been speculated. If I had inner peace regarding my own death, it could possibly make me callous, smug, or even indifferent to the dying of my fellow man. As well exemplified in countless articles, although we fear death — we must not be afraid to face it, to come to grips with it in a *realistic* manner, not only in our patients, but in ourselves.

Having listed these characteristics I find helpful in dealing with terminally ill patients, let me suggest a few practical hints in dealing with patients on a day-by-day basis.

Availability

With the exceptions of vacations, a physician caring for his patients should try and make himself available 24 hours a day. Patients and their families should be given his home and office telephone number. Most of the time they do *not* call; many times they do not call when they *should*. "We didn't want to bother you at home, doctor," they say, and I give them hell for this! Whether they call or not — this act of giving, involved in the patient's knowing that their physician does not mind being bothered, is perceived as an overt act of caring that I find immensely helpful.

I try not to share my patients with incurable illnesses with my associates. I may assign a student or resident to see my patients as outpatients; however, I always make the patients feel they are seeing me through a surrogate. Occasionally my associates see my patients in my presence — but again the same process holds true. It is extremely important that patients with incurable illnesses not feel abandoned or passed back and forth. It is cruel when one has leukemia to be turned loose in a clinic to see first one doctor and then another. All patients want to identify with one primary physician. This is even more apparent for those patients with cancer and other incurable diseases. It takes a good deal of one's time, patience, and persuasion to keep open the lines of communication between doctor and patient. Many times these lines are never opened and we only hear about our patient's needs through the nurses, ward technicians, laboratory technicians, chaplains, or social workers. In addition, group practice, as such, does not work well in these surroundings, nor in my opinion is it humane.

The most difficult thing for me to do in my practice is to tell a critically ill patient I am leaving town or will be away. This is perceived as indifference, or abandonment by some. I once had a patient ask me, "You're *not* going out-of-town now that I'm so sick?" It is a tough decision that one makes — a decision usually made in favor of oneself and one's family *versus* one's patients. In regard to not sharing patients with one's associates, I believe this definitely limits the total number of patients for whom one can aptly care. One physician can render adequate care to only a finite number of sick patients. Whether that number is 15 to 20 inpatients or 20 to 30 outpatients a day is dependent on any one individual's talents, dedication, thoroughness, and drive. However, it is easy to delude one's self into believing that one is invincible and can "do it all." Patient care suffers, and the physician falls into a standard of practice that is unacceptable. The physician should take no more patients than he can care for or to whom he can give ample time. He should not fool himself.

Attentiveness

On rounds one can easily observe that those patients doing extremely well are allotted the most time and those closest to death, the least. In practice, it should be reversed. But, attentiveness cannot be measured in minutes alone. It is many things. It is making the patient comfortable. It is telling the patient where he is with his disease and dealing with his family by also telling them where he is. It is a willingness to continue therapy if there is hope, but also it is, a wish to cease all but the most minimal aspects of care if the situation is hopeless. It is a desire to prolong life but not suffering. It may be recognizing the desire of the patient and his family to leave the institution (80% of us will die here) and return home, and allowing him to do so. One may also demonstrate his attentiveness in other ways. I have heard a well-known thanatologist stress the importance of sitting when conferring with a patient.[9] I believe this is a most helpful therapeutic maneuver. When we are standing, patients know that our motors are running and we are in gear to move on. This is especially likely to be the case with our most terminal, hopeless cases. There can be no dialogue. In this mode, the questions asked usually demand one-word answers and that is what they receive. "How are you doing, Mr. Jones?" "Fine, fair, same, poor, or lousy." Occasionally a patient recognizes this and throws it back in our faces. "How do you think I'm doing?" Your answer also can only be one phrase, "Oh, about the same, a little better, or a little worse." Little constructive can come from such an encounter. If, on the other hand, one sits and stays as long as necessary, he is demonstrating to his patient an honest desire to carry on a meaningful conversation. "Well, Mr. Jones, what's on your mind today?" "Doc, I was thinking about what you said yesterday. What are my chances of getting better?" Here, the physician may want to tell the patient where he is in the dying process. He may want to probe his concepts of dying and death. He may wish to hear about or inquire about his patient's problems, be they financial, emotional, family, or personal. As opposed to the typical outpatient, whose presentation of a long list of complaints is often viewed as tantamount to "crockery," hysteria, or hypochondriasis, a physician may encourage dying patients to make up lists of such questions. "Doc, I can always think of a million things to ask you when you're gone!" I reply, "Write them down and we'll go over them point by point tomorrow." I find this especially helpful in the early phase of one's disease. After the initial diagnosis has been made and confirmed, I sit down with my patients and their families (who have been previously called together for the occasion), and in most cases, all aspects of the disease and its ramifications are discussed in frank terms. I have learned through painful experience that "evasiveness" at this point is worthless. I use shock words—*cancer, leukemia, incurable, you have the worst kind of . . .* , etc.; for if one tries to evade these terms, eventually we are asked, "Is this a malignant tumor or a cancer?" "Is this problem with my white cells leukemia?", "Do I have the type of leukemia that causes you to die within a short period of time?" Many times, following this conference (a time when I also find myself feeling very uncomfortable), I notice that the patient has heard only the first few sentences—those confirming his or her worst

premonition. Prior to this point there was always the possibility of a wrong or benign diagnosis. Now the escape route has been closed. Frequently the patient hears very little after the initial few words. The rest of my discussion falls on deaf ears. The same story must be reiterated again and again, and here the list of questions is most helpful. "I'm sure I've told you more than you can possibly take in. Sit down and write all the things that concern you about what has been said, and we will cover these, item by item." This technique requires an immense expenditure of time and patience. It also shows a great deal of concern and is a concrete way of caring. In my opinion, a patient and his family have the right to know everything they wish to know. They should know all one can relate about the disease, its treatment, and prognosis. What are the toxic or side effects of therapy? Will there be suffering, and if so, what will be done? Approximately how long will he be hospitalized? Can he return to work? How will he die? What are the predicted and even unforeseen complications of his disease and its treatment? Virtually nothing is held back. By the same token one is not overly optimistic if optimism is unwarranted. Neither is one pessimistic. The door is always left ajar. These are the nuances of hope, caring, and real concern. Once a contract such as this has been established, the patient then will have trust and confidence in his physician to proceed along this one-way street. Without it, his trip may be very lonely and laden with anxiety.

Propitiation or Making the Unfavorable as Favorable as Possible

In this, the next overt act of caring and caregiving, not only is the physician the patient's advocate who intercedes in his behalf with the nursing and medical staff, but he is also a buffer against the effects of his illness. Dr. Kübler-Ross has categorized the various levels or stages of adjustments to one's terminal illness.[10] These we know as Denial, Anger, Bargaining, Depression, and finally Acceptance. However, as she acknowledges, the phases may be admixed.[11] Thus a patient may be in shock and denial while depressed, angry yet accepting, bargaining while depressed, etc. It would be far easier, perhaps, if each patient followed this protocol in an orderly fashion. I'm reminded of a close friend, a mother of three young daughters, who having finished reading a contemporary book on the rearing of children, tried out the newly acquired technique. She was appalled to find chaos in the ensuing dialogue and stated; "My kids don't know their lines!" Those of us dealing with terminally ill patients have also found that our patents do not know their lines in terms of following an orderly progression in their adjustment.

The interventions aimed at propitiation dictate that the physician be at his most tolerant level of functioning. He allows the patient to become angry with him (the doctor), his staff, the nurses, his family, and friends. He consoles and sympathizes yet perseveres in his plan of management. He accepts the responsibility of the many incidential irritations accompanying patient care, yet he remains within his team of caregivers in an accepting manner. He absorbs all the abuse that goes with this responsibility. The patient, in return, takes advantage of this position and loads his doctor with much of his concern. "What are *we* going to do if that doesn't work?" "I thought I'd be out of here by now!" "You told me your last case went into remission on this treatment in two weeks." "Is this the same treatment that Mr. Jones had (the one who died!)?" "You didn't tell me I'd lose all my hair." "Why aren't the antibiotics stopping the fever?" "I thought you said the platelets would stop my nose bleeds." In addition to receiving this type of subtle hostility from patients, the same questions or phrases may be asked by the patient's family. Acts of propitiation are an attempt to place these disquieting moments into proper prospective—an attainment of harmony. Here a sense of humor may be an invaluable tool and a means of dealing with this anger, depression, and frustration in a favorable way. Very few patients object to this ploy. "If you don't get better, don't pay your bill!" "We're giving a dollar a platelet, so you best get busy and make some!" "If I were you, I'd *hire* a doctor who knew something about leukemia, your present one hasn't done so well!" "I can't do much for your marrow (at present), but I can treat the hell out of your hemorrhoids!" Statements

such as these may seem simplistic, trite, or even self-effacing, but it reminds the patient of our mutual frustration. They lend a common cause and identity to pressing problems. If he is not getting better, it is good for the doctor to remind him that he (the physician) *also* is swept up in the dilemma. This does not reflect an indifference or callousness to the patient. An ability to joke or kid about one's infirmities reflects a rather "healthy" atmosphere. It also shows that the grimness which surrounds the patient is not absolute or impervious to transition. Any change for the better should constantly be a reminder for the patient to persevere during these difficult times.

The Ability to Identify with Patient's Desires and Needs

The fourth aspect of patient care is the physician's having the ability to identify with the patient's needs. Here, I mean the ability of the physician to be perceptive enough to be able to sense and to predict just where the patient is and intuitively become engaged in his problems. There is a oneness in such a relationship—the doctor placing himself in the patient's position, and conversely the patient's seeing the doctor's dilemma. It sometimes gives us the green light to go ahead with aggressive therapy and all its sequelae. It may also be the red light which tells one to stop, back off, and allow the patient to gather his strength for the time he may have remaining. There is no magic formula for such levels of conviction. Many times the patient will give the physician those clues which signal a go-ahead or conversely, to put on the brakes. "You're not going to quit, are you, Doc?" "It looks bad now, but you've got other tricks up your sleeve, don't you?" Such questions reflect a will and desire to continue with therapy. "When are we gonna call it quits, Doc?" "Do all your patients react as poorly to treatment and hate it as much as I do?" "We've about shot our wad—have we not?" The latter is the patient's way of telling us to back off! There are many subtle forms of communication between a doctor and his patient, and often these are nonverbal. In this regard, one is reminded of Keats' lines, "Heard melodies are sweet, but those unheard are sweeter . . ."[12]

The game of mutual pretense has been mentioned. As stated previously, in most cases I try to be as frank and forthright as possible, but in some circumstances the patient knows what he has and where he is, but sometimes does not want it verbalized. At times this is also true of his diagnosis. He does not want you to be explicit. On the other hand, some patients want it all spelled out. They are interested in their blood counts, chemistries, x-rays, marrows, doses of chemotherapy, and are frank about asking or telling you. Some of the latter groups may be your most anxious patients. On the other hand, the casual ones may also be denying their illness and its complications. I am reminded of a patient with acute leukemia. We discussed virtually everything except his illness. If I probed him on his feelings regarding his disease — which was in a very acute stage, complete with anemia, leucopenia, purpura, and bleeding — his answers were curt, evasive and rather vague. The housestaff was very concerned because of his aloofness. This type of denial usually vanishes in the waning phases of one's illness, but these patients fill their caregivers with uneasiness. Patients who can verbalize their feelings seem to be easier to care for, but not always. I can also remember an attractive 18-year-old high school senior who hardly ever spoke about her illness. We had great rapport, yet for the life of me, I could not get her to talk about her disease, her anxieties, her symptoms, or any of her deeper feelings. Her answers were always short and evasive. She was a devout Roman Catholic and I did get her to talk to one of the young priests in her parish. Outwardly, I could never discern any cracks in her facade. She went on for almost two years in this manner. She wanted to live through Christmas and died quietly and serenely on Christmas Eve. For this particular young girl, a tight-lipped adjustment seemed most successful in her adaptation.

Those of us dealing with the multiplicity of backgrounds, cultures, educational levels, family ties, socioeconomic levels, intellectual endowment, and regional geographic factors, must be able to adapt our approach to our patient's background. One cannot talk in depth to an aged person from a rural area in the same fashion as one does with a university professor. One cannot handle a teenager with leukemia in the same manner as a dejected, angry executive or bank president. The ability of the caregiver to adapt his approach to this diverse clinical population is reflected in how successful he is in dealing with each patient *individually*.

At this point, it might be well to look more closely at the physician caretaker who must deal with these patients, the majority of whom are dying or have incurable illnesses. Almost daily we are beseiged with questions of the following type: "How do you do this day in and day out?" "Don't you ever want to quit and do something else?" This is driven home to me repeatedly by our residents in medicine who rotate through the service each month. In all candor, I really do not know what the answer to these questions is or should be. We all have certain "innards" that make us individually distinct. It is the traits that constitute what I call "a well integrated defense system" that sustains those of us treating dying patients. The precise nature of this system is undefinable in most cases. It is an objectivity that keeps us from getting involved with our patients to the extent that we become so emotionally "wrung out" that we are rendered incapable of the sound medical judgment needed to manage such patients. It is not an aloofness, a callousness or a lack of caring; it merely means "not losing one's cool" and keeping science and caring in balance. One thing that is helpful to me personally, is not to "take the patients' problems home." I try and solve most of the medical and managerial problems on the hospital wards and in the clinics. I seldom take them home. I usually am successful at this, but some cases do tend to "break through" and plague me during the night. I also believe it is important that we have hobbies or distractions that hold our interest outside of our working area. This seems to dilute some of the gloom and depression that may stick to us as we leave the hospital each day. Interests outside of work are useful. Personally, I hunt and fish. Patients have asked me how I could kill anything, especially after I direct all my energies in an effort to save lives. I answer in terms of my stomach; I hunt small game (doves, quail, ducks, and geese) because I love to cook and eat. Travel is another way to "get away" or escape from the tensions, pressures, and responsibilities of this kind of patient care. However, this may require extensive periods of time away from my work, and I try not to be gone more than one or two weeks at the maximum. Strong family ties and family interests are also a good deterrent to the maudlin state such patients tend to create in us all.

The Relationship with the Family

The next aspect of caregiving concerns the physician's relationship with the family. With adults this does not present the same set of problems or "ground rules" that one encounters in a pediatric practice. In the latter, the mother's (especially) relationship with the child is one of intense identification. Children are incapable of coming to grips with dying and death in the same manner as adults. There the physician's relationship with the mother or parents is much like that of the internist to his patient.

Families are just that—relatives—be they husband, wife, mother, father, or siblings. Sometimes even these immediate family members are not present and we must deal with guardians or close personal friends of the patients. I must again stress that it is *not* the family member or friend who is dying or ill. It is our patient, and his rights and privileges must come before those of the family. Families in their emotionally distraught state may make or try to make demands on the physicians that are not in the patient's best interest. The classical statement when family members find that their loved one has an incurable illness is "Please don't tell him, doctor, he can't take it." The "can't take it" statement bespeaks a fear of the possibility of the patient's "going to pieces," "killing themselves," "having a nervous breakdown," and what have you. What the family is telling us is "don't tell him, *I* can't stand it." I may add parenthetically, that it is rare indeed to have a patient "go to pieces" when one tells him about the nature of his illness. The issue of suicide in incurable illness is debatable, but in my experience it is a rare entity. Only a very few such incidents have come to my attention in the past 20 years of my practice. One was a patient with an intolerable home situation—an immigrant who had been abandoned by her husband and whose children were unhappily placed in foster homes. The second was an elderly man with multiple myeloma with many painful lytic bone lesions. He was given pain medication in one of our recently developed "child-proof" bottles and left alone at home for a day. Unable to take his pain medication because of difficulty opening the container, he smashed the bottle of pain pills, took them all and shot himself for good measure. I have had one other patient who feigned suicide when he was separated from his family and sent out-of-town for a bone marrow transplantation. He cut his wrists (superficially) with a watch crystal and was promptly sent back to us (and his family) for care. He made no other attempt to take his life during the remainder of his illness and frankly admitted that he did it to "get back home." A number of my patients have either threatened to kill themselves or told me quite candidly that they were considering it, yet never made an actual attempt. I have never had a patient who had a "nervous breakdown" or "went to pieces." The preoccupation with adjusting to or adapting to illness seems to channel their energies in a positive fashion. Some do become despondent or depressed and may require psychiatric support, but all in all, these reactions are of a rather minor degree. One patient of mine recently required psychiatric hospitalization for severe depression which was intensified by his having a malignant lymphoma, though the lymphoma was in relatively good control.

When fears, such as those mentioned, are expressed by the family one must be assertive at this point and calmly assure the family that these fears are unlikely to come to fruition. It is wise to point out the families' concern and to show them what they actually fear lies in themselves and not necessarily the patient. As the diseases progress, the family may want you to tell them (in no uncertain terms) when the patient will die, what hope there is in pursuing therapy, how much he is suffering, and other probes directed toward obtaining absolute answers to unanswerable questions. Certainly the family is entitled to ask such questions. They are entitled to know virtually everything that has been told to the patient. Thus, I try to have all concerned members of the family present at the inception of the illness when the patient is told (in lay terms) what his illness is, what his prognosis is, and what he can expect during the course of his illness and its therapy. It is also helpful to have family members present during one's daily rounds. Many times, family members will introduce pertinent information withheld by the patient. "Did he tell you about his chill last night?" "What do you think is causing the blood in his stool?" "Did he show you that place on his skin?" In this way, family members are made to feel part of the care-giving process, as they should. On the other hand, one must not spend all one's time answering the questions of family members. It is a form of entrapment to be caught talking *about* the patient *in front* of the patient, regarding his problems. Conversing *only* with a family member, the patient may well feel left out. It is a rather *impersonal* way of caring for the patient's needs, as if one were speaking with an interpreter. I try never to discuss the patient with the family *outside* his room. It leads the patient to believe that I am telling the family something I have withheld from him.

There may come a time when family or family members may be an obstacle to good patient care. We have mentioned the "Don't tell him" aspect, but it may go even deeper. This aspect of family intervention is the "He's suffered enough," or conversely "Is that all there is to do, isn't there some other drug or some other hospital" aspect of family involvement. The latter can usually be handled with ease if the patient and the family has sufficient confidence in their physician. One always likes to hear "We know you're doing all that is humanly possible, doctor." This is a confirmation of confidence. However, some family members are constantly searching for newer methods or cancer centers with notoriety. At no point do I discourage this. I tell my patients candidly that I am doing all I can to be contemporary. I keep up with the latest in pertinent literature and journals, and I go to as many meetings as time will allow. However, I gladly furnish the names of centers which specialize in the patient's specific illness. By the same token, if it is true — and so often it is — I am quick to say, "At this point in time

they have little to offer that you can't get here."

The "He's suffered enough" aspect is more difficult to deal with. It is important to recognize that the family often makes subjective judgements that are not always in tune with the patient's feelings or his clinical status. I am reminded recently of an incident in which a patient's children as well as her referring internist, approached me about ceasing all supportive measures (antibiotics for infection and fever; blood and platelet transfusions) and allowing the patient, an elderly lady with acute leukemia, to return home to die. When discussing this issue with the patient, these were not her wishes. We persevered; she went into complete hematologic remission and went home in a relatively good state of health. The attrition of prolonged, debilitating illness takes its toll — both emotionally and financially — on family members. Repeated hospitalizations for fever, bleeding, inanition, and infections with the resulting sometimes temporary correction of these serious sequelae of malignancy, exhausts families. Each family member keeps asking himself, "Why won't he die?" or "When is he ever going to die?" Such ambivalence extracts quite an emotional price on that individual. His only recourse is to face the doctor for the ultimate solution as if to say, "Let him die, won't you — end *my* suffering!" As stated, this is not always in the best interest of the patient. It is at this point that the physician must rally the entire family. He must allow family members to verbalize their frustrations and even point out the ambivalent features of their wishes while being sympathetic and understanding, yet firm. Here, the physician reiterates that all are concerned with the best interests and desires of the patient. To further exemplify this process of care, I would like to relate an incident in the care of one of my patients that I consider exceptional.

In an ongoing relationship with one of my patients who had leukemia, it had become apparent that he desired control and active participation in his care. When he reached the terminal stage of his illness, we continued to allow him the prerogative of being the "master of his fate." His platelets were quite low and bleeding became a problem. During his final days he suffered a "small" intracerebral hemorrhage with dysphasia — the inability to speak in an integrated or meaningful fashion. He maintained his receptive ability and understood what was said, but could not respond verbally in an intelligible way. Some persons felt that treatment efforts at this point were too vigorous. They brought pressures to bear on those of us intimately concerned with his care. Those involved in his care called a conference in which all the alternatives were stated. The patient was told to indicate affirmatively or negatively (which he could do with appropriate signals). His choices were: 1) to discontinue all present efforts including transfusions of platelets, blood, the use of antibiotics, 2) to continue with the present supportive methods as outlined, 3) or a variation of these plans. The patient chose support, but it was left open-ended so that he might change his mind on a day by day basis should he desire. The patient died two days later, after another intracerebral bleed. He had always wanted his medical management charted in a conjoined method, yet one in which *he alone* made the final decision. This may be the ideal way to deal with dying patients, but it is not applicable to all or many patients. It is much too open, too frank for the majority, who prefer to leave it in the hands of their family and caretakers. Although I find the incident a rather utopian exercise in patient care, unfortunately it remains just that. The deterrents to this type of care lie with the patient, his family, and the amount of time, energy, and effort the caretaker is willing and able to give to each individual case. In summary then, family members closest to the patient and his needs, require involvement and identity as part of the total team providing care and managing their loved ones. This is an important job of the caretaking group — to incorporate family and friends into an active role in the care of their loved ones — but within the limits determined and controlled by the group.

Presence and the Laying-on-of-Hands

An integral part of the physician-patient-family interaction involves "presence." I have alluded to the fact that I give patients and their families my phone number and encourage them to call if problems arise. I also try to be present every day while the patient is hospitalized. I have not directed attention to non-verbal communication, but this is a vital part of the doctor's ability to deal with dying patients. A downcast look, a seemingly undetected tear, a sigh, an expression, or an inappropriate laugh can reveal a great deal about one's patients and his anxieties in dealing with the death dilemma. One must be present at these times. Also, it is mandatory that one be present during the event of dying itself. Here the patient is usually or may be comatose. The family relies on your presence more than your words; for mere presence has a very stabilizing effect during these moments. Certainly after death has taken place, I try to be present with the family; and we relive the illness and direct our conversation toward the patient, his relationship with the family, and with me. This reviewing process has some similarity to what Weisman describes as a "psychological autopsy."[13] It also gives the family and me the opportunity to openly grieve. It is at these times that I allow myself to become tearful. You will note this implies some previous control, for prior to death, like a family member, I (probably) would not want the patient to see me in a grieving or maudlin posture.

The laying-on-of-hands takes place throughout the entire illness. In my opinion, touching may be an appropriate form of caring. It is another form of person-to-person contact and a vital form of non-verbal communication. A pat is for reassurance, a hug or kiss is an overt sign of affection or compassion, or an arm around a person's shoulder is a form of consolation. Recently I had the mother of a dying teenager look at me very soulfully while asking about her son. I caught myself taking her face in my hands and telling her (what she knew but did not want to hear) that her son was dying and most likely would not leave the hospital. As I recall the incident, it was a most paternal gesture — as a father would react to his daughter or, even deeper, as a husband would react to his wife. The taking of her face in my hands was symbolic of the deep affection that I had for her steadfast devotion to her son, my patient, whose side she never left. At the time of death, when I let my hair down, and openly grieve, I often do this in the arms of a close family member—husband, wife, mother, etc. I may occasionally hug or grasp a male family member, but we usually shake hands—a firmly gripped, sustained, meaningful hand shake.

In all candor, as mentioned heretofore, one does not enter into this intimate form of relationship with *all* of one's patients and their families. When I do, there is a receptiveness, a cue that I perceive that determines how intimate I may become. Some people are rather rigid, cold, and standoffish in their relationship with me. I accept this. Others are openly receptive and encourage the interplay that I have outlined above. Again, every situation is different and must be clearly "read" by the caregiver as comfortable for the person involved and himself.

THE CARE-GIVING TEAM

The final part of this chapter is devoted to a description of the care-giving team and the allotment of responsibility to its members. I must admit that my attitude toward this aspect of patient care has changed radically during the past years. This change is related largely to an enlightenment, an objectivity that I was incapable of seeing or feeling in the past. Heretofore, I have assiduously avoided the use of the term *"role"* in this chapter. I have, in the past, defended the role of the physician as the central and dominant figure in such a relationship. All other care-takers took on a secondary or a subordinant role. After all, was not HE the ONE who prescribed the medications that were life-saving? Was not HE the ONE who made the decision to treat or not to treat, to save or not to save, and finally to live or let die? In Figure 1 I have depicted the classical care situation as it has existed. Note that the physician occupies the center of one circle. Surrounding him are his subordinates who, under his tutelage, care for the patient, his family, and immediate friends. This is the situation that presently exists in most hospitals. Nurses, ward technicians, housestaff and the like, operate on a secondary level

beneath the power of the physician. My confreres in nursing, pastoral counseling, social work, and philosophy were quick to point out the foolishness of such a scheme. If one cost-accounts time, day in and day out, who spends the *least* time with the family? It is the physician. Who is involved in the minute-by-minute, hour-by-hour care giving? It is *not* the physician! The ward technicians and nurses have much more intimate contact with the patient. Why should they be excluded from decision-making in the patient's care? Often patients engage in more significant relationships with individuals such as nurses and ward technicians, than they do with their doctors, families, or even their ministers. The reasons for these relationships are obvious. These are people who administer medications, bathe them, rub them down, touch them, clean up their excrement, and involve themselves in all the overt physical acts of caring. This was well demonstrated in Tolstoy's "The Death of Ivan Ilych."[14] Here the dying, suffering Ilych tells us that the person whose *role* is the most meaningful in his care, is the orderly who bathes him and rubs and positions his legs to relieve the ever-present pain. So be it on our modern wards today. On the other hand, some physicians tend to continue to remain aloof, always scientific, and even insensitive to a patient's everyday needs (how many times will a contemporary physician sit down and discuss a patient's bowel habits?). As physicians, we sometimes tend to be more interested in the patient's disease (blood counts, chemistries, blood gasses, x-rays, etc.) than we are in him! A constant ego boost is provided by the physician's parade through the wards followed by his retinue of residents, students, nurses, and chaplains. It is rewarding to us to have this relationship with the other caregivers and as has been noted, it is seemingly an easily defended position. In reality it is archaic! The patient's interests are best served by an arrangement indicated in Figure 2, entitled "The Ideal Caring Situation." This diagram is a representation of a conjoined effort—a team effort, in which each member brings *his* special talents, training, skills, and expertise to the caring situation. The physician with his science, in

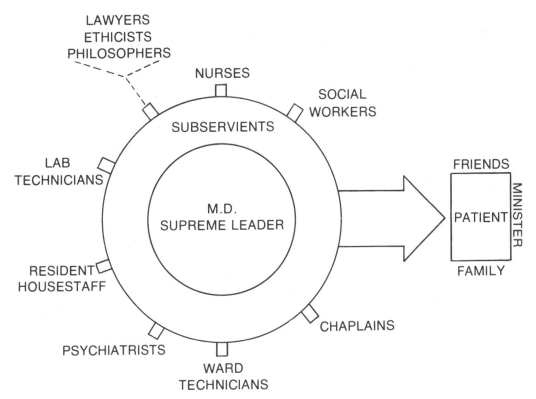

FIGURE 1. The Classical Caring Situation

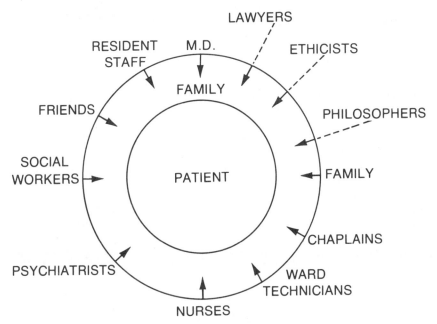

FIGURE 2. The Ideal Caring Situation

some cases, is just as expendable as the ward technician's back rubbing and bed-pan emptying. Present-day attitudes of patient care must change. We *all* must care for patients' needs together. This union of care-givers has been designated with labels such as the "Dying Team." I suggest, however, that this team approach should be used on ALL patients, whether their disease is incurable or not. Communication is the common denominator in such an arrangement. By the same token, nurses must shed the aged subservient relationship with doctors. They must speak up and speak out! Other members, such as philosophers, ethicists, and lawyers, should likely be put on the team. Some would be there not so much in a day-by-day "front-line" caring situation, but in care supporting efforts such as ethics committees, which deal with the thorny problems of life and death that our newspapers are so full of each day. Here the committee functions *only* in an advisory capacity.

Finally a word about the temporality of man! Often, after the shock of telling a patient he had an incurable illness, especially of the more chronic variety, I find myself returning to the phrase — "The most dangerous thing we all do — day in, day out — is start our automobiles!" Knowing that fifty per cent of the American population will be killed or involved in a serious automobile accident really provides little comfort for the incurable, yet it is a way of putting life expectancy in a proper prospective. One merely has to stop and think of one's immediate friends and classmates who have died, to be aware of the temporal nature of us all. No one knows what the day or morrow holds! Our own lives and those of our loved ones may be snuffed out at a moment's notice. Thus, we (the living, the well) must live under this sword — as well as our patients. All of us repress or suppress this temporality — yet it remains inside us all and is constantly stirred (knowingly or unknowingly) each time we face the dying patient. This knowledge — regarding our own death — should be allowed the freedom to surface. Books such as this one and the courses and conferences alluded to in this book allow this surfacing. We must all try to come to grips with our own death — openly and honestly — as difficult as this may be.

REFERENCES

1. Michaelson MG: "Death as a Friendly Onion," in *The New York Times Book Review,* July 21, 1974
2. Rees WD: The Distress of Dying. *Amer Heart J 86:*141–142, 1973
3. Wilkes E: Where to Die. *Brit Med J 1:*34–35, 1973
4. Robitscher JB: The Right to Die. *Hastings Cent Rep 4:*11–21,1972
5. Cassell EJ: Learning to Die. *Bull N Y Acad Med 49:*1110–1118, 1973
6. Vaisrub S: Dying is Worked to Death. Editorial, *JAMA 229:*1909–1910, © 1974, American Medical Association
7. Caroline NL: Dying in Academe. *New Phys 21:*655–657, 1972
8. Netsky MG: Dying in a System of "Good Care": Case Report and Analysis. *Pharos Alpha Omega Alpha, 39:*57–61, 1976
9. Weisman AD: The Dying Person: Relationships and Responsibilities. Symposium, Vanderbilt University, Nashville, Tennessee, March 8, 1973
10. Kübler-Ross E: *On Death and Dying.* The Macmillan Company, London, 1969
11. Quizzing the Expert: Kübler-Ross on Coping with a Job You Dread. *Hosp Phys 9:*30–32, 26,29, 1973
12. Bush D (Ed): *John Keats' Selected Poems and Letters.* Houghton Mifflin Company, Boston, 1959
13. Weisman AD: *The Realization of Death: A Guide for the Psychological Autopsy.* Jason Aronson, New York, 1974
14. Tolstoy L: "The Death of Ivan Ilych," in *The Death of Ivan Ilych and Other Stories.* New American Library, New York, 1960

14

DETERRENTS TO THERAPEUTIC CARE OF THE DYING PERSON—A NURSE'S PERSPECTIVE

Ann B. Hamric, R.N., M.S.

"The modern hospital is the greatest enemy of meaningful death."[1] Spoken by the brother of a dying man, this statement is an indictment of the care given by nurses in hospitals as much as that care given by any other professional group. It is the nurse who is most consistently at the bedside of the dying patient, and the nurse is often the most important health professional in the patient's dying experience. She* has the most direct contact with the patient, and it is she on whom the patient depends for his immediate needs.[2]

An abundance of articles and books related to the therapeutic care of dying persons has been written by nurses and other health professionals. Recently, this area has been increasingly studied and discussed. How, then, with all this attention given to the care of the dying patient, could the modern hospital setting come in conflict with meaningful death? Although more nurses than ever are being taught the principles of caring for the dying, this knowledge is infrequently translated into practice. The real problem is applying knowledge, skills, and theory and "practicing what is preached." In writing this chapter, rather than repeat what has already been written about the area, I have chosen to focus primarily on those constraints encountered by the practicing nurse attempting to provide care for dying patients. Five major and realistic issues (no doubt others exist) impede the transition from knowledge and

theory to practice. These are: (1) hospital system pressures; (2) conflicting expectations placed upon the nurse; (3) the nurses' lack of adequate training in caring for dying persons and their families; (4) problems of teamwork among health professionals; and (5) conveying and exchanging diagnostic information. Although there are no simple solutions to the problems generated by these matters, their ramifications will be discussed and suggestions given that will, it is hoped, help the nurse creatively manage these difficulties.

BACKGROUND

Caring for the dying person has been a recognized area of nursing concern since the 1950's.[3] As increasing numbers of people die in hospitals, more nurses are exposed to the problems of dying patients. A recent survey published in *Nursing 75* indicated that the majority of the responding nurses dealt with dying patients two to three times per month.[4] Critical care units have also increased the nurse's contact with death, and 60% of the critical care nurses responding in this study reported that they care for a dying patient once a week or more often. However, this increased contact with dying patients has not led to increased satisfaction or confidence. Forty-seven per cent of the responding nurses in this same survey stated that they seldom or never had feelings of satisfaction or fulfillment from working with

---

* Although the author recognizes and supports the nursing profession's attempts to increase its male membership, the profession remains predominantly female. For the sake of consistency, the nurse will be given a feminine gender in this chapter.

a dying patient. Seventy-two per cent of this latter group stated they felt slightly or not confident in their abilities to manage the psychological needs of patients. These findings indicate that although nurses are being increasingly called upon to meet the needs of the dying patient, they are often dissatisfied with their work and feel ill-prepared for this role.

A second consequence of more people dying in hospitals is that in many cases, more responsibility for terminal care rests with the hospital personnel than with the family.[5] The nurturing functions of the extended family have increasingly been transferred to the nurse, and she is expected to meet both the patient's physical and psychological needs. One reason for this transfer of functions is undoubtedly the intimate dependence of the patient on the nurse. Also many families are unfamiliar with and frightened of the foreign hospital environment, and are relieved to surrender their responsibilities to nurses, who are traditionally seen by society as nurturing, supportive persons (a stereotype which will be discussed in more detail later). One must question the extent to which the nursing profession has responded to these expectations.

Generally, the nursing literature has supported the notions that nurses have primary responsibility to provide care and comfort, and to psychologically support the dying person and his family through the dying process. In the last 10 years, the expectation that nurses help the patient with the psychological aspects of dying as well as attend the physical aspects of care has increased. Nursing educators are now "more comfortable with dying."[6] It should be mentioned, however, that one of the major problems for the nursing profession is the continuing disunity between education and service. Practicing nurses may not accept their role as it is presented in the literature. Yet it is common to see at least one new published article per month dealing with some aspect of nursing care of the dying patient. However, much of this literature is " . . . philosophical, theoretical, or anecdotal."[7] It can still be argued, as Quint did in 1967, that although the literature says what to do, it does not always prepare the nurse for actual implementation, or delineate those problems which may well be encountered along the way.[8]

Aspects of the nurse's role are changing. Nurses were traditionally taught to avoid conflict, to be passive, and to be accepting. In the last few years, however, a shift to a different set of behaviors is evident, and many nurses have moved toward developing independence in judgment, active rather than passive problem solving, and improved colleagueal relationships among health team members. These new behaviors are likely to cause conflict in a hierarchically structured system such as the hospital, and this conflict may well have a direct effect on patient care.

The way in which other health professionals, consumers, and the society as a whole view the role of the nurse also affects the perception of her function. Although commonly held expectations of nursing practice will be discussed later, at this point two general determinants of nursing care delivery are worth noting. First, the societal mandate is definitely cure-oriented. This expectation has caused the medical and nursing professions to place a high value on cure, and created a consumer expectation that he be cured. Death is often viewed as a failure, and health professionals direct more of their efforts toward the patient who can be cured rather than the patient who cannot. Many health professionals are beginning to ask for a shift from a cure-oriented focus to a care-oriented one, but this has not been accomplished in most acute care hospitals. Second, health professionals tend to have rigid perceptions of each others' roles.[9] Often these are circumscribed and stereotyped, and result in poor communication, lack of trust and even hostility between professional groups. Fragmentation of effort, lack of teamwork, and a behavior best characterized as "staking out one's territory" are all end-products of this emphasis on roles. These behaviors can devastate the care of dying patients and their families. All health-care professionals are products of role-oriented training. Indeed, this chapter is being written from the perceived role of a nurse. Importantly, the issue is not to negate our roles, but to use them creatively to provide optimal care to the dying person.

DEFINING THERAPEUTIC NURSE-PATIENT RELATIONSHIP

Prior to discussing the practical issues which impede care, it is necessary to look more closely at some general aspects of the nurse-patient relationship. The term "therapeutic nurse-patient relationship" is frequently used as a standard for effective care of patients. Before proceeding, it is necessary to discuss the meaning of this phrase as it specifically relates to the dying patient.

Both verbal and nonverbal actions are important to create a therapeutic nurse-patient relationship. Such activities include: sitting down with the patient, listening for clues to the meaning behind the patient's words, accepting and reflecting the patient's expression of feelings, and creating an environment in which the patient is free to express his anxieties and feelings without censure. Focusing interactions on the patient, and, at times, sharing one's own feelings with the patient are important. Both behaviors give the patient a feeling of worth and importance. Some specific suggestions for openings to communication are: "Let's go talk"; "How are you really doing?" "You are having some pretty strong feelings—I'd like us to talk about them"; "What do you know about your illness?" Rinear notes that a caring posture is more important than feeling qualified.[10] Importantly, not all nurse-patient interactions need to be at a serious level or emotionally charged to be therapeutic. Patients do not need to discuss their feelings continuously. Indeed, sometimes patients and their families have a need to avoid the reality of their situation. When this occurs, they should be allowed to retreat and maintain their adaptive defenses.[11] Sustained contact, and a willingness to talk about how the patient feels are the most important factors in maintaining a caring position.

Numerous authors have found that patients fear isolation and abandonment more than death.[12, 13] Thus, one factor in a therapeutic relationship is simply presence, *i.e.,* sustained, meaningful contact between the patient and nurse. This does not mean the nurse is in constant physical attendance; rather it means that the patient knows she is available, and he is not alone. Feelings of isolation can also be decreased through giving the patient some sense of control through participation in his own care. Setting goals, making realistic plans, and allowing the patient to make decisions about certain activities are all means to this end.[14]

Interaction with and between family members is an important part of care. Here, there are two aspects of family involvement: nurses must consciously involve the family in the caring process; family members must understand that this involvement is important for their own grief. To accomplish these goals the nurse can encourage open communication between the patient and his family, provide support for the family so that they can then support the patient, encourage the family to remain close to the patient and help the family to provide direct care to the extent which they are able and have the need.[10] Therapeutic family participation was evident when the daughter of a comatose patient trimmed her mother's hair to help with her care. After doing this, the daughter said, "I think it helped my mother, but mostly it helped me." The subtleties of family participation are further illustrated by another example. The daughter of a woman dying of a brain tumor was unable to deal with her mother's death, and would leave the room whenever the patient tried to talk about death. She knew her mother wanted to go home, but did not think the family could manage her. The nurse caring for the patient recognized that the daughter would be unable to help her mother until she herself could begin coping with the loss and her feelings about her mother's death. Recognizing this, the nurse talked with the daughter alone over several days. They talked about her feelings, what the loss of her mother meant to her, her mother's need for close contact with one loved family member on a continuing basis, and specific ways she could respond to her mother's comments about death. After these sessions, the daughter said, "Now I can give Mother some of the things she's given me all these years." The family was able to take the patient home, where she died two months later.

With these underlying principles in mind,

it now becomes appropriate to examine more closely the problems which hinder the nurse in implementing these therapeutic relationships.

HOSPITAL SYSTEM PRESSURES

The first major deterrent faced by nurses in caring for the dying patient is the hospital system itself—specifically, time pressures and the hospital milieu. A frequent complaint made by nurses is, "I don't have the time." A high degree of organizational skill is often required to complete the administrative and physical aspects of care (checking off doctor's orders, administering medications, bathing patients, and performing treatments. It often takes all of the nurse's time and energy to see that these basic aspects of care are completed. The dying patient often requires far more complicated nursing care than the average patient. In the survey of nurses mentioned earlier, 62% of the respondents said care of the terminal patient was "more demanding than that of other seriously ill patients."[4] The psychological demands of these patients may be greater than the physical demands, but often do not receive as much attention. There are numerous reasons for this discrepancy. Nursing has traditionally valued physical care over the psychological aspects of care. Although nursing educators have advocated the importance of psychological care for a number of years, this has not been consistently reflected in practice. The hospital system rewards one for "getting work done" and keeping the organization running smoothly. Nurses have traditionally been designated as having primary responsibility for efficiently managing the ward and organizing activities of patients. This expectation will be discussed in more detail later in this chapter. A consequence of this delegation of management responsibility is that nurses fail at times to judge whether certain aspects of physical care could be omitted in favor of meeting the patient's psychological needs.

There are other reasons why psychological aspects of care are infrequently translated into practice. Physical measures tend to be more related to the important societal value of saving or maintaining life, and nurses themselves sometimes get more satisfaction out of tasks performed because there is visual evidence of accomplishment. Talking with patients is less structured and the rewards may appear less apparent and tangible. Nursing continues to place greater value on a clean patient in a clean bed with a clean bedside table than a patient who has been helped to express his feelings. Nurses have reported conflict with their superiors related to spending too much time talking with patients,[8] and nurses may even use physical care tasks to avoid talking to patients.[5] Sometimes the path of least resistance is to get entrapped in administrative details: equipment, paperwork, and staffing problems. In many hospitals, nurse's aides spend more time with patients, while the professional nurse only coordinates and manages the care process. Under these circumstances, the trained nurse has little chance to establish a therapeutic relationship with a dying patient. However, the untrained aide who has the time often lacks the knowledge required to enter into such relationships.

Another factor inhibiting psychological care is related to the difficulty in taking time to confront and manage one's own feelings when there is so much work to be done. Many strong, often negative emotions are generated in working with dying patients. Nurses need time and support to work through these feelings. Jones states, "Perhaps nurses assumed an attitude of detachment so they could face the painful, disturbing, distressing problems of their patients, and at the same time handle clerical, dietary, administrative and many other responsibilities."[15] After a number of years in a system that provides rewards only for physical aspects of care, nurses may become insensitive to the psychological needs of patients. Sinton's article provides a disturbing reminder that indifference to the dying patient does exist.[16]

Besides time pressures, the other major setting pressure that impedes care is the hospital environment. Two examples of environmental barriers in the hospital setting will be mentioned briefly. First, although all caregivers recognize the patient's right of and need for privacy, it is not always easily attained. Intensive care units are designed to treat critically ill patients who require expert monitoring of numerous physiological parameters. These units are often designed without walls or doors, in order that nurses may quickly observe three to four patients at any given time. In these settings it is difficult for the nurse to give patients either the time or the privacy needed to deal with their feelings. Visiting hours are usually very limited, and the patient's interaction with his family is likely to be minimal. This setting creates a considerable challenge for the nurse in trying to humanize patient care. A similar problem with privacy occurs in four- to six-bed wards found in many hospitals. In addition to the problem of privacy, hospital routine presents another barrier to humanistic care. This routine can take precedence over individual's wishes and all too often, the patient is expected to conform to the prevailing practices of the hospital, rather than the practices flexibly changing to meet patient needs.

To deal with the problem of time pressures, one may focus on the quality rather than the quantity of time spent with the patient. Although many factors impede them from spending time with patients, nurses are most proud of the fact that they work primarily at the bedside. What is done with that time? Is it spent actively creating a climate of trust, caring, and openness, or merely spent in routinized, social conversation? There are few activities with as much potential for closeness as the direct ministrations nurses provide for dying patients. Physical care measures (bathing, treatments, etc.) combined with skillful communication can be used to achieve a therapeutic relationship in a remarkably short period of time. As Kübler-Ross notes, the patient is often anxious for meaningful communication. "Dying patients who have such a limited time do not waste precious hours. It is not the number of hours spent with them that counts . . . It [working with the dying] is exhausting because of its depth and intensity, but it does not require many hours."[11] Giving direct physical care is not the only way to achieve a therapeutic relationship, but it is a necessary activity for the working nurse and can be used effectively to facilitate patients' verbalizing their feelings. Pa-

tients, especially those dependent on the nurse for their physical needs, are very sensitive to their nurse's competence and openness. When the nurse is directly responsible for the patient, she can demonstrate these behaviors quickly, and a trusting relationship can be formed. Often, after a few days of giving direct care, I have found that the patient views me as "his" nurse, and that the relationship, once initiated in this mode may continue without further direct care. Nurses must reorient themselves to view physical care as a vehicle, rather than an impediment in achieving effective communication, for they can care for the psychological needs of patients while still caring for their physical needs. A nurse must necessarily, however, feel relatively competent in the physical care area before she will be able to achieve this blending of care. Nurses must also examine their implicit communications with patients. Too often, we say, "I'm not too busy," but we are conveying the message "I'm in a big hurry, but can I help you?" It is, in many cases, clear that patients have picked up on the latter message.

Another suggestion for dealing with time pressures is to evaluate the way patient care assignments are made in the care setting. Frequently the psychological needs of a patient are not considered in such assignments. Staff nurses who are interested and capable of working in depth with dying patients should be consistently assigned to these patients, and given lighter assignments so they will have time to provide this type of service. To facilitate effective assignments, information about patients' psychological as well as physical needs should be shared at report. Continuity of care, although difficult to achieve, is important to both the dying patient and his family. Primary nursing (assigning each patient to one nurse who is then responsible for coordinating his care throughout his hospitalization) is one answer to this problem but it may not be feasible in certain settings. Assigning a small team of two to three nurses to work with a certain patient may be more practical than the assignment of one nurse. This alternative enables the nurses on the team to support each other while still providing the patient with a sense of continuity. The point is to creatively experiment with methods of assigning staff to patients, taking into consideration the needs of the patient, the capabilities of the staff, and the limits of the care setting.

While time pressures may be difficult, system pressures present even more difficult barriers, because there is frequently little the nurse can do about structural or administrative problems. But recognizing what barriers exist and how they create problems is a step toward finding solutions. For example, nurses cannot always place a dying patient in a private or semi-private room, but they can recognize the patient's need for privacy and give him time alone by drawing curtains or partitions around the patient when he so desires. Conversely, recognizing that a private room can cause isolation, nurses can encourage the patient's family to stay with him, or make a point of visiting the patient frequently, even when there is no task to be performed. Transferring patients from one unit to another, or from a unit to a specialized care setting, disrupts the caring process. Until the patient and family become comfortable with the new staff, efforts can be made by staff familiar with the patient to maintain some continuity through sharing information, and systematic visits. As Rinear states, "We mustn't be so easily intimidated by the hospital's functional operation that we lose sight of priorities."[10]

Sometimes, the nurse must face the fact that she cannot do anything about these pressures, that on any particular day, inadequate staffing, or events such as a cardiac arrest may interfere with her spending time with patients. It is precisely at this point that the nurse needs the most support. For if she cannot bear the guilt of being unable to meet the dying patient's needs, she will either withdraw from these patients or become insensitive to their concerns. Nurses cannot be everything to every patient, though that is often the expectation they set for themselves. Saunders has stated this well: "Sometimes the staff have to bear their inability to understand, to feel as if they are not helping at all, yet still go on staying close to the patient."[17] An example may help illustrate some of these points. A nurse had worked closely with a dying patient who was transferred to another unit because of a medical complication. The day of his death, the nurse felt guilty and helpless because she had only seen the patient three times after his transfer, and now she said, "It's too late for me to help." She was encouraged to go talk with another dying patient for whom she was caring. In encouraging her to work with the other patient, the clinical specialist was in essence saying, "It's not too late for this patient." The nurse did begin working with the other patient, and reported that it helped her positively manage her guilt.

EXPECTATIONS PLACED UPON THE NURSE

It has been previously mentioned that other professionals often have stereotyped notions of nursing (and, no doubt, vice versa). These expectations, whether justified or not, present real problems to the nurse attempting to give therapeutic care to patients. Certain expectations and stereotypes deserve brief mention here, for they are often at work in the hospital setting. These views of the nurse include the nurse as a ward manager, the nurse as the physician's servant, the nurse as a technician, and the nurse as a mother surrogate.

Perhaps the strongest expectation is that of the nurse as a ward manager. Although many hospitals now employ clerks and management personnel to both relieve the nurse of some of these managerial duties and to ensure that the unit might be operated more efficiently, the majority of other hospital personnel still look to the nurse as the primary administrator. This perception is reinforced by the fact that nurses are expected to supervise clerks and on the night shift, to function as clerks and managers in many hospitals. One author suggests that the role of the nurse has degenerated into that of traffic director.[18] Added to the pressures of the expectations of others are those of the nurse herself. Many nurses see certain ward-managerial functions as their primary responsibility, and have difficulty drawing the line between nursing and non-nursing management areas.

The expectation that the nurse be the

physician's servant is diminishing, but is still a strong force in the public's eye as well as in the nurse's self-image.[18] In a recent survey, 80% of those responding felt they were sometimes treated as servants by physicians.[19] This stereotype emphasizes the view that the nurse's primary role is to follow the doctor's orders and carry out his wishes. This expectation has been reinforced by the traditional sex difference between the two professions, the stereotype being the authoritarian male physician and the submissive female nurse. This view of the physician-nurse relationship still has strong, emotional force.[9] However, as a result of many factors, it is weakening. There is increased movement toward equality of the sexes in society in general. Larger numbers of women are entering medicine and increasing numbers of men are entering nursing. There is greater education of nurses toward independent judgment-making. And, significantly, a changing legal position holds nurses accountable for their own actions regardless of physician directive. The emphasis this legal position gives to independent nursing judgment is illustrated by the following statement. "Under no circumstances should the nurse carry out a physician's order which directs her to commit an act which she knows, or *should* know, to be unlawful. If she does, she will subject herself to criminal liability, whether or not the patient suffers injury, and she cannot avoid such liability by claiming she was merely following the doctor's orders."[20]

The view of the nurse as a technician is largely an outgrowth of the development of critical care areas, such as intensive care and coronary care units. This stereotype holds that the nurse is more concerned with the care of machinery surrounding the patient than with patient care. Most nurses in special care areas reject this stereotype, and hold firmly to the conviction that they " . . . nurse patients, not equipment or physicians."[21] In critical care areas, however, the physiological care of the patient is given priority, and the nurse must often attend first to the physical monitoring of the patient. These highly complex and technical measurements may create time pressures which interfere with caring for the patient's psychological needs. In addition, the posture in most critical care areas, and indeed, in most hospitals, is toward sustaining life. Death is an enemy; our sophisticated technology is viewed as the main weapon against it. In such an atmosphere, patients may be unwilling to voice fears of dying, or desires to die, and staff may be too busy with monitoring the patient's physical status to listen.

One of the cherished self-images nurses hold is that of comforter, nurturer, and mother surrogate to patients. There is little objective evidence to indicate whether or not patients share this image, for there are few studies detailing patients' expectations of nurses. White's study on non-acutely ill patients showed that they placed the highest priority upon nurses following the doctor's orders, with performing physical care measures "readily and cheerfully" also being listed as important.[22] In an earlier study, Tagliacozzo found that over 90% of the patients she interviewed after discharge felt that nurses were too busy and too hurried, which caused patients to be unwilling to make any additional demands on their time. Over half of the patients questioned said that nurses expected them to be cooperative. They repeatedly stated that only physical needs were legitimate, and emotional needs were to be managed by the patient alone.[23] Although neither of these two studies actually dealt with critically ill or dying patients, they suggest that the nurse's expectations of caring for and supporting the patient's psychological needs are not sufficiently realized in practice to cause patients to expect such care. These findings may also indicate that patients do not have a clear understanding of what is meant by the therapeutic nurse-patient relationship, and thus do not see it as part of the present health-care system.

Many aspects of the expectations discussed above have an integral role in the nurse's image of herself. She is expected to follow orders (to a greater or lesser extent), to keep the ward running smoothly, to handle technical aspects of care with ease and efficiency, and to be busy and task-oriented. Also, in her training the nurse has been expected to be calm and supportive, to spend time with patients, and to actively establish therapeutic relationships with them. It is easy to see how the need to integrate these often conflicting expectations could result in significant constraints when dealing with the dying person and his family. An example serves to illustrate the point. A nurse noticed that her patient seemed very upset. Upon questioning her, the nurse discovered that she had just been told by the doctor that she had cancer, and that "there was nothing more he could do." The patient began to express her fears and feelings of hopelessness, crying and holding the nurse's hand. After a few minutes, the nurse was interrupted by an aide who said that another patient needed pain medicine. The nurse told her cancer patient that she would "be right back," and went to give the pain medicine. While doing that, she was interrupted by a call from the blood bank about an improperly completed requisition, and by an irate housekeeper complaining that the bedpan hopper had overflowed for the third time in five days. It was fifteen minutes before she returned to the upset patient's room. When she did, the patient stated she no longer felt like talking and turned away from the nurse. An important opportunity had passed.

Often the idealized expectations of training give way to the real demands of the work setting. It is difficult for anyone to trade the known, set expectations found on most hospital units for poorly defined ones such as "spending time with patients" or "therapeutic listening." For the nurse who does not feel adequate in dealing with the dying patient, the expectations of the work environment become a screen behind which to hide. It is often easiest to follow orders or focus on managing ward activities when one is uncomfortable or unsure of oneself. New graduates are especially insecure in their abilities to perform procedures, and their focus of orientation is usually on learning routines and policies of management. Unless significant others in the work setting encourage beginning nurses to move beyond these routines and skills, they will continue to focus their attention on them rather than attempt to understand the total needs of the patient. Too often, this latter emphasis ends when the student graduates.

For therapeutic, psychologically oriented care to dying patients to be realized fully in practice, other providers in the health-care system must move beyond the stereotyped views of nurses. They must reward the nurse for providing psychological care as well as managerial expertise. Nurses also have a responsibility to articulate their need for physical and psychological support to carry out these functions. Two such support systems are already well known and in use, with varying degrees of effectiveness: a unit management system which relieves the nurse of managerial functions, and the primary nurse concept mentioned earlier. Some authorities feel that dying patients should be placed together, with a staff especially trained to meet their needs. Dr. Saunders describes care in a British hospice designed strictly for terminal patients.[24] Many nurses are opposed to this idea, feeling instead that each ward should have a few specially trained staff to work with these patients.[4] Some nurses are experimenting with new roles in an effort to better meet the patient's needs. Three examples of these new directions are the oncology clinical specialist who works throughout the hospital only with terminal patients, the nurse in the intensive care unit who works only with patients' and families' psychological needs, and the nurse who is employed by a physician to focus on psychological support. These nurses are not responsible for staff nursing functions. This frees them from systems constraints and leaves them with time to work with patients. The nursing profession needs more experimentation in developing such models.

Perhaps the most crucial factor in legitimizing therapeutic nursing care is psychological support. The nurse must recognize and accept that she needs a network of individuals who share common recognition of the value of psychological care if she is to be able to continually involve herself in this difficult area. As previously mentioned, the health-care system does not recognize her in this role, nor do many significant others. Consequently, support must come from informal sources: other nurses on the floor, concerned physicians, chaplains, the patients themselves, or a head nurse or supervisor who will defend the nurse when she fails to get all her "work" done. Eventually, such informal support groups may become formalized.[25] However, in most hospitals the nurse must take the initiative to find supporting persons or be able to recognize when they do not exist in a given system. In the latter case, she must decide whether or not to remain in the system. A system which does not provide any recognizable support for psychologically oriented care can be overwhelming to any nurse, and have a serious effect later on her abilities. Quint deals in depth with the need for support within the reality of hospital work.[8]

Wagner states that all nurses need to be taught principles related to care of the dying as part of their basic nursing preparation.[26] Although this is important, and students should have the opportunity to go into depth in this area if they so desire, serious questions must be raised about expecting every nurse to work in this area. It may be unrealistic to expect all nurses to be willing to enter into and be capable of establishing therapeutic relationships with dying patients. Perhaps the emphasis should be placed on supporting those nurses who are skilled in this area and facilitating training in the area for those who desire it.

An additional necessary factor in legitimizing nursing interventions with dying patients resides with nurses themselves. They must become as responsible for their actions and interactions in the psychological aspects of care as in the physical aspects. Glaser and Strauss have discussed this point, stating that psychological aspects of terminal care are not part of an accountable, visible process, but rather they rely on the individual nurse's initiative. They maintain that planning and review must be given to these aspects of care, and that personnel must be made directly accountable for their actions.[27] Educational programs will play an important role in making this level of accountability a reality.

THE NURSE'S LACK OF ADEQUATE TRAINING IN CARING FOR DYING PERSONS AND THEIR FAMILIES

The third deterrent to the provision of care for dying patients by the nurse is her lack of training and feelings of incompetence in dealing with the subject of death. As Popoff states, "Satisfaction and self-confidence in one's ability to provide care to terminally ill patients tend to go together."[4] Quint's study remains the major treatise describing the influence of initial training (or lack of it) on the nurse's behavior toward the dying patient. Based on her findings, she states,

There is no orderly progression of student experience with death and dying, and there are differences in the amount and kinds of experience students have during their basic education as nurses. . . . For the most part, the interaction model the teachers present is one emphasizing avoidance of dying patients. . . . Among the students participating in this study, the majority had limited opportunities to learn how to achieve satisfaction from assignments to dying patients: they developed a nurse identity primarily committed to recovery care.[8]

Although numerous attempts to improve the quality of undergraduate education in this area have been reported in the literature,[6,26,28] a study of their effects as broad as Quint's has not been attempted. While the basic theoretical notions about dying and death are probably dealt with in most undergraduate schools of nursing, there undoubtedly remains a wide variability in the amount and quality of direct clinical experience students receive.

Quint also reported that many teachers felt uncomfortable working with dying patients and, therefore, transmitted that discomfort to their students.[8] Strauss and Glaser go even further, characterizing medical and nursing faculties as having "deep-seated professional attitudes that social, psychological, and organizational matters are irrelevant or minor in the cure of illness and the care of patients."[27] Consequently, students may receive lectures on dying and death but have no opportunity to work through their feelings, or have structured, supported actual experiences with dying patients. It is this latter area of providing clinical experience to students that is lacking. Various reasons for this deficit include the near impossibility of guaranteeing such an experience for each student, the lack of competent role models for students to observe and emulate, and the disunity between education and service. Whatever the causes, they result in a practicing nurse being forced into experiences with death, even though she has not had adequate preparation as a student. The *Nursing 75* study on nurses' perceptions of caring for the dying indicates that about 50% of the respondents felt uncomfortable when a terminal patient brought up the topic of death.[4] One study found that although nurses recognized the need of dying patients for someone to talk to, they were unable to meet that need themselves.[2] The fact is that talking with patients about dying is both painful and difficult, and, at the same time, extremely worthwhile. But there are no easy responses that will automatically make the patient feel better. One nurse described her feelings when asked to sit with a dying patient:

I wondered what I would spend my time doing. . . . Gladly, I busied myself. . . . Then I ran out of things to do. . . . I excused myself to help pass trays. I felt terrible. . . . Just sit there? Oh, I can't do that. . . . I felt so guilty; if she [the patient] only knew how hard it is doing nothing with someone who is dying.[29]

The issue of how to best prepare healthcare professionals to care for the dying is crucial. This chapter will not attempt to deal with the content material of such training courses, but rather with some problems related to process. The first is the importance of one's attitudes about dying. Most studies contend that training does influence attitudes and behaviors but some authors contradict this. Golub and Reznikoff found that early career experiences influence attitudes about death and dying.[30] Yeaworth, Kapp, and Winget found that ". . . important shifts in attitudes about death and dying can result from the nursing education."[7] Lester, Getty, and Kniesl found that increasing a nurse's professional education decreased her fear of death and dying.[31] On the other hand, Quint and Knutzen reported separately that the nurse's potential ability in the area of terminal care is largely unaffected by her education, mainly because of inadequate clinical experience as students.[8,32] An additional issue is whether attitudes influence performance. Shusterman and Se-

chrest found that "Apparently a nurse's assessment of her ability to comfort dying patients is not related to her own personal fear of death and dying."[2] Conversely, in the *Nursing 75* survey, nurses stated they were more comfortable caring for the dying patient if they had ". . . come to terms with fear of their own death."[4] Thus, the literature is not consistent. However, I feel that exploring one's attitudes and beliefs about dying should be undertaken as part of a student's training experience. It is important that the nurse at least be aware of, if not completely comfortable with, her feelings, and understand how they inevitably influence her care. All practitioners need to be aware that their attitudes may facilitate or block the caring process.

In my view, the two goals of instructors working with students are to develop their ability to *be with* the dying person and his family, and to create an open atmosphere in which students' feelings can be discussed, and meaningful support given. How does one structure training programs to achieve these goals? Certainly some basic theory is necessary. Theoretical knowledge related to stages of dying, grief, and crisis intervention are helpful points of reference and give a framework within which the students can begin to understand their own feelings and responses and those of their patients. Many excellent materials are available for this purpose. However, although theoretical material is necessary, it is not sufficient. As Quint states, "Class discussions about death and dying are of limited value without concomitant planning for first assignments to dying patients under conditions that maximize the chances for positive outcomes for the student."[8] This position is supported by the findings of the *Nursing 75* survey that ". . . having experienced some kind of positive feedback from terminally ill patients or their families is a key element in the makeup of nurses who are able to provide care and comfort to those who are about to die."[4] This would suggest that all courses on death and dying should contain a direct experience component. This can be achieved in numerous ways, the most desirable of which would be directly supervised clinical experience, utilization of students' experiences in other courses, or selection of one patient for the student to follow in the community. If none of these alternatives were available, a simulation of the practice setting might be attempted through contact in class with dying patients. Filmed interactions between nurses and patients or role-playing exercises might be employed. It is crucial to approximate practical situations in order that students may have the opportunity to experience the difficulties and rewards in working with dying patients, and, perhaps more importantly, have the opportunity to begin to see themselves as competent in caring for the dying. Readings, interpersonal process recordings, and discussion of interactions can all serve to support students as they deal with problem areas. The growth potential of positive patient contacts must be recognized and incorporated into the teaching effort. As Kübler-Ross says, "My best teachers were my dying patients."[33]

Teachers must recognize the necessity for providing both emotional and practical support for students and be prepared to do this. This support may involve taking time for students to verbalize feelings, giving concrete suggestions for responding to difficult situations, or helping a student analyze a certain interaction. An example illustrates these functions. A dying patient with whom a student nurse had previously worked was admitted to the floor on which she was assigned. She was assigned to take the patient the next day, as the instructor and the staff were excited over the possibility that the student might give them insights into his present confused behavior. Later that day, the student approached the instructor, saying that she could not be assigned to that patient. She stated that it was painful for her to see him so sick and restrained, and that he reminded her of her own father who had died a few years before. The student was able to verbalize many of her feelings. She felt she could not care for his wasted body and confused mental state, and at the same time, give him psychological support. She and the instructor agreed that until she was ready she would not be assigned to provide his direct physical care, but would work with his psychological needs by going in to talk

with him. In this way, she was given some time to deal with her own feelings. After a few days, the student was able to resume working with the patient, and subsequently provided valuable input to the staff regarding his care. As Wise states, "It is exhausting [for teachers to help students] to deal conscientiously with feelings, and a certain commitment is necessary for this approach."[6]

Three additional factors are important in maximizing students' learning in courses on death and dying. The first is the necessity for the student to feel some beginning competence in performing physical care activities. As previously stated, students without such competence will focus their energies on procedural and organizational skills, rather than interactional skills. The second factor is the importance of contacts between nursing and other health professional students in training courses. Admittedly, this is difficult outside a university setting. However, having faculty from different disciplines participate in a course can achieve much the same goal. Interdisciplinary contacts do much to dissolve stereotypes, foster colleagueship, and encourage a unified approach. Within an atmosphere conducive to learning, students have a chance to explore the feelings of other professionals and the constraints placed upon them. Students observe the role models provided by various faculty working as a team to develop common approaches to the dying patient, and supporting each other in the process. In many cases, it has been traditional for physicians to teach nursing students, but rarely are medical students taught by nurses. In caring for dying patients it is especially important that beginning physicians see nurses as knowledgeable colleagues, rather than less intelligent functionaries who simply follow orders. The third factor in maximizing students' learning is giving increased attention in training programs to hospital setting constraints that impede care for the dying. There is a great need to better prepare students to deal creatively with the problems of the work environment.

But what of the nurse who received her basic education before principles of terminal care were included in nursing school curricula? For nurses with little basic training, continuing education becomes very important. These nurses have considerable experience, but much of it may have been negative. Those who have become oriented only toward managerial and physical care priorities need to be resensitized to the psychological needs of patients. Strauss, Glaser, and Quint recommend a variety of methods, including training courses, workshops, and unit discussions. Expression of participants' feelings in this area, reasons behind them, and tactics available to deal with patient and system problems should be included. They further recommend that any method be interdisciplinary.[34] Numerous continuing education programs are available. Murray reports one such program and its effect on participants' death anxiety.[28] However, as important as any workshop may be, it must be followed up and supported in the clinical setting. Indeed, ongoing programs at a staff level are necessary to cope with feelings individual patients may engender, to deal with continuing system problems which require intervention, and to provide regular support to staff members.

THE PROBLEM OF TEAMWORK AMONG HEALTH PROFESSIONALS

Many professionals provide care and are involved with the dying person and his family. These include nurses, physicians, social workers, chaplains, and physical therapists among others. The composite of those individuals caring for a given patient is considered the team.

One serious barrier to giving coordinated therapeutic care to the dying person is lack of teamwork among health-care providers. Although much has been written about teamwork, and its advantages are obvious, it is infrequently practiced in the modern hospital. In large part, this is due to the rigid hierarchical structure of the health-care system, which places the physician at the head of the team, with other health-care personnel somewhere below him. Generally, personnel from varying disciplines have not been trained in working together as a coordinated group. The patient comes to the hospital to receive medical treatment (managed by a physician), and the actions and focus of health-care providers are directed toward that end. As a consequence, the orientation of the individual physician often has a great deal to do with whether a team approach is realized.

Much lip service is given to teamwork; it is a popular concept and easily discussed. In reality, however, it is quite difficult to practice colleagueal relationships in a hierarchical structure. In addition, there are few working models of effective team relationships from which others can learn. Nurse practitioners have made strides toward colleagueal relationships with physicians, but hospital-based nurses have not kept this pace. The multiplicity of health-care workers and multiple consulting services further complicate the problem. Five different disciplines may be working with the patient, minimally sharing information. Even if the physician and nurse have a good working relationship, teamwork may not be realized. A further problem is that because the hospital team is organized chiefly for promoting and saving lives, death is often viewed as the team's corporate failure. Team members may feel, "We didn't do all we could," or conversely, "We did more than we should have." It is difficult to expose such feelings unless considerable trust exists between team members.

The nurse has some specific problems as a member of the health-care team. She is continually based on a given unit for extended periods of time and often has the most direct interaction with other health-team members. Thus, she is in a pivotal position to coordinate the efforts of the team. In practice, however, she is most often a "coordinator without portfolio." There are a number of reasons for this lack of recognition. Nurses are not always willing to assume the role of coordinator. Nursing as a profession is not valued by some other professions as being equal in stature or deserving of this role. Also, there is a constant turnover of nurses (due to shift changes, assignment changes, high attrition rates) which decreases the individual nurse's sense of accountability for ensuring effective team functioning. Even the nurse willing to take on this responsibility is often confronted with a physician who sees team conferences as "a waste of time," or a threat to his position as head of the team. As one physician informed a nurse when told of her concern over a patient's not knowing his diagnosis, "Worry about it on your own time, honey." Use of the sexual stereotype by referring to the nurse as "honey" or "one of the girls" is often employed by physicians, and is very difficult for nurses to handle. It places interactions on a sexist, hierarchical level rather han a professional one.

Another practical difficulty in getting team members together is found in coordinating schedules. The time may be good for the nurse, but not for the social worker or the chaplain, and the larger the team the more difficult the problem. This results in each person "doing his own thing" with the patient, and only sporadically communicating with others. The busy, concerned nurse is likely to give up in frustration. Quint states, "Many difficulties faced by dying patients stem directly from lack of communication between doctors and nurses."[8] Perhaps those two groups are the worst offenders, but social workers, chaplains and other health-care workers also communicate inadequately, resulting in poor teamwork. Nurses can do much to improve this communication, but all professional groups have equal responsibility.

Ten years ago, Quint stated that effective team work would involve " . . . moving out of the traditional nurse role with its emphasis on delegated medical tasks and comfort care into a more active role in which communicating with and on behalf of patients is a primary concern."[8] The nursing profession, with its traditional focus on caring, is in a position to help the rest of the team move toward helping people die dignified deaths rather than maintaining life at all costs. To this end, nurses are beginning to define their role on the health-care team as patient advocate and coordinator of team efforts. They are beginning to see themselves as primarily accountable to the patient, not the doctor or the hospital. These definitions give nurses clear responsibilities on the team: to take initiative in communicating with other team members; to assess the patient's needs and interpret them to the rest of the group; and to facilitate getting

the patient and the rest of the team together. First, nurses must improve communication among themselves, so that all staff share the same information. They must make an effort to involve those team members such as community clergymen, who may be important caregivers or have important information, but who are less visible in the hospital system.

Nurses must be flexible enough to recognize that too rigid a definition of one's role may not best serve the patient. As Epstein states, "Different members should take on the leadership role when their own particular skills are especially needed to solve a particular problem."[9] As early as 1949, Hiltner advocated a "fluid-role team" (*versus* a "fixed-role team") in which the major counseling responsibilities are assigned to the worker who is best able to counsel a particular person.[35] This person may change from patient to patient. What is important is that the nurse take some responsibility for identifying, and helping the patient identify for himself, those health professionals best suited to help with particular needs; and that she initiate and facilitate communication between team members. The patient has the right to at least one primary caregiver with whom he can best relate. This notion of teamwork is quite difficult to achieve, and will not work unless all health-care disciplines recognize and support the necessity for communication and unity of effort. Physicians especially need re-education about the importance of colleagueal relationships between team members. The nurse must accept the responsibility of being part of the team, and other health professionals must acknowledge her responsibility in this area.

Adequate support systems for the caregivers are a vital part of providing care for the dying person. Support for the nurse has been discussed. All members of the team must allow ventilation of others' feelings, share the difficulties they are experiencing, and have their own needs met to be able to work continuously with the dying patient.[33] It will take a reorientation of approach, best begun in the student experience, to make teamwork and peer support among health professionals a reality.

An additional point should be mentioned. At times, any health professional may have the need to withdraw from a certain situation. In a good team, the person can be allowed to do this, and other members can substitute. An impersonal attitude or withdrawal can be a necessary coping mechanism employed by the nurse. It would seem preferable to develop teams that allow members to retreat from painful situations, and replace them with others, than to have overburdened personnel demonstrating uncaring attitudes to patients. We must recognize and support our own humanness without compromising patient care. This cannot be done without a cooperative team approach.

CONVEYING AND EXCHANGING DIAGNOSTIC INFORMATION

The last major practical problem to be discussed in rendering therapeutic care to dying patients is the issue of diagnostic information and the manner in which it is communicated. The nurse has no sanctioned role in telling the patient his diagnosis. This is the physician's responsibility and most patients look to their physician for this information. However, a patient may ask the nurse, especially if the physician is reluctant to give the diagnosis, or if he infrequently visits the person. Glaser and Strauss have categorized the situations that develop from various degrees of informing the patient as "awareness contexts," and have studied the resultant behaviors in depth.[36] Three specific situations will be discussed here: the physician who does not tell the patient his diagnosis; the nurse who does not know what the patient has been told; and, the nurse and physician who hold differing views of what the patient should be told.

In the first instance, the physician chooses not to tell the patient. Numerous studies have shown that nurses find it more difficult to care for the dying patient or converse with him when he has not been told his diagnosis.[5] Kübler-Ross notes that the problem of physicians not informing patients of their diagnoses results in a dilemma frequently faced by conscientious nurses.[33]

In the second, perhaps more common situation, the nurse does not know what the patient has been told. Often a patient asks the nurse for information first, because he is more comfortable with her. Shusterman and Sechrest state, "If a nurse does know a patient's condition, she is unlikely to tell him, and the worse his condition, the less likely she is to communicate with him."[2] There is considerable fear among many nurses of accidentally "giving away" the patient's diagnosis and causing distress to the patient and trouble for themselves. As one nurse graphically states: "I don't recall ever being actually forbidden or ordered not to answer a patient honestly when he or she asked about death, but in every single hospital I've worked in, I have always felt that such honesty would cause serious problems for me, and possibly cost me my job."[4] Rather than lead the nurse to seek information from the doctor, this anxiety often causes her to avoid the patient.

In the third instance, the nurse and physician hold differing views on what the patient should be told. The *Nursing 75* survey reports that 60% of nurses responding felt the patient should be told his diagnosis as soon as possible.[4] Physicians, however, seem more reluctant than nurses for the patient to know. Shusterman states, "Much of what has been written about revealing the truth to dying patients is anecdotal, but indicates that the majority of doctors do not reveal a fatal prognosis to the patient."[5] This puts the nurse in an extremely difficult position, especially if the patient is asking her for information. The following example illustrates this dilemma. A nineteen-year-old adolescent developed a terminal illness. Neither his family nor his physician wanted him told the extent of his illness, saying, "He would not be able to take it," and "We're not going to let him get depressed." One evening, a nurse found him crying. When asked what was wrong, he blurted out, "Am I going to get well?" The nurse, knowing he was not to be told, but not wanting to lie, said, "I don't know. What do you think?" He replied, "I used to think I would get well, but I don't know anymore." He proceeded to tell her about his progressing symptoms. The nurse listened and reflected the patient's comments, without adding her own. The next day she was confronted by the patient's angry parents, who told her that he was depressed, and was saying that the doctors had told him he was not going to get well. The nurse was never able to convince the family that she was not responsible for the patient's knowledge.

Another area in which nurses and physicians may differ is that of patient's denial of diagnosis and prognosis. Denial may result when the physician does not tell the patient his diagnosis, or when the patient is unable to accept it. Physicians, who see their patients for short periods of time, may be comfortable with denial. But because of their daily contact with the patient, nurses are often uncomfortable and frustrated even to the point of anger with the denying patient. For example, a patient with metastatic bone cancer told the nursing staff repeatedly that she had "arthritis," and that she planned to return to her home where she lived alone. After ascertaining that the physician had told the patient her diagnosis and prognosis, the staff became angry, saying, "Doesn't she know she's dying?"

The options in all the above situations are limited and difficult. The nurse can avoid the patient (the most commonly chosen option). She may go to the physician for information, or tell the patient and risk the wrath of the physician and/or the family. She may try to get the patient to come to his own conclusions through reflective listening (the course chosen in the first example). In the extreme, she may change her situation to one in which she is not confronted with dying patients at all (described by Quint).[8]

How then can nurses deal with the problems related to conveying diagnostic information? Although it can be argued that the nurse should be able to tell the patient his diagnosis if she is the one with whom he has the strongest relationship, I do not feel this is presently a practical goal for most hospital nurses. Most physicians feel that the giving of the diagnosis is their responsibility, and most nurses agree with this position. Consequently, most of the suggestions in this section relate to increasing communication about diagnostic information between physician, nurse, and patient, and fostering a climate within which the patient can work through his feelings about his illness.

Craytor points out that the first and most important step for the nurse is to determine the patient's own perception of his illness.[14] Patients may claim they have not been told anything, even when the doctor says he has explained the diagnosis carefully. Patients sometimes are too shocked to comprehend the meaning of the words used, or they employ the mechanism of denial or simply block the information because they do not want to hear it. Assessing what the patient thinks he has been told, and what he *wants* to be told, as well as the physician's and family's perceptions of the same information are important first steps in deciding how to proceed. Often the patient must be told his diagnosis repeatedly with time for discussion and reflection before it begins to "sink in." Some physicians seem to be impatient with the need for such reinforcement. However, just because they told the patient does not mean the patient is psychologically ready to integrate the information. Less frequently, it may be that the patient understands his diagnosis, but does not wish to talk about it. However, the nurse may prematurely assume this when, in reality, she has not given the patient a chance to talk.

It is extremely important that all the health-care providers working with the patient know what information he has been given. Because of their position in the system, nurses have a pivotal role in seeing that this is done. This may mean going on rounds with physicians to hear what they tell patients, or setting up interdisciplinary team conferences or informal one-to-one discussions on the hospital unit. Regardless of the form, sharing patient information among team members is a logical nursing function for which nurses must take responsibility. This does not absolve the physician from his responsibility to take more initiative in communicating with other team members.

The problem is different if the physician does not want the patient told. If the patient is asking for the information, however, the nurse has the responsibility to communicate this to the doctor. Many doctors feel, "When the patient is ready to know, he will ask me." Unfortunately, many patients feel, "When the doctor is ready for me to know, he will tell me." Thus they do not approach the doctor, but rather ask the nurse. In this situation, the nurse should offer her support to the patient through a statement such as, "I'll be here when Dr. S. comes to see you, and we can ask him together."

The accepted standard action when the patient asks about his diagnosis is to reflect the question back to him. Examples of this technique are, "What are you feeling now that caused you to ask that?" or "If you did have cancer, what would that mean to you?" Although these responses can be viewed as avoiding the question, they can also be valuable tools in opening the way for a meaningful dialogue between the nurse and the patient. The nurse's main role is to help the dying patient deal with his dying in whatever manner and at whatever level he is best able. She is a listener, a facilitator, a sounding board, a support. It is important that the nurses not forget these vital functions in the confusion over whether or not the patient "knows." Therapeutic nursing interventions are dependent only on the nurse's abilities, not how much information the patient has or has not received.

COMMENT

Strong, negative emotions may result from work with the dying patient, and are among the most difficult feelings with which nurses must deal. The following feelings and thoughts occurred on the day one of my own patients died:

Mr. C. has just died. As I left his room, I wondered what I'm doing writing a chapter on care of the dying. Feelings of guilt, helplessness and grief. Guilt that I didn't spend the time with him and his wife I should have: "I'll see her tomorrow, as soon as I've caught up." Avoiding? We never did have the talk I promised, and now it's too late. Helplessness—what can you say? "We loved him." Grief—for his wife, remembering the picture of how strong he was, the loss of him to the family. Remembering the day I shaved him, and finally did it right and we both laughed. Feeling so stilted and artificial standing in that room full of people, chaplain, two nurses, mother, son, and wife, a "cast of thousands." Not wanting her to misunderstand, not wanting to leave. How do you show that you cared? Sadness. Relief.

Many times, there are no obvious answers to how to cope with these feelings. Meeting the dying patient's needs is demanding and draining, but at the same time tremendously rewarding. I recognize that all the suggestions presented in this chapter are more easily written about than accomplished. But they represent positive steps that can be taken to counteract the real problems of the work setting, and maximize the rewards of working with the terminally ill. There are few experiences as satisfying as helping a patient deal with his own death. Through training, support, and acceptance of responsibility nurses can do much to both humanize the hospital environment and give thoughtful, compassionate care to the dying person.

REFERENCES

1. Carmody J: A Death, a Radicalization. *Christian Century 91*:639–640, 1974
2. Shusterman LR, Sechrest L: Attitudes of Registered Nurses Toward Death in a General Hospital. *Psychiat Med 4*:411–426, 1973
3. Morris CM: The Nurse and the Dying Patient. *Amer J Nurs 55*:1214–1217, 1955
4. Popoff D: What Are Your Feelings About Death and Dying? Part One. *Nursing 75 5*:15–25, 1975
5. Shusterman LR: Death and Dying: A Critical Review of the Literature. *Nurs Outlook 21*:465–471, 1973
6. Wise DJ: Learning About Dying. *Nurs Outlook 22*:42–44, 1974
7. Yeaworth RC, Kapp FT, Winget C: Attitudes of Nursing Students Toward the Dying Patient. *Nurs Res 23*:20–24, 1974
8. Quint JC: *The Nurse and the Dying Patient*. The Macmillan Co., New York, 1967
9. Epstein C: Breaking the Barriers to Open Communication on the Health Team. *Nursing 74 4*:65–68, 1974
10. Rinear EE: Helping the Survivors of Expected Death. *Nursing 75 5*:60–65, 1975
11. Kübler-Ross E: "The Dying Patient's Point of View," in *The Dying Patient*, Brim OG Jr, Freeman HL, Levine S, Scotch NA (Eds) Russell Sage Foundation, New York, 1970
12. Feder SL: "Attitudes of Patients With Advanced Malignancy," in *Death and Dying: Attitudes of Patient and Doctor*. Group for the Advancement of Psychiatry, New York, 1965
13. Thomas JM, Weiner EA: Psychological Differences Among Groups of Critically Ill Hospitalized Patients, Noncritically Ill Hospitalized Patients and Well Controls. *J Consult Clin Psychol 42*:274–279, 1974
14. Craytor JK: Talking With Persons Who Have Cancer. *Amer J Nurs 69*:744–748, 1969
15. Jones EM: Who Supports the Nurse? *Nurs Outlook 10*:476–478, 1962
16. Sinton J: Another One Gone! Were You on Duty? *Nurs Mirror 140*:59, 1975
17. Saunders C: "The Moment of Truth: Care of the Dying Person," in *Death and Dying*, Pearson L

(Ed) The Press of Case Western Reserve University, Cleveland, 1969

18. Kellar NS: The Nurse's Role: Is It Expanding or Shrinking? *Nurs Outlook 21:*236–240, 1973

19. Nursing Ethics. *Nursing 74 4:*34–44, 1974

20. Bernzweig EP: *The Nurse's Liability for Malpractice,* 2nd Ed. McGraw-Hill, St. Louis, 1975

21. Zschoche D, Brown LE: Intensive Care Nursing: Specialism, Junior Doctoring, or Just Nursing? *Amer J Nurs 69:*2370–2374, 1969

22. White MB: Importance of Selected Nursing Activities. *Nurs Res 21:*4–13, 1972

23. Tagliacozzo DL: "The Nurse From the Patient's Point of View," in *Social Interaction and Patient Care,* Skipper JK (Ed) J. B. Lippincott Co., Philadelphia, 1965

24. Saunders C: The Last Stages of Life. *Amer J Nurs 65:*70–75, 1965

25. Everett MG: How Health Professionals Help Each Other. *Amer J Nurs 75:*1355, 1975

26. Wagner B: Teaching Students to Work With the Dying. *Amer J Nurs 64:*128–131, 1964

27. Strauss AL, Glaser BG: "Patterns of Dying," in *The Dying Patient,* Brim OG Jr, Freeman HL, Levine S, Scotch NA (Eds) Russell Sage Foundation, New York, 1970

28. Murray P: Death Education and Its Effect on the Death Anxiety Level of Nurses. *Psychol Rep 35:*1250, 1974

29. Croushore T: It's Hard to Sit With Death. *Amer J Nurs 73:*1060, © 1973, The American Journal of Nursing Company

30. Golub S, Reznikoff M: Attitudes Toward Death. *Nurs Res 20:*503–508, 1971

31. Lester D, Getty G, Kniesl CR: Attitudes of Nursing Students and Nursing Faculty Toward Death. *Nurs Res 23:*50–53, 1974

32. Knutzen AL: "Cultural Beliefs on Life and Death," in *The Dying Patient,* Brim OG Jr, Freeman HL, Levine S, Scotch NA (Eds) Russell Sage Foundation, New York, 1970

33. Kübler-Ross E: Letter to a Nurse. *Nursing 73 3:*11–13, 1973

34. Strauss AL, Glaser BG, Quint JC: The Nonaccountability of Terminal Care. *Hospitals 38:*73–87, 1964

35. Hiltner S: *Pastoral Counselling.* Abingdon Press, Nashville, 1949

36. Glaser BG, Strauss AL: *Awareness of Dying.* Aldine Press, New York, 1965

15

ISSUES FOR CLERGY IN THE CARE OF THE DYING AND BEREAVED

Liston O. Mills. Th.D.

Pastoral responsibility for the care of the dying and bereaved is not a recent development. Prior to our rediscovery of death in professional circles in the fifties and sixties, clergy were considered gatekeepers of death, a function others were perfectly willing for them to perform.

Any number of developments fostered a change in this understanding. The breakdown of christendom and the emergence of a pluralistic society in which one cannot assume general agreement on the meaning of living and dying was one. Another was the mobility of the American people and the frequent absence of family to care for the dying and sustain the bereaved. Advances in medical technology constitute an important dimension of this change. Prolongation of life and the emergence of the hospital as the locus of care meant hospital staff faced terminal illness more frequently and with more of a sense of responsibility for care than before.

Clergy generally welcome heightened sensitivity and more direct involvement on the part of other professionals in the crisis of death. We have profited greatly from the concerted attention and research that have flowed from other professions. At the same time the efforts of others in this sphere require us to be more precise in the meaning of the care we give and offers a group of potential colleagues to whom we may turn.

In this chapter I attempt to address a few of the issues that affect clergy in light of these developments and our responsibility to care for the dying and bereaved. I will not deal with intricate questions of medical ethics but will instead seek to respond to the question: "What are the issues confronting clergy seeking to care for a dying person and his family?" by commenting on the clergy's person and role, the hospital setting, and the patient and his family.*

ISSUES OF PERSON AND ROLE

Regardless of their particular religious orientation, clergy operate out of a tradition and set of meanings which occasion both possibilities and frustrations. The perception of this tradition, and thus of the clergy's place and function with the dying and bereaved, leads to some of these hopes and disappointments.

For centuries clergy have been looked to in times of human distress. Pope Gregory, John Calvin, Jeremy Taylor, and Richard Baxter were among those who instructed them to attend persons in trouble, especially the sick and dying.[1] Beneath this expectation of presence lay a view of illness and death as a potential crisis of faith. It acknowledges that life in its unvarnished form may effect not just our physical well-being but the entire set of meanings and relations which undergird it. One continues to see the wisdom of this observation in the loneliness of the dying and bereaved. To clergy ques-

---

* I hope my use of the term "clergyman" and of the masculine pronoun when referring to ministers and patients will not offend women readers. I am quite aware of the significant work women are doing in ministry generally and in the care of dying persons particularly, but have yet to find a felicitous way of acknowledging this.

tions about the goodness of God, whether his love can finally be trusted, still attest to the potentially devastating effects of the crisis of death on people.

Also beneath this view of death and dying as a crisis of faith lay a set of meanings and commitments about the religious person's responsibility. Creeds and confessions demand care and attentiveness to those in distress: to love God is to love and care for one's neighbor. Thus those in the throes of illness and death need consolation; they need someone to stand with them so as to make misery more bearable and to reassure them that death does not negate love and hope.

The presence of clergy, then, symbolizes this tradition of care in the face of a crisis of faith. Ministers represent to the patient and family a network of meanings about living and dying; their function is to care. "Care" in this sense usually means a tender and solicitous concern.[2] It means to sustain another in the face of an irreversible situation. Often the word comfort is used to describe the clergy's work in such circumstances, and if it refers to its root meaning of lending courage or taking heart it is a proper term. The point is that clergy do not usually understand their task either as providing false hope or as encouraging resignation to a hopeless situation. Instead they encourage patients and families to take heart in the face of difficulty. I think it important to underscore that such care understands pain, suffering, guilt, and death as part of the stuff of life. To be sure such experiences are not sought. But their presence and the subsequent crisis are understood in most religious communities as opportunities to see life and values more clearly. Thus clergy do not seek to avoid the descent into hell but see it as a prerequisite to a frank dealing with life and to the emergence of hope. This understanding of care, it seems to me, forms the basis for some of the issues we shall discuss later.

I have described this tradition because it seemed essential in order to understand both the possibilities and the frustrations clergy experience in their efforts to work with the dying and bereaved. For example, theological students and younger clergy are often astounded at the power of their symbolic role. Often they are credited with a trustworthy motive, and, unless a person's experience has been quite negative, even non-believers seem to assume that the clergy's commitment is to them and their well-being. Strangers may say, "I've never gone to church much myself," and then proceed to discuss the most personal and difficult aspects of their lives. Moreover, as representatives of a religious community, clergy often serve to remind people of present ties or ones lost in a distant past. In either case the ties are or have been real and function to link us to meanings and persons which help to overcome isolation. Clergy also sometimes symbolize hope to people. They serve to bring to mind the ways in which omissions, defeats, failures, and disappointments may be dealt with and one's life make sense again.

At the same time, however, the expectation that clergy care for the dying often spawns personal crisis and frustration. It calls for personal involvement with the dying patient, and it assumes both competence and the capacity to care on the part of clergy. Yet ministers know that ordination insures neither competence nor compassion. They know that the awesome privilege of dealing with the unknowable, of brushing shoulders with death, threatens them just as it does everyone else.[3] They know they are not exempt from the temptation to deal with death by routine practices or by ignoring and denying it. Unless they have had opportunity to deal with their own feelings about death and dying, an opportunity their education by no means insures, their tradition of care becomes a burden and their competence a perfunctory routine. I have known clergy who became ill when it was their responsibility to care for a dying patient. I have known others who simply avoided such visits, preferring the stigma as a "non-visiting minister" to the anxiety aroused by death.

Clergy respond to the threat of death and the demand for care in different ways. For some it becomes an occasion for self-discovery and a more faithful ministry to those in trouble. Others may over-identify with patients, becoming their champions against the forces of depersonalization, *e.g.*, doctor, nurses, and hospitals. Frequently they don a mask that may serve to make care impersonal and perfunctory and to shield them from anxiety. The collar or the dark suit, the tone of voice, the use of the Bible and prayer book, prayer itself, and the observance of ceremony and symbolic act—all these beguile the clergyman into thinking he is caring, being the professional, and at the same time enable him to keep his distance. It is not that ritual and symbol are unimportant to care. But ritual acts and practices should open us to each other, not serve as obstacles to meeting.

Clergy may also "handle" death and the demand for involvement by a resort to doctrine. As their anxiety increases, so does their authority to speak finally about the unknowable. This retreat to doctrine is understandable when one realizes the emphasis placed on concepts, verbal facility and the ability to intellectualize in American theology and theological education. Clergy are frequently asked to speak on death and they are expected to have thought through the "theological problem of death." The tendency is to equate "talking about death" with dealing with one's own feelings about death, to assume that because one has a well-worked out view of evil and suffering, one has come to terms with death personally. It results in the feeling that if one can explain a phenomenon he has mastered it, and that he helps others by explaining it to them.

Finally, the expectation to care may precipitate personal crisis in its assumption of faith on the part of the clergy. As men of faith, clergy are often self-conscious about their lack of it on occasion. Confrontations on a pediatrics ward with the raw injustice of innocent suffering cause most of us to pause. Yet clergy sometimes feel they should rise above such experiences. They may feel they should not have, let alone admit and confess, such thoughts and feelings. As a result their caring does not come through as authentic, as stemming from anything deep within them. Having never dealt with their own doubt, they may not see it as essential to a life of faith and simply reject those who own it freely in the same way they have rejected themselves. Again, doubt by clergy may express itself in argumentativeness with patients about this or that point of view. The minister may protest too much

that the patient must "give in" and believe as he says and rob his parishioner of the opportunity to deal with the human dilemma which may lay behind his view of life.

A second set of issues in caring for the dying results from the ways clergy are perceived by others. Both positive and negative stereotypes amuse, irritate, or anger the clergyman, depending upon how much they interfere with his work or demean his purpose or distort the meaning of his presence.

Since I have described some of the positive functions of these projections, I think it important to point out that their effect occasionally distorts a situation and is quite negative. Sometimes both patients and other professionals assume they know what the minister's coming means and that they would be better off without him. He may be greeted by a patient with, "I'm glad to have a visit but please don't try to convert me." Many among the staff and patients see the clergy as some sort of spiritual head-hunter who regard the dying and the bereaved as fair game. They are suspicious of his motivation and wonder whether his words and attention do not really have something other than their welfare in view. Again, others see him as a miracle worker. He is often greeted by doctors with, "Well, I'm glad you're here. We've done all we can and it's up to you." Families meet him with the exclamation that they have been told that their relative will die but they know God will change that. Some of the medical staff also see clergy as anti-scientific.[4] They represent dealings with the "spiritual" as opposed to the "real" world. They represent the hereafter whereas the scientists are concerned with the practical here and now. And again, to some clergy represent judgment. On occasion this is felt as a judgment on the way the dying are neglected. More often it comes through as simply the assumption that ministers are likely to be judging and rejecting persons and to represent an order of reality which revels in castigating helpless people. A friend of mine was once greeted by an intern with the phrase, "Oh, you're one of J.C.'s boys. You know, you're one of the glory boys, Jesus Christ's boys. You're just in time, he won't last much longer."

Clergy usually deal with distortions from

patients and families and count it as part of their pastoral task. However, there is more ambivalence about the failure of professional colleagues to attempt to understand the clergy's commitments and intent. More mature clergy write it off as the failure of others to deal with their own religious histories and beliefs. But ministers whose self-esteem is not so sure are intimidated and angered by the slights and comments. They become reluctant to take initiative in relating to medical colleagues, or they become part of the chorus whose song is hostile criticism of the "medical establishment." But primarily their stance stems from feeling that their work is not understood and their efforts are not appreciated.

In concluding this section on person and role I think it important to suggest that most clergy are not selfish with their care. Although they come out of their traditions with notions about care and commitments about the meaning of life and death, clergy do not make the offer of their care conditional. To be sure, there are some who are intent on coercing or badgering a patient into mouthing certain statements of belief. And on occasion hospitals must ask such persons to leave or not to call on given patients. But by and large clergy do not offer care on a confessional fee for services basis. Seward Hiltner observes:

Like the ministry of healing, that of sustaining is not confined in the intention and availability of the pastor and church to those who are officially of the faith. It is offered to any who need and want this service, whether they want the whole faith or not. Or so goes the goal and intention, whatever the deficiencies in its execution. Whether the cup of cold water heals and restores him whose sole problem is thirst or merely soothes the one with a rising fever, the cup is offered to all even if they are unprepared also to eat the bread and drink the wine.[2]

ISSUES WITH HOSPITALS AND OTHER PROFESSIONS

Ministers who visit dying patients in hospitals often feel isolated and an outsider. There is no objection to their coming; on the contrary, they are usually welcomed. But what they encounter is a fundamentally different understanding of care and patient need and an institution organized to insure that its own assessment of need is met. What they encounter is a system with its own rules and procedures, its own hierarchies and status systems, and its own language and networks of communication. This system and its view of care affects the clergy's work with patients and families. Its understanding of care must be broadened if collaboration in caring for the dying is to take place.

General hospitals are committed to the diagnosis and treatment of disease and acute medical problems. Their sophisticated equipment, their highly trained and responsible staff, their organization and routine reflect this commitment. Moreover, doctors and nurses receive their professional rewards as a result of dealing with the challenging or exotic case. Since recognition is always desirable, the staff naturally expends itself in those ventures likely to elicit it. All of this is to say, then, that hospitals prefer health, not dying and death.

As understandable as this sense of mission and its subsequent attitudes are, it leads to two results unfavorable to the dying patient and his family. First the emphasis on health and efficient treatment lead to a restricted notion of care. Medical care refers to cure which in turn refers to relief from pain and physical distress. Pain and suffering are always the enemy so that elaborate routines and techniques are employed to insure accurate diagnosis. Sophisticated procedures are utilized to come up with the proper treatment. But through all this process, one looks and listens in vain for any reference to a notion of care which is inclusive of a person's personal, social, or religious history. A view of life in which suffering is endemic to life and the source of much of our meaning is lost in the preoccupation with technology, diagnosis, and cure. As Edward Dobihal points out, "The patient's life began on his admission, except for the previous physical symptoms that brought him to the hospital, and will end on his discharge."*

A corollary to this emphasis on health and treatment is the need to control the patient's life. Hospitals and medical personnel feel

---

* I am indebted to Edward Dobihal for many of the insights expressed in this section of the paper (see Ref. 4).

responsible for the outcome of illness and thus, again in Dobihal's phrase, understand themselves as "*the* caring ones." The staff, those committed to the treatment, know each other, understand each other, and function efficiently in relation to each other. Patients are told in countless subtle ways that the inconveniences, embarrassments, nudity, menus, routines, and personal questions are "normal." They are not to worry; they are to let the staff do its work and all will be well. In short, the staff, those who belong, will, with the patient's compliance, restore health. Obviously this control

" . . . cannot be shared if it is to be sustained. To share it would quickly demonstrate its delusional quality and threaten the closed system which is in reality more closed by the staff than the patient. They simply are more expert at keeping out the realities of life which the patient, families, and other outside persons are left to deal with on their own . . . "[4]

I hope it is understood that I have no wish to demean either hospitals or their staffs. Their mission is essential and often is carried out with great thoughtfulness for and kindness to the patient and consideration for the family. My point is that this restricted understanding of care and the emphasis on control sometimes lead to a neglect of those very persons and factors which might make the dying's last days bearable. Moreover, these notions foster the practice of heroic medicine, interfere with truth-telling, and fail to acknowledge the ways in which others, *e.g.*, clergy and families, can contribute to the dying.

When I say that this narrow view of care fosters the practice of heroic medicine, I am suggesting that our responsibility to the dying differs from that to the living or to the ill with the prospect of longer life. So long as the prospect of restoration remains, all that can be done must be done. But I am asking whether physicians do not have the responsibility to determine (imperfectly to be sure) when health and the removal of symptoms are no longer realistic goals of treatment, and whether, when this judgment is made, "there does not arise the duty *only* to care for the dying, simply to comfort and company with them, to be present to them."[5] Only a physician can make this judgment,

and, if Glaser and Strauss describe accurately the various dying trajectories, despite the uncertainty they do make such distinctions.[6]

Such a shift in attitude would call for a fundamental change in the medical understanding of care. It would suggest that, as Paul Ramsey points out, the "treatment" for a patient "irreversibly doing his own dying . . . is care, not struggle."[5] It would suggest that there are things we can do when "there's nothing more to do" but that these acts consist of gifts of time and compassion, the goal of which is simple comfort to one who will not live.

Again, it seems that a narrow view of care gets in the way of confiding to the patient and the family the fact of impending death. Studies suggest that medical personnel are at least as anxious about death as the general public.[7] When this fact is coupled with the knowledge that their training has been technical, that they have been taught to diagnose, to treat, and hopefully to heal, it is not surprising that the dying are isolated in certain sections of the hospital and doctors are reluctant to share the truth with them. Truth in this instance is a confession that the system has failed or that "I have failed." It calls for the medical staff to offer more to the patient than their technical skill. It raises the anxiety of not knowing what to do or be when what I have been trained to do and be is of no avail.

Ministers are often angered by this circle of closed awareness and/or suspicious awareness. Often the support they might offer to a dying person is denied because they do not know how to respond to the person's questions and cannot get information from the staff. I recall as a young pastor calling faithfully on a 78-year-old widow who was a parishioner. She was a remarkable and courageous woman whose only family, a son, lived some distance away. I called on her frequently during her hospitalization and saw her return home. A few days later she died. I asked her physician later the cause of death and he reported that she had been dying for months. I asked him if she was aware of her condition and he replied that he did not think so, that he had never discussed it with her. "I did not think she could deal with that," he said. In my judgment he was wrong in his estimation of this woman's resources. In any event his somewhat arbitrary decision, made without benefit of consultation with others who also felt responsibility for her care, meant that some acts and words went undone and unspoken.

This episode leads to a final observation about a narrow understanding of care and a closed system, namely that they lead to the exclusion of other helping persons. Ministers, the family, social workers do not contribute directly to the missions of hospitals, and if the special needs of the dying are not acknowledged these others have no place. Seldom, however, does any direct consultation between medical staff, ministers, and families take place concerning the sort of care which would be most helpful for the dying. To be sure clergy hear phrases such as, "We've done all we can; it's in your hands now." And occasionally a nurse will take it upon herself to inform a minister of a patient's condition. But primarily clergy depend upon the family for their knowledge of the patient's condition. The sorts of contributions they could make in enlightening the staff about the person's history, about those commitments and meanings which have enriched their lives, go unmade. They and the family are outsiders.

It would seem, then, that before the clergy can minister to the dying and their families effectively a new and broader understanding of care by hospitals and the medical community is called for. Some effort to affirm both the necessity and legitimacy of care as healing and the special needs of dying persons may be seen in the growth of the hospice as an institution devoted to the care of the dying.

As important as this institutional development is, I do not see it as a solution to our common problem. That solution must come in the lives of professional practitioners, doctors, ministers, nurses, social workers, etc. It will come when they are given opportunity in their training to become acquainted with, to appreciate, and to trust each other. It will come when their training includes confrontation with their feelings about life and death as well as the development of professional skill. It will come when we realize the relation between competence and compassion.

ISSUES WITH PATIENTS AND FAMILIES

Clergy who understand their responsibility to the dying and their families often speak of it in terms of faithfulness. They feel obliged to be available, to offer relationship and sustenance. They hope that persons will avail themselves of the offer and come to terms with their life and death. Deep down they may wish that persons die believing. But the belief they covet for the dying person is not so much in this or that creed or confession as it is in the triumph of love and hope and meaning over death. And coming to belief or indeed a constructive use of the minister's availability is not a condition of care. It is instead sometimes a result of faithfulness.

In the course of the dying person's pilgrimage, clergy are confronted with every issue man is heir to. Fundamentally, however, the direction or thrust of many dying patients is characterized by what one writer calls a built-in need for completeness.[8] Many dying persons have loose ends to tie up, old business to attend, meanings they intended to explore and never got around to. The late Andras Angyal said that life had an intrinsic purpose which made it comparable to a work of art which the individual seeks to create, shape, perfect by living, and, if he is fortunate, put the finishing touches on it.[9] He suggests that even an uncreative life retains a thrust to meaning, a wish to add up the years in some creative fashion.

The form this quest will take cannot be easily anticipated. It does seem, however, that it is consistent with one's past; one cannot look to overturn the history of a life in its last days. A woman, active in her church, who did not see a physician until cancer had broken through the skin on her chest, died as she had lived, self-contained and alone, relying on her minister's ritual acts for reassurance. There are those who, like this lady, keep their own counsel, apparently resigned to their fate. Others seem to welcome death as release from pain or from a life which seems intolerable.

Issues in the pastoral care of dying persons arise first, then, at the point of assessing what a given person needs and how he chooses to use the relationship to the minister. Issues arise, secondly, as persons seek to deal with their life and death with clergy.

One of the more difficult of these issues is the patient's denial. Many ministers, having read and not understood Kübler-Ross, think of denial in negative and moral terms. It is difficult for them to tolerate.[10] They want patients to move on and to face their deaths. A chaplain became distressed when a soldier who had been diagnosed as terminal began acting out his denial by buying a mobile home. The chaplain felt he had to force the man to face the situation.

A more difficult form of denial for clergy is that which comes cloaked in the language of faith. Many ministers are convinced that if dreams are a "royal road to the unconscious" then the use of religious language may provide a thoroughfare to understanding a patient and his reactions. They try to be careful not to allow the use of favorite phrases to seduce them into thinking that the patient is dealing well with death. Questions about the afterlife or whether the patient will recognize loved ones in heaven may suggest a need to grieve more than a concern with theological sophistries. The preoccupation with the soul's final abode may indicate a nagging guilt more than a wish for theological dialogue.

These observations point up two issues clergy frequently encounter. The first is the need simply to sanction grief in the dying person. The family grieves the loss of one person; the dying grieve the loss of all relationships. If grieving means the reliving of our significant moments, acknowledging our important relationships, and attending our hopes, dreams, and disappointments, accepting their emotional content, and letting them go, then the dying's grief is more easily understood. One way this loss of all relationship appears to the clergy is as religious doubt. And this doubt underscores the importance of staying with the patient. The Apostle Paul speaks of the sting of death as sin. We may interpret him to say the sting is separation and the hopelessness this engenders. What the dying seek is some assurance that they may grieve and not despair of hope. They long to continue to be able to believe in life and love even while losing life and the love they know. This was well illustrated recently when a student chaplain called on a man who had learned the day before that his illness was terminal. A grandfather, retired, he spoke of his family for a time and then suddenly broke into tears exclaiming, "I can't accept it, damn me. I just can't accept it. I love them so."

Another issue for the clergy stems from their efforts to deal with guilt. Anxiety over failures, neglects, omissions, slights, and wrongs done to others is part of all our life stories. At times, usually depending somewhat on one's religious tradition, dying persons can deal with this sense of wrongdoing in general terms or by means of the sacrament. At other times, however, nothirg will substitute for a telling of the story.

The whole question of guilt was raised for a minister when he was requested to visit a woman in a nearby hospital. At the nurse's station he learned she had been in an automobile accident, probably would not live, and that her male companion had been killed in the accident. When the minister introduced himself, she immediately became attentive and said, "I thank you for coming. I wanted to talk to a preacher because I want to know how to get saved. Can you tell me how?" He asked her to tell him how this had become a concern for her and she related a story of divorce, work in a bar, loss of her children because she and her former husband were declared unfit parents, remorse, and an intention to "make things right." The accident occurred while she and her former husband were on their way to visit their children. He had been drinking to excess and, according to the patient, deliberately drove the car into a concrete wall. Her request for a minister and her questions about salvation, she went on, were attempts to follow through on her decision "to be different" even through she would not be able to rear her children. The minister gave her steadfast attention. Though she died with many of her conflicts unresolved and many of her questions unanswered, her guilt provided an occasion for her to gain some measure of fellowship and meaning.

The final issue we will discuss sometimes appears initially as guilt. Many persons search their past for a wrongdoing which will account for their plight. This is especially true of untimely deaths, the young and middle-aged, and of the parents of children who are terminal. "Why?" is their question and it is frequently undergirded with considerable rage and anger. Those who are frustrated over lives cut short and dreams unfulfilled often complain bitterly of a cruel God or fates. And the father of a ten-year-old boy who was dying asked his pastor, "Now you tell me, just tell me! What good does any of it do? I've lived right but what damn difference does your church or your God make? Where is the justice?"

The sense of being punished or of injustice at the hands of a cruel deity is but a prelude to their deeper question. What begins as attempt at explanation of personal calamity sometimes ends with the question, "Why pain, why innocent suffering, why death?" For these we have no answer. We may intellectualize about the "problem of evil," but those who have stood dumb before death's mystery in a pediatrics ward know how little solace and assurance it brings to parents. Before this onslaught the minister does not speak with glib conviction of the theological "solutions" he has read. Instead he simply stands and points. His standing with the person shows him as mortal, too, caught in the same suffering, facing the same death, and in need of the same comfort with which he seeks to comfort others. His pointing is to the source of his faith, the God who beckons us to trust that covenant and hope abide. The clergy can only hope that this willingness to stand with the dying and to bear witness to a faith will lead the patient back into an affirmation of his oneness with humanity and a trusting hope that death can be overcome.

I have spoken of pastoral issues in the care of the dying patient. The comments would hardly be complete, however, without some mention of the patient's family. They also are objects of the minister's attention and, on some occasions, the sole recipients of his care.

Perhaps the foremost issue for clergy in ministering to families is to attempt not to assume anything about their reaction to the death. He cannot assume, for example, that their grief will appear as sorrow. Instead he

must be prepared to deal with the whole range of emotions, with denial, with misunderstandings of the patient's behavior and attitude, and with the family's perplexity at their own feelings.

Some families have great difficulty accepting an illness as terminal. They may take the patient from doctor to doctor, from medical center to medical center, seeking a confirmation of the rightness of their denial. In this process they usually isolate the patient and sentence him to loneliness. They may strive to cheer the patient, pick up his spirits, and accuse him of being morbid and not trying when he broaches the subject of death with them.

A more common problem for families is the feeling of abandonment and the ways this complicates their grief work and their relation to the patient. Not only is the patient leaving them but if the illness is of any duration friends also begin to neglect them so that they are left alone to deal with their grief. When the relation to the dying person has been poor, family members frequently are guilt ridden because their anger or jealousy is not replaced by sorrow. Again, families frequently finish their grief work and wonder about their wish not to go back to the hospital or their relief when the relative dies. Considerable assistance can come to families in helping them understand these feelings.

Just as important as the family's own feelings are their misunderstandings of the patient. They need an interpreter to comprehend the patient's denial or his ambivalence or his loss of interest in this or that family member or project.

One instance of family care involved the parents of an eighteen-month-old child and is suggestive of ways ministers relate to families. The child had a malignant brain tumor which was inoperable. The parents called for a minister and told him of their shock and grief. It was like a dream, the wife said. "Sometimes I feel like I'm on the other side of the room looking at myself. It's funny and unreal." It was more difficult, she continued, because they felt alone. They had talked to a social worker and other parents and that helped, but their families were avoiding them. Both parents came from large families and their brothers and sisters assured them they would be with them, but they had not. One mother visited for an hour but they had to comfort her. The wife's only help came from sitting in the chapel until finally she decided to call a minister. When asked if she resented the neglect she admitted she did. Her anger towards her family worried her; she wondered if it would affect the child's illness. She wondered also whether all these feelings she was having were normal; she was somewhat frightened and disturbed by them. She asked the minister to pray with them, then paused and wanted to know if it was all right. It seems she had not been attending church.

When death comes the clergyman's whole attention turns to the family. At times there are questions about an autopsy or funerals which make it helpful for him to be present at the time of death. Regardless of the timing, however, the minister's task becomes one of helping the family grieve its grief and reaffirm its life.

In his work with the bereaved the clergyman has ample opportunity to serve them. For example, he can attempt to counteract the denial of death in present funeral practice by the way he comforts the bereaved and conducts the funeral. He can sanction grief in the funeral—at times simply by getting the family out from behind the modern-fold doors—and make it a service of common worship in which the family is supported by the community of faith. Finally, the clergy have access to the bereaved as does no other professional group. Not only are they expected to continue their relation but they can marshal the resources of their congregations.

SOME CONCLUDING THOUGHTS

To conclude this paper, I should call attention to two other issues in the care of the dying which trouble some clergy. They arise from reading the research and literature on the subject and from experiences with patients in hospitals. One issue has to do with the fact of social class and stratification as this appears in the care of the dying. A second issue follows upon reflection on some of the norms which seem to be popular among those with responsibility for care of the dying.

There is a certain sense of moral outrage undergirding the literature on death and dying. Although it is usually low key, one cannot avoid feeling indicted when he becomes aware of our neglect of death in order to maintain illusions of life and immortality. At the same time, however, ministers observe and David Sudnow describes the social class overtones implicit in our attitudes to death and dying.[11, 12] It seems that even in death, social worth plays a part in determining the care people are felt to deserve.

Clergy visit many people in many different settings. Thus they often are impressed with the sensitivity of staff in one kind of hospital as opposed to another. Those of us who have stood in the stench of a county hospital, peopled with society's outcasts of drifters, prostitutes, and panhandlers, wonder whether they too should not receive care. Yet I have heard discussions on the availability of a bed the next morning because "he won't make it through the night" at the foot of a dying man's bed. I do not wish to suggest that this crassness is typical. But clergy do feel that our empathy for the dying, our sense of rightness and justice, should be less socially provincial and should be inclusive of all sorts and conditions of men.

Second, the suggestion by some of the literature that there is a proper way to die bothers some clergy. The notions of stages and dynamic progression can be construed as the emergence of a new norm, a "right" or "better" way to do it. Sociologists have described our former ideas of a "good patient" as one who died quietly. And ministers have long been accustomed to accusations that they sought to coerce conformity and confession from the dying. One of the great gains of research on death has been the exposing of these stereotypes and a renewed acquaintance with lived fact. Yet one cannot avoid a word of caution lest our more recent reflections harden as a new tyranny of expectation. The new priests, those who care for the dying, must also avoid coercing conformity and introducing a secular canon of perfection, a more noble way to do it.

What these observations call for, indeed what all our comments call for, is a more humane treatment of our fellow man. There is a sameness about the questions various professionals are asking about the care of the dying and bereaved and the sameness consists of its moral seriousness. Despite issues and orientation, clergy will gladly join hands with morally serious colleagues when the issue is faithfulness to those in distress.

REFERENCES

1. Clebsch W, Jaekle CR: *Pastoral Care in Historical Perspective*. Prentice-Hall, Inc., Englewood Cliffs, New Jersey, 1964
2. Hiltner S: *Preface to Pastoral Theology*. Abingdon Press, Nashville, 1958
3. Reeves RB, Jr: Professionalism and Compassion in the Care of the Dying. *Pastor Psychol 22:*7–14, 1971
4. Dobihal EF, Jr: "Problems Which Confront the Minister," in *Death and Ministry: Pastoral Care of the Dying and the Bereaved,* Bane JD, *et al* (Eds). © The Seabury Press, Inc., New York, 1975
5. Ramsey P: *The Patient as Person: Explorations in Medical Ethics*. Yale University Press, New Haven, Connecticut, 1970
6. Glaser B, Strauss A: *A Time for Dying*. Aldine Press, Chicago, 1968
7. Feifel H: "The Function of Attitudes Toward Death," in *Death and Dying: Attitudes of Patient and Doctor*. Group for the Advancement of Psychiatry, Vol. V, Symposium 11, October, 1965
8. Bowers, M, *et al:* Counseling the Dying. Thomas Nelson and Sons, New York, 1964
9. Angyal A: *Foundations for a Science of Personality*. Commonwealth Fund, New York, 1941
10. Kübler-Ross E: *On Death and Dying*. Macmillan, London, 1969
11. Sudnow D: *Passing On*. Prentice-Hall, Inc., Englewood Cliffs, New Jersey, 1967
12. Duff RS, Hollingshead AB: *Sickness and Society*. Harper and Row. New York, 1968

16

THE ELDERLY WHO FACE DYING AND DEATH

Daniel T. Peak, M.D.

It is often difficult to put ourselves "in another person's shoes" or on some cases "in another person's wheelchair or bed," but this is what may be necessary if we are to understand older persons who are faced with the prospect of death. There is a common tendency in our society to turn away from things that are not viewed as appealing and this applies to our view of aging older people, particularly those who have entered into the last phase of their lives. We have taught ourselves that the best way to handle old people is to turn away from them. In many cases we do not manage their problems or we work with them by default. Little documentation is needed to show that this is the case. Such references to nursing homes as "warehouses for the dying," treatments as "pulling out the plug" of "giving him the brown bottle," and general care of the dying as "life sustaining," is evidence to show that we are not dealing with the crucial problems at all. In most cases when we take a close look we find no basic treatment plans. Instead we are likely to find "non-plans" where each caregiver is "on his own" when placed in the position of caring for the dying elderly person.

The fact that most of us have had little exposure to this phase of life is described by Magraw[1] when he states "probably no culture in the history of the world has had as little day to day contact with death as has ours. We manage to conceal the fact of death so that it is no longer a part of life, thus sick people are put into hospitals and death, when it comes, or becomes immi-

nent, is dealt with behind closed doors of hospital rooms so that only those intimately associated are aware of it in any immediate way. The rituals of funerals and death also tend to protect us from reality; thus, the whole subject of death is swept under the rug. We cannot help but be caught up in the usages of our culture. We are apt to have many neurotic and unrealistic attitudes toward death and have not always developed a philosophy which encompasses death and dying."

In this chapter we will present and discuss a number of issues. We will describe the state of the older person who is dying, his concerns during this period of life, and the type of help he or she may need to allow a comfortable journey out of it. We will focus on the problems of caregivers and their attempt to provide optimum and humane care. We will also focus on the family, the relationship to their dying relative, and the relationship of caregivers to the family. Finally, we will offer suggestions for improving and delivering care to the dying elderly.

WHAT IT IS LIKE TO BE OLD AND DYING

Most of us at one time or another have found ourselves in a position where we felt very much alone, very much out of what was happening around us and hoped and prayed that somehow, someone or something would intervene so that we would once again get to feel a part of things. We make feeble attempts to reach out and make contacts, but after a number of failures there is a natural tendency to withdraw, turn into ourselves, to lose hope, and finally, we become locked into ourselves. In many cases this describes the position of the older person who is faced with death. Most of us have experienced such feelings only briefly and transitorily, but when they occur they are of such magnitude that we wish to avoid them if at all possible. People who have the ability and insight to understand such feelings make good candidates to care for older people who are dying, for they are not threatened by such feelings.

In essence, the aging process is a falling away of supports. All older people, although generally most older people are healthy, do find that certain physical attributes are no longer present. For example they may tire more easily, have certain newly acquired aches and pains, need to watch their diet and to get more sleep. They worry about physical losses, although in most cases these can be compensated for and they are not too disturbing for most older people. A much smaller number may show a fairly rapid physical decline, particularly when they have a disease process such as severe arthritis, cardiovascular diseases, etc. Probably more threatening however, are the psychosocial and cultural losses that one becomes aware of as he ages. There is a dropping away of family, friends, and acquaintances, so that gradually the sphere of interpersonal contacts is reduced. Along with this comes a gradual realization that they are being excluded from the mainstream of life, particularly in this country, since our society tends to be youth-oriented. Only fairly recently have we made the older person feel "welcome" in our society. We usually do not provide specific provisions for them such as easy accessibility to public facilities, transportation, and the like. In general the attitude we have had is for them to "shift for themselves."

The behavior of older people faced with death varies and is determined by a number of factors. In most cases there is a tendency for individuals to react to death as they have to crisis situations in the past. Their behavior results from a conscious or unconscious awareness that death is imminent and the attempt of the individual to adjust to this awareness.

In general we may describe the behavioral characteristics of older people who are faced with death by three groups. The first group includes people who have, through a process of adjustment and foresight, faced the prospect of inevitable death and have become comfortable with it so that it does not stir up strong feelings. Such people have laid out realistic plans to be carried out when it is clear that death is imminent. We find that such people do not shy away from discussions of death and dying and have become quite comfortable with them. They do not react strongly when discussing specific details of their own demise. For example, several older relatives in my own family have discussed burial plans, financial costs, funeral arrangements, etc., in a very realistic non-emotional way. There seems to be a natural tendency in younger people, including myself at times, to react and conjure up ideas of being "placed in the cold ground" when thinking of death, while these people obviously do not react in such a way.

The second group of people includes those who have not allowed themselves to face the fact of death and continually put it aside for future reference. Such people tend not to plan for the future, have probably not planned adequately for their retirement, and tend to live exclusively in the present. They have probably done things this way most of their lives. They would probably not show an immediate reaction to a discussion of death because they would see this as not directly applicable. The third group of people consists of those who become quite emotionally upset about the thought of their own death or the death of those close to them. This third group is by far the least in number. Looking into the background of such individuals we would find that they have probably had trouble throughout their lives adjusting to many situations and crises which occur normally. We would probably find elements of emotional disturbances, patterns of instability, and difficulties in adjusting to earlier stages of life.

In light of these groups of elderly, it is helpful for caregivers to have had some idea of the type of older person with whom they are working. It is important as part of the treatment plan and evaluation to do a good background history. One should focus on patterns of adjustments to earlier critical periods; for example, the adolescent period, marriage and child rearing, responses to death of close relatives in the past, the response to losses in general, and particularly the response to menopause or the retirement from one's occupation. These will provide clues as to how one would respond to the ultimate; the loss of one's own life.

To support and elaborate on the behavioral responses of older people to death, studies of groups of elderly dying persons have been conducted. Birren[2] has grouped such persons as "Welcomers, Acceptors, Postponers, Disdainers, and Fearers". DeRopp[3] on the other hand, has categorized such people as "Cerebrotonics (people who are observed to face death freely and joyfully)," "Somatonics (people who react by expressing aggressiveness, boisterousness, and fearlessness)," and "Full-bellied Viscerotonics (people who have a devil of a time adjusting and react as if life is being torn away by its roots)." These classifications reflect the basic types of reactions mentioned above. The first is of those people who have faced and accepted the prospect of death and have adjusted to it. These might be the "Welcomers" and "Acceptors" of Birren or the "Cerebrotonics" of DeRopp. The second is of those who tend to avoid the idea by pushing the thought out of awareness. These might be the "Postponers" (Birren). The third is of those who react strongly to thoughts of death with anxiety, fearfulness, and the need to actively fight such thoughts and feelings within themselves. These are the "Disdainers" and "Fearers" of Birren, or the "Somatonics" and "Full-bellied Viscerotonics" of De-Ropp.

Certain psychological defenses are employed by each of these three groups. Jeffers and Verwoerdt[4] have described defensive patterns in older people and these patterns can be related to the above groupings. They describe those defenses which are aimed at *mastery* and *resolution;* those which are based on *denial;* and those which are designed to allow *retreat* from *anxiety.*

In the first group the person is basically psychologically well adjusted. The defensive maneuvers employed allow them a fairly comfortable and easy course through this phase of life and death. Such people do not deny the possibility of death but have accepted it and its realities for them. Such people do not dwell on the idea but have adjusted to living with it. Mastery also implies control and the feeling of being in control of any situation, leads to feelings of comfort and security. However, in order to accomplish this, a certain degree of denial is necessary, since the concept of the finality of death is so overwhelming. In my own observations of dying elderly, I have seen that it is entirely possible for people to have accepted the idea that they were dying and that this was a part of being old and a part of the life cycle. Once this was accomplished, they were free to use their energies as they wished in the remaining months or days.

In some cases this adjustment is not complete. One may see older people who have become overactive in an attempt to make the most of time remaining and such behavior may become pathologic if not properly modulated. Here one observes older people who are constantly on the go. They seem to be trying to make up for lost time. They may feverishly flit from one project to another without really seeing any one through to its completion or fruition. One sees that they do not have a clear goal in mind, but the goal seems to be to somehow fill up time, rather than specifically accomplish a project or act. I have recently observed a man who rather suddenly lost his wife due to a stroke. He became swept up in a feverish flurry of activities that led to a state of severe emotional and physical exhaustion. He went through several stages of attempting to find relief by first turning to members of his family in hope that they could replace the needs that were served by his wife. When this was not successful he developed physical symptoms for which he was hospitalized and also did not find relief. It was then clear that he was having emotional difficulties in adjusting, and mentally accepting the loss of his wife, and on a deeper level thoughts of his own death had become prominent. Fortunately, he was then referred for the proper treatment of this emotional state.

A healthy use of such energy in the remaining time may be the pursuing of ambitions or projects which one has wished to accomplish during his or her lifetime. I have recently witnessed the demise of a fine professional woman who spent much of her lifetime working with and for the elderly. She spent her terminal months, while dying of metastatic carcinoma, writing a book of memoirs which focused on her own feelings regarding death. Projects such as these not only keep one busy, but also relate to a phenomenon described by Butler[5] which he refers to as the "life review." He describes this as a process which occurs in the latter stages of life where one recalls and reviews his or her life as a whole and comes to some conclusions about it. Such a life review leads to a feeling of peace and contentment that comes with the idea that things are in order when life is coming to a close.

The second category, the "Deniers" is made up of those who avoid accepting the reality and inevitability of death. These people at some level are aware of this reality, but must unconsciously and in some cases completely, deny it. As mentioned previously, some degree of denial is necessary and helpful, but total denial inhibits persons from making proper plans and preparations which might allow them to adjust comfortably. In such cases, one may see a denial of incapacitation and/or physical limitations. These persons may attempt to do things which they feel they have missed in life and this inevitably results in feelings of frustration, which leads to irritability and depression since they are caught up in unrealistic and impossible pursuits of pleasure and comfort which they cannot possibly achieve by these means. Such unrealistic denial of limitations may in some cases actually hasten death since the stresses may be too great. Excessive drinking and overexerting to the point of physical and emotional exhaustion are examples.

The third group, those that retreat from anxiety, is observed to regress, withdraw, and tend to disengage from surroundings. This may lead to what Engel[6] describes as "giving up." He hypothesizes that this "giving up" may facilitate a biological change which sets up a condition which is conducive to death. A tendency to give up may also

lead to suicide, which may be viewed as a form of surrender. Another form of retreat is that of focusing on one's own body with over concern about one's health, leading to a state of hypochondriasis. In hypochondriasis one turns away from the external environment and focuses primarily on the body and internal environment. This defense is frequently used by older people since most aging persons have some infirmities which may be psychologically magnified. There is a purpose and function behind such hypochondriacal reactions and in some cases these may be used as a cry for help or intervention. I am reminded of a 78-year-old lady who was admitted to a general hospital suffering mainly from severe gastrointestinal problems. She was having severe vomiting, nausea, inability to retain her food, and was becoming debilitated. She went through a number of tests and it was found that in general there was no severe physical pathology. However, while she was in the hospital it was noted that she seemed to be somewhat depressed, and a consultation with a psychiatrist was requested. The patient was a woman who was not very sophisticated, lived in the rural part of the community, and was basically a very pleasant, warm, likeable person. The psychiatrist learned that her husband had died about 6 months previously. She recounted the events leading to his death in great detail. Following his death she had planned to have her sister move in with her. However, the sister, in this period of time, suffered severe physical problems herself so that she had to be hospitalized and eventually necessitated total care, and therefore could not move in and share living quarters with her. This lady, in the course of events, talked about her own death and being a religious woman she had fairly well resolved her feelings about it so that this did not frighten her and she was psychologically quite well prepared for it. However, the problem was that she was feeling helpless and hopeless in regard to the intervening years since she did not know how to do the very basic chores and tasks that were done mostly by her husband. For example she did not know how to shop for groceries, to handle money, take care of the bills, etc. She had depended on her husband for these things, so that while she was an enterprising, energetic woman and very capable in many respects, there were certain aspects of her life which she feared she could not handle. After several sessions her fears and problems became clear and a program was set up whereby someone would teach her to handle these aspects of her life. She left the hospital and after a short time she was relieved of her physical symptoms and was having so much fun learning to shop and be successful in these other tasks that she in essence, found a whole new part of her life opening up. She actually looked forward to taking care of these things which she previously felt she could not handle. This case represents not so much the fear of one's own death, but the fear of inability to manage the latter aspects of one's life.

The defense mechanisms described here are not necessarily mutually exclusive and it is common to find mixtures of them. However, they tend to fall into the three patterns. In summary, we see three types of reactions: (1) those who face the prospect of death and handle it by active means within their capacities; (2) those who completely block out ideas of death; and (3) those who spend much time and energy trying to avoid the fears and anxieties it excites. It is important to keep in mind that all elderly people do not react alike to the prospect of death and people who care for the dying must be alert to the type of person with whom he or she may be dealing.

In order to understand each individual older person a comprehensive work-up is necessary. A good history of physical, social, and family problems is needed. It is important to record the types of personal interactions, and particularly the responses to earlier critical periods in their lives. Such information will determine the type of reaction presently observed and eventually guide us to the proper interventions that may be necessary. This information can be collected in a formal way when the patient first arrives, or more informally when the caregiver, through a series of contacts, may get to know the older person, discuss his past life, then record such information. Of course it is necessary to have the basic vital

facts readily available early in the contact, *i.e.,* age, family structure, etc.

THE PROBLEMS ENCOUNTERED BY CARETAKERS OF OLDER DYING PEOPLE

Caretakers of the dying elderly find themselves in a difficult and perplexing situation. In some cases they may have had little or no training in the care of such people. They are often left to their own devices as to how to handle them and as so often occurs, the whole caretaking process becomes one of indecision. Difficulties arise in such cases. One is the relative difference in the age of the patient and the caretaker. Usually the caretaker is younger and has vastly different concepts of death. It has been shown that younger people react to death differently than the old. They tend to view it in a much more negative and immediate way. Kogan and Wallach[7] have shown this to be true. They compared college students with older people using word stimuli suggesting death and found that there was considerably less negative and urgent responses to words connected directly or indirectly with death in the older group.

In general, the death of a young person is viewed as much more tragic and threatening than that of an aged person. It is often conceived of as "crushing" or "stamping out" of a young, vigorous developing life as one would crush a flower that was about to bloom. This is not so in the case of the older person. They have in most cases "had their chance." They have tasted of the fruits of life, invested their energies in their pursuits, and have arrived at a position where the work of life is over and the tasks and other burdensome aspects are no longer necessary. Therefore, in many cases we find that the caregiver and the older person are operating and reacting from two very different frames of reference. The older person may not find the concept of death frightening, distasteful, or particularly exciting. Jeffers and Verwoerdt[8] in another study found that older people had thoughts of death frequently during the course of a day, but most of them did not feel that it interfered in any way with carrying out their daily activities. Cameron, Stewart, and Biber[9] conducted a survey of over 4000 people of all ages and found that young adults had the least thoughts of death. They found that older people (and women in this group) thought and dreamed about it more often than the young, and/or men. What appears to emerge from these studies is that thoughts of death become more tolerable as one gets older. It is as if people gradually allow themselves to think about something that is initially distasteful, and in the process it becomes less frightening and less threatening and more acceptable. Also the fact that older people have more frequent thoughts of death does not necessarily mean that they are more concerned about it. In fact the reverse is probably true. More frequent thoughts of death, more thoughts over a lifetime, and more exposure to death itself, appears to have the effect of reducing fear and anxiety about it. In the process of aging, older people have been subjected to other losses such as loss of physical abilities, loss of friends and relatives, social contacts, job, and status in society and within the family structure. In most cases they have been able to assimilate these losses within their lives and adjust to them. Adjustment to losses can be conceived of as a preparation for the final and greatest loss of all, one's own life.

This process of working through and the increased comfort about death however, may not always be allowed to proceed, particularly if conflictual elements of the personality get involved. In such cases a normal adjustment process does not occur and may result in problems such as were alluded to earlier in this chapter.

Age differences may lead to failure in communication. The older dying person is very adept at reading both the verbal and non-verbal cues of those around him and may quickly perceive that the subject of death is taboo and should not be discussed. He may see that the caregiver believes it might upset him to talk about it or because it makes the caregiver too uncomfortable. In this case, direct communication ceases, which then results in insufficient interchanges to allow proper planning and preparations necessary for the last months and days of life. It is important to be aware that most older people would welcome discussion, and the astute caregiver watches for

cues as to when it is proper, and allows such discussions to proceed. In these discussions it is important to allow the older person to set the pace. There is often a strong tendency for the caregiver to impose his or her own attitudes and feelings on the person. This occurs not only in reference to attitudes toward death, but also in relation to the plans and preparations the older dying person may wish to make. The wishes of the older person should always be considered as primary. We must learn to listen without letting our own feelings interfere.

There are specific issues which the older person would like to discuss during this period of life. It is not uncommon for older people to wish to speak quite openly about planning for their death. They may wish to discuss the type of burial they would like, the ceremony, certain religious rites, the gravemarker, and particularly the cost involved so that these things will be properly taken care of at the right time. They are also concerned with time and how much they have left. This is important since they may fear incapacitation in the latter years which would prevent them from doing certain things they might wish to do. For example, they may wish to take one final trip, to visit children or other relatives. They may wish to visit grandchildren they have never seen. They may wish to visit a certain place which has been a life-long ambition. They may wish to accomplish some act or donate money to be used as a memorial. Often if they could accomplish these things they could die happily. They may also wish to speak about the effect their death may have on their families and how they wish to make it as burdenless as possible for them.

As the proximity of death increases they become more concerned about personal issues such as "Will there be pain as death approaches?", or "Will I be able to talk about it?", also, "Will there be a loss of mental functions so that I cannot cope and carry out daily tasks?", and the final and probably the most significant, "Will I be alone at the end?". The last issue brings up the controversy of whether it is better to die in one's own home or elsewhere, such as a hospital, nursing home, etc. One cannot categorically say which is best for all people.

This is an individual matter which depends upon the circumstances within the family structure. In some cases there is a large family and the home setting is conducive to caring for the older person. They then have frequent contact with a variety of people within the family and it may be desirable for that person to be at home in the last stages. However, many times this is not the case and it may be more feasible for the individual to be in an organized setting where contact with people is more frequent even though these people may not be close relatives. It is interesting to note how important certain relationships may become for the older person at this time. For example, certain nurses, aides, attendants, maintenance personnel, and others may take on a special meaning. Such individuals have a consistent and daily contact with the older person and they often become invested with deep feelings since this relationship is serving the need for the older person to have someone close at hand. Also relationships between certain patients or residents become important, and in some cases most important, where both of them may be sharing a common problem that of approaching death.

A particular difficulty for those working with the dying elderly concerns the decision about who should assume responsibility for the care and planning during this critical stage of life. It is often left by default to whomever is around. It may be left to the physician, the nurse, social worker, minister, nursing aide, or others. At a conference held at Duke University on the subject of death and dying,[10] the participants of a seminar, which included people from all disciplines, each stated singly that they felt the basic responsibility for the care of such persons was theirs. The internist claimed the responsibility, the social worker felt it was hers, the minister his, and finally the funeral director related that people frequently turned to him because no one appeared ready, willing, or able to adequately handle the situation and care for specific needs. It was clear that there was no common agreement on where the basic responsibility stood. In reality all of these disciplines play a role in helping a dying person, but very few groups are organized so that such re-

sponsibility may be shared, as it should be, and not left to any one particular person. Just as treatments are set up for various disease entities, treatment plans which handle all aspects of the aged who are dying should be a part of comprehensive planning. There should be a core group to develop a plan. It should consist of a physician, nurse, social worker, and in most cases a member of the clergy. The physician should have the basic responsibility for developing the appropriate medical regime, including treatments which may alleviate or ameliorate the physical problems. The nurse and nursing staff should have the job of carrying out the orders of the physician, and aid in making the individual more comfortable, but also they are the ones that will have the most personal contact and their interaction on a daily basis will be most significant. The social worker should enter in to assess the family situation and to help the older person carry out his or her final wishes. They should also work with family members in making appropriate plans as they relate to the older person. The clergy should be available to deal with religious beliefs and feelings and in planning proper ceremonies.

A problem particular to physicians, nurses, and the rest of the medical profession is that of viewing death and dying as a threat to one's own skill and knowledge. In effect, dying persons may be viewed as therapeutic failures, or professionals may view their problems as entirely out of their realm of treatment since the goal in some cases may be only palliation. This concept is applied not only to the dying elderly but also sometimes to the elderly in general. Many professionals avoid working with this age group because treatments may be supportative rather than definitive. However, just as birth is an event of life, so also is dying and death, and just as our knowledge and techniques have improved the birth process, so should we improve the death process. It is important therefore, that the medical profession accept the fact that relief of suffering may be just as important as the goal of total cure. Another problem faced by many practitioners relates to the decision as to when it is proper to "throw in the towel" and change the treatment from cure to palliation. Like many other critical decisions, this probably is the most difficult for those who have been trained to preserve life at all costs. In extreme cases the battle lines are drawn and death is seen as the spector or enemy which must be conquered at all costs. This concept is very pervasive and is based in the roots of our culture which dictates that we must have an enemy to fight and the most final and definitive one is death. A solution to this dilemma may involve a rethinking and a change in therapeutic perspective. Many practitioners have worked out systems which allow them to be objective and apply proper treatments. One such approach is proposed by Kast[11] who says "it is important to deal with the realistic appraisal of illness in all its aspects and in open discussion. It adds to the self-respect of old people to inform them (without cruelty) about their disease and treatment. Such discussions express implicit trust in the personality strength of the older person and so add much to their dignity and stature." The idea of the finality of death often leads us into all or none situation. However, in most cases dying is a gradual event and treatment plans can and should be formulated and changed whenever appropriate.

Those who wish to deliver proper care and are concerned with the elderly dying have few guidelines to follow. A major purpose of this book is to develop such guidelines so that the whole approach in caring for the dying may be seen as less pessimistic and impossible. Techniques are being developed and just as in other problems of health, we must begin with a conceptual or philosophic rethinking, and from this develop more technical applications.

THE FAMILY AND THE DYING OLDER PERSON

The event of death occurs only rarely in most families and therefore, when faced with it, most people do not know how to respond. People feel at a loss and their actions are guided by their feelings which are often distorted at this time. Therefore people often do not react in a well thought out way. Goals become vague, disjointed, and disorganized. This is usually because each individual is reacting to his or her own con-fused and mixed feelings about death and this interferes with open and proper communication. It may lead to an overreaction on the part of family members whereby they avoid speaking objectively of proper planning, and in some cases they may even try to talk the older person out of the fact that death is a reality and is in fairly close proximity. Again it is important to allow the older person to take the lead in expressing his concerns and wishes.

Martin Berezin[12] describes a process that occurs in family members of dying elderly persons. He terms this a "partial grief reaction" or "partial grief state." He describes these as states that occur during the period preceding the death of the older relative, resulting from observations of certain losses during this period indicating that death is a real possibility. The realization that death is imminent may come into awareness either at a conscious or unconscious level. He states "such partial grief which is unresolvable brings about many reactions on the part of responsible relatives and friends which at times make extended care difficult if not impossible. It is well known that the issues that confront the physician in extended care more often than not involve the family more than the patient. The reactions and attitudes of the spouse and children require more attention and tactful management than does the care of the patient himself. The passive reactions in family members may vary from anxiety and guilt to mature understanding and appreciation of the realities of the situation. When guilt becomes the steam motivating family members, reactions can be quite extreme, irrational and unmanageable."

Such reactions are related to what Berezin calls "partial losses." These may be such things as increasing degrees of infirmity, reduction in the social sphere, retirement, manifestation of organic changes in the brain such as memory loss, disorientation, and finally the presence of severe and possibly terminal illness. He describes these as "partial" losses relative to the total demise of the individual. Therefore, he contends that the grief reaction can only proceed to a certain point at which time the process is suspended and such limbo-like states may produce the behaviors we see in relatives and people who are close to the dying person.

One aspect of such a state is the feeling of helplessness which family members often suffer at this time. They are driven by feelings that they should "do something" for the dying person and therefore one often sees exaggerated and unnecessary catering and ministering which is actually unwanted by the dying person and and certainly by the caregivers. Another factor is the gnawing feeling or wish that one could bring about a resolution of this state. This of course would mean that death would have to occur. Such a wish or thought may be intolerable and therefore one may have to deny that it even exists. Berezin goes on to further state "the partially grieving family member may also be caught in the terrible dilemma of wishing an aging person dead – a wish which often remains unconscious and denied. The wish for the old person to die may be handled by reaction formation in which the opposite is expressed or yearned for: that the elderly patient is not going to die, in fact some family members deny that the patient is even sick. Some of us have had the experience of observing a spouse or child talk to an aged person with a far advanced organic brain deterioration as if they were holding an understandable conversation. I have witnessed such "conversation" conducted with patients who are totally unconscious and in coma."

Interrelationships of family members are often brought clearly into view during this period. Problems which have lain dormant for long periods of time may emerge in bold relief. Probably the most common of these are feelings of guilt within family members, relating to events recent or past for which in some way they feel responsible. They may feel that they have hurt the dying person through their behavior or in some cases feel responsible for not being more concerned or helping more during the course of terminal illness and death. The behavior then becomes one of attempting to "make up for lost time" or to some way make amends before it is too late. For example, one may find the family spending an inordinate amount of time fawning and doting over the older person. They may believe that they are supplying comforts and pleasures. This may run contrary to the wishes of the nursing staff and to the patient himself. They may bring food such as candies, sweets, etc., which in actuality may be harmful to the patient, and the older person may feel obliged to eat them simply to please the relatives. For the nursing staff this may be a problem, particularly if there are dietary restrictions. They may be constantly trying to make the person more comfortable by changing their position, altering the beds, etc., when in actuality the older person would simply like to rest. The family may increase the number of contacts and phone calls they make to the nursing staff where little can be said regarding progress or change in condition and this may take time away from nursing duties. Family members may become so concerned about their own feelings and atonement that they simply cannot or do not hear and observe the messages that the older person is trying to send out to them. In some cases families feel that they simply have to be near the older person and they may hover in lounges, in coffee shops, in the waiting rooms, etc., when it may be quite unnecessary for them to be there. This is not to say that there might be an appropriate time for them to be close at hand, but often such behavior occurs when the older person is not particularly critical and it would be better for all concerned if they carried on their daily activities.

Regarding the social aspects at this time, it is important for the patient to stay involved since it will maintain a sense of control over his life and in this case, his death. The involvement should consist of a basic schedule of daily activities that is within his or her capacities. This may consist of planning so that a certain part of the day is spent in "work" pursuits such as working on financial affairs, etc. Part of the day should be spent in leisure activities which may simply be watching television, reading a book, or visiting with family or friends. The other part of the day should be spent in rest periods and treatments of various types. The involvement, of course, would vary greatly from person to person, but some concept of a basic schedule is necessary for the person to maintain a feeling of being in control of the situation. This is particularly particularly true of the older person who has always been very independent. They may have been handling many of the family affairs and in essence have taken care of the other members of the family. However, they may have come to a point where they are no longer able to do this. The family has accepted this position of being cared for and the transition from being taken care of to that of caretaker may be a difficult one for them. It may be equally upsetting for the older person to assume the role of being cared for. This leads to a problem commonly called the "role reversal problem" and occurs in families where the above conditions exist. This role reversal relates to the authority structure within the family system and the making of decisions. Certain of these responsibilities should be relegated to other family members at the appropriate time. A very real and critical problem occurs when it is necessary to remove the older person from the family home at the point when it becomes evident that care and treatment are necessary and cannot be provided in that setting. Such families need particular help at this time. Other problems may exist when the physical capacities of the older person are insufficient to allow carrying out certain tasks such as driving an automobile, operating dangerous machinery, or taking medications when they are confused and forgetful.

While this may be a time for problems, it also may be a period when old problematic family relationships may be resolved. It is important, if the grief process is to be successful, that feelings of guilt and anger be resolved; and it is my contention that such resolution can occur either before or after death, a concept somewhat different from that of Berezin's. It may be beneficial if such resolution occurs prior to death, then good relationships may exist for a time preceding it and any incomplete grieving following death may be reduced. In order to facilitate this process the caregiver must be aware of these factors and must provide the communication with the family members either in formal or informal sessions so that they may be supported during this period. It is impor-

tant for them to have an opportunity to ventilate some of these feelings and it is often very beneficial to do this with the family as a group. They will then realize that such feelings are not unique to themselves and that others are struggling with similar concerns. In my own work, I use this approach and others who deal with the elderly have also found it helpful. Berezin[12] also advocates this approach and states "in such a conference, the family is confronted with reality of a given situation and the prognosis is openly discussed. Reactions, especially those of helplessness are discussed with the family and the need for unity within the family structure is stressed. The appeal is to the realities both of the aged one and the uncomfortable struggles among the grieving one. The awareness of this significant mode of management has grown so that the family conference has become procedure in many social service agencies and hospitals."

APPROACH TO OPTIMUM CARE OF THE DYING OLDER PERSON

People who work and deal with older persons must be prepared to handle and face the process of dying. They must accept this as part of their treatment responsibility and be prepared to handle death directly or indirectly and the subjects related to it. It should be as much a part of the treatment plan in this age group as all other ameliorative therapies. One must first have a basic plan in mind. In formulating such a plan it is important to recall the reactions and behaviors described above, then certain approaches can be used when the appropriate time arrives. One should feel ready to deal with these subjects just as one deals with the details and variations in the physical disease processes that are being treated. It is necessary for a person who works in this area to come to grips with the subject of death in his or her own mind so that when the subject arises it may be dealt with objectively. This can be accomplished through introspection either alone or in group discussions. One must understand such feelings regarding aging and death and attempt to circumvent the taboo which has built up around it. It is a task that must be accepted or it will continue to be avoided when active intervention is necessary. Group discussion should be an activity of every treatment team that works with the elderly. Such discussions tend to share the burden and responsibility since no one person should assume the total responsibility. This leads to a feeling of lessened fear and anxiety and will allow a more appropriate response on the part of all caregivers. The goal is to correct misconceptions, to become comfortable with the concept of personal aging and death, and to face this inevitability realistically. It is also important to take advantage of seminars when they are offered; in some cases it may be necessary to organize such training programs if they are not available.

In order to achieve the proper balance of care, caring, and distance, it is important to develop the feeling of sharing mentioned above. Each person in the team has a specific role to play and through planning, individual caregivers will provide the necessary services for which they are best suited. In most cases the physician is the "coach" of the team since he or she has ultimate responsibility for the physical care of the dying person. In addition to the core group, the team may include all levels of nursing staff, social workers, paramedical personnel, and adjunctive therapists, if such are available, such as occupational therapists, rehabilitation therapists, physical therapists, etc. A psychiatrist or psychologist is helpful if one is available. In terms of the time spent with the patient it is clear that the nursing personnel spend the most time in direct contact. Therefore, this group is usually most involved and should be particularly prepared to deal with these problems. It is frequently left to them to carry out the daily and consistent type of contact in the supportive and understanding way that has already been outlined. The social worker deals with the family members and should act as liaison for the purpose of keeping family members informed of the condition of the patient and also in working through family interrelationships and feelings. The psychiatrist or psychologist should be involved as a consultant, or if available, in a direct way, for working through some of the conflictual feelings described above. The so-called adjunctive therapists are helpful in

terms of keeping the older person involved and active within his own capacities and limitations. The clergy are helpful to those who have a religious belief and desire counseling in this area. It is important that communication exists between the team members to achieve this end. When successful, the effect will produce a feeling of security in the patients regarding those who are caring for them and will lead to the idea that someone will be available to handle their needs at all times.

A number of misconceptions already mentioned should be emphasized. It must be realized that all older people are not afraid to die. It is clear that many older people look forward to it as the end of a life well lived or for other reasons, and that we must allow them to express their feelings if we are to understand how they actually feel. In some cases discussion of the subject of death may be approached prior to the time they are actually dying. Such discussion may solve many later problems. The misconception that death is the enemy and must be fought at all costs is important. This type of thinking, while understandable, may produce the dilemma where helping professionals are caught in heroic measures not to save life but to fight death. With our knowledge of disease processes, a fairly good estimate and approximation of death can usually be made and the approach should be to comfort the patient and to supply the appropriate adjunct at the right time during the process of demise. I am not advocating active measures to hasten death, but those measures which are beneficial to anyone whether he dies the next day or in six months. The extent of a person's illness should be shared with him and mediated by our knowledge of the individual's ability to handle such information. It is clear that older people fear isolation and disability much more than death itself. It is therefore important to avoid the conspiracy of silence and avoidance that often exists in those who care for the dying. There is a need for the elderly dying person to feel involved throughout this period. In formulating a plan of involvement, this should include the areas of social relationships, physical and mental activities, and involvement in one's own physical well being. In formulating the plan these levels of involvement should be equated to the limitations of the individual and his desires. For example, as one approaches death the social contacts often become reduced to the more important friends or family. Physical stamina may fail and therefore physical activities should also be reduced appropriately. In the final stages, the individual may really desire a minimal amount of interaction with other people. Such a plan therefore should have a built-in flexibility where the involvements may be reduced as approaching death occurs. The feeling that there is a plan of treatment carried out by those who care for them, in itself, will produce comfort and the knowledge that they will be cared for when the time comes. Again one must battle the irrationality of feelings and use judgment based on the real needs of the patient.

The above ideas are not necessarily meant to be applied verbatum. They are meant rather as guidelines for those of us who are concerned and work with older people. It is difficult to set out specific plans of operation since there are so many different types of individuals and facilities who deal with the elderly. As mentioned above, we may be the only ones who are available to care for a dying person and to such people it is hoped that the comments will be an aid to them in understanding their charges and in providing the comfort and peace we would all wish if we were to trade places. To those who are part of a larger system of treatment services it is hoped that these comments will lead to a rethinking, reformulating, or reorganization of services where the final result will again be the increased comfort of the patient, client, friend, or relative. If we can begin with a better understanding we may find that working with such older dying people may not be so pessimistic and unrewarding as it may seem on the surface. I believe there is no more profound experience than to see, observe, and to be involved with an older person who has resolved the conflicts, problems, and misconceptions which surround death in his life and to share in the peace and contentment that results.

REFERENCES

1. Magraw R: The Doctors, The Relatives and The Cancer Patient. *Lancet 81:*381–384, ©, 1961, The New York Times Media Company, Inc.
2. Birren J: *The Psychology of Aging.* Prentiss-Hall, Inc Englewood Cliffs, New Jersey, 1964
3. De Ropp R: *Man Against Aging.* St. Martins Press, New York, 1960
4. Jeffers F, Verwoerdt A: How The Old Face Death, in *Behavior and Adaptation in Late Life.* Busse E, Pfeiffer E, (Eds), Little, Brown & Co., Boston, pp 163–181, 1969
5. Butler R: The Life Review: An Interpretation of Reminiscence in the Aged, in *New Thoughts on Old Age.* Kastenbaum R (Ed), Springer, New York, 1964
6. Engel G: *Psychological Development in Health and Disease,* W. B. Saunders Co., Philadelphia and London, pp 392–394, 1962
7. Kogan N, Wallach M: Age Changes in Values and Attitudes. *J Gerontol 16:*272–280, 1961
8. Jeffers F, Verwoerdt A: Factors Associated with Frequency of Death Thoughts in Elderly Community Volunteers. Proceedings of The Seventh International Congress of Gerontology. Vol. 6. Vienna Medical Academy, 1966
9. Cameron P, Stewart L, Biber H: Consciousness of Death Across The Life Span. *J Gerontol 28:*92–95, 1973
10. Peak D: Death and Dying, in *Successful Aging.* Pfeiffer E (Ed), Duke University Press, Durham, pp 124–128, 1974
11. Kast E: On Being Old and On Dying. *J Amer Geriatr Soc 20:*524–530, 1972
12. Berezin MA: The Psychiatrist and the Geriatric Patient: Partial Grief in the Family Members and Others Who Care for the Elderly Patient. *J Geriatr Psychiatr 4:*53–64, 1971

17

CARING FOR THE CHILD WHO MIGHT DIE

Jan van Eys, Ph.D., M.D.

No human interaction is possible without involvement. One cannot be an unbiased observer of other people: mere presence alters the life of the one observed. There is a sequence of phenomena that are to a greater or lesser degree recognizable in the person with terminal illness. However, one cannot observe their unfolding, rehearse the necessary reaction that is thought to be required for the next step in the dying process, and in that way cope with the dying person, let alone that one can thus care for him. The reactions of those that are in the environment are part of the dying process and their feelings and concepts result in positive care or negative neglect of the dying. This is always true, but never more than when caring for the dying child. The child has expectations of the nurturing adult that adults do not anymore expect to be met by their caring age peers. Conversely we have feelings about the death of a child that are far stronger than our reactions to the dying adult. It is not the purpose of this chapter to catalogue the phenomenology of the dying child. Rather it will try to describe the dynamic interactions between child and caring adult. It is the thesis that self-awareness makes it possible to care through continued person-to-person contact.

THE SCOPE OF THE PROBLEM

The death of any child is an emotionally traumatic event. However, were it only an occasional happening then it might be possible to ignore it as a major issue. Unfortunately children's death is not exceptional.

While accidents and poisonings are the most common cause of death in children, cancer is the most common cause of death by disease. To cancer deaths one must then add less frequent but significant causes: renal disease, cardiac disease, and a variety of genetic disorders. Medical knowledge has made such diseases treatable—almost all children with cancer can be helped to some degree: palliation is often meaningful; life can frequently be significantly prolonged. Therefore we are often dealing with a slowly dying child,[1] a child for whom the dying process is extended over months to years, with the attending needs developing very slowly. Needs for comforting are readily perceived and it is now actually fashionable to want to help the child and his family cope with the impending death. But that can become attempts at psychological euthanasia. The family seeks medical help and their initial expectation is cure. If that were a purely futile aspiration, our optimal care would be preparation for the inevitable. But medicine has progressed and we are just now at the 50% cure rate when averaging all childhood cancers admitted to our ward. In other words, cure is indeed almost the norm. That hope cannot be denied nor minimized to the parents or the child. For physicians it is easier to expect death and reap cure as a reward, than it is to expect life and have to accept death as undersirable outcome. One must approach each child with life-threatening illness as a child who might die, not as a child who will. Clearly I am not talking about the child who is on a respirator, or comatose, or otherwise beyond any medical retrieval. Rather, I am placing childhood life-threatening illness in the perspective of today's reality, which is different from that of an octagenarian adult whose death is imminent under any circumstances.

PROBLEMS UNIQUE TO LIFE-THREATENING ILLNESS IN CHILDHOOD

In addition to the general concepts stated so far, there are a number of unique problems with children. First of all, no child is truly independent. Illness of the child affects the whole family. It is far more the emotional investment that parents have in their children. Each child is precious and each child represents, what amounts to an almost narcissistic undertaking to extend our existence.[2]

One must also not underestimate the frequent youth and inexperience of parents in dealing with such new realities of life-threatening illness in their child. There is great analogy between the predicament of the parent with the handicapped child and the parents with a chronically ill child, whether the illness is life-threatening or not. Progressively fewer young parents have had a direct exposure to death. They are therefore very poorly prepared to deal with the protracted illness and the slow dying. In addition they are rarely financially prepared for the costly illness. There is a great threat to family stability when a child dies or is dangerously ill.[3]

The needs of the family have been well described by various oncologists, sometimes in a personal mode,[4] and sometimes in a more detached manner.[5] There is as much need to support the family as there is to provide support for the child, and that responsibility of the caregiver does not stop after the child dies.[6] A survey of parents after the death of their child clearly suggested needs of the parents for discussion with professionals.[7] Not all authors concede significant family problems after the child's death. Lascari and Stehbens interviewed families of 20 deceased leukemic children and encountered no major emotional difficulties among parents and only occasional minor problems among siblings.[8] This is, however, not the experience of many who deal with families of children with fatal ill-

nesses.[9] These differences of opinion appear to be functions of the social norms of the families and the concepts of needs as perceived by the observers.

Since the child cannot deal with his own fate alone, but is intertwined in the family, it is impossible to truly dissect out his own concepts of death.

There is a substantial body of literature on the child's concept of death. The most frequently quoted are by Nagy[10] and Anthony,[11] but many other examples exist. A historically interesting account by von Hug-Hellmuth[12] should be cited. Another well-written discussion is by Kastenbaum.[13] There are several lines of inquiry involved: What does a child perceive, how does he acquire his perception, and is the perception pragmatically significant in dealing with life threatening illnesses. All these discussions elaborate the thoughts that the concept of death in children follows a sequence: up to two, no concept of death; between two and four, separation; between four to six, mutilation; and finally the idea of death as permanent and irreversible. There is an easily discerned correspondence to the stages of development as described by Erikson.[14] Erikson describes first a stage which he calls basic trust *versus* mistrust. The child is in an oral-sensory state only. He does not yet have a concept of self as autonomous. This comes later, at the stage Erikson called autonomy *versus* shame and doubt. The concept of autonomy allows separation as a concept. The next stage is called initiative *versus* guilt. Actions are discerned as perceptions in a framework of cause and effect. Mutilation as synonymous with death is readily perceived. The stage called industry *versus* inferiority begins to allow death as final and permanent. It must always be remembered that Erikson did not mean that these stages represent achievement scales, but rather incorporation of necessary and stepwise demands.[15] Not every child approaches critical illness mentally healthy. A child may still struggle with the problem of a previous stage which is unsatisfactorily resolved. This may indeed result in a seemingly childish definition of death. Such stepwise definitions of death by children to a degree follow not only Erikson's concepts of psychological maturation but also Piaget's description of the conceptualization of the physical universe and separativeness of objects.[16] Children must develop the concept that what is out of sight is not necessarily non-existent. But such developments do not concede a concept of death, anymore than adults have a clear concept of non-existence. Children believe far more in immortality; in fact they conceive of no other state.

Death concepts of children are not concepts in the adult sense, *i.e.,* a mental image and intellectual emotional "reasoning out" to cope with inevitable dissolution. Rather, they are to a child definitions of a word. Such studies clearly indicate that the child knows the word and tries to answer questions about death. But again the healthy child's concept of non-being is not an adult one, and an adult's symbolic allusion about death may be taken quite concretely by the very young.[17]

The child will eventually perceive dying; *i.e.,* an exorable progression into the final. Recently, Bluebond-Langner translated this gradual dawning of awareness into a recognizably stepwise continuum in children with cancer—the child realizes his serious illness; the names of his drugs and their side effects; treatments are learned, procedures and their purpose are acknowledged; the relapse/remission cycle is recognized; the finiteness of this cycle is acknowledged; and lastly the final prognosis is internalized.[18] Only then does the child gain a concept of death. By that stage even very young children seem to have a real awareness of death.[19] This may represent a growing up of the child, a maturation beyond actual chronological age.

But we adults rarely allow a child to be a child. We have our own images conjured by the word death, and when a child uses that word, we cannot perceive any other image than our own. Unfortunately our adult concepts, which are intellectually reconciled with our own inevitable death, do not allow a child to die.[20] Whatever rationalizations we may have about death, there are in most of us one of two concepts involved: either we accept the satisfactory completion of life, or death is the consequence of the intervention of some higher power. When the process of dying is perceived as unpleasant, it is

only tolerable for onlookers when death is meaningful or at least acceptable. We cannot truly accept a meaningful death of a child, nor can we fully conceive a higher power who allows a child to die. Yet, a thirteen-year-old boy once said: "Why are you afraid? I am the one who is dying."[21] The answer is of course that we cannot avoid testing our own *"weltanschauung"* and, if we are religious, our concepts of an all-loving God, and we very often fall short in accepting.

MUTUAL INTERACTION

Earlier in this chapter the mutual interaction between the child and the caregiver was stressed. One cannot care for a child in an *a priori* posture of mature adult guiding a child with problems, but rather the opposite is frequently the case, for it is the child that progresses through a natural and average process of dying, cared for by an adult who has major problems acknowledging the process. This interaction between the adult and child invariably demands an examination of how the adult views the child and the child views the adult as fellow humans, for by definition they do not meet each other as peers. While generalizations in this area are perhaps dangerous and often unfair, in caring for the child who might die it is important to reflect on this vital child-adult interaction. We approach other people with a graded evaluation. First we may or may not accept the individual as human, and, once accepted as human, we may or may not accept the human as a person. Acceptance of a person's humanity implies their acceptance as a member of the community (human herd) and the granting of personhood establishes the person as an individual member of the community with independent rights. Such rights are not automatic; rather they are bestowed by the human contacts in the community. We allow another invididual to be a person whenever we accept that that fellow human can make independent decisions, and whenever that fellow human, that person, is allowed to differ in opinion without losing our love or generating our displeasure. Of course, interpersonal contact is mutually defining—an individual is not a person unless he has bestowed personhood on at least some of his human contact in return. You cannot claim personhood among humans unless you treat and respect some fellow humans as persons yourself.

In ordinary healthy interpersonal development the acceptance of another as human occurs somewhere around birth, and the acceptance of another as a person occurs as a gradual process somewhere beyond adolescence. A great deal might be said about the healthy transition of a well loved, well cared child from humanity to full personhood. But the point here is that those people we have accepted as humans are our responsibility, *in toto,* physically as well as mentally, until they are given personhood, at which time they assume their own responsibility for their physical and mental being.

As adults, we have great difficulty bestowing personhood on children, especially our own or those under our care. This is, at best a slow and arduous process. They have, as yet, no independent existence and therefore have, as yet, no independent rights. However, the one and only inviolate right of a person is the right to die. Children are not allowed to do that in fact, because they are human, but not yet persons. Not only do we want to continue to view them as dependent on us, we are actually fiercely protective of their lives. We go even further: we try to keep them ignorant of the problems. We say that the burden of knowledge is for the parent, the adult, the person, while ignorance of problems constitutes childhood.[20] Yet children can and do die. If they are allowed to do so as persons, and if we, as caring adults, can bestow that personhood on the child it is liberating for both caring adult and dying child.

It becomes important to reflect further that we have no conflict if we have not accepted the child as human. A non-human does not need, nor deserve, protection from the community and therefore can die, be discarded as it were. We all have our definitions of humanity. Some fiercely defend the idea that humanity begins at conception. Others have more restricted ideas and will reject the physically deformed, the mentally retarded, even the culturally deprived. Joseph Fletcher once said that creative joy and happiness are intelligent pleasures and an essential ingredient of being human.[22, 23] This is usually extrapolated further. Humanity is defined when one can perceive the capacity of being creative and happy. A premature infant in the nursery may be lost after valiant medical effort with little more feeling than that related to the failure of technical skill, but we cannot see an older, previously health child suffer.

Yet, children are persons. Each child is an individual with a separate will and a separate ability to learn. Once he has accepted trust and mistrust in the world, then the child is on his way to becoming a separate entity. Therefore, to die is that child's right and we cannot and should not deprive him of that right.

How does the child then view us. The sobering realization is that each faltering step toward the independence of the child is an attempt to separate the caring adult from his existence. We are far more persons to a child than the child is to us. That does not mean that a child rejects the caring adult. Far from it, rather the situation is the other extreme. All caring adults are brought into the child's extended family — and are viewed, and to a degree judged by the degree of involvement. Children seek friendship, much as lonely adults do, just to talk about their problems. However, the death itself is met alone — and adults may actually not participate nearly as much as they want to, for a child grows up during the terminal chronic illness. There are a number of articles that relate data showing that nurses and doctors avoid the dying patient and are actually further away from the bed and enter the room less frequently. A recent study tends to suggest that the child not only perceives this, but actually seems to prefer it this way for whatever reason.[24]

These considerations of personhood and humanity are the focal point for generating problems in the adult, not the child. Care of the child who might die is not an exercise for the mature adult to help a child cope with his problems, but is as often as not a struggle for the adult to reconcile his view of the world with the concept that a child can indeed die. In either case communication is only possible between persons who are allowed to define their own concepts. Only when this occurs does the caring adult indeed help.

These observations are not meant to negate the clinical descriptions of the phenomenology of dying, as described by Kübler-Ross,[25] Pattison,[26] and many others. Children are no different than adults in that respect. Denial, anger, bargaining, depression, and even acceptance all are discernable in children as well as in adults. But these so-called stages of dying are descriptive and do not indicate a sequence which must necessarily be completed. A child may not follow the sequence, without expressing symptoms of psychological maladjustment, just as adults may not fit Kübler-Ross's scheme, without having significantly maladaptive reactions to dying.[27] Nor do these observations deny the possibility of poor adjustment in parents who then may require therapeutic intervention. Many times parents do need help in coping with the problem. But in the vast majority of cases medical, psychiatric or psychological intervention is not necessary for parents.

However, I am writing this for those health care professionals who care for the dying, often without the ability, expertise and indeed inclination, to diagnose psychiatrically or to treat the psychologically morbid. Those health care professionals, and indeed anyone who falls in the circle of nurturing adults, still need to deal with the terminally ill child in a way that allows their own feelings to exist without causing mental upheaval and yet a way that supports the child-person in his own rightful life.

TELLING THE CHILD

In the context of the discussion to tell or not to tell is almost a meaningless question. A person should be allowed to react to his fate. However, this is one of the fiercest tests of our ability to grant personhood. A touching and well written article by Evans and Edin suggests that a child should be told no more than is appropriate for his age and understanding.[28]

A variant on this theme suggests that the question is not what a child should be told, but how he should be told.[29] Earlier, however, the idea that children should not know

was strongly rejected by Vernick and Karon,[30] but that was not uniformly well received.[31]

Many have discussed this same topic.[32, 33] A large number of authors do not agree with Vernick and Karon, but one perceives almost always an element of denial. One article was honest in saying: "Mostly we pray the question will not arise or even go out of our way to prevent its arising."[34]

The concept of a child's fear of death is a large element in such considerations. The idea is often put forth that below a certain age a child has no adult concept of death, and hence no fear of death. Therefore, telling him about something he does not conceive is either futile or shattering. However, the fear of death has been the subject of studies by Knudson and Natterson[35] and Morrisey,[36] and these investigators showed that children do fear death.

In either case, the discussion has little relevance, for invariably we tend to confuse the definition of the word "death" and the integration of death as a concept. Fear of death, the word, need not come into play, and fear of death, the realized concept, is unavoidable because death is going to occur whether we tell or not. Not conveying the nature of the illness creates a block between parent or caring adult, and the child. And a child can rarely be fooled because we communicate nonverbally the information we would hide. A child always reacts positively to sincerity and honesty and it is far more important how news is conveyed than what is related.[37] Not to tell is incompatible with a mutually respecting interpersonal relationship. If we truly accept the child as a person, we would like for him to be cognizant of what happens in his life, his body and his future, to the same extent any human can be aware.

How to tell can not be decided *a priori* based on the idea of a given child's age and the thereby presumed level of understanding. How to tell will follow naturally from the adult's empathy with the child. If one truly tries to communicate, one should attempt to evaluate whether it was successful. Each child will respond clearly to the adult if the adult truly tries to tell the child something important to both.

CARE THROUGH AVAILABILITY

We are then dealing with the dying child in an interpersonal relationship which extends beyond our role. We are not dealing solely with a doctor-patient, nurse-patient, socialworker-family relationship, for a child perceives those roles only superficially — and to a degree the same is true for the family. A child may ask the dietitian about his operation or a janitor about his pills. The anxiety and uncertainty behind those questions are the real issues and need to be answered. However, that does not imply that the fears of the respondent need to be allayed by the answer. There are questions parents and doctors are afraid to ask, and the answers to these questions are usually the ones that are thought to interfere with the professional relationship but would not disturb a truly interpersonal relationship.[38] The professional interaction would only allow: "When will I go home," the genuine interpersonal relationship might allow "Will I die?" Availability to the family and the patient means availability of the person, which is so easily hidden behind the masks of professional language, materiality, impersonality, ritualized action, and hospital routine.[39] To be sure, befriending is traumatic — one cannot use anger as releasing emotion when losing a friend, only sadness will prevail; but befriending is involvement with another person, and only then is one available, not for physical care but for mental succor.

One is available to someone but availability does not mean servitude. To the contrary, availability means a person listening and talking to another person. From this it follows that children should participate in their disease process, they should be part of the decision making.[30] Again, our professionalism often blocks us from allowing the child's participation. Rothenberg called this attitude of the physicians the consequence of the unholy trinity — activity, authority and magic.[40] Patients who are ill come to the physician expecting that the physician take away the disease with the authority and the magic of medicine. At times this can be beneficial and in fact result in a placebo effect. But if the physician limits himself to that level of interaction with the patient

then he has avoided total interaction and he has failed to evaluate the patient as a person, he has only dealt with the disease. A child can participate in decision making in many ways, from where his IV should be started (and they often know the veins better than the random intern) to whether treatment should be continued at all. Some teenagers do indeed refuse treatment, and should be allowed to do so.

Thus far, few references to age differences have been made. Of course they exist and children accept and assimilate at their level of understanding. Discussions must be interpreted in light of the milestones which have been achieved by the child. But that emphatically does not mean that the truth is only partially allowed to surface and that this partial hiding of the truth is graded according to a presumed understanding of the child. The truth is for the child to assimilate to his ability. After all, if you ignore the disease as not part of the true child, or if on the other hand you only focus on the disease and not on the living aspiring human, you do not accept the child as he is. The dying child is the whole child — he is death and growth combined — take away the illness and you have a different child that he will never be. Moustakas has described this conceptual difficulty well in his therapeutic sessions with a leukemic child.[41] This concept is not unique to a dying child. It is also forced on us through the grossly malformed child, for whom we readily conceive a poor quality of life. Yet, that is that child's total being, it is that child's total life and uniquely his. When we reconcile ourselves with our gender role we have given up half of the potential humanness, yet that limitation shapes our being. It seems a far extrapolation to accept malformation or life threatening illness in that way but that is not truly the case. To restate: Ignore the illness in a child and you have denied that child his reality.

However, our ability to approach a child simply but truthfully is largely a measure of our own mental and healthy psychosocial development. The stages of development as envisioned by Erikson continue to evolve until the wisdom of old age might be achieved.[14] One's own achieved milestones are as important in the care process at any age as those presumed to have been achieved by the child.

PROBLEMS UNIQUE TO THE CHILD

To this point only generalities have been discussed. In a sense, these generalities sugest that the endowment of personhood could serve as a common denominator in dealing with the terminally ill child. To a large degree that is true. This is akin to Joseph Fletcher's "situation ethics"[42] where it is presumed that love (agape) for others will solve each unique problem according to its own specific need. Allowing the child to be a person does set the stage for each specific encounter to resolve toward mutually rewarding interaction without set scenario, as each situation approached through love might resolve itself without fundamentalistic ethics.

But the concept of agape eventually becomes insufficient when it is not sustained by an ethic which supports the distinction between love for all and love for self. Similarly interpersonal relationships falter when one's personhood is threatened by an interpersonal encounter. And that is frequently the case in one's encounter with the dying child. It is not easy to accept a child's questioning of one's faith as requiring serious reflection; rather it is threatening, because we give children no right to challenge such axioms. But if one grants personhood to a child, then sooner or later one has to develop in one's encounter with deadly serious children, and I mean that term literally, an ethic or belief, or a certainty that it is alright not to know. Communication is only possible if one's own basis of thought is not anxious uncertainty about the event of death. And children, of whatever age, are honest and straightforward and expect this in return. Honesty implies that no apology need to be given for one's thoughts. And after all, faith is only possible with doubt — therefore not knowing, not being certain is quite compatible with supporting faith whether faith is religious or secular. Therefore, one is forced to abandon pure "situation friendship" and embark on a posture of being oneself a real and definable person. That means in this context being a person who has his own

views of humanness, personhood and even one's own personal concept of right and wrong, good and evil.

These pressures toward defining one's own basis of identity become critical in any encounter where one to one relationships are threatened by the realities of modern medicine. I would like to discuss some examples of such situations using, where appropriate, specific cases. The extreme nature of the cases does not negate the realities of equally difficult ethical and moral dilemmas of friendship with the child and his family in settings with far less pressure.

THE MANIPULATION THROUGH SYMPTOMS

Lest this development of the care of the dying child gives the impression that all children are naturally adapted to dying, there needs to be some discussion of excessive or counterproductive attempts at coping on the part of the child. Even then, one needs to be careful not to view dying as a disease in and of itself,[43] or to view the stages of dying, the adaptive phenomena to cope with dying, as pathological. There is nothing wrong with denying unless and until it interfers with otherwise necessary adaptive functions. In a sense, the adaptation to dying is somewhat analogous to the reaction of inflammation by a noxious stimulus — there is heat, redness, pain — all pain — all part of the process of coping with the stimulus. Only when this process fails to deal with it do we need to intervene, although palliation (antipyretics, cold compresses) may be applied to help at any time. And the analogy is flawed, since dying is not a noxious stimulus; dying is a natural process.

As recently pointed out by Plumb and Holland,[44] teenagers as a group are more concerned with symptoms than they are with the overall process of life-threatening illness. This is in line with all of our own observations of the preoccupation of a teenager with physical and mental self-images, even in the face of life-threatening illness. For example, a teenage girl with Hodgkin's disease was admitted to our ward for a complicating illness accompanied by a severe weight loss. This weight loss was so extreme that it became understandingly and appropriately a major concern of the caring physicians as well as the mother. The girl was well aware of her basic malignancy, the stormy course it had taken and the eventual prognosis. How much of this was internalized is uncertain and even immaterial. However, because of their preoccupation with the weight loss which had no obvious physical explanation, the physicians accepted as the primary concern the symptom instead of the illness, and soon entered into bargaining with the girl implying that she would regain well-being were the anorexia to be cured, or alternatively explaining much of the status of the illness by the marasmus. This clearly did not constitute care of the whole child. The use of the symptom from the part of the girl was in effect beyond the ken of most of the family of caring adults. The situation finally required the assistance and reassurance of a psychiatrist. One should never feel reluctant to ask for consultation in situations one cannot handle, be it somatic illness or psychological maladjustments. But this situation should not have needed psychiatric intervention. Had house officers and nurses reacted to the child as a whole person, one would have avoided this extreme coning down on a symptom, ignoring the disease.

PARTICIPATION IN EXPERIMENTAL THERAPY

Modern medicine has made life-prolongation a realizable goal, but to a large degree only with such expenditure of medical knowledge, biomedical engineering, and the clinical pathology skills that a very large proportion of our children with life-threatening illnesses are referred to medical centers. That in turn suggests experimental therapy. In and of itself, experimental therapy is not wrong. Since we do not know how to cure the disease with certainty, experimental therapy may be the best therapy — at least it should be theoretically the best.[45] Research, even when therapeutically intended, is always morally demanding when applied to children.[46] Even when the science is impeccable, and the ethics are examined clearly, experimental therapy still remains a dilemma for the medical worker who partic-

ipates in the care of the child. And when the child inquires and the adult had uncertainties, then what is the right course to take?

Recently, we had a protocol for leukemia where the various alternative modes of therapy were not predictably diferent in outcome but there emerged a clear difference in toxicity and thereby morbidity. These protocols are experimental designs wherein various alternative modes of therapy are compared. Usually, these protocols are designed to match the best known treatment to date against another that is theoretically better, but untested in practice. That one mode of therapy might be different in toxicity does not invalidate any of the compared schemas of treatment, since therapy to tolerance may be required for optimal outcome. Nevertheless, there developed among the house officers and nurses, who had professionally no secondary gain to expect from the outcome, a real aversion to this therapeutic modality. How does this become translated into human interaction?

One is that one appeals to the child for help — that is a role reversal that occurs only too frequently. In a sense we have the expectation for dying persons that they think kindly of us. After all they may die and one does not readily tolerate unresolved crisis. In any interaction between two persons, if one cannot mutually solve a problem, the one who is most perplexed appeals to the other for help. We do that with any dying person, including children. In fact this is one way in which we do let the concept of personhood to the child creep into care.

But as desirable as our acceptance of personhood in the child is, this is not the solution, because in this particular child-caregiver interaction the adult must take the lead. The experiment was the adult's idea, therefore, one should rather muster the faith in the role in which one is placed and admit the inherent doubt — then one remains oneself the person one needs to be.[47] In fact, it is quite conceivable that the reluctance to participate in the overall care of the child, *i.e.* the experimental therapy, might materially influence the outcome by altering the child's ability and willingness to continue the therapy, and even his perception of the treatment.

A given individual relationship with the child should be a one-to-one interpersonal relationship, but in the care of the child the entire team should function as a unit with, to a degree, defined roles.[48] One must anticipate conflicts between the demands imposed by the role in the care team and the personal friendships. A personal ethic and conviction is a necessity if one wants to avoid resolving such conflicts towards the soothing of one's own psyche, rather than by placing first the care of the friend that the child should be.

LIFE PROLONGATION – PERSONNEL NEEDS VERSUS FAMILY AND CHILD NEEDS

No greater struggle in medical ethics exists than the question surrounding unnecessary life prolongation. Such dilemmas are compounded when one deals with children. There is a legitimate need to allow the dying process run its final course undisturbed. But the wish for the problem of the dying child to go away as a burden and responsibility invariably results in easing the barrier against discontinuation of life support, be it through the use of a respirator or infection specific drugs.

We had on our ward a 5-year-old girl with a pontine glioma (a nonoperable brain tumor), who in spite of attempts at chemotherapy progressively deteriorated until her ability to communicate ceased except through restlessness. The restlessness coincided with situations when discomfort could be surmised. There was no one, health care personnel or family, who wanted to prolong the life by extraordinary means. The argument arose that anything which prolonged the survival at all was extraordinarily heroic. However, the child would get restless from infiltrated IV fluids, inadequate caloric intake, and other potential sources of discomfort from lack of ordinary support or care. This lasted for weeks and the personnel came to openly admit that they hoped the child would die. This admission was clearly not in the best interest of the support needs of the family. Only when the issues were examined with a view that caring means the best for the child and only the child, in contrast to the caregiver, was it possible to deal with the situation.

PARENTAL NEEDS VERSUS THE NEEDS OF THE CHILD

A child does not act independently during illness and dying. Many of the decisions are practically and legally made by the parents. Parents would have grief under any circumstances, but participation in decision making generates the need in the parents to do the right thing—to make the right decisions with their own value system, in such a way that the parents, who will survive the child, can live with those decisions and their consequences. Frequently those decisions are in conflict with the desires and considerations of the caring health professionals. Not all parents approach the death situation as mentally healthy. But one should always remember that the parent is an adult with an almost infinitely greater mental commitment to the child than the health care professionals. Therefore, all of the problems of the hospital personnel are also present in the parents. Assuming pathological adjustments in the parents is almost always a defense maneuver. Anger in response to one's own indequate feelings is very readily displaced to the parents, and the parents may have even stronger feelings of anger towards you. It would be easy to try to change the outward expression of the parent's feelings, justifying this on the basis of perceiving the parents adaptation to the child's dying as undesirable. In so doing we would in essence try to deal with our own problems without having to be self-critical. Yet that is non-helpful to the parent and clearly unfair.

A 5-year-old boy, with a medulloblastoma (a brain stem tumor), had been treated with surgery, radiation, and chemotherapy. The latter was successful at first, but when he became resistant to those drugs a trial of new experimental drug only resulted in severe neutropenia. The child developed a urinary tract infection, sepsis, Klebsiella pneumonia, became comatose, and developed profuse gastric hemorrhage, obvious from repeated bouts of vomiting of blood. He could only be kept alive (biologically) by superheroic combinations of antibiotics, oxygen, blood, platelets, and parenteral hyperalimentation. There would have been no difficulty in allowing the body to die, even without withholding of specific needs, since the survival was dependent on an extreme vigilance and superhuman effort from the houseofficers, and this was provided with reluctance. The parents, however, were in no way ready to give him up and requested that anything be tried. A mode of therapy never before tried was offered and they readily and rapidly consented. To deny all hope at that point by saying (and that would have been truthful), that all known remedies had been tried and had failed might have been accepted *per force,* but the parents were in no way prepared to hear this. Interestingly, the therapy was a spectacular success. The child regained much of his neurological function, and three months later was talking, playing, coloring, and beginning to walk again. He regained control over urine and bowel function. Once again we had to prepare the parents again that this was a last-ditch stand. But that outcome was really immaterial; this boy illustrates the extreme impact of parental needs to be sure that everything is being done, and how those needs supersede personnel needs.

Another extreme example may be given. A 4-year-old boy was in the last stages of leukemia. His mother was in no way ready to give him up and he was placed on a phase II drug.[50] He developed a neurological syndrome with somnolence and migratory neurological deficits, for which a specific etiological cause could not immediately be diagnosed. About 24 hours after these symptoms started he had a sudden cardiac-pulmonary arrest. Because the possibility of a treatable central nervous system disorder was not ruled out, cardiopulmonary resuscitation was instituted twice, each time with transient success. Throughout this ordeal, the mother stayed in the room. This is extremely unusual and not really considered desirable by the staff because efforts at resuscitation, even when successful, are not pleasant sights. When we had to declare him dead, she told me: "I had to stay in there. If I had waited outside the room I would always have wondered if you really tried everything and now I know you did and that there was really nothing more you could do. I want to thank you for all you have done".

For both patients we went to great extremes, far beyond what is normally done, or desired by parents. In both cases, the indication was the parent's mental health and desires and not truly the child's. After both incidents, the medical and nursing staff were at ease with the decisions, even though that hindsight reversed a great deal of previous doubts. In a sense one treats a whole family and one needs to chart the best course to deal with child and family. In those circumstances when a conflict has to be resolved on the basis of considerations of and for the child, and has to go to great length to explain to the parents that after all the child is the patient and that was why they brought him. Usually that helps the parent's difficulties but not always, and there is often no right or wrong in such situations.

PERSONNEL NEEDS VERSUS THE NEEDS OF THE DYING CHILD

In spite of cases in which the decision might appear to have been decided against the best interests of the child, the usual conflict is between the needs of the medical care team and the desires of the patient. These conflicts often have to be resolved for the patient.

This is best illustrated by the case of a child, nearly thirteen, who had a diagnosis of Hodgkin's disease since age four. His family had moved away from their home town to a distant city where he had been vigorously and successfully treated. However, his remissions were ever more dearly bought and when the family moved back to home he had extensive extralymphatic disease. The father brought him to our hospital and asked us to try any new treatment we might have. We instituted a chemotherapy regimen to which he had not been as ye exposed. He was a friendly and cooperative boy but he never allowed the house officers to discuss his prognosis with him; so much so that they decided he was more than situationally depressed. Interviews with a consulting psychiatrist made it very clear that the boy had come home to die. Even though the return to our care was seemingly the parents' need for unemployment assistance and family help, the boy had obviously been the overriding concern and had actively participated in the decision to return home.

The boy was appreciative of our efforts but he went along with them only to please his father. He expected to die and was ready. The house officers could not accept this, especially since treatment appeared somewhat successful, and they doubled their efforts in optimizing therapy.

One day the resident was in his room adjusting his IV fluids when he looked at her and said: "Now I am going to die." And he did. She was unprepared and very shaken. Very few of the staff had approached this boy as the person he was, and only the psychiatrist truly befriended him on his own terms. It is likely that this boy needed less support than most, and he taught us the lesson that one must avoid satisfying one's own needs, otherwise one is not able to listen to the child.

The death of a friend is saddening and the temptation to avoid emotional involvement is great. If this avoidance is an absolute necessity for the caregiver's own mental stability then he should not try to care for the children who might die, because the conflicting demands often cannot be resolved.

I do not mean to imply that dying while being a natural proprocess, may not be difficult for the individual patient. Some normal processes are harder to face and to cope with than others, and in that sense, the dying person needs more support and more opportunity to discuss his problems than one who has a crisis of less major proportions. But that makes the opportunity to befriend all the more challenging. It does not take a special skill or knowledge. However, it demands that one does not hide in the crowd, a phenomenon that is so prevalent in the usual treatment centers.[51]

TEACHING CARE FOR THE CHILD WHO MIGHT DIE

One must always bear in mind a point already alluded to — that most caring adults are not ultimately responsible for the management of the patient. However, all members of the care team have human contact with the child. We are often prone to talk about care teams that address themselves to the mental health of the patient. Such teams are undoubtedly useful for assisting the staff with their feelings, but they do not avoid the problems of individual interpersonal interaction with the patient.

Frequently the adults in the environment of the dying child are not necessarily interested in thanatology. The number of house officers, students, student nurses, paramedical personnel that are brought in contact with the dying child by circumstance and not by choice is very large.

The infrequent occurrence of the dying child in a general hospital brings the whole staff, mature or not, in that position. There is a need to learn to deal with the problems.

I have stated before that dying is not a disease in and of itself. However, the view that dying is a disease, requiring therapy, could be considered correct, but only as an iatrogenic disease, engendered by the modern medical center with its impersonal demands and routine responses. And then it is only a disease of the community and the social context: parents, patient, and medical staff combined, and not of any individual. The reactions of the patient and parents are the pathophysiological basis for the disorder, but no disease would exist if the community as a whole reacted appropriately.

It is clear then that members of the community have a responsibility to help each other. This is most acutely apparent and necessary with the involuntary newcomer. There are many published considerations of the impact of the dying child on the staff and the ways to help them deal with it. Schowalter divided the response of house officers into three periods: impact, battle, and defeat.[52] But first and foremost it must again be stressed that friendship, which is the only basis for interaction, cannot be taught. What can be done is to help the staff to realize the reasons for their inadequate responses.

Indeed all health professionals have a need to be successful, and physical cure is often the measure of success. But this picture is incorrect. Care of the total child is necessary, and the death of a child is often not seen as defeat but more as a relief that the suffering is over. More house officers, students, and nurses becrie "last-ditch stands" than the event of death. If indeed they become friends as well as nurturing adults, what they are not prepared for is the fear, anger, guilt, and sadness that they have to cope with, not only from the patient, not just from the family but in themselves.[53] The caring adults must hold back anger more than the patient or parent, and then another feeling, depression, frequently becomes a problem.

Teaching in medical centers is usually done by the person who is the one next higher in the hierarchy. As pointed out by Omsted, this may not be so in the care of the dying.[54] Rather, it will be that person who is most at ease with the patient and who allows and can encourage the staff to talk about and discuss their own feelings. If that be mental health team members, then such teams have a vital function. But it can be anyone with sufficient psychological integrity to have his feelings about the dying child examined by others. Finally, if it is a group problem, as has repeatedly been found true, group evaluation of the problem should be useful.[55]

The ward community that is truly concerned about the patient reacts very much like a family unit, and in this regard an illustration might be useful: A group of new house officers on a cancer ward had all the emotional reactions to the situation that one would hope and expect from young, capable and empathetic physicians. However, the faculty of their general pediatric training program had described their rotation on the cancer service as basically an experience where acute medicine is learned in quantity, which is of course a true but inadequate description of the rotation. Those house officers that were not capable of coping, reacted with a barrage of complaints about the physical details of the ward setting. Nursing was inadequate, the ward was overcrowded, there were too many procedures, etc. A lively discussion occurred during a called meeting. During this meeting misgivings over the setting were voiced by the permanent staff at the parent hospital as well: fear of emotional involvement with death is not unique to the professionally young. One of the residents, who began as a fierce critic, did concede the human values, the therapeutic experience and the diagnostic challenges inherent in the oncology ward.

When I said to him that he did not have to like the place, he said: "As long as you remember that, then I can deal with it." Many did a good job thereafter, and complained less over the unavoidable crush of labor. Most allowed themselves to be sad at times of loss and glad at times of success.

Our reactions are too often what we think others want them to be, and this occurs at the expense of the liberating experience of being ourselves. The days in which that emotional involvement with the patient was thought to be undesirable are hopefully gone forever.

CONFLICTING CONVICTIONS

If one participates in the care for a child who might die as an involved nurturing adult and with all the efforts aimed towards bestowing true personhood, then all the reactions that the child shows become shared. Sooner or later one has to define a basis for answering or knowingly leaving unanswered the various questions inherent in the altered life of the child. The initial shock of having to cope with the problems involuntarily, as so many health care professionals have to do, makes them sometimes grope for a coping basis from past religious or ethical teachings. These frameworks for coping with anger, grief, guilt or even despair may not be truly adequate, but sometimes are clung to in desperation. This work for oneself but inevitable conflicts arise when the child has his own methods and wording to define the concepts around dying within his own social and religious constraints. Nothing can be more threatening to the barely compensated.

Since the child's thoughts may appear primitive in relation to the adult concepts of the words used, the tendency to overpower the child's thoughts is very great indeed. That, of course, is precisely denying personhood to the child, for the adults' concepts about the enormity and infinity of dying are no better than the child's. One cannot claim to be significantly closer to the sun by standing on a hill.

A presentation on dying children was discussed by three chaplains of various faiths. One of them said: "The physician need never apologize for his own religious convictions." Later he added: "this, of course, is not a time for making converts—it is a time for one human being to offer all that he has for the benefit of another."[56] Realizing and acknowledging conflicts when they arise help avoid turmoil. Recently a speaker summarized the situation well when he described an anecdote about a chaplain intern who was assigned to an Emergency Room. One of his first nights on the assignment he was accosted by a distraught relative who grabbed him by the lapels of his coat and shook him shouting: "Do something, do something." He must have looked very uncertain and shaken and the relative said: "You are new at this aren't you?" He answered: "Yes ma'am, and it looks like we are going to learn together."[57]

CONCLUSION

This discourse can be summarized in several points: the death of a child is sad but no more unnatural than the death of an adult. Children must be treated as persons, and the availability of an interpersonal friendship to the child makes caring for the child who might die possible. To be able to deal with the inevitable conflicts imposed by the consequence of medical decision making, one has to develop an individual and personal ethical and moral foundation, on which the problems of the dying child can be resolved.

The needs of the child are inexorably entwined with the needs for the whole family and conflicting demands cannot always be resolved with the child exclusively in mind. The parents and caregivers are an integral part of the care process. Finally, full involvement with the child may evoke all the same reactions in the health care professional that are seen in parents or children. Those feelings must be recognized and one must learn to deal with them rather than trying necessarily to alter the feelings of the parents and child and thereby avoiding granting personhood to all concerned.

REFERENCES

1. I am indebted to Dr. L. J. Singher for this phrase, from his article, Singher LJ: *Clin Pediatr 13:*861–866, 1974
2. Howell SE: Mental Health of Mothers Who Have Handicapped Children. *St Joseph Hosp Med Surg J* (Houston) *10:*37–44, 1975; Also, Psychiatric Aspects of Habilitation. *Pediatr Clin NA 20:*203–219, 1973
3. Cobb B: Psychological Impact of Long Illness and Death of a Child on the Family Circle. *J Pediatr 49:*746–751, 1956
4. Examples. Easson WE: The Family of the Dying Child. *Pediatr Clin NA 19:*1157–1165, 1972; Friedman SB: Care of the Family of the Child with Cancer. *Pediatrics 440:*498–504, 1967; Binger CM, Ablin AR, Feverstein RC, Kushner JH, Zuger S, Mikkelson C: Childhood Leukemia, Emotional Impact on Patient and Family. *N Engl J Med 280:*414–418, 1969; Weiner JM: Reaction of Family to the Fatal Illness of a Child, in *Loss and Grief: Psychological Management in Medical Practice,* Schoenberg B, Carr AC, Peretz D, Kutscher AH (Eds), Columbia University Press, New York, 1970, pp 87–101
5. Friedman SB, Chodoff P, Mason JW, Hamburg DA: Behavioral Observations on Parents Anticipating the Death of a Child. *Pediatrics 32:*610–625, 1963; Futterman EH, Hoffman I: Crisis and Adaptation in the Families of Fatally Ill Children, in *The Child In His Family: The Impact of Disease and Death,* Anthony EH, Koupernik C (Eds), Vol. 2, John Wiley & Sons, New York, 1973, pp 127–143; Natterson JM, Knudson AG: Observations Concerning Fear of Death in Fatally Ill Children and Their Mothers. *Psychosom Med 22:*456–465, 1960. Again this list is in no way complete but gives representative examples of semidetached observations.
6. Taylor G: The Mother and Father of a Child With Catastrophic Disease. *Can Bull 26:*107–109, 1974
7. Lewis IC: Leukemia in Childhood, Its Effects on the Family. *Austr Pediatr J 3:*244–247, 1967. This paper was discussed in a later editorial: Freedman AR: Interview The Parents of a Dead Child? Absolutely! *Clin Pediatr 8:*564–565 1969
8. Lascari AD, Stehbens TA: The Reactions of Families to Childhood Leukemia. An Evaluation of a Program of Emotional Management. *Clin Pediatr 12:*210–214, 1973
9. Binger CM: Childhood Leukemia, Emotional Impact on Siblings, in, *The Child in His Family, The Impact of Disease and Death,* Anthony EJ, Koupernik C (Eds), Vol. 2, John Wiley and Sons, New York, 1973, pp 195–209
10. Nagy MH: The Child's View of Death, in *The Meaning of Death* Feifel H (Ed), McGraw-Hill, New York, 1959, pp 79–98
11. Anthony S: *The Discovery of Death in Childhood and After.* Basic Books, Inc., New York, 1972
12. von Hug Hellmuth H: Das Kind und seine Vorstellung vom Tode, Imago, I. 286–298, 1912. This was translated by Kris AO: The Child's Concept of Death. *Psychoanal Quar 34:*499–516, 1965
13. Kastenbaum R: The Child's Knowledge of Non-Existence. *J Exis Psychiat 2:*193–212, 1961
14. Erikson EH: *Childhood and Society.* 2nd Ed, W. W. Norton & Co., New York, 1963. Also, *Identity, Youth and Crisis,* W. W. Norton & Co., New York, 1968

15. Evans RI: *Dialogue With Erik Erikson*. E. P. Dutton & Co., New York, 1969
16. Piaget J: *Six Psychological Studies*. Vintage Books, New York, 1964. Dr. Piaget has a very large oevre dealing with the intellectual and conceptual development of children. The cited work contains a number of papers that help delineate his own development of these theories.
17. Maurer A: The Child's Knowledge of Non-Existence. *J Exis Psychiat 2:*193–212, 1961
18. Bluebond-Langner M: I Know, Do You? A Study of Awareness, Communication and Coping in Terminally Ill Children, in *Anticipatory Grief*. Schoenberg B, Carr AC, Kutscher AH, Peretz D, Goldberg IK (Eds), Columbia University Press, New York, 1974, pp 171–181
19. Spinetta JJ: The Dying Child's Awareness of Death. *Psychol Bull 81:*256–260, 1974
20. van Eys J: The Dying Child. *Can Bull 26:*105–106, 1974
21. This question was the theme of a letter written by a boy named Ronald Wayne Klingbeil, with the help of his parents.; it was submitted to the *Cadillac Evening News* (Michigan). It came to my attention in a column by Dr. S. Kapel published in the *Houston Chronicle* on March 27, 1974. There is no way to judge the authenticity of the concepts, but the letter does illustrate that the points are under consideration by afflicted families.
22. Fletcher J: The Pursuit of Happiness – Being Happy, Being Human. *Humanist* Jan–Feb, 1975
23. Fletcher J: Indicators of Humanhood: A Tentative Profile of Man. *Hastings Cent Rep 2:*1–4, 1972
24. Spinetta J, Rigler D, Karon M: Personal Space as a Measure of a Dying Child's Sense of Isolation. *J Consult Clin Psychol 42:*751–756, 1974
25. Kübler-Ross E: *On Death and Dying*. Macmillan, New York, 1969
26. Pattison EM: The Experience of Dying. *Amer J Psychother 21:*32–43, 1967
27. Branson R: Is Acceptance a Denial of Death? Another Look at Kübler-Ross. *The Christian Century*, May 7, 1975, pp 464–468
28. Evans AE, Edin S: If a Child Must Die. *N Engl J Med 278:*138–142, 1965
29. Vore DA: A Child's View of Death. *South Med J 67:*383–384, 1974
30. Vernick J, Karon M: Who's Afraid of Death on a Leukemia Ward? *Amer J Dis Child 110:*393–397, 1965
31. An example is a Letter to the Editor written in response to the attitude voiced in Ref, 30. Lee HF: What Should the Child With Leukemia Be Told? *Amer J Dis Child 110:*703–704, 1965
32. Howell DA: A Child Died. *J Pediatr Surv 1:*2–7, 1966
33. Editorial: The Dying Child. *Med J Austral 1:*1011–1012, 1968
34. Yudkin S: Children and Death. *Lancet 1:*37–41, 1967
35. Knudson AC, Natterson JM: Participation of Parents in Hospital Care of Fatally Ill Children. *Pediatrics 26:*482–490, 1960 (see also Ref. 5); Natterson JM: The Fear of Death in Fatally Ill Children and their Parents, in, *The Child and His Family:*

The Impact of Disease and Death, Anthony EJ, Koupernik C (Eds), John Wiley and Sons, New York, 1974, pp 121–125
36. Morrissey JR: Children's Adaptation to Fatal Illness. *Soc Work 8:*81–88, 1963; Morrissey JR: A Note on Interviews with Children Facing Imminent Death. *Soc Case Work 44:*343–345, 1963
37. Zeligs R: *Children's Experience With Death*. Charles C Thomas, Publisher, Springfield, Ill., 1974, especially p 80
38. This topic was dealt with more fully in a taped talk; van Eys J: "Answers to Questions Parents of Children With Cancer are Afraid to Ask." Dial Access System #684, Southern Medical Association Cancer Education Service, 1975
39. Byrd JL: Ministry to the Dying Patient Through Availability. *Can Bull 26:*115–118, 1974
40. Rothenberg MB: The Unholy Trinity – Activity, Authority and Magic. *Clin Pediatr 13:*870–873, 1974
41. Moustakas C: The Dying Self Within the Living Self, in *Existential Child Psychiatry,* Moustakas C (Ed), Basic Books Inc., New York, 1966. Reissued also as *The Child's Discovery of Himself*. Ballantine Books, New York, 1972
42. Fletcher J: *Situation Ethics: The New Morality*. Westminister Press, Philadelphia, 1966
43. Weismann AD, Kastenbaum R: *The Psychological Autopsy*. Community Mental Health Manuscrips #4, Behavioral Publications, New York
44. Plumb MM, Holland J: Cancer in Adolescents: The Symptom is the Thing, in *Anticipatory Grief*, Schoenberg B, Carr AC, Kutschen AH, Peretz D, Goldberg IK (Eds), Columbia University Press, New York, 1974, pp 193–209
45. This concept is vigorously promoted by Dr. E. J. Freireich, Chairman of the Department of Developmental Therapeutics at The M. D. Anderson Hospital and Tumor Institute, Houston, Texas. He was written much and spoken publicly even more about that concept. It is true, but one should guard against the many extrapolations that could be made from such a statement, such as omitting controls from clinical studies and similar prejudgments. It must therefore be kept in mind that an experiment is and must remain just that. It should be honestly conceived and responsibly executed, but the results must not and can not be prejudged.
46. Schwartz AM, Sturges JS: Medical Experimentation on Children, in, *Should Doctors Play God?,* Frazier CA (Ed), Broadman Press, Nashville, 1971, p 83
47. van Eys J: Faith, Hope and the Dying Child, in *Medical Ethics as Seen by Doctors,* Frazier CA (Ed), in press
48. van Eys J: What do we mean by the truly cured child?, in *The Truly Cured Child,* van Eys J (Ed.), University Park Press, Baltimore, 1977
49. The current parlance is "death with dignity." It is debated whether that is either ever truly possible (Freireich EJ: Death with Dignity? *Can Bull 26:*110–114, 1974), or ever truly deniable (St. Paul, I Corinthians 15, v. 50, *The Bible*). However, at best, the young children speak the views their parents inculcated. The term is therefore

meaningless for children and should be avoided if it is used to describe one's own wishes.

50. Research drugs go through a sequence of experimental testing: Phase I, Toxicity evaluation; Phase II, testing of spectrum of effectiveness, usually done in late stages of the disease; Phase III, incorporation of the new drug in combination chemotherapy with drugs previously found effective.

51. This is frequently described. One good example, whenever he discusses treatment settings, is: Schortz FC: *The Psychological Aspects of Physical Illness and Disability.* Macmillan, New York, 1975

52. Schowalter JE: Death and the Pediatric House Officer. *J Pediatr 76:*706–710, 1970

53. Rothenberg MB: Reactions of Those Who Treat Children With Cancer. *Pediatrics 40:*507–510, 1967; Rothenberg MB: The Fear-Anger-Guilt-Sadness Syndrome, in *The Effect of Hospitaliza-* *tion on Children,* Oremland EK, Oremland JP (Eds), Charles C Thomas, publishers, Springfield, Ill., 1973, p 204

54. Omsted R: Teaching Medical Students and House Officers. *Pediatrics 40:*514–515, 1967

55. Heffron WA: Group Therapy Sessions as Part of Treatment of Children With Cancer, in *Clinical Management of Cancer in Children,* Pochedly C (Ed), Publishing Sciences Group, Inc., Acton, Mass., 1975, pp 247–248

56. Reed AW: Commentary on Toch R: Management of the Child with Fatal Disease. *Clin Pediatr 3:*418–427, 1964

57. Oates WE: Standing Together in Times and Stress. Address at the 2nd Annual Benefit Dinner of the Institute of Religion and Human Development, Houston, May 13, 1975

INDEX